PAUL IN ECSTASY

Although many readers of Paul's letters recognize how important his experience was to his life and thought, biblical scholars have not generally addressed this topic head-on. Colleen Shantz argues that they have been held back both by a bias against religious ecstasy and by the limits of the biblical texts: How do you responsibly access someone else's experience, particularly an experience as unusual and debated as religious ecstasy? And how do you responsibly account for the role of experience in that person's thought? *Paul in Ecstasy* pursues these questions through a variety of disciplines – most notably neuroscience. This study provides cogent explanations for bewildering passages in Paul's letters, outlines a much greater influence of such experience in Paul's life and letters, and points to its importance in Christian origins.

Colleen Shantz is assistant professor of New Testament studies in the Faculty of Theology at the University of St. Michael's College and at the Toronto School of Theology, the consortium of seven theological schools at the University of Toronto.

Paul in Ecstasy

*The Neurobiology of the Apostle's
Life and Thought*

COLLEEN SHANTZ

St. Michael's College at the University of Toronto

*To Brick,
the most handsome
neuropsychologist I have
ever met!*

Colleen Shantz

CAMBRIDGE
UNIVERSITY PRESS

CAMBRIDGE UNIVERSITY PRESS

Cambridge, New York, Melbourne, Madrid, Cape Town, Singapore, São Paulo, Delhi

Cambridge University Press
32 Avenue of the Americas, New York, NY 10013-2473, USA

www.cambridge.org
Information on this title: www.cambridge.org/9780521866101

First published 2009

Printed in the United States of America

A catalog record for this publication is available from the British Library.

Library of Congress Cataloging in Publication Data

Shantz, Colleen.
Paul in ecstasy : the neurobiology of the Apostle's life and thought / Colleen Shantz.
p. cm.
Includes bibliographical references and indexes.
ISBN 978-0-521-86610-1 (hardback)
1. Paul, the Apostle, Saint. 2. Ecstasy. I. Title.

BS2506.3.S53   2009
225.9′2–dc22   2008045751

ISBN 978-0-521-86610-1 hardback

Contents

v

Acknowledgments

I would like to express my thanks to and acknowledge the contributions of several people who helped to improve the ideas presented here.

My doctoral supervisor, Leif Vaage, served alternately as trade wind and dry dock as I tried to create something seaworthy. As occasion required, he was generous in his encouragement of the pursuit of intuitions and insightful in his interventions. The process was more fruitful for his part in it. In addition, my doctoral examiners, Professors Terrence Donaldson, J. Dorcas Gordon, L. Ann Jervis, and Alan Segal, were thoughtful and gracious readers whose comments were most helpful and encouraging in subsequent stages. Of the three anonymous readers for Cambridge, only Carol Rauch Albright subsequently revealed her identity to me. I thank her especially for her thoughts about the use of neuroscience outside laboratory settings. I am grateful also to the two other readers for their suggestions, and especially to "reader C," who misconstrued my tone in a way that highlighted the potential for others to do the same! I hope the final version better demonstrates that occasional use of humor need not be antithetical to respect.

A number of people read portions of the manuscript for accuracy and intelligibility. Among them, Dr. Deirdre Dawson, of the Kunin-Lunenfeld Applied Research Unit, kindly checked the science sections of Chapter 2. Her expertise is greatly appreciated, and it goes without saying that any shortcomings that remain in that chapter are solely my responsibility. Other colleagues and sharp-eyed friends read portions of the manuscript. I thank my excellent colleague Professor Jennifer Harris, as well as Claudine Carlson, Professor Zeba Crook, and Michael Mills (the last of whom read the whole manuscript at one point or another and tolerantly served as conversation partner even after his native interest had run out). Ryan Wettlaufer prepared the indexes of ancient sources and modern authors (and even entertainingly documented the process). I am indebted to all for their suggestions and assistance.

A few additional people deserve acknowledgment for their practical and/ or moral support along the way. At key points, Professor Brent Strawn offered both kinds of aid, for which I am very grateful. Professor Robert Jewett proved himself to be that most wonderful of species: a generous and encouraging senior scholar. AndyBeck, religion editor at Cambridge, has been a genial guide throughout the publishing process. Finally, my children, Chloë and Jonah, are the most excellent companions I know for just about any adventure. (Thank you, my dears, for dinner-table hilarity and learning not to ask when the book would be done.)

PAUL IN ECSTASY

Introduction

Whenever theology touches science, it gets burned. In the sixteenth century astronomy, in the seventeenth microbiology, in the eighteenth geology and palaeontology, in the nineteenth Darwin's biology all grotesquely extended the world-frame and sent churchmen scurrying for cover in ever smaller, more shadowy nooks, little gloomy ambiguous caves in the psyche where even now neurology is cruelly harrying them, gouging them out from the multi-folded brain like wood lice from under the lumber pile.

— John Updike

In any field, find the strangest thing and then explore it.
— John Archibald Wheeler

IT WOULD BE PRESUMPTUOUS IN A FIELD LIKE PAULINE STUDIES TO claim that one had found the strangest thing because we are indeed blessed with many. Instead, this book is an exploration of the coincidence of two curiosities. The first curiosity, and the major interest of the chapters that follow, is Paul's ecstatic religious experience. This interest begins with the premise that a certain set of Pauline texts not traditionally read together forms an inherently meaningful grouping. In part, they belong together because in each text Paul is describing occasions in which he considered himself to be in contact with nonhuman agents (spoken of mainly as spirit – whether spirit of God, spirit of Christ, holy spirit, spirit of sonship, etc.). In another way, these texts also belong to the broad category of religious experience and, more precisely, can be categorized as involving altered states of consciousness (henceforth designated by the abbreviation ASCs). Furthermore, the same diversity of experiences reflected in this group of Pauline passages is frequently studied together in disciplines other than biblical studies. In short, these texts are a particular kind of data whether described from the inside (emically) or studied from without (etically); yet they are not often considered as a whole in Pauline studies.

The relevant passages touch on ecstatic forms of worship, visions, spirit possession, and glossolalia. The latter is probably the most frequently studied in New Testament scholarship because Paul also gives it proportionately more attention – including his admission that he speaks in tongues more than any of the exuberant Corinthians (1 Cor 14:18) – while other of Paul's comments about his own ecstatic religious experience are often made in passing. For instance, he mentions ecstatic prayer (Rom 8:26; 1 Cor 14:14–15a) and singing in or with the spirit (1 Cor 14:15b); he alludes to "signs and wonders" that he was able to perform (Rom 15:18–19; 2 Cor 12:12)[1] and also the general category of being ecstatic for God (which he contrasts with being in his right mind; 2 Cor 5:13); and he speaks of revelations (in general, 2 Cor 12:1, 7; and, in particular, Gal 1:12, 2:2) and visions of the risen Christ (1 Cor 9:1, 15:8). Perhaps most noteworthy among these incidents, because it includes a description of the experience itself, is Paul's account of his ecstatic journey to heaven (2 Cor 12:2–4). Taken together, these details suggest that ecstatic religious experience was a frequent and significant aspect of Paul's life and his apprehension of the divine. These data also suggest that the drive toward religiously oriented ecstasy was an aspect of Paul's personality and social setting, not just a circumstantial contingency. In other words, Paul was not someone who was merely surprised by an unsolicited encounter with the divine in the course of his everyday business; Paul was, among other things, an ecstatic.

The second curiosity is not a feature of Paul's letters themselves but rather of method and what is possible in our scholarship on Paul. For some time, New Testament studies have been explicit in declaring that Paul cannot be thought of as a systematic theologian and that his writings are occasional – that is, driven by the needs of and ongoing conversations with particular communities. That fact seems to have been integrated to varying degrees into our actual readings, which now take more account of the audience and its social and rhetorical context. Likewise, exegesis is increasingly informed by attention to cultural influences, including material culture. The challenge that remains is how to integrate such contextual awareness into a full-blooded portrait of a human agent who does more than pick and choose from a menu of cultural options. Thus, although the view of the letters as communication has developed and the world in which they were written has become ever more interesting, often the understanding of the person behind

[1] For now, I will assert the performance of signs and wonders as an ecstatic state without offering the explanation for that assumption, which will be provided in Chapter 4.

the letters persists implicitly as that of the rational, if not systematic, generator of theological ideas. Yet an overly narrow focus on Paul's thought and words alone risks creating a distortion of both Paul and Pauline christianity[2] – as if speaking and thinking in themselves adequately constitute the man and the movement. When we consider the whole picture of what is produced in Pauline scholarship, even though more and more exceptions are appearing, it is the body that tends to remain absent or partial.

So, although much corrective work is under way, the second curiosity in this study is the scholarly construction of what amounts to a disembodied Paul. In some cases, Paul is disembodied by exegesis that is restricted to the analysis and comparison of texts. I hasten to add that these questions and approaches are not wrong in themselves. Obviously, there is much that is both necessary and methodologically sound about such approaches because the surest access to Paul is through the texts he created, and concerns for accountability and responsibility in interpretation are met when one works from the evidence of the texts themselves. Thus, the problem is not attentiveness to the texts per se but perhaps begins when the nature of texts as words and ideas is allowed to be sufficient explanation. At some point, the monopoly of the text risks creating a misrepresentation. Two examples will illustrate this concern. These examples were not chosen because they are particularly glaring occurrences of this pattern; rather, the arguments are quite standard examples of New Testament exegesis and very useful in their own right.

The first example is taken from Luke Timothy Johnson's comments on Romans 8 in his commentary on that letter.[3] In his discussion of Rom 8:18–27, Johnson notes Paul's appeal to common knowledge: "For we know that the whole creation groans together and labors together in pain until now" (Rom 8:22). Johnson asks rhetorically how it is that Paul can confidently assert that everyone knows this, and he answers with the proposal that Paul "must be referring to the shared world of Torah." Johnson then supports that claim with a short string of prophetic texts that includes birth imagery as an expression "of hopefulness" or "of eschatological tribulation."[4] The proposal is quite reasonable within New Testament exegetical discourse, yet when we imagine Paul's letter first being read to the assembly in Rome, it at least seems worth considering other aspects of "shared world" that might be even more salient to the auditors than that of the "world of Torah." Their

2 The lowercase "c" is intentional here, and throughout, in reference to early christians and christianity. I describe the purpose of this anomaly at the end of the introduction.
3 Luke Timothy Johnson, *Reading Romans: A Literary and Theological Commentary* (New York: Crossroad, 1997).
4 Ibid., 128.

shared world included, for instance, the fact that the population density of
Rome was greater than that of present-day Manhattan or Mumbai (Bom-
bay) and that most of the christians likely lived in tenements having windows through which the sounds of neighbors' daily lives were audible.[5] Thus,
their shared world ensured that everyone would at some point be privy to
the birth of a child through the thin walls that subdivided the upper stories
or the uncovered windows of their buildings. Given the high death rates in
childbirth in antiquity, it is also safe to assume that everyone would have
been privy to tragedy on some of these occasions as well.[6]

   If we try to imagine a shared understanding of the suffering of creation in
the passage, we also have recourse to something in addition to Torah. Rome
in particular, but also many other parts of the empire, showed signs of
environmental degradation of which ancient writers were well aware.[7] Both
Pliny and Vitruvius speak of the dangers of lead and other contaminants and
the need for purification of drinking water.[8] Furthermore, the human and
animal sewage that was not immediately washed into the Tiber littered the
streets of Rome.[9] During heavy rains and flooding, the water and sanitation
systems were known to reverse, causing the fountain in the coliseum to
spout sewage (hardly the stuff of tourist brochures). Other authors recognized especially the deadly effects of air pollution from industry in particular
and urban life in general.[10] They did not rely on Torah to establish the
suffering of creation in its decay, not only because they were not Judean
but also because more palpable evidence was at hand. So, in this case,
analysis that is restricted to textual correlates may in fact mask much that
is more relevant to the meaning of the passage.

[5] Peter Lampe catalogs the evidence for the geographical and social location of the earliest
   christians in Roman tenements in his study *From Paul to Valentinus: Christians at Rome in
   the First Two Centuries* (London: T. and T. Clark, 2003), 19–47. For a discussion of population density, see Rodney Stark, *The Rise of Christianity: A Sociologist Reconsiders History*
   (Princeton, N.J.: Princeton University Press, 1996), 149–51. For a colorful description of
   some of the effects of such crowding, see Juvenal (*Satires*), whose third satire is devoted to
   complaints about the city.
[6] Mary Harlow and Ray Laurence, *Growing Up and Growing Old in Ancient Rome: A Life
   Course Approach* (London: Routledge, 2002), 8–9. Harlow and Laurence report that the
   infant mortality rate in ancient Rome was roughly three in ten. That high probability of
   death was not matched again until individuals reached the age of 65 or 70.
[7] For an excellent discussion of ancient awareness of and theorizing about environmental
   pollution, see J. Donald Hughes, *Pan's Travail: Environmental Problems of the Ancient
   Greeks and Romans* (Baltimore: Johns Hopkins University Press, 1994), 51–53.
[8] Pliny, *Natural History*, 36.173; Vitruvius, *On Architecture*, 8.6.12–15.
[9] For example, Strabo (*Geography* 5.3.8) mentions the filth on the streets and in the river.
[10] They include Xenophon, *Memorabilia*, 3.6.12; Strabo, *Geography*, 3.2.8, 16.2.23; Pliny, *Natural History*, 33.122; and Artemidorus, *Interpretation of Dreams*, 1.51, 2.20.

The second illustration of this interest is taken from Andrew Lincoln's study of "the role of the heavenly dimension in Paul's thought," *Paradise Now and Not Yet*.[11] Lincoln's comments offer a more subtle example and hence possibly also a more provocative one. One of the texts that he considers is 2 Cor 4:16–5:10. After describing the epistolary context of the passage, offering a reconstruction of the purported background views of Paul's opponents, and examining the construction of the section along with its special vocabulary and its possible sources in other literature, Lincoln concludes:

> In the midst of decay and affliction Paul concentrates on the as yet unseen heavenly realities and *knows* that if he dies before the parousia he will assuredly still receive a heavenly body when Christ returns. He longs to be able to put on that body without first experiencing death. For him the disembodied state, though possible, is undesirable and he *knows* that ultimately God has prepared him for the reception of the heavenly body and has in fact guaranteed this by giving him the Spirit. In the light of this he is of good courage and *knows* that even if he dies before the parousia this is something to be preferred because it will mean that he will be present with the Lord.[12]

The recurring language of knowledge is one of the most striking features of the quotation. Doubtless here Lincoln is exercising appropriate academic restraint; he is describing rather than claiming to be able to explain how such knowledge came to be. Yet in the absence of either a caveat about the methodological limits of assessing Paul's knowledge or a less emphatic verb, the simple assertion of knowing is taken as sufficient explanation of the theological facts.

It is my sense that we might want to supplement such a description by considering how it is that Paul came to know such things, lest the certainty of the language become a distortion of the circumstances.[13] I raise this concern particularly as someone who is writing from within a department of theology and therefore bears some responsibility for the truth claims of institutional Christianity. An unintended effect of Lincoln's summary is that

---

[11] Andrew Lincoln, *Paradise Now and Not Yet: Studies in the Role of the Heavenly Dimension in Paul's Thought with Special Reference to His Eschatology*. Society for New Testament Studies 43 (Cambridge: Cambridge University Press, 1981), v.

[12] Ibid., 69, emphasis added.

[13] In general, Pauline scholarship indulges the reconstruction of Paul's opponents (complete with their purported belief systems and history of engagement with Paul), to whom Paul barely alludes; however, it is quite intolerant of attempts to reconstruct Paul's own experiences of the Lord, of whom Paul speaks directly and at length.

Paul's knowledge, like the authority of the biblical text itself, is a priori in nature. Paul's theological commitments do not need to be grounded in anything beyond the text itself. In part, this epistemological silence results from the recognition of the real limits of what can be claimed about Paul's knowledge. But the silence also serves in understanding the text as a particular kind of revelation. Perhaps, for example, somewhere between the idea that Paul invented Christianity[14] and the view of scripture as hermetically revealed there is room – and need – to consider fuller notions of knowing and coming to know.

So, to ask another set of rhetorical questions: At what point does attention to textual interplay function as a de facto denial of other, more common forms of knowledge? At what point does disciplined specificity become distortion? Driving these questions is an epistemological concern because it is precisely at the level of *knowing* that the curiosity of Paul's ecstatic religious experience and the curiosity of the sometimes-disembodied scholarly imagination of Paul and his religious life are connected. These questions of theory and method cannot be pursued at much length in this project. They do, however, constitute a subtext that runs throughout the ensuing chapters. Throughout this examination, it is worth considering not just the fact that Paul alludes to or reflects on ecstatic experiences in his letters but also that they took place "in Paul." It is worth exploring not only how one talks about such experience but also how it feels, why one might want to talk about it, and how it is fundamentally constitutive of theological reflection. For some time, others – for example, art theorists, philosophers, and historians of other periods – have been interested in the meaning-making that takes place apart from language.[15] "Human reason is a polyglot," as William Grassie puts it, and some of the "languages" that it speaks are not verbal at all.[16]

With these questions in mind, this examination of Paul's ecstatic experience is lodged in the larger and much broader category of "religious experience." Religious experience is a term with a substantial and significant

[14] Hyam Maccoby, *The Mythmaker: Paul and the Invention of Christianity* (New York: Harper and Row, 1986).

[15] In the 1960s, these questions were addressed in art theory in Rudolf Arnheim, *Visual Thinking* (Berkeley: University of California Press, 1969), and from a philosophical perspective in Susanne K. Knauth Langer, *Mind: An Essay on Human Feeling*, 3 vols. (Baltimore: Johns Hopkins University Press, 1967). The historian Margaret Miles has worked at historical reconstruction from nontextual, experiential, bodily bases; see, for example, her *Image as Insight: Visual Understanding in Western Christianity and Secular Culture* (Boston: Beacon, 1985).

[16] William Grassie, "Postmodernism: What One Needs to Know," *Zygon* 32 (1997), 88.

history, especially in the philosophical study of religion. In real
might be accurately applied to any experience connected with or
life or to participation in any religiously construed occasion. I
practice, it has often been mired in philosophical debates
possibility of direct knowledge of God. In fact, William James
the category of religious experience precisely in order to account for what he
took to be a distinct, and objectively trustworthy, source of knowledge of the
divine; he described religious experience as "pure experience" distinct from
(and untainted by) other ways of knowing or apprehending.[17] For the better
part of the twentieth century, the term was caught up in a debate about
whether or not one can have "a veridical experience of the presence or
activity of God."[18] In that debate, the term "religious experience" functioned
with a more limited range of defining characteristics, which have been
summarized by William Alston. First, this early definition of religious experience was concerned with the experiential – rather than with "abstract
thought" – as the means to knowing. Second, religious experience was
understood to be a direct apprehension of the divine as opposed to "being
aware of God by being aware of something else." Third, and closely related
to the second, it was described as "completely lacking in sensory contact,"
which is not to say that it has no bodily or sensory manifestations; rather,
this point is a more specific expression of the previous one. Finally, according to Alston, religious experience comprised a "focal experience" in which
"awareness of God attracts one's attention so strongly as to blot out all else
for the moment."[19]

Partly in response to such views, some theorists have argued that all
religious ecstasy is inherently and essentially cultural. Certainly it is true
that in many societies the means to attain mystical ecstasy, the adept's
behavior while in trance, and the interpretation of the trance can all be
informed by culture. So, for example, the Christian Shakers of St. Vincent
and the Christian Apostolics of Yucatan, who share the same religious texts
and who claim possession by the same spirit, nonetheless demonstrate
significantly different behavior while in trance.[20] Ethnographers have

---

[17] William James, *The Varieties of Religious Experience* (New York: Triumph, 1991); first published New York: Longmans, Green and Co., 1902.
[18] William P. Alston, "Religious Experience," in *Routledge Encyclopedia of Philosophy*, vol. 8,
ed. Edward Craig (London: Routledge, 1998), 250–55.
[19] Ibid., 250–51.
[20] See Felicitas D. Goodman, "Apostolics of Yucatán: A Case Study of a Religious Movement,"
and Jeannette H. Henney, "The Shakers of St. Vincent: A Stable Religion," in *Religion,
Altered States of Consciousness, and Social Change,* ed. Erika Bourguignon (Columbus: Ohio
State University Press, 1973), 178–218, 219–63, respectively.

documented these differences in numerous societies, and members of such groups themselves sometimes recognize their distinctiveness in almost precisely the same categories. For example, in his study of a ritual trance cult in Jamaica, William Wedenoja notes that the participants themselves identify (1) the process of transformation from temporal consciousness to a trance state, (2) "the ritual means for effecting transformation," (3) the expected behavior while in trance, and (4) "the 'gifts' and obligations" of participation as aspects peculiar to the distinct subculture of the cult.[21] On the basis of such observations, some argue that mysticism is nothing but a cultural construct.[22]

Perhaps the most zealous champion of this position is Steven Katz,[23] who ascribes not only the ritual accoutrements and the preconditioning of religious experience to cultural control but also the character of the experience itself: "The ontological structure(s) of each major mystical tradition is different and this pre-experiential, inherited structure directly enters into the mystical occasion itself. As a consequence, Christian mystics, as we have shown, have Christian experiences . . . while Jewish Kabalists meet Elijah and 'see' the *Merkabah*"[24] and "The Hindu mystic does not have an experience of x which he then describes in the, to him, familiar language and symbols of Hinduism, but rather he has a Hindu experience, i.e. his experience is not an unmediated experience of x but is itself the, at least partially, pre-formed anticipated Hindu experience of Brahman."[25]

Katz's position is known as constructivist; that is, the understanding that all experience is constructed by the terms, beliefs, and particularly the *language* that the subject brings to them. In effect, constructivism extends the cultural control of religious ecstasy into a kind of absolute: Without language, there is no experience.

---

[21] William Wedenoja, "Ritual Trance and Catharsis: A Psychological and Evolutionary Perspective," in *Personality and the Cultural Construction of Society: Papers in Honor of Melford E. Spiro,* ed. David K. Jordan and Marc J. Swartz (Tuscaloosa: University of Alabama Press, 1990), 275–307 at 279.

[22] It is noteworthy that none of the ethnographers I have cited here make this argument themselves but are rather drawn to the similarities between cultures.

[23] Also in this company are Wayne Proudfoot, *Religious Experience* (Berkeley: University of California Press, 1985), esp. 123; and Gershom G. Scholem, *Major Trends in Jewish Mysticism* (New York: Schocken, 1961). See also Nils G. Holm, "Ecstasy Research in the 20th Century – An Introduction," in *Religious Ecstasy,* ed. Nils G. Holm Scripta Instituti Donneriani Aboensis (Uppsala: Almqvist and Wiksells, 1982), 7–26 at 7.

Steven T. Katz, "The 'Conservative' Character of Mystical Experience," in *Mysticism and eligious Traditions,* ed. Steven T. Katz (Oxford: Oxford University Press, 1983), 3–60 at 40. ɨ., 4. Katz's argument may have more validity in the case of the "masters" in various ɨical traditions, from whom many of his examples are drawn. But in many ways even ɨre the exception that proves the rule.

Not surprisingly, Katz's subordination of experience to cultural control goes beyond the tolerance of some who are otherwise sympathetic to the idea of cultural influence, and indeed it goes beyond the claims of this book.[26] One of the most significant and convincing objections is represented by Sallie King.[27] King counters Katz's view with the criticism that it reduces experience to language – that language is in fact inextricable from culture, but that religious ecstasy, like all experience, cannot be reduced to the attempt to describe it. In other words, the whole of the mystical experience cannot be subsumed in the adept's description of that experience. In fact, there are many who find that mystical experience is in its very nature a nonlinguistic experience. Thus, as Wayne Proudfoot argues, terms such as "ineffable" and "paradoxical," which are often applied to religious ecstasy, are not vague reports of the experience but in fact quite precise descriptions of what it is.[28] These views are supported by Natika Newton's observation that language was a tool for communication before it became a primary shaper of cognition. Thus, says Newton, other forms of cognition still exist alongside this newer linguistic dominance.[29]

More recently, the term "religious experience" has been freed from the debate about veridical experience and has come to be seen as interesting and valuable in itself rather than only for what it may demonstrate about the nature and existence of God. This interest has grown partly through a lively interdisciplinary conversation between philosophers, theologians, and

---

[26] See especially the volume of essays in Robert K. C. Forman, ed., *The Problem of Pure Consciousness: Mysticism and Philosophy* (New York: Oxford University Press, 1997). This is not to say that all counterproposals are well reasoned. For example, some object that a mystical experience exists that transcends cultural confines because it is in fact an encounter with the "Absolute." For example Huston Smith, "Is There a Perennial Philosophy?" *Journal of the American Academy of Religion* 60 (1987), 553–66, esp. 560–64), appeals to Piaget's model of higher-order thinking in general, and to the concept of "decentration" in particular, as corroborating evidence for his view of an acultural mysticism (558). However, his description is so ideologically loaded – in part with the baggage of social Darwinism – that it serves more to illustrate Katz's viewpoint than to refute it. Smith's explanation of the acultural mysticism is as follows: "[T]here is one God. It is inconceivable that s/he not disclose her saving nature to her children, for s/he is benevolent: hence revelation. From her benevolence it follows, too, that her revelations must be impartial, which is to say equal; the deity cannot play favorites. ... The great historical religions have survived for millennia, which is what we would expect if they are divinely powered (562)." He continues on with several equally circular arguments.

[27] Sallie King, "Two Epistemological Models for the Interpretation of Mysticism," *Journal of the American Academy of Religion* 56 (1988), 257–79.

[28] Proudfoot, *Religious Experience*, 125.

[29] He outlines the behavioral, evolutionary, and neurocognitive findings that support his thesis in Natika Newton, *Foundations of Understanding* (Philadelphia: John Benjamins, 1996).

scientists, and culture is now understood as a contributing factor rather than an absolute limit on such experience.[30] The theories of Pierre Bourdieu, for example, have helped us to imagine how human behavior can be both culturally conditioned and innovative, while the philosopher Maurice Merleau-Ponty has discussed the indeterminate nature of perception, in which the human body is the grounds and basis of knowing.[31] With this shift has come a greater focus on what such experience reveals about human thinking, knowing, practice, and culture, as well as a turn toward the "socially informed body."[32] Minimally and most importantly in the context of this project stands the claim that human experience includes elements that are known apart from language; elements that are essentially human, not cultural. Although I will touch on cultural contributions throughout the book, the primary focus of the ensuing chapters will be these embodied elements.

In the renewed conversation about ecstasy, the broader valences of both "religious" and "experience" are active, so the term religious experience functions as a "vague" category.[33] Although that designation sounds pejorative, it is used to define precisely what can be most useful about categorization. As the philosopher Robert Cummings Neville explains it,

[30] Among those interested in a reinvigorated conversation about religious experience are Carol Rausch Albright and Joel Haugen, *Beginning with the End: God, Science, and Wolfhart Pannenberg* (Chicago: Open Court, 1997); James B. Ashbrook and Carol Rausch Albright, *The Humanizing Brain: Where Religion and Neuroscience Meet* (Cleveland, Ohio: Pilgrim, 1997); Eugene G. d'Aquili and Andrew B. Newberg, "Religious and Mystical States: A Neuropsychological Substrate," *Zygon* 28 (1993), 177–200; Eugene G. d'Aquili and Andrew B. Newberg, *The Mystical Mind: Probing the Biology of Religious Experience Theology and the Sciences* (Minneapolis: Fortress, 1999); Bstan Dzin Rgya Mtsho et al., *Consciousness at the Crossroads: Conversations with the Dalai Lama on Brainscience and Buddhism* (Ithaca, N.Y.: Snow Lion, 1999); Andrew B. Newberg, Eugene G. d'Aquili, Vince Rause, and Judith Cummings, *Why God Won't Go Away: Brain Science and the Biology of Belief* (New York: Ballantine, 2001); Proudfoot, *Religious Experience*; Fraser Watts, "Cognitive Neuroscience and Religious Consciousness," in *Neuroscience and the Person: Scientific Perspectives on Divine Action*, ed. Robert J. Russell (Berkeley, Calif.: Center for Theology and the Natural Sciences, 1999), 327–46; Wesley J. Wildman and Leslie A. Brothers, "Religious Experience" in Russell, *Neuroscience and the Person*, 347–416.

[31] The watershed studies for the two authors are: Pierre Bourdieu, *Outline of a Theory of Practice*, trans. Richard Nice, Cambridge Studies in Social and Cultural Anthropology 16 (Cambridge: Cambridge University Press, 1997), originally published as *Esquisse d'une théorie de la pratique* (Geneva: Droz, 1972); and Maurice Merleau-Ponty, *Phenomenology of Perception*, trans. Colin Smith (New York: Humanities Press, 1962), originally published as *Phénoménologie de la perception*, 15th ed. (Paris: Gallimard, 1945).

[32] This phrase comes from Thomas J. Csordas, "Embodiment as a Paradigm for Anthropology" *Ethos* 18 (1990), 5–47.

[33] The notion of vagueness was first articulated by Charles Peirce and has been described in Robert C. Neville, *Normative Cultures* (Albany: State University of New York Press, 1995), esp. 61–68.

theoretical vagueness allows for a broad field of comparison that is nevertheless meaningful in the minimal level of similarity that it identifies. He illustrates it through the metaphor of translation: "Translation has to do with expressing the relatively specific in terms of the relatively vague, and then doing the same with some other relatively specific category, so that both specific things are expressed in the language of the vague level of categories that function as their unifying context."[34]

Vague categories can counterbalance the distorting tendencies of specificity. They assert the significance of foundational similarity between specific incidences that have been elaborated in diverse directions, they provide a perspective within which given differences can be seen according to their actual proportions and significance, and they help theorists to see much more than they otherwise might.

It is in that capacity that the vague category of religious experience is especially useful to a study of Paul and his letters. Pauline scholarship is quite adept at accounting for the specific. Luke Timothy Johnson has described the way some of these specific categories can blind scholarship to the larger and often more necessary issues:

> On one side, we possess marvelously intricate and methodologically sophisticated scholarship about early Christianity, a veritable mountain of learning about every word of the New Testament and its milieu, every literary seam, every possible source, every discernible pulse of historical development. On the other side, we are virtually ignorant concerning a remarkable range of statements in the New Testament that appear to be of first importance to the writers, that seem to express fundamental convictions, that demand some kind of account, but that all of our learning does not touch. This range of statements has to do with religious experience.[35]

If Paul's theology takes place in the complex context of experience, so, equally, does our discussion of his experience take place in the complex context of this historical moment. Contemporary interest in religion has shifted both in its perspectives and its motivations. Postmodernism's vital, if scant, conclusion that we have constructed not only the means by which we come to know but the objects of knowledge themselves has given new, albeit diffuse, impetus to the examination of religion. More direct provocation arises from the fact that the broad and troubled context of international relations continues to be played out against religious backdrops. In response,

---

[34] Ibid., 61.
[35] Luke Timothy Johnson, *Religious Experience in Earliest Christianity: A Missing Dimension in New Testament Studies* (Minneapolis: Fortress, 1998), 3–4.

factions within world religions vie with one another for authoritative descriptions of their own traditions with renewed urgency. Coincident with these changes in ideological context, an intriguing bit of happenstance has provided new means by which religion might be assessed. Neuroscience is now probing the pathways to its own description of religious phenomena, and evolutionary psychology is theorizing about the origination of religious impulses.

The interplay between these two sets of contexts – the social-political and the scientific – holds potential for important correctives of and tempered insight into religion. Unfortunately, all too often, their combined effect makes religious experience vulnerable to competing totalizing claims. Reductionisms abound on all "sides." Even some recent philosophical contributions have been cast in simplified either-or propositions. *Breaking the Spell: Religion as a Natural Phenomenon*, the latest contribution of the well-known philosopher of mind Daniel Dennett, is a case in point. However complex and nuanced his views are at heart, Dennett's argumentation often presents the situation as one of a single choice between purely religious explanations on one side and purely scientific on the other. As one reviewer put it,

> Dennett lives in a world in which you must believe in the grossest biologism or in the grossest theism, in a purely naturalistic understanding of religion or in intelligent design, in the omniscience of a white man with a long beard in 19th-century England or in the omniscience of a white man with a long beard in the sky.[36]

Because of the importance of Paul's letters to Christian religious claims, it seems necessary that this larger context affect the objects and means of knowledge in Pauline studies as well. In addition to their crucial critique, postmodern perspectives make a constructive contribution through the obligation that we pursue both approaches and solutions – means and ends – that are inherently complex. (In fact, because this book is an attempt to describe *experience*, one might assume that complexity is a necessity.) I have argued earlier that the practice of traditionally good exegesis in itself is prone to creating unintentional distortions; likewise, some of the other methods employed most energetically in this book are predisposed toward their own totalizing visions. For these reasons, this study is fundamentally interdisciplinary. It is concerned not only with viewing Paul's religious experience

---

[36] Leon Wieseltier, "The God Genome," *New York Times*, February 19, 2006, online at http://www.nytimes.com/2006/02/19/books/review/19wieseltier.html?ex=1147924800&en=c0448e8f57c4bb21&ei=5070.

from many perspectives but also with the ways in which each of those diverse perspectives require the tempering and completion found only in their relation to the others. They come to their fullest expression through interrelationships rather than in isolated articulation, no matter how lucid it may be.

Before launching directly into this tour of the several facets of Paul's ecstasy, a moment of orientation to the chapters that follow is in order. Readings of Paul's letters have proceeded quite nicely with little more than a curious or embarrassed footnote or two to the possibility of Paul's occasional exuberance. The premise of this book is that ecstasy is actually a significant feature of Paul's life and impetus to his thought, and thus it seems necessary to account for its absence in the usual journeys through the letters. Chapter 1 of this study begins with an assessment of the ideological influences that make it difficult not only to view ecstatic experiences positively but even to discern them as present in the biblical texts. New Testament scholarship has been affected by broader cultural biases against ecstasy: In European, Russian, and North American cultures, there is a long history of viewing the use of ASCs as psychologically and socially deviant. In the formative generations of academic anthropology, shamans, for example, were routinely understood to be either mentally ill or socially manipulative. These evaluations were supported by a pervasive tendency in modernity to value the rational over all other forms of knowing, a tendency that Michael Harner has dubbed "cognicentrism."[37] Even while anthropology was publishing those early biases, biblical studies were taking them up in confessional polemics. For example, in the nineteenth century and much of the twentieth, mysticism became one of the means by which the contest for authoritative Christian origins was waged.[38] Mysticism, in some discourse, served as shorthand for many phenomena, including most forms of ecstatic religious experience. Furthermore, mysticism was routinely depicted as world-negating and solipsistic. By extension of these arguments, it was important for Protestants (who were the vast majority of biblical scholars) to show that Christian origins were free of "Catholic" tendencies, including the sacramental and the mystical. Paul, in his role as the "patron saint of thought in Christianity,"[39] provided a Protestant champion against these

---

[37] Michael J. Harner, *The Way of the Shaman*, 2nd ed. (San Francisco: Harper and Row, 1990).
[38] The broader effects of these polemics on early historiography are outlined in Jonathan Z. Smith, *Drudgery Divine: On the Comparison of Early Christianities and the Religions of Late Antiquity*, Jordan Lectures in Comparative Religion 14 (Chicago: University of Chicago Press, 1990).
[39] This image is from Albert Schweitzer, *Die Mystik des Apostels Paulus* (Tübingen: Mohr, 1930), translated into English as *The Mysticism of Paul the Apostle*, trans. William Montgomery (New York: Henry Holt, 1931), 377.

Catholic "abuses." It was in such circumstances that Albert Schweitzer was able to write an entire book on Paul's "mysticism" that barely touched on any of Paul's ecstatic experience. For example, Schweitzer devotes a chapter to Paul's ethics (thus demonstrating the apostle's engagement in the world) but attributes Paul's "conversion" to an epileptic seizure.[40]

Although these broader confessional and cultural views have changed, their effects have been encoded in certain patterns of interpretation of Paul's letters. One of these patterns is the preference to see the christian assemblies as susceptible to ecstatic abuses while viewing Paul as an opponent of those tendencies. Therefore, the second half of Chapter 1 examines some of the means by which Paul has been viewed as an opponent of ecstatic religious experience. That examination focuses on two test cases: 1 Cor 14:18 and 2 Cor 12:1–4. In these two passages, Paul's own religious experience is mentioned explicitly, and therefore the attempts to subvert it even here are all the more noteworthy. Finally, Chapter 1 considers the fact that the occasion of Paul's conversion and/or call has remained the one relatively widely accepted category in which Paul's experience can be considered.

Part of the argument in Chapter 1 is that exegetical method (necessarily) favors certain questions and obstructs others. As Paula Fredriksen put it with regard to historical Jesus studies, "once method determines our perspective on our sources, *how* we see is really what we get."[41] Because of that inherent difficulty, and because Paul's ecstatic experience has fared poorly in much exegesis, the ensuing chapters are deliberately interdisciplinary in their perspectives. Chapter 2 begins the process of accounting for Paul's ecstasy by lodging it, in the first place, as firmly and physically as possible in Paul's own person. For a number of reasons, the examination relies on medical science, and the relatively new field of neurocognitive science in particular ("new" at least in terms of what can now be measured), as a primary tool in this process. The primary and most obvious among these reasons are the fact that medical science is of manifest relevance to understanding human bodily experience and that neuroscience is the only direct means to describe brain functioning during normal and altered states. Thus, neuroscience provides a lens through which some details that are normally out of our range of vision can be brought into focus. It also provides a language with which to discuss what has been observed and the means to compare variant forms of a

[40] Schweitzer, *Mysticism of Paul the Apostle*. The chapter on ethics comprises pages 293–333. The diagnosis of Paul's "seizure" appears on page 153. The book was less an examination of religious experience than it was an attempt to rehabilitate the category of mysticism.

[41] Paula Fredriksen, *Jesus of Nazareth, King of the Jews: A Jewish Life and the Emergence of Christianity* (New York: Knopf, 1999), 7.

phenomenon. Thus, it has robust explanatory power for this question. Another invaluable feature of neuroscience is its investment in both experience and understanding. The second set of reasons for choosing neurology concerns academic responsibility. The use of data from the natural sciences is recommended by the fact that such findings are inherently falsifiable. The ability to falsify the claims seems especially important in an examination of human experience, where there is concern both about undue subjectivity on the one hand and opacity on the other.

However, scientific approaches are not without their pitfalls, and I have tried to keep these in mind while choosing and evaluating scientific conversation partners. One of the dangers of the "hard sciences" is, as mentioned, their inherent intolerance for phenomena that cannot be directly tested and measured. Still, the tendency to reduce God to neural blips is no stronger in science than is the parallel tendency in theology to abstract God from embodied knowing. At the very least, each set of interests provides a natural check on the absolute claims of the other. At best, the two make fruitful conversation partners, as demonstrated, for example, by the ongoing consultations between the Dalai Lama and a group of neuroscientists.[42] The neurological model of religious ecstasy used in Chapter 2 is unabashedly scientific, but not reductionist. It was developed by Eugene d'Aquili in collaboration with Andrew Newberg,[43] but it is built on generations of clinical observation of and experimentation on the functioning of the brain and central nervous system. Although the authors attempt to describe as fully as possible the mechanisms of human neurology that accompany religious ecstasy, they do not believe that religious experience is merely neural noise. Put another way, they do not claim that God is generated by the brain, but they do claim that God cannot be known apart from the brain.[44]

After presenting the model and the rationale for a neurological approach to ecstatic religious experience, Chapter 2 applies that work to Paul's account of his experience of ascent to paradise (2 Cor 12:1–4). This account is noteworthy among Paul's various comments because it is the fullest description and, arguably, the most powerful of the experiences that Paul

[42] Transcripts and commentary on the proceedings are published in Bstan Dzin Rgya Mtsho et al., *Consciousness at the Crossroads*.
[43] The model is outlined in greatest detail in d'Aquili and Newberg, *Mystical Mind*.
[44] Furthermore, they argue, if human certainty about the reality of an object is the measure of its realness, then God as experienced in religious ecstasy "wins hands down." See Eugene G. d'Aquili and Andrew B. Newberg, "Liminality, Trance, and Unitary States in Ritual and Meditation," *Studia Liturgica* 23 (1993), 33. The comment on "realness" is based on reports of ecstatics' sense that their visions of God are "more real" than anything they experience in ordinary states of consciousness.

discusses. Two authors in particular – Alan Segal[45] and James Tabor[46] – have assessed the passage in some detail, and both of them approach it primarily through comparison with other texts and interpretive traditions. But these assessments cannot adequately account for two details in Paul's brief description. The first is Paul's repeated claim that he does not know the status of his body during his trance, and the second is his claim that he heard "unutterable utterances." The remainder of the chapter attempts to show that these details are intelligibly described as neurological features of a particular bodily state.

Chapter 3 expands the conversation to consider how such rich experiences are constitutive of Paul's theological reflection. Here the focus broadens in two ways: First, it moves from primary experience to secondary reflection on it, and, second, it moves beyond the close examination of a private and superlative event to follow its ripples through a number of passages and themes from Paul's letters. Following a detailed examination of one of Paul's ecstatic events in Chapter 2, Chapter 3 shifts to considering what difference an understanding of such experience can make to a broader reading of Paul's letters and circumstances.

The focus on Paul's religious ecstasy, by its very nature, moves experience to a more central place in exegetical reconstruction. As a result of reading from experience, certain features of the text that are frequently glossed over are instead seen to be unpolished attempts to express what is known apart from words. Reading from experience also reorders what is privileged in any given passage. For example, passages such as 2 Corinthians 3–5 and Romans 8 have been comfortably discussed under traditional (etic) rubrics of pneumatology and eschatology. However, some of these taxonomies are quite slippery and loosely defined, and it is not at all clear that such labels identify the most meaningful and distinguishing features of the discourse. For example, both the Romans and the 1 Corinthians passages mention the future and Paul's claim that change is already under way, but recognition of that content says little about how Paul came to understand the present in this way. Instead, I argue that Paul is speaking out of both his experience of an alternate reality of his own body and his ecstatic relationship to the figure of the resurrected Jesus. If religious experience is epistemologically significant (and that, you may have guessed, is the wager of this book), then its influence cannot be limited only to the specific occasions in which it took

---

[45] See especially Alan Segal, *Paul the Convert: The Apostolate and Apostasy of Saul the Pharisee* (New Haven, Conn.: Yale University Press, 1990), 34–71.

[46] James D. Tabor, *Things Unutterable: Paul's Ascent to Paradise in Its Greco-Roman, Judaic, and Early Christian Contexts*, Studies in Judaism (Lanham, Md.: University Press of America, 1986).

place. So Chapter 3 considers the way its residual presence – the afterglow, if you will – is perceivable as part of the conversations Paul carried out with various christian assemblies. The chapter is, in short, an attempt to provide a fuller account of Paul's first-order reflection on the basis of his ecstatic experience.[47]

A second set of textual interests in Chapter 3 is all those details that are sometimes grouped together as Paul's "Christ-mysticism."[48] These include Paul's talk of being in Christ, participating in the death and resurrection of Christ (Rom 6:5–6), being transformed into the same glorious form as Christ (2 Cor 3:18), and of being united with Christ (1 Cor 6:15). The distinctive Pauline language of participation in Christ has been a problem primarily because there is no theological category that can comfortably account for it. However, Paul's various claims are rendered more intelligible when they are seen as responses to the bodily phenomena of ecstatic experience in which neurochemical analgesics and euphorics are released, in which the pain and weight of human flesh is neurologically numbed, and in which our cognitive constructs of personal boundaries are temporarily blurred. Paul's "Christ-mysticism" is not so much a theology in search of a metaphor as an ecstatic experience struggling with the limits of words.

Chapter 4 both thickens the description of ecstasy and serves as a test case for the preceding chapters. Ecstasy exists at once as both an intensely personal experience (the focus of Chapter 2) and a thoroughly social and cultural one. Such communal concerns are perhaps nowhere more salient than in 1 Corinthians 12–14. The passage provides far more information about the social circumstances of ecstatic practice than any other portion of the Pauline corpus. Furthermore, the passage is significant in this consideration because it also provides the largest potential obstruction to the book's claims about Paul and his ecstasy, for there Paul seems to be rejecting ecstatic practice by limiting the number of people who speak in tongues and by relegating "exuberant" expression of glossolalia to a place below that of the "controlled" practice of prophecy.

---

[47] There are clear indications of second-order thinking in the passage as well; for example, the interpretation of the *rhēmata* as superhuman speech and the assigned destination of the third heaven. However, eschatology is an academic category, as is apocalyptics. It represents a tertiary systematization of ideas that lies well beyond Paul's thoughts in this passage. What was there for Paul before the system? What made it meaningful to speak in ways that have since been called eschatological?

[48] Adolf Deissmann coined the term "Christ-mysticism" in *Paul: A Study in Social and Religious History*, trans. William E. Wilson (New York: Harper and Brothers, 1957). The term has persisted despite the inability to fully incorporate this category of Pauline thought into Paul's theology.

So, the thickness of the description in Chapter 4 derives from the modeling of a number of anthropologists applied to the social and material history of Corinth. In particular, Erika Bourguignon and Michael Winkelman have described the value of ASCs in human communities. They have also documented the social patterns that correspond to different kinds of deployment of ASCs. Their shared categories of spirit possession, shamanism, and mediumship can classify the various ecstatic practices taking place in Corinth and, furthermore, explicate how Paul's advice participates in a cross-cultural social logic. Bourguignon and her colleagues found that some form of ASC was institutionalized as part of a religious setting in 90 percent of the societies in their worldwide sampling.[49] The christian community in Corinth was no different. The chapter argues that whereas most New Testament exegeses see Paul opposing ecstatic practice, he is in fact urging the development of a form of ASC that he feels is better suited to the evolving circumstances and well-being of the community.

The decision to use neurological, exegetical, and social anthropological perspective approaches also grows out of the concern for responsibility on two specific fronts. First, because the topic of Paul's religious ecstasy remains something of a curiosity in New Testament studies, it seems prudent to demonstrate its explanatory power over a range of Pauline texts and issues; if experience is truly a significant and critically neglected aspect of the texts, then it should be possible to demonstrate its relevance in several ways. Second, anyone else's experience will always remain partly veiled from us. Because Paul's ecstasy cannot be accessed directly, it seems even more important to choose more than one vantage point from which to consider it. Thus, it is my assumption that where cognitive neuroscience, textual exegesis, and social anthropology converge, the contours of Paul's experience will be outlined more fully than they would be through any one approach alone.

Finally, two choices of language deserve preliminary explanation. The first is my use of "christian" with a lowercase "c." What to call the movement that became Christianity is always a problem. Whatever term is used needs to signal that the movement was in some way Jewish, because two distinct religions did not yet exist, and yet that it was distinguishable from that larger conglomerate in part by its connection with Jesus, who was called Christ. My solution is pragmatic and convenient rather than either elegant or exacting.

---

[49] Erika Bourguignon, "Introduction: A Framework for the Comparative Study of Altered States of Consciousness," in Bourguignon, *Religion, Altered States of Consciousness, and Social Change*, 11.

I have chosen to use the most common term "Christian" unmodified by hyphenated qualifications. At the same time, it appears with a lowercase "c" when it signals the unofficial status and unsystematized character of the movement in the first century. So, "christian," with no capitalization, will serve as merciful shorthand for that phase in the evolution of a Jewish sect before it fully developed into a formal and socially recognized independent religion, and "Christian" refers to the culture that now interprets this precursor.

The second choice is the decision to use the phrase "ecstatic religious experience." The utility of "religious experience" has been outlined previously, but the further designation of "ecstatic" also warrants comment. I use "ecstasy" to designate the biological, chemical, and neurological – in short, bodily – state in which Paul experienced various phenomena. In other treatments of this same topic, the term "mysticism" is used. That term can suffice to designate both the notion of extraordinary experience and something of the cultural interpretative framework in which it exists. However, I have chosen to avoid it for a number of reasons. On the one hand, mysticism has a history of misrepresentation in New Testament scholarship – it has been made to represent the straw man of irrationality and self-serving solipsism. On the other hand, where mysticism retains positive connotations, it generally describes a primarily textual artifact and a tradition of interpretation. My own interest here leans more toward the comparative and experiential and therefore away from the mystical in these senses. From time to time, I will also use the phrase "altered state of consciousness" (or the abbreviated ASC) and the term "trance" as synonyms for ecstasy. I use them more for the sake of lexical variety than for taxonomic precision. Both terms are routinely used in the scientific literature as synonyms for ecstasy.

So, with some sense of the route ahead and a few tips on the local dialect, we can proceed to an examination of the ideological opposition, methodological concerns, and, in some cases, historical accidents that have blocked examination of ecstatic elements in Paul's letters.

1

∾

What Ecstasy? An Assessment of the Misregard

"As a rule," said Holmes, "the more bizarre a thing is the less mysterious it turns out to be. It is your commonplace featureless crimes which are really puzzling."

– Arthur Conan Doyle

To an imagination used to the perspectives of dignity and glory, the naked gospel scheme seems to offer an almshouse for a palace.

– William James

RELIGIOUS ECSTASY IS RARELY TAKEN UP AS A CATEGORY OF Pauline studies and even less often as a window into the historical character of Paul himself. This is not to say that ecstatic elements in Paul's letters have gone wholly unnoticed, but rather that they have not typically been addressed as an aspect of his life and thought. Among the labels applied to Paul – apostle, convert, Pharisee, apocalyptic, even tentmaker – that of ecstatic is seldom used.[1] In fact, it is often forcefully resisted. This chapter examines that resistance both within Pauline studies in particular and within the larger culture in general. Why the extraordinary effort to avoid the ecstatic in Paul's life? What has, in benign form, prevented people from attending to this feature and, in more tendentious forms, motivated them to work so hard against the more obvious meaning of the text? On occasion, the misregard of ecstasy seems significantly more "bizarre" than the fact that Paul experienced it; yet, more often, the misregard is merely the product of habits of seeing – where

---

[1] Even John Ashton, *The Religion of Paul the Apostle* (New Haven, Conn.: Yale University Press, 2000), who nonetheless has recently addressed many of the issues that are near the heart of this examination, does not pursue this category.

we look, the perspective from which we look, and the lenses that focus our attention.

The resistance to the image of Paul as an ecstatic can be seen as one example of a more pervasive cultural aversion that crosses academic disciplines and in fact is not even restricted to academia. In a culture that "believes in" an initiatory cosmic explosion but not, for example, in animate spirits, anyone who claims to interact with such spirits is not likely to get expansive hearing. In fact, the cultural resistance to religious ecstasy is not expressed merely through the ethnocentric claim that no one *here* does that; rather, it has often been extended into arguments about what no one *anywhere should* do. Conventional psychology has been especially effective in its antagonism toward ecstatic religious experience. For generations, diagnostic manuals described behaviors related to religious ecstasy in pejorative terms. Diagnoses of epilepsy, hysteria, and schizophrenia have been most frequently applied to ecstatic trance. In the mid-1970s, the Group for the Advancement of Psychiatry published a study entitled *Mysticism: Spiritual Quest or Psychic Disorder?*[2] The case of religious ecstasy is further complicated by the fact that, within the discipline of anthropology, the anthropology of religion has more recently been marginalized.[3] Thus, the very subdiscipline that might reform or revise narrowly modern views of such religious experience has a hard time even finding a stage.

Within this larger set of biases, the ethnographic studies of shamanism provide an apt case study of the changing attitudes of anthropologists toward the practice of religiously interpreted altered states of consciousness for at least two reasons. First, because the work of shamans entails the regular

[2] See discussions in Roger Walsh, "The Psychological Health of Shamans: A Reevaluation," *Journal of the American Academy of Religion* 65 (1997), 105–14; Joan B. Townsend, "Shamanism," in *Anthropology of Religion: A Handbook*, ed. Stephen D. Glazier (Westport, Conn.: Greenwood, 1997), 454–56; and Richard Noll, "What Has Really Been Learned about Shamanism?" *Journal of Psychoactive Drugs* 21 (1989), 47–50.

[3] Stephen D. Glazier, ed., *Anthropology of Religion: A Handbook* (Westport, Conn.: Greenwood, 1997), 1. For instance, Glazier highlights the fact that only five of the American schools with graduate programs in anthropology even offer a concentration in religion. In a comparable, if less statistically oriented, description, a philosopher of religion observes: "If you are in a company of people of mixed occupations, and somebody asks what you do, and you say you are a college professor, a glazed look comes into his eye. If you are in a company of professors from various departments, and somebody asks what is your field, and you say philosophy, a glazed look comes into his eye. If you are at a conference of philosophers, and somebody asks you what you are working on, and you say philosophy of religion..." (Renford Bamborough, "Editorial: Subject and Epithet," *Philosophy* 55 (1980), 289–90).

use of ASCs, and because their role involves communication with spirits and travel in the spirit world, shamans have been vulnerable to incriminations on a number of fronts. Second, because shamans attracted anthropological attention early in the development of that discipline, their practices provide a longer history to be traced than do some other practices of ASC. The European academic study of what came to be identified as shamanism began in eighteenth- and nineteenth-century explorations of Africa and was colored by the worldview that accompanied colonialism: "We were white, they were black. We were civilized, they were primitive. We were Christian, they were pagan. We used science, they used magic."[4] But it was the ethnography of Siberian shamanism (which gave us the term shaman) that most thoroughly shaped the contours that continued to define the study for generations.

The avenues of inquiry opened by these first records of Siberian practitioners set interpretive directions that have been difficult to reroute. Descriptions tended to the extremes of romanticizing or vilification. Others have shown how these early studies were often also colored by a particular Marxist evolutionary view of religious behavior.[5] But, most tellingly, in his thorough review of Soviet literature on the topic, Andrei Znamenski recounts how a single account of an ecstatic séance recorded in the 1840s "by an anonymous Russian missionary" "remained for a long time the only available complete record of a shamanic session."[6] That account focused exclusively on the means by which a particular shaman achieved an ASC through vigorous dance and dramatic vocalization. The account was abstracted from the observation of its occasion and its effects on the community, as well as any more comprehensive description of the part the shaman played within the society. Thus, the possibility of viewing shamanism as a role encompassing a range of tasks and a wider repertoire of behaviors within the context of enduring relationships was effectively pushed out of view. Znamenski further traces the path of the account from the record of an oral account delivered to the Orthodox missionary Vasilii Verbitskii (1870), to the German academic Wilhelm Radloff, who first published it (1884), through to twentieth-century accounts. This one highly dramatic occasion was made the early exemplar of the entire phenomenon.

---

[4] E. Fuller Torrey, "Spiritualists and Shamans as Psychotherapists: An Account of Original Anthropological Sin," in *Religious Movements in Contemporary America,* ed. Irving I. Zaretsky and Mark P. Leone (Princeton, N.J.: Princeton University Press, 1974), 331.

[5] Townsend, "Shamanism," 429.

[6] Andrei A. Znamenski, *Shamanism in Siberia: Russian Records of Indigenous Spirituality* (Dordrecht: Kluwer, 2003), 11. My thanks to an anonymous reader for alerting me to Znamenski's work.

Thus, a combination of historical circumstances and cultural antipathies eventually focused attention on the shamans themselves as a target for pejorative descriptions. As I. M. Lewis describes it, ethnographers frequently became "absorbed in often quite pointless debates about the genuineness or otherwise of a particular trance state."[7] In many descriptions, it was not merely the religious practices of shamanism that were questionable but the characters of the shamans as well. Their relatively high degree of influence in their societies was accounted for by the fact that they were accomplished charlatans and manipulators.[8]

The work of L. B. Boyer illustrates the persistence of such views well into the twentieth century. In 1961, Boyer published this assessment of an Apache shaman: "He was shown to suffer from a personality disorder, with impulsive and hysterical traits, and to have characteristics of the impostor. His principal fixations were oral and phallic. There were suggestions he lacked clear masculine identity and suffered from problems resulting from latent homosexuality."[9]

That same year, Boyer published a second study, in which, on the basis of his questionable observations, he extrapolated from that single shaman to the conclusion that all Apache shamans were mentally ill.[10] To his credit, over the next three years, Boyer met with eleven more Apache shamans and eventually published a reversal of his earlier opinion, concluding that these shamans were actually healthier than the average members of their communities.[11] Although his later opinions may also be overstated, they at least have the benefit of drawing on more than a single example as evidence.

---

[7] I. M. Lewis, *Ecstatic Religion: An Anthropological Study of Spirit Possession and Shamanism*, 2nd ed. (Harmondsworth: Penguin, 1971), 26.

[8] Such views were recorded as early as 1751 by travelers such as botanist Johann Georg Gmelin, who wanted to confine Siberian shamans "to the Urgurian silver mine, so that there they might spend the rest of their days in perpetual labor," cited in Jeremy Narby and Francis Huxley, *Shamans through Time: 500 Years on the Path to Knowledge* (London: Thames and Hudson, 2001), 28. The editors of the volume point out further that Gmelin's wishes were more or less fulfilled two centuries later when "Soviet authorities interned Siberian shamans in camps, or executed them" (27). In contrast to these views, a century later, geologist Petr Chikhachev noted that the shamans "did not demand any honors" and carried on lives indistinguishable from the rest of their communities (cited in Znamenski, *Shamanism in Siberia*, 6).

[9] L. B. Boyer, "Notes on the Personality Structure of a North American Indian Shaman," *Journal of Hillside Hospital* 10 (1961), 14–33.

[10] L. B. Boyer, "Remarks on the Personality of Shamans," *Psychoanalytic Study of Society* 2 (1961), 233–54.

[11] L. B. Boyer, "Comparison on the Shamans and Pseudoshamans of the Apaches of the Mescalero Indian Reservation: A Rorschach Study," *Journal of Projective Techniques and Personality Assessment* 28 (1964), 173–80.

Such psychological condemnations of shamans continued into the 1970s. Typically, the diagnoses were applied without sensitivity to cultural differences and the distinct functions that a single behavior might serve in diverse contexts. The evaluation of transvestism, where it appeared among Plains Indians, is a case in point. Cross-dressing was offered as (sensational and titillating) proof of mental instability without any attention to its interpretation in that society and evaluation by that culture.[12] As a final example, in a description that is distinguished primarily by the economy with which so many cultures are damned so comprehensively, one commentator described shamanism as follows:

> The general process of becoming a shaman is, indeed, remarkably similar throughout the world: a phase of *schizoid identity* dissolution is followed by a phase of *paranoidal identity* restitution, the new identity being that of the shaman, and with community support and encouragement for the development of a controlled *hysterical dissociability* during which the shaman is able to visit, speak to, see, or be entered by his *supernatural alter ego*.[13]

In such depictions, shamanism illustrates the glossary of psychological disorders at least from "a" (alter ego) to "s" (schizoid).

The last quarter of the twentieth century included systematic efforts to view shamanism in a more nuanced light and with increased cultural awareness, including awareness of both the culture being observed and the interpreting culture. For instance, in one study, Richard Noll closely compared the ethnographic reports about shamans with the description of schizophrenia in the *Diagnostic and Statistical Manual of Mental Disorders* (DSM-III).[14]

---

[12] Torrey discusses the research of A. L. Kroeber in this context; see Torrey, "Spiritualists and Shamans as Psychotherapists," 331–32. Contemporary studies of gender and sexuality would, of course, add even further grounds for dismissing the pejorative evaluations of Kroeber et al.

[13] Anthony F. C. Wallace, *Religion: An Anthropological View* (New York: Random House, 1966), 145, emphasis mine. Wallace evaluates "mysticism" similarly: "The prolegomena to the mystic experience must be, as with the shaman, a profound sense of dissatisfaction with one's secular identity, a feeling of anxiety or fear, a desperate sense of the need to be saved before being damned by some final disaster" (152).

[14] Beginning with the publication of the third edition of the DSM, disorders were described in the pattern of infectious diseases. This change coincided with ideological shifts regarding mental disorders (e.g., a primarily biological understanding and illness paradigm that subverted cultural tendencies to see mental illness as a character flaw) and allowed sexual difference to be removed from the manual. However, as Allan Young argues, it also discouraged consideration of environmental and circumstantial contributors to mental health. See Allan Young, "Notes on the Evolution of Evolutionary Psychiatry," in *New Horizons in Medical Anthropology: Essays in Honour of Charles Leslie,* ed. Mark Nichter and Margaret M. Lock (London: Routledge, 2002), 221–39.

Noll's goal was to show that, even in its own terms, psychiatry could not dismiss shamanism as mental illness. He concludes that: "[U]nless all shamans are suffering from a mysterious organic brain disease the symptoms of which they can willfully control, or until a better case can be made for a type of schizophrenia in primitive societies the symptoms of which are also willfully controlled over a lifetime, the schizophrenia metaphor for shamanism presents a false and misleading analogy."[15]

So, the blanket assertions of dysfunction have abated. Furthermore, closer and more balanced examination of the evidence has made it possible for students of shamanism to observe that, for some practitioners in some societies, the role of shaman actually required levels of mental health and social maturity higher than those of the general population. This reevaluation is possible, in part, because work in cross-cultural psychology has helped to show how ethnocentric our constructions of human mental health have been, and definitions of mental health have expanded to include more cultural and individual variation. In addition, the traditional psychotherapeutic categories have been applied more impartially to shamanism. Joan Townsend's work is characteristic of the more recent and nuanced evaluation of shamanism. She describes the shamans she has met in the course of her fieldwork as "quintessential 'normal, average' people." Furthermore, she distinguishes them from past portraits as follows:

> Mentally disturbed people are burdens on others. Shamans are intelligent, balanced, and capable individuals who must move into dangerous conditions in spiritual reality – a feat that a neurotic person could not handle successfully. The shaman's society might consider him a strange or difficult person because he is an individualist and he traffics in a dangerous world. Handling the dangers of spiritual reality and dealing with emergencies and threats in his own society demand a competent, very sane individual.
>
> I do not deny that some people who are shamans also happen to have mental problems.... What I question is the allegation of a functional relationship between shamanism and mental illness.[16]

Shamanism is not the only form in which the practice of religious trance has been routinely recognized and studied. The other major anthropological category of religiously altered states of consciousness is spirit possession, and its cultural evaluation follows a similar trajectory. As in the case of shamanism,

---

[15] Richard Noll, "Shamanism and Schizophrenia: A State-Specific Approach to the 'Schizophrenia Metaphor' of Shamanic States," *American Ethnologist* 10 (1983), 454.

[16] Townsend, "Shamanism," 456. Here she is summarizing, in part, the work of R. Gilberg, "How to Recognize a Shaman among Other Religious Specialists," in *Shamanism in Eurasia*, ed. Mihály Hoppál (Göttingen: Herodot, 1984), Part 1, 21–27.

"the spectacle of spirit possession has driven Western man to produce the most lurid descriptions of possession as well as the most abstract, objectivistic, indeed rarefied, analyses of the condition."[17] This negative evaluation is especially interesting in light of the oft-cited study by Erika Bourguignon that found that 90 percent of the societies for which information was available were reported to have "one or more institutionalized culturally patterned forms of altered states of consciousness."[18] It is appropriate to consider whether the combined fascination and revulsion have as much to do with the issues of the interpretive culture as with those of the culture being observed.

Throughout this history, modern interpretive cultures seem to be the primary source of the "problems" with religious ecstasy, and mental illness has provided a convenient way to legitimate our discomfort. At a more fundamental level, Michael Harner has described the essence of Western discomfort as an orientation toward a certain way of thinking that he calls cognicentrism. Cognicentrism is a kind of prejudice that, in Harner's words, "is the counterpart of ethnocentrism between cultures."[19] The bias of cognicentrism is rooted in the constructs of scientific enlightenment, especially the idea of objective truth as the product of critical thinking stripped of personal investment. A cognicentric stance purports to arbitrate what counts as acceptable knowledge as well as what counts as acceptable ways of coming to know. Thus, it has come to judge mental health and even intelligence. The use of ASCs, particularly in religious contexts, is only one victim of this prejudice. Although ASCs are tolerated in Western therapeutic contexts such as hypnosis, where they are controlled by a professional, and even in some meditative practices, their use in virtually every other context is seen as mental weakness at best and pathology at worst.

I will give the final word on this bias to Noll, who, although he does not use the term cognicentric, nonetheless describes its valences well:

> The psychopathological model has been adopted by adherents of three philosophical systems that are pervasive in shamanism studies – scientism, psychoanalysis, and Marxism-Leninism. They all share a common characteristic: They base their legitimacy on a polemical devaluation of religion and religious experience. Furthermore, as is clear from shamanism scholarship, adherents to these world views often resort to psychiatric terminology as a powerful technique for the devaluation of such an important human

---

[17] Vincent Crapanzano and Vivian Garrison, *Case Studies in Spirit Possession,* Contemporary Religious Movements (New York: Wiley, 1977), 4.
[18] Bourguignon, "Introduction," 11. Bourguignon's findings are based on an examination of records from 488 societies distributed throughout the world.
[19] Harner, *Way of the Shaman,* xx.

experience.... [The schizophrenia model of shan
Western (and Soviet) ethnocentric distortion based
of psychiatric/medical schemata to experiences enc[

1.2 THE VIEW FROM HERE: BIASES
TESTAMENT STUDIES

When we turn to the treatment of religious experien
studies, we might expect some tempering of the broader cultural bias. Of
course, the location of biblical studies within academia ensures that some of
the cognicentric assumptions just described spill over into this field as well.
And Paul, in particular, has been vulnerable to being cast in the role of
systematic theologian and enlightenment reasoner. However, one might
expect biblical scholars, as a whole, to be less likely to hold the same ideological
disregard for religion. Unfortunately, that assumption, although true in general, does not tend to extend to religious experience because a general attitude
of openness has been partially offset by confessional polemics regarding mysticism, with the parties on either side of this divide typically, if somewhat
broadly, identified as Catholic and Protestant. So, although one might assume
that ecstatic religious experience would fare better under the gaze of theologians and biblical scholars, who in many cases are more sympathetic to religion, this has not been the case with the study of Paul; instead, the generalized
cultural bias against religious ecstasy placed its practitioners almost irretriev-
ably in the category of Other, while Paul was firmly the exemplar for Us.

1.2.1 *Cognicentrism in New Testament Studies*

In many ways, the cognicentric bias against ecstatic religious experience has
also been conveyed through a kind of straw man labeled "mysticism." In the
first half of the twentieth century, mysticism was frequently portrayed as
devoid of ethical content and as mere sentimentality. For example, as Ernst
von Dobschütz described it: "Proper to mysticism is especially the tendency
to become only one thing with the Deity, to become free of the 'I,' to become
lost in the infinite. Mysticism is always only a religion of feeling, delirious-
ness in the love of God, a retreat of ethical and active aspects. And this
simply cannot be said of Saint Paul."[21]

---

[20] Noll, "What Has Really Been Learned About Shamanism?" 48.
[21] Ernst von Dobschütz, *Der Apostel Paulus* (Halle [Saale]: Buchhandlung des Waisenhauses,
1926), 24.

in glove with the concern about subjective experience was the
tion that Paul's gospel must have been "objective." If Paul's gospel is
haped by his experience, then its absolute authority is weakened. Hans
Conzelmann, in particular, is insistent on the objective truth of Paul's
preaching, which, although it may have borrowed from "the linguistic
milieu of 'enthusiasm,'" was at heart a "juridical," not mystical, category.[22]
By declaring Paul to be without mystical influence, these early scholars
strove to insulate Paul's theology from Paul's own thinking and experience,
to make it something more trustworthy.

Likewise, the desire to translate Paul's letters into contemporary contexts
hindered the discussion of some experiential elements in his thought. For
example, in a discussion of Paul's widely acknowledged emphasis on "participation in Christ," James D. G. Dunn summarizes some of the reasons why
earlier interest in religious experience died away throughout the twentieth
century. In brief, he writes that the changing intellectual context of the twentieth century made it increasingly difficult to present "Paul's imagery of incorporation into another person" in meaningful language.[23] Albert Schweitzer's
Die Mystik des Apostels Paulus is an interesting case in point. Schweitzer stands
out from his contemporaries because he both championed mysticism as a
prevalent and central aspect of Paul's thought and, at the same time, reduced
that mysticism to *conceptual* constructs stripped of any but incidental *experiential* components. So, on the one hand, Schweitzer uses the term "Christ-
mysticism"[24] and introduces the notion of "being in Christ" to describe Paul's
distinctive insights. For example, he discusses the "natural" (or "quasi-phys-
ical," the suggestive rendering of *naturhaft* in the English translation), "cos-
mically conditioned" aspects of Paul's understanding of redemption; and,
breaking with the dominant interpretation of his time, he describes Paul's
understanding of righteousness by faith as merely "a subsidiary crater which
has formed within the rim of ... redemption through the being-in-Christ."[25]
These observations are compelling and distinctive for their time.

[22] Hans Conzelmann, *An Outline of the Theology of the New Testament*, trans. John Bowden (New York: Harper and Row, 1969), 208–12.
[23] James D. G. Dunn, *The Theology of Paul the Apostle* (Grand Rapids, Mich.: Eerdmans, 1998), 393.
[24] In fact, Adolf Deissmann used the term "Christ-mysticism" (along with "Christ-intimacy") first, but Schweitzer made it most famous. See Deissmann, *Paul*, esp. 135–57.
[25] Each of these views can be found at various points in Schweitzer, *Mysticism of Paul the Apostle,* but representative examples are as follows: for being in Christ, 3; for the "natural" character of redemption, 219 (in fact, he highlights Paul's inability to transcend the "prim-itive" attachments to concrete, physical experiences of what for Schweitzer should be universal theological propositions, 3–5); and for the subordination of righteousness by faith to being-in-Christ, 225.

On the other hand, for Schweitzer, the mysticism of the apostle is always a synthetic, intellectual construct, and the relation of Paul's actual experience to his mysticism is incidental and perhaps confirmatory, but never initiatory. So, for example, according to Schweitzer, "[T]he logic of his mystical doctrine compels Paul . . . to treat suffering as a form of manifestation of the dying with Christ" and not the other way around.[26] That is, for Schweitzer, Paul's occasions of suffering did not provide for him an experience, best conceived as dying with Christ, that he was then able to articulate as a principle; rather, because he had formulated the principle of suffering as dying with Christ, he was then able to see his own experience in that same light. Implicitly for Schweitzer, such experience has no meaning without the template of articulated doctrine. With characteristic conviction, Schweitzer speaks of the "violent" (*gewalttätig*) quality of Paul's thinking that empowers Paul to contradict the observable order of things in order to follow rational presuppositions to their logical ends.[27]

Schweitzer frequently admits that the reasons behind Paul's various theological positions remain undeclared, and yet he asserts that only the most linear reasoning lies behind them, reasoning that Schweitzer himself must often supply.[28] So, for example, when Paul declares that the Elect are "already supernatural beings," Schweitzer asserts that he is solving the logical puzzle of "how natural men can be in union with the already glorified person of Jesus."[29] Throughout Schweitzer's exegesis, both Paul's "solution" and the unstated logical "problem" that occasioned it are the products of Paul's cogitation, uninformed by any somatic phenomena or apprehension of union with the risen Christ. Perhaps more to the point, it is usually pretty difficult to imagine how the problems Paul addresses would have arisen naturally as theological dilemmas. In the end, despite the fact that Schweitzer claims that at heart Paul's own religion is mystical ("for when all is said and done, Pauline personal religion is in its fundamental character

---

[26] Schweitzer, *Mysticism of Paul the Apostle*, 147. All of Chapter 9 is devoted to an examination of Paul's reflections on and experience of suffering.

[27] Ibid., 111.

[28] This argument is stated perhaps most baldly in the following passage from *Mysticism of Paul the Apostle*, 138: "The problems which made his mysticism necessary, and the general conception on which it is based, are never expounded by Paul. Indeed even the doctrine of being-in-Christ is never systematically developed; its implications are simply stated as though they were self-evident. But behind the phrases in which he expresses his mysticism lie the problems by which it was called into being, and the fundamental conceptions out of which it arose stand forth with such clearness that they would always have been visible if only theologians had had the courage to endeavour to understand."

[29] Ibid., 110. See similar attempts to explain the reasoning behind Paul's assertions on 111 and 141.

mystical . . . its own essential life lies in the mystical"), there is little recognition of any connection between mysticism and religious experience.

On occasion, Schweitzer makes explicit his distrust of the category of experience as an interpretative key to Paul's writings. The two occasions that I will consider here are his discussion of scholarship on Paul's "Damascus road experience" and his own theories about Paul's ascension to the third heaven as described in 2 Corinthians 12. In the first case, Schweitzer uses Karl Holsten as his interlocutor because "Holsten was the first to explain the special character of the Pauline thought as a psychological result of the unique Damascus experience."[30] For Schweitzer, Holsten's interpretation is altogether too convenient because as he reads Holsten: "Whatever remains unexplained after the psychologising, the depotentiation, and modernisation, is referred to the peculiar character of the religious experience which the Apostle is supposed to have undergone in the vision on the Damascus road."[31] In this critique, Schweitzer has a legitimate complaint. The category of conversion can be used as an untestable explanation of much in the letters of Paul (a problem that I discuss in Section 1.3.2). But the point here is how much is brushed aside through Schweitzer's critical gesture. Rather than claiming simply that the appeal to a conversion experience is an inadequate explanation for Paul's thought, Schweitzer asserts that religious experience per se is inadmissible as a contributing factor. Here he uses the negative connotations of psychology to eliminate emotional, embodied, or psychosocial – in short, experiential – contributions to Paul's thought. As John Ashton summarizes it, "If Schweitzer had portrayed Paul as a real mystic instead of simply applying the language of mysticism to what, on the evidence of his own language, he actually conceived to be rational thinking, then he would have had no trouble in meeting the most serious criticisms that can be made of his fascinating book."[32]

In the second case, Schweitzer discusses Paul's visionary experience recounted in 2 Cor 12:1–4. Here again, Schweitzer subordinates ecstatic experience to normal, conscious propositional reasoning. Schweitzer does not deny that Paul had the experience that he describes as ascent to the third heaven; rather, he suggests that the "most natural hypothesis" for the occurrence is "that Paul suffered from some kind of epileptiform attacks, which does not by any means necessarily mean that he was a real epileptic."[33]

[30] Ibid., 35.
[31] Schweitzer, *Paul and His Interpreters: A Critical History,* trans. W. Montgomery, Schocken Paperbacks SB79 (New York: Schocken, 1964), 40.
[32] Ashton, *Religion of Paul the Apostle,* 151.
[33] Schweitzer, *Mysticism of Paul the Apostle,* 153.

Furthermore, the fact that on his way to Damascus Paul "hears voices" and "suffers afterwards a temporary affection of the eyesight" can be explained by the fact that he had another such attack.[34] Schweitzer cites the notorious "thorn in the flesh" (2 Cor 12:7) and Paul's illness in Galatia (Gal 4:13–14) as additional evidence of these attacks. To Schweitzer's mind, it is Paul's faithful genius that allows him to view such events as "special mercies" and, in particular, to interpret them using Jewish cultural norms. What seems most remarkable in this case is the length to which Schweitzer has gone to avoid the category of visionary experience in assessing Paul. He is not alone in this aversion, but he is distinctive in that he desires so thoroughly and insightfully at one and the same time to explore mystical *thought* and equally thoroughly reject mystical *experience*.

More recently, Luke Timothy Johnson's work on religious experience struggles a little within the confines of cognicentrism. Unlike Schweitzer, Johnson sets out deliberately to (re)instate religious experience as an important and neglected aspect of Christian origins as part of "what escapes the scan of scholars."[35] In Johnson's case, the immediate focus of his analysis is glossolalia, a topic that he treats with some restraint. In his discussion, he reviews the mixed nature of the evidence for the reception of glossolalia in Pauline communities and delineates what he sees as the uncertainties that impede its study in antiquity. That being said, at one point in Johnson's analysis, his scope subtly expands to include all ecstatic religious experience, and he goes on to draw two broad conclusions, both of them negative in nature: "Two inferences about that first period are therefore emphatically *not* supported by the evidence: that tongues was a normal and expected accompaniment of the Holy Spirit (and therefore, by implication, a necessary indicator of the authentic presence of the Spirit); and, that tongues demonstrates how the first Christians lived in a charismatic fog of trance or dissociation."[36]

One suspects that the first of these conclusions has more to do with contemporary polemics of religious identity and its authorization than with clarification of the circumstances in the first-century Corinthian assembly. The second inference is also somewhat tendentious, although much harder to position against any real religious practice. We may all agree with Johnson that of course the first Christians did not live in a "fog of trance or dissociation." That said, I am not sure how agreement with such a pejorative generalization furthers the understanding of religious experience in the New Testament. However, the exaggerated notion of trance states does serve a

---

[34] Ibid.
[35] Johnson spells out this position in the first chapter of *Religious Experience in Earliest Christianity*, 1–37. The quoted portion is the heading on page 12.
[36] Ibid., 118.

rhetorical purpose, and that is to discredit the experience of trance states in general. Regardless of Johnson's intentions (which, given the overall thrust of the book, seem generous), the effect of his statement is to denigrate ecstatic religious experience.

Between Schweitzer and Johnson, one finds a range of other examples. Many of these positions employ theology in the way other cognicentric categories are used in secular contexts. In some cases, the subcategory of eschatology is used as a hedge against experiential, participatory statements in Paul. For example, Rudolf Bultmann claims that Paul's "in Christ" language "denotes an eschatological and not a mystical fact."[37] Here Bultmann is not even contrasting a conceptual possibility with an experiential one but rather contrasting two worldviews (one primarily temporal and the other primarily spatial), both of which are conceptual. Gunther Bornkamm is among those who admit to religious experience in Paul's biography – in particular, a conversion experience – but explicitly deny its effect on Paul's life or its value as an object of reflection. According to Bornkamm, Paul may have had a conversion experience, but his few references to it have little effect on the content of his gospel. Furthermore, when Paul talks about revelation in Gal 1:15–16, he cannot mean revelation "taken as vision and experience" but must mean "an objective world-changing event through which God in his sovereign action has inaugurated a new aeon."[38] William Wrede put it more tersely: "The religion of the apostle is theological through and through; his theology is his religion."[39]

On occasion, biblical scholars fall back into cognicentrism through their use of anthropology and psychology. Once again, Johnson illustrates this possibility. After relating Paul's muted appreciation for glossolalia, Johnson goes on to introduce a variety of psychological studies that find that those who speak in tongues tend to be imitative, prone to influence, able to be hypnotized, submissive to authority, and disruptive to community[40] – in short, of inferior character. Even apart from questions of cross-cultural

---

[37] Rudolf Bultmann, *Glauben und Verstehen: Gesammelte Aufsätze* (Tübingen: Mohr, 1933), 257.

[38] Günther Bornkamm, *Paul,* trans. D. M. G. Stalker (Minneapolis: Fortress, 1971), 21.

[39] William Wrede, *Paulus,* 2nd ed., Religious geschichtliche Volksbücher für die deutshce christliche Gegenwart. 1. Reihe, 5/6. Heft. (Tübingen: Mohr [Siebeck], 1907), translated into English as *Paul* (Lexington, Ky.: American Theological Library Association Committee on Reprinting, 1962), 76. Strangely, Wrede makes this comment even though he, like Bornkamm, allows for Paul's visions as religious experiences and not only theological reflection (*Paul,* 6–11).

[40] L.T. Johnson, *Religious Experience in Earliest Christianity,* 126–27. All of the studies he cites were published in the 1970s. In a further interesting take on the evidence, Johnson uses Paul's own glossolalia as an indication of Paul's opposition to glossolalia: "As for Paul, he could hardly emphasize more strongly that, in his view – and he was a speaker in tongues himself (14:18) – glossolalia is an intrinsically noncommunicative form of utterance" (*Religious Experience in Earliest Christianity,* 112).

applicability (particularly on issues of individual and group identity), the use of these studies in this context results in a kind of ad hominem attack. Johnson concludes that "[i]t is certainly conceivable that the party spirit of those who cried out, 'I am for Paul' or 'I am for Cephas' (1 Cor 1:12) could be correlated with the sociopsychological tendencies of submission to authority figures, elitism, and divisiveness attributed to contemporary glossolalists."[41] Studies such as those on which Johnson draws suffer somewhat from ethnocentrism. What feels like submissiveness in North Atlantic contexts looks like a dyadic self-construction in the Mediterranean region. What marks character strength in one context interferes with the human good in another.

In each of these examples, ethnocentric and cognicentric biases color the interpretation of Paul. The scholarly imagination is understandably, though unnecessarily, limited by its own cultural parameters. Even those who recognize elements of religious experience attempt to explain them as theological deductions wrapped up in "mystical" language. Despite Paul's references to multiple ecstatic religious experiences, Enlightenment sensibilities continue explicitly and tacitly to bracket out such experiences as a contributing factor in Paul's writing.

1.2.2 Ecstatics Are Catholic, Aren't They?

Much of this reading through Enlightenment values has been exacerbated by confessional polemics. Like claims of impurity, the accusation of religious exuberance has often served as a means to indict one's confessional antagonists. In this section, however, I will focus the analysis on Catholic–Protestant polemics because the debate endured there longest and perhaps most thoroughly. As illustrated earlier, Protestant New Testament scholarship has used the term "mysticism" to designate bad or sloppy theological thinking. It has also attempted to describe ritual, magical, and even ecstatic elements in Christianity as Catholic distortions of Christian origins. More than any other contemporary author, Jonathan Z. Smith has drawn attention to the polemics fueling the description of Christian origins. Smith has argued persuasively that the relation of formative christianity to Hellenistic Mysteries has served, in the words of one of his reviewers, "as a proxy-war between denominational superpowers reluctant to step into open combat."[42] In Smith's own words:

---

[41] L. T. Johnson, *Religious Experience in Earliest Christianity*, 127–28.

[42] Robert M. Price, "Review: *Drudgery Divine: On the Comparison of Early Christianities and the Religions of Late Antiquity*," *Journal of Higher Criticism* 3 (1996), 137. Although Smith makes this argument most thoroughly in *Drudgery Divine*, see also Jonathan Z. Smith, "The Temple and the Magician," in *Map Is Not Territory: Studies in the History of Religion* (Chicago: University of Chicago Press, 1993), 172–89.

The scattered polemic references in the early reformers – a Melanchthon or a Calvin – to the "pagan imprinting" on Roman Christianity, to this or that detail of Catholic praxis being the result of syncretism, gave way to a full-blown history, to the quest for origins and the narration of progressive degradation, whether as a result of "infiltrations" from the non-Christian environment, or diabolical "intervention" or "invention."[43]

In elaboration of this claim, Smith argues that comparisons with paganism have been used to distinguish the purported "'petitionary,' 'inward,' and 'ethical'" nature of authentic primitive Christianity from the later corruption of "pagano-papism," which introduced concepts of the magical efficacy of ritual.[44] Eventually, as Smith shows, deists and rationalists used the same sorts of comparisons to argue that Paul himself began the process of tainting an originally pure Christianity with Hellenistic influences.[45] What is central to Smith's analysis is the use of Hellenistic religious parallels as an ineffective and miscalibrated test for fidelity to Christian origins; that is, it neither measures what it was meant to nor is it based on an accurate picture of ancient difference. What is central for me in repeating Smith's analysis is the convenient way in which Hellenistic religious parallels seem to line up with biases against ecstatic religious experience, an element that Smith does not take up explicitly.

The confessional bias against elements of ecstatic (or "mystical") practice in the New Testament is more frequently expressed in general terms than in specific exegeses of Pauline texts. Albrecht Ritschl and subsequently Adolf von Harnack are sometimes credited with cementing the division between proper Christian faith and mystical religion. Ritschl decried mysticism as nothing more than reconstituted Neoplatonic metaphysics.[46] Protestantism seems to have followed this general line of thinking throughout much of the twentieth century. Emil Brunner could simply assert the opposition between reformation and mystical piety, "reformatorischer und mystiker Frömmigkeit," as self-evident declaration of the superiority of the former – ". . . was

---

[43] J. Z. Smith, *Drudgery Divine*, 13–14.

[44] J. Z. Smith, "Temple and Magician," 188; see also J. Z. Smith, *Drudgery Divine*, 16–26. It should be noted that denominational polemics can run as easily in the other direction, as they do for Luke Timothy Johnson, who faults Smith for not going far enough in his critique: "By showing how thoroughly the NT was immersed, like Judaism, in the language of the mysteries, Smith could rescue earliest Christianity from its Protestant protectors and restore it to its messy but Catholic birth" (L. T. Johnson, *Religious Experience in Earliest Christianity*, 34).

[45] See especially the discussion of the correspondence exchanged by Thomas Jefferson and John Adams in J. Z. Smith, *Drudgery Divine*, 1–9, 26–27.

[46] Albrecht Ritschl, *Theologie und Metaphysik: Zur Verständigung und Abwehr*, 2nd ed. (Göttingen: Vandenhoöck and Ruprecht, 1902), 27–28.

wollen wir mehr?" (what more could we want?).[47] William James agreed to a general, superior "spiritual profundity" of Protestantism but still offered a few qualifications of that basic stance. In particular, he described Catholicism as more attractive in its "multiform appeals to human nature," including its ability to entertain myth and mystery. In contrast, James concluded that the Protestant devotion to the literal "will always show to Catholic eyes the alms-house physiognomy."[48]

Although alternate views may have thrived undaunted in Catholic circles, they were not frequently published. Until approximately the midpoint of the twentieth century, only two Catholics contributed significant discussions on the topic of Paul's mysticism. They were Joseph Huby in 1946[49] and Alfred Wikenhauser in 1955. When Wikenhauser wrote *Die Christusmystik des Apostels Paulus* (The Christ-mysticism of the Apostle Paul), he self-consciously introduced his work as "the first study of St. Paul's mysticism to appear from a Catholic source."[50] Further, he stated that his study was intended in part to address Protestant "antipathy" as the source of the "theory that Christian mysticism is an offshoot from New-platonism, and that it is a debased form of Christian piety."[51] Wikenhauser had identified "mysticism" as one of the issues that split the scholarship along confessional lines. Still, even some Catholics eschewed the idea of mystical elements in Paul. For example, Lucien Cerfaux, in a line that could have been written by Martin Dibelius, declared that "Paul is fond of precise theological ideas and not a vague mysticism" and, further, that mysticism "is not suggested by Pauline vocabulary and even partly contradicts it."[52] Cerfaux's comments illustrate the same sort of misunderstanding or even misrepresentation of ecstatic experience that was common among Protestants. In his massive history of Christian mysticism, Bernard McGinn finds that "German Protestant

---

[47] Emil Brunner, *Die Mystik und das Wort: Der Gegensatz zwischen moderner Religionsauffassung und christlichem Glauben dargestellt an der Theologie Schleiermachers*, 2nd ed. (Tübingen: Mohr, 1928), iii.

[48] James, *Varieties of Religious Experience*, 502.

[49] Joseph Huby, *Mystiques paulinienne et johannique* (Bruges: Desclee de Brouwer, 1946).

[50] Apparently he was unaware of (or unimpressed by) Huby's book. See Alfred Wikenhauser, *Die Christusmystik des Apostels Paulus*, 2nd ed. (Freiburg: Herder, 1956). The citation is from the English translation: Alfred Wikenhauser, *Pauline Mysticism: Christ in the Mystical Teaching of St. Paul* (New York: Herder and Herder, 1960), 9.

[51] Wikenhauser, *Pauline Mysticism*, 14. Walenty Prokulski, "The Conversion of St. Paul" *Catholic Biblical Quarterly* 19 (1957), 456, assessed the split more bluntly, stating that among critical scholars "all Catholics . . . regard Paul's conversion as a miracle, in the true sense of the word, wrought in his soul by the resurrected and glorified Christ, who appeared to him in person."

[52] Lucien Cerfaux, *Le Chrétien dans la theologie paulinienne*, Lectio divina 33 (Paris: Éditions du Cerf, 1962), 326 and 328, respectively.

scholars saw mysticism, at least God-mysticism or the mysticism of union with God, as essentially world-negating and solipsistic."[53] So it is not surprising that through the rest of the century, he can count only four noteworthy Protestant scholars who contributed to reflection on mysticism.[54]

There are some examples of more direct application of this orientation to Pauline exegesis. For instance, in classic Reformation categories, Ernst Käsemann posed "the Pauline doctrine of justification" as "protection . . . against enthusiasm and mysticism."[55] Apparently protection is not enough because Käsemann also insists that "faith must be *rescued* from the dimension of recurrent religious experience."[56] Thus, illustrating another dimension of Protestantism, he prescribes the combined use of doctrinal prophylactics and the avoidance of multiple religious experiences as the antidote. (The precise nature of the disease is less clear.) In Käsemann's case, the term "mysticism" can substitute for an overt reference to Catholicism.

In other cases where mysticism is used, "theology" is typically posed as its alternative.[57] James Dunn is not unaware of some elements of bias in Pauline scholarship. For example, in discussing the category of "Christ mysticism," he notes the neglect of certain themes and disproportionate attention to others: "In comparison with the amazingly vigorous contemporary debate on justification by faith, interest in our present theme, even the thoroughly and distinctively Pauline 'in Christ' and 'with Christ' motifs, has been modest and marginal. . . . For, in fact, study of participation in Christ leads more directly into the rest of Paul's theology than [does] justification."[58]

But despite recognizing one of the prominent fault lines in the Protestant–Catholic divide, Dunn nonetheless presupposes the same dichotomy between thought and experience when assessing other Pauline themes. For example, in his discussion of Paul's statements about the body of Christ, he makes it clear that the most important point "is the *theological* insight implicit in the very concept of 'the body of Christ.' The overlap with the language of 'participation in Christ' can readily distract the thought into an *otherworldly mysticism.*" According to Dunn, the "corporeal" nature of

---

Bernard McGinn, *The Foundations of Mysticism*, vol. 1: *The Presence of God: A History of Western Christian Mysticism* (New York: Crossroad, 1991), 275.

[54] McGinn, *Foundations of Mysticism*, vol. 1, 266–91.

[55] Ernst Käsemann, *Perspectives on Paul*, trans. Margaret Kohl (Philadelphia: Fortress, 1971), 73–74.

[56] Ibid., 82–83; emphasis added.

[57] Pitting theology against mysticism is in some sense simply a reiteration of the cognicentric bias. That said, the terminology warrants attention for its distinctive contribution to confessional polemics.

[58] Dunn, *Theology of Paul the Apostle*, 395.

Paul's thought "points in the other direction."[59] Dunn's invocation of material, bodily realities raises issues that are addressed in the next chapter. For now I will emphasize only that the separation of ecstatic religious experience from bodily investments represents a significant misconception of ecstasy. Typically the category of *theology* constitutes an equal or greater disembodiment. At any rate, the comment demonstrates just how much a particular characterization of mysticism has tainted the conversation about religious experience.

A final example is drawn from a source that is explicitly and self-consciously evangelical in its interpretive commitments. *The Dictionary of Paul and His Letters* includes an entry on "Mysticism," in which the author is at pains to assert the sort of definition of mysticism that fueled the polemics at the beginning of the twentieth century. Peter T. O'Brien insists that Paul's language of union with Christ derives from the fact that, like other believers, Paul "was personally united with his Lord in the salvation-historical acts of the cross and resurrection." Thus, the union is a forensic and conceptual one; Paul and Jesus are united by the legal equation. According to O'Brien, one must understand further that "this important event is misunderstood when dissolved into a subjective, mystical experience. The apostle does not isolate the individual and focus on the inner experience as mysticism does."[60] I do not disagree with O'Brien's effort to avoid dissolving Paul's construct of "union with Christ" into a single simplistic explanation; however, dissolving it into only a theological premise seems equally partial and tendentious. Such a statement echoes the misrepresentations of a previous generation without any effort to substantiate the depiction of mysticism. O'Brien also resists the idea of Paul's mystical experience because he sees it as a threat to the "objectivity" of Paul's knowledge. He takes issue with Alan Segal in particular because Segal's analysis "does violence to Paul's emphasis on the objectivity of Christ and his salvific work."[61] In this reading, confessional commitments seem to squeeze out any margin for religious experience as an informing element in Paul's thought.

---

[59] Ibid., 563.
[60] Peter T. O'Brien, "Mysticism," in *Dictionary of Paul and His Letters*, ed. Gerald F. Hawthorne, Ralph P. Martin, and Daniel G. Reid (Downers Grove, Ill.: InterVarsity, 1993), 624.
[61] As an illustration of this objective reality, O'Brien asserts (citing F. F. Bruce) that, "Paul's theology was not based on experiences which might be called mystical, but 'on Jesus, the fulfiller of God's promise and purpose of salvation; Jesus, the crucified and exalted Lord; Jesus, the divine wisdom, in whom God creates, maintains and brings to consummation everything that exists; Jesus, who here and now lives within his people by his Spirit.'" Surely, "objectivity" is not precisely the word for the distinction O'Brien is trying to make.

1.3 PAULINE OVERSIGHT

The persistence of this broad perspective is frequently worked out in particular Pauline texts, even though the line between the bias and the means that perpetuate the bias is not always clearly circumscribed. Both the emphasis on articulate reason and the sort of confessional prejudice just discussed can, of course, also be used as strategies for reading the text; however, two particular exegetical habits have further contributed to the neglect of ecstatic religious experience as a category in Pauline studies. They are, first, an overemphasis on the negative aspects of ecstatic practice in Pauline communities and, second, the assumption that the disparate texts in which Paul mentions his own ecstatic experience are all allusions to a single event.

1.3.1 *Paul, Opponent of Ecstatic Abuses*

The first of the emphases begins with an observation that is partially accurate for the letters to Corinth at least: Paul does address some "ecstatic abuses" in that community. The problem with the attention to abuses is that it has not (either within individual articles and monographs or in the scholarship as a whole) been balanced by attention to the positive role of ecstatic experience often expressed in the very same passage.[62] The result of the imbalance is a tacit argument that Paul was the sensible opponent of early Christian irrational exuberance. In some other readings, the immediate context of Paul's statements is ignored and his specific complaints are transformed into absolute principles. In the following analysis, I will consider the scholarship on 1 Cor 14:18 and 2 Cor 12:1–4 only because (apart from the possibility of a conversion experience) these are the two texts that are most routinely recognized as statements of Paul's own ecstatic practice. Thus, they provide the clearest test case for bias against an ecstatic Paul.

In 1 Corinthians 14, Paul is continuing a discussion of "spiritual things" (*pneumatika*) begun in 1 Cor 12:1 with the characteristic περὶ δε that marks most major sections in this letter. Twice in Chapter 14, he speaks of his appreciation of glossolalia: In v. 5, he declares that he would like all the Corinthians to speak in tongues, and in v. 18 he gives thanks for his own superlative practice of

---

[62] There are some exceptions to this one-sided reading of ecstatic religious experience. Feminist scholarship in particular has addressed the positive role that spirit possession may have played in the lives of women in the Corinthian assemblies. See, for example, Antoinette Clark Wire, *The Corinthian Women Prophets: A Reconstruction through Paul's Rhetoric* (Minneapolis: Fortress, 1990); and Mark C. Black, "1 Cor 11:2–16: A Re-investigation," and Carroll D. Osburn, "The Interpretation of 1 Cor 14:34–35," both in vol. 1 of *Essays on Women in Earliest Christianity*, ed. Carroll D. Osburn (Joplin, Mo.: College Press, 1995), 191–218, 219–42, respectively.

glossolalia. Some commentators also include v. 15 (in which P
intention to continue both lucid and esoteric prayer forms) a
Paul's positive attitude.[63] Paul does, however, qualify his app
in the case of the Corinthian assembly. He argues that the p
nature of their assemblies requires a more discerning use of gif
that suit the communal nature of worship – including glossolalia when accompanied by interpretation – should be preferred. In the commentary literature,
there are some authors who do recognize that Paul does not disparage, but in
fact values, the practice of tongues. Further, they recognize that his relative
ranking of glossolalia and prophecy pertains specifically to public worship[64]
and perhaps even exclusively to the Corinthian assemblies.[65] Theirs is the most
straightforward interpretation of the passage. It is not, however, the only one.

The second text is the description of Paul's ascent to the "third heaven"
recounted in 2 Cor 12:1–4. The account is noteworthy for several reasons. For
students of Jewish mysticism, it provides the only extant first-person account
of an ecstatic experience by a Jew from the first century.[66] In some treatments,
Paul's repeated ignorance of his bodily status during the ascent ("whether in
the body or apart from or out of the body I do not know") provides a

---

[63] See, for example, Gordon D. Fee, *The First Epistle to the Corinthians*, New International Commentary on the New Testament (Grand Rapids, Mich.: Eerdmans, 1987).

[64] Among those who recognize Paul's advocacy of the private practice of glossolalia are John Stanley Glen, *Pastoral Problems in First Corinthians* (Philadelphia: Westminster, 1964), 180–82; Jean Héring, *The First Epistle of Saint Paul to the Corinthians* (London: Epworth, 1966), 151; Karl Maly, *Mündige Gemeinde: Untersuchungen zur pastoralen Führung des Apostels Paulus im 1 Korinther-brief*, Stuttgarter biblische Monographien 2 (Stuttgart: Katholisches Bibelwerk, 1967), 202; C. K. Barrett, *A Commentary on the First Epistle to the Corinthians*, Harper/Black New Testament Commentaries (New York: Harper and Row, 1968), 321; Hans Conzelmann, *1 Corinthians: A Commentary on the First Epistle to the Corinthians*, Hermeneia (Philadelphia: Fortress, 1975), 239; Charles H. Talbert, *Reading Corinthians: A Literary and Theological Commentary on 1 and 2 Corinthians (New York: Crossroad, 1987)*, 87; Raymond F. Collins and Daniel J. Harrington, *First Corinthians*, Sacra Pagina 7 (Collegeville, Minn.: Liturgical Press, 1999), 503; and Anthony C. Thiselton, *The First Epistle to the Corinthians: A Commentary on the Greek Text*, New International Greek Testament Commentary (Grand Rapids, Mich.: Eerdmans, 2000), 1076, 1109.

[65] The peculiar circumstances of status struggles within the Corinthian community are widely accepted for this section in particular and for the letter as a whole. On the former issue, see especially Dale B. Martin, "Tongues of Angels and Other Status Indicators," *Journal of the American Academy of Religion* 59 (1991), 547–89, who is now frequently cited in this regard. For the latter, see Gerd Theissen, *The Social Setting of Pauline Christianity: Essays on Corinth* (Philadelphia: Fortress, 1982); Alan Christopher Mitchell, "I Corinthians 6:1–11: Group Boundaries and the Courts of Corinth" (PhD dissertation, Yale University, 1986); Peter Marshall, *Enmity in Corinth: Social Conventions in Paul's Relations with the Corinthians*, Wissenschaftliche Untersuchungen zum Neuen Testament 2; Reihe 23 (Tübingen: Mohr [Siebeck], 1987); Margaret M. Mitchell, *Paul and the Rhetoric of Reconciliation: An Exegetical Investigation of the Language and Composition of 1 Corinthians* (Louisville, Ky.: Westminster/John Knox, 1991).

[66] Scholem, *Major Trends in Jewish Mysticism*; and Segal, *Paul the Convert*, 36.

tantalizing peek at the state of "mystical doctrine" in this same period.[67] In its epistolary context, 2 Cor 12:1–4 is part of the climax to Paul's "fool's speech" (2 Cor 11:21b–12:10).[68]

Paul associates this particular revelation with a subsequent and enduring affliction – his much discussed "thorn in the flesh" (v. 7). This two-part (vision and aftermath) and paradoxical (exaltation and debasement) experience compels Paul to provide an explanation for the unexpected twist of events. In Paul's view, the "over-raising" ($\dot{\upsilon}\pi\epsilon\rho\alpha\acute{\iota}\rho\omega$) provided by his ascent is counterbalanced by the humiliation of his painful treatment ($\kappa o\lambda\alpha\phi\acute{\iota}\zeta\omega$). This pattern of exaltation and debasement is being repeated in Paul's interactions with the Corinthians;[69] although he is their apostle, he is being treated as if he were nothing to them. So, Paul describes these private events in order to reinforce a social point, and the effectiveness of his persuasion here depends on the fact that his elation will be recognized by others as an occasion of special beneficence and, indeed, as something that he cherished as such. If it is not viewed positively, then its reversal will be less dramatic and the point will be lost. Some scholars have recognized the autobiographical significance of this account and the door it opens to a larger unexplored territory in Pauline studies.[70] As Andrew Lincoln

---

[67] For example, Segal, *Paul the Convert*, 39.

[68] In turn, the rhetorical unit of the fool's speech is part of the larger section of Chapters 10–13. I hold to the majority view that these chapters constitute what remains of the "letter of tears" mentioned in 2 Cor 2:3–4, 9, 7:8–12. Because for the most part I am interested in an enduring feature of Paul's life and person, this argument is not dependent on a definitive outline of Pauline chronology. Therefore, I will not discuss the evidence for partitioning and dating, which is well covered elsewhere. See, for example, Hans Dieter Betz and George W. MacRae, *2 Corinthians 8 and 9: A Commentary on Two Administrative Letters of the Apostle Paul* (Philadelphia: Fortress, 1985); Linda L. Belleville, "A Letter of Apologetic Self-Commendation," *Novum Testamentum* 31 (1989), 142–63; C. Blomberg, "The Structure of 2 Corinthians 1–7," *Criswell Theological Review* 4 (1989), 3–20; D. A. Carson, *From Triumphalism to Maturity: A New Exposition of 2 Corinthians 10–13*, Biblical Classics Library 20 (Carlisle: Paternoster, 1996); D. A. DeSilva, "Measuring Penultimate against Ultimate Reality: An Investigation of the Integrity and Argumentation of 2 Corinthians," *Journal for the Study of the New Testament* 52 (1993), 41–70; D. A. DeSilva, "Meeting the Exigency of a Complex Rhetorical Situation: Paul's Strategy in 2 Corinthians 1 through 7," *Andrews University Seminary Studies* 34 (1996), 5–22; P. B. Duff, "2 Corinthians 1–7: Sidestepping the Division Hypothesis Dilemma," *Biblical Theology Bulletin* 24 (1994), 16–26; Hans-Georg Sundermann, *Der schwache Apostel und die Kraft der Rede: eine rhetorische Analyse von 2 Kor 10–13*, Europäische Hochschulschriften Reihe xxiii, Theologie 575 (New York: Peter Lang, 1996).

[69] Earlier in this section, Paul also constructs a version of his own history following this same pattern (2 Cor 11:21b–29; cf. Phil 3:4b–9).

[70] For example, Tabor, *Things Unutterable*; Segal, *Paul the Convert*; Ernst Benz, *Paulus als Visionär: Eine vergleichende Untersuchung der Visionsberichte des Paulus in der Apostelgeschichte und in den paulinischen Briefen*, Verlag der Akademie der Wissenschaften und der Literatur (Mainz: F. Steiner Wiesbaden 1952), 77–121; H. Saake, "Paulus als Ekstatiker," *Novum Testamentum* 15 (1973), 154, 156, 160; Ashton, *Religion of Paul the Apostle*, 116–120.

says, "[t]hat Paul does not anywhere dwell on this side of Christian existence [i.e., the ecstatic] must not be taken to mean that it was not a valid side or that it only played a very minor part on the periphery of his life.... Clearly, lack of frequent reference does not necessarily mean lack of frequent experience."[71]

However, many scholars are not prepared to admit a positive role for either ecstatic speech or visions and revelations in the practice or estimation of Paul. In the most extreme case, there are those who would argue that Paul did not have either experience.[72] In the case of tongues, some commentators, seizing on the use of $\mu\hat{\alpha}\lambda\lambda o\nu$ in 1 Cor 14:18, argue that Paul is referring not to greater quantity of experience but rather a qualitative difference.[73] In other words, although the Corinthians may have been engaging in ecstatic speech, Paul was doing something superior (but often unidentified). Even in the case of Paul's ascent, a few commentators have argued that the experience was not Paul's. For example, Michael Goulder has taken the third-person speech literally and proposed that Paul is recounting the experience of a friend.[74] In another essay, Goulder attempts to divest Paul of any extraordinary religious experience by asserting rigid lexical distinctions between the "visions" and

---

[71] Lincoln, *Paradise Now and Not Yet*, 72.

[72] Perhaps the most effective means of denying the experience is simply to ignore a passage altogether. I have not found any commentaries that manage to wholly ignore 2 Cor 12:1–4, but it is not an uncommon phenomenon in the case of 1 Cor 14:18. This avoidance is especially noteworthy in commentaries or discussions that are otherwise providing verse-by-verse exegesis. So, for 1 Cor 14:18, the neglect began early, with the likes of John Colet. See John Colet, Bernard O'Kelly, and Catherine Anna Louise Jarrott, *John Colet's Commentary on First Corinthians: A New Edition of the Latin Text, with Translation, Annotations, and Introduction* (Binghamton, N.Y.: Medieval and Renaissance Texts and Studies, 1985), 273–75; and Arthur Penrhyn Stanley, *The Epistles of St. Paul to the Corinthians: With Critical Notes and Dissertations*, 5th ed. (London: John Murray, 1882), 269–72. More recent examples include: Margaret E. Thrall, *The First and Second Letters of Paul to the Corinthians*, Cambridge Bible Commentary: New English Bible (Cambridge: Cambridge University Press, 1965), 99; David Prior, *The Message of 1 Corinthians: Life in the Local Church*, Bible Speaks Today (Downers Grove, Ill.: InterVarsity, 1985), 245–47; Graydon F. Snyder, *First Corinthians: A Faith Community Commentary* (Macon, Ga.: Mercer University Press, 1992), 181; Kevin Quast, *Reading the Corinthian Correspondence: An Introduction* (New York: Paulist, 1994), 84–86; and Ben Witherington, *Conflict and Community in Corinth: A Socio-rhetorical Commentary on 1 and 2 Corinthians* (Grand Rapids, Mich.: Eerdmans, 1995), 284.

[73] F. F. Bruce, *1 and 2 Corinthians*, New Century Bible (London: Oliphants, 1971), 132: "The context requires us to understand him to claim a richer endowment *of glossolalia* than theirs"; Thiselton, *First Epistle to the Corinthians*, 1117: "It is a *qualitative* rather than a *quantitative* use of mallon"; and John J. Kilgallen, *First Corinthians: An Introduction and Study Guide* (New York: Paulist, 1987), 121. The most remarkable claim by far is the view of Fred L. Fisher, *Commentary on 1 & 2 Corinthians* (Waco, Tex.: Word, 1975), 225, that Paul was speaking authentic foreign languages for the purposes of evangelization. To his credit, Fisher does not argue that this was a different skill than one the Corinthians practiced.

[74] Michael Goulder, "Vision and Knowledge," *Journal for the Study of the New Testament* 56 (1994), 53–71.

the "revelations" of 2 Cor 12:1. "Visions are distinct from revelations," Goulder asserts, "in that revelations take place on earth, whereas in a vision one is caught up to heaven."[75] Certainly Paul had feet-firmly-on-the-ground revelations, claims Goulder, but he knows of otherworldly visions only secondhand – through a "friend in Christ." If such fixed distinctions are even to be entertained, surely the lexical evidence supports the case diametrically opposed to Goulder's: "Revelation" (*apokalypsis*), not "vision" (*optasia*), is the word used consistently for otherworldly journeys and in fact has lent its name to the genre of writings about heavenly journeys. In an argument akin to Goulder's, L. Hermann reasons circuitously that the "man in Christ" is Apollos.[76] Morton Smith has championed the case that Paul is speaking of an experience that Jesus had.[77] Finally, on the basis of apocalyptic literature, Martha Himmelfarb presupposes that every account of a mystical journey is strictly literary and always written pseudepigraphically, and therefore that this account cannot get us to Paul's experience, whatever it may or may not have been.[78]

Most attempts to suppress the ecstatic are more modest in their methods. Typically they are based on rhetorical grounds. In one set of arguments, the opposition to Paul's ecstatic religious experience is expressed through an overemphasis on Paul's reluctance to talk about it. Only extraordinary circumstances, so the argument goes, forced Paul to recount what is at best embarrassing and at worst repugnant to him.[79] In the case of tongues, it is sometimes maintained that Paul speaks about his own ecstatic speech only because the Corinthians must have raised it in the letter they sent to him. Thus, Paul, who has since had a change of heart about such exuberance, must address his past practice despite his preference to leave it behind. In the same vein, some commentaries argue that the Corinthians must have

---

[75] M. D. Goulder, *St. Paul versus St. Peter: A Tale of Two Missions*, 1st American ed. (Louisville, Ky.: Westminster/John Knox, 1995), 49, emphasis original.

[76] L. Hermann, "Apollos," *Revue des sciences religieuses* (1976), 330–36.

[77] Morton Smith, "Ascent to the Heavens and the Beginning of Christianity," *Eranos-Jahrbuch* 50 (1981), 403–29. Here he takes the grammatically plausible, but contextually implausible, minority position that the genitive κυρίου of v. 1 is subjective.

[78] Martha Himmelfarb, "The Practice of Ascent in the Ancient Mediterranean World," in *Death, Ecstasy and Other Worldly Journeys*, ed. John Collins and Michael Fishbane (Albany: State University of New York Press, 1995), 123–37. Before Himmelfarb, William Baird ("Visions, Revelation, and Ministry: Reflections on 2 Cor 12:1–5 and Gal 1:11–17," *Journal of Biblical Literature* 104 (1985), 651–62), offered this "solution." See also Christopher Rowland, who allows for the possibility at least in *The Open Heaven: A Study of Apocalyptic in Judaism and Early Christianity* (New York: Crossroad, 1982), 244.

[79] For example, this seems to be the implication of Thiselton's wording (*Epistle to the Corinthians*, 1075): ". . . even if Paul knows what it is to allow his inner self to well up 'in tongues' in private devotions (v. 18)."

accused Paul of being unspiritual.[80] Others argue that they would have done so if given half a chance and that therefore Paul was (judiciously) beating them to the punch![81] Either way, commentators construct an argument from silence in which the positions and actions of Paul's opponents are reconstructed as the mirror opposite to Paul's statements through "mirror exegesis."[82] Against this, Conzelmann argues that 1 Cor 14:18 "has no polemical point. In Corinth it has apparently not yet been called in question that he is a genuine pneumatic, as was to happen later (2 Cor 10–13)."[83]

Although mirror exegesis can provide a measured means to generate hypotheses about diversity in earliest christianity, if taken too far it can also introduce a fatal circularity into the interpretation of a text. For example, in 1 Cor 12, some interpreters begin with the assumption that Paul is combating an organized and explicit party of spiritual enthusiasts.[84] On that basis, they reconstruct the views of this group by inverting

[80] Fee (*First Epistle to the Corinthians*, 573, 661, 709, 734) suggests that "the Corinthians have called Paul into question for his lack of spirituality." Therefore he responds with this revelation (709). See also John Coolidge Hurd, *The Origin of I Corinthians* (Macon, Ga.: Mercer University Press, 1983), 185, 194.

[81] Thus, in the opinion of these authors, Paul is issuing a preemptive rhetorical strike required by the knowledge that the Corinthians would resort to such tactics. The sense of rhetorical contest is perhaps strongest in Richard B. Hays, *First Corinthians*, Interpretation, a Bible Commentary for Teaching and Preaching (Louisville, Ky.: John Knox, 1997), 237–38: "Paul has held back one important bit of information. . . . Paul has now played his ace, seeking to trump the Corinthians' claims. He could beat them at their own game of superspirituality." More sympathetic are John Calvin in T. H. L. Parker, *Calvin's New Testament Commentaries* (Grand Rapids, Mich.: Eerdmans, 1971), 294: "Paul did not want to give the impression that he is decrying the gift of tongues through ill-will or jealousy"; Bruce, *1 and 2 Corinthians*, 132: "If the Corinthian enthusiasts were disposed to maintain that no one who lacked the gift of glossolalia could rightly claim to have received the Spirit or to be able to discern spiritual realities, Paul makes it plain that they cannot object to his argument on this score"; William Barclay, *The Letters to the Corinthians,* rev. ed., Daily Study Bible Series (Toronto: G. R. Welch, 1975), 128–29; and Leon Morris, *The First Epistle of Paul to the Corinthians: An Introduction and Commentary,* 2nd ed., Tyndale New Testament Commentaries 7 (Grand Rapids, Mich.: Eerdmans, 1985), 196: "What Paul has been saying is not due to 'sour grapes'. Paul himself exercises the gift of tongues more than all the Corinthians."

[82] Among the several authors who recognize the possible methodological pitfalls of mirror reconstructions, Jerry L. Sumney, *Identifying Paul's Opponents: The Question of Method in 2 Corinthians,* Journal for the Study of the New Testament Supplement Series 40 (Sheffield: JSOT Press, 1990), has most systematically addressed the issue. Drawing on the work of David Hackett Fischer, *Historians' Fallacies: Toward a Logic of Historical Thought* (New York: Harper and Row, 1970), Sumney describes it as one of the most significant methodological problems of historical reconstruction in Pauline scholarship. Although Sumney's point is well taken, it is somewhat overstated. Some disciplined reconstruction of Paul's interlocutors on the basis of Paul's comments is obviously in order.

[83] Conzelmann, *1 Corinthians*, 239.

[84] They assume that Paul is combating opponents rather than, for example, simply introducing a corrective to their worship or answering a query through which they had sought his advice. The passage does not require opposition in order to be intelligible.

Paul's own – a maneuver that then provides evidence of opposition. As a result, because that set of hypotheses would have Paul opposing ecstatic religious practice, any statement he makes in favor of it cannot be taken at face value. Thus, when Paul speaks his thanks for his own gift of tongues, he must be doing so ironically[85] or even sarcastically,[86] may be using hyperbole,[87] or perhaps is merely quoting a slogan.[88] At any rate, according to these readings, Paul's intention in one way or another is to communicate the opposite of what he has written. Certainly there are points at which the circularity of this reasoning exceeds the permissible benefit of the doubt.

As the comment from Conzelmann suggests, mirror exegesis is also a common means to interpretive leverage in 2 Corinthians 10–13. In this case, it is much clearer that Paul is addressing circumstances in which he perceives real opponents. He names them, in vv. 11:5 and 12:11, as "super-apostles" ($\dot{\upsilon}\pi\epsilon\rho\lambda\acute{\iota}\alpha\nu\ \dot{\alpha}\pi\sigma\sigma\tau\acute{o}\lambda\iota$). Most students of the letter also agree that throughout Chapters 10–13 the relative estimations of Paul and the more recent apostolic arrivals are the focus. So, in this section, it is quite appropriate to look for signs of a position at odds with Paul's. The classic reconstructions of the opponents are those of Gerd Lüdemann and John Gunther, who imagine pneumatic Judaisers; Walter Schmithals, who finds gnostics; and Dieter Georgi and Gerhard Friedrich, who propose divine men.[89]

---

[85] R. H. Horsley, *1 Corinthians* (Nashville, Tenn.: Abingdon, 1998), 185: "He too (supposedly) values the personal edification of tongues"; Hurd, *Origin of 1 Corinthians*, 188; John S. Ruef, *Paul's First Letter to Corinth* (Harmondsworth: Penguin, 1971), 150: "The tone could be somewhat ironic, i.e. this is the subject of his thanksgiving."

[86] Allen Rhea Hunt, *The Inspired Body: Paul, the Corinthians, and Divine Inspiration* (Macon, Ga.: Mercer University Press, 1996), 127, n. 16.

[87] Horsley, *1 Corinthians*, 185; and Fee (*First Epistle to the Corinthians*, 674), who says that the comment "is probably somewhat hyperbolic" and adds (n. 53) that Paul couldn't have known how much the Corinthians spoke in tongues.

[88] Thiselton (*First Epistle to the Corinthians*, 1097) parenthetically raises the possibility that it "is a quoted slogan."

[89] John J. Gunther, *St. Paul's Opponents and their Background: A Study of Apocalyptic and Jewish Sectarian Teachings*, Novum Testamentum Supplement 35 (Leiden: E. J. Brill, 1973); Gerd Lüdemann, *Paulus, der Heidenapostel* (Göttingen: Vandenhoeck and Ruprecht, 1980), esp. 112, 136–137; Walter Schmithals, *Gnosticism in Corinth: An Investigation of the Letters to the Corinthians* (Nashville, Tenn: Abingdon, 1971), esp. 209–18; Dieter Georgi, *The Opponents of Paul in Second Corinthians: A Study of Religious Propaganda in Late Antiquity* (Philadelphia: Fortress, 1986); and Gerhard Friedrich, "Die Gegner des Paulus im 2 Korintherbrief," in *Abraham unser Vater; Juden und Christen im Gespräch über die Bibel*, ed. Otto Betz, Martin Hengel, and Peter Schmidt, Arbeiten zur Geschichte des Spätjudentums und Urchristentums (Leiden: E. J. Brill, 1963), 231–53. Whether or not subsequent writers concur with the details of these reconstructions, the work of these authors has determined the lens through which Paul's promotion of his own ecstasy is understood.

Each in turn explains 2 Cor 12:1–10 as Paul's response to his opponents' claims of ecstatic prowess. [90]

A final way in which Paul is made to oppose ecstatic practice is through lack of attention to the context of his statements. In this case, exegetes are sometimes quite sensitive to the purported context that compels Paul to discuss ecstatic experience and insensitive to context when they draw conclusions about the merits of such practice. To put it another way, Paul's particular concerns about some aspects of ecstatic practice are generalized into absolute opposition to all religious ecstasy. In the case of tongues, Paul's relative ranking of *uninterpreted* glossolalia *in the assembly* is transformed into a comprehensive denigration of ecstatic speech.[91]

A final quotation from Jerome Murphy-O'Connor illustrates the way in which many of these perspectives (and a few additional ones) amplify one another. In this passage, Murphy-O'Connor is speaking of the rhetorical use of third-person speech in 2 Cor 12:2–4:

> By attributing it to someone else Paul underlines the irrelevance of the experience for his ministry. It did not change him in any way and it did not furnish him with any information which he could use. The unstated critique of his opponents is obvious. If their experience was the same as Paul's, it contributed nothing. If their experience was something they could talk about, it was less ineffable than his.[92]

---

[90]   In addition to pinpointing specific methodological errors in these reconstructions (for example, he discusses overreliance on secondary sources from as much as three centuries after Paul [69]) and the presupposition of "a single front of opposition for all of Paul's letters" (70), Jerry Sumney describes the erroneous assumptions behind the act of reconstruction itself. In particular, he argues that "any time a reconstruction determines the interpretation of a passage, that passage cannot be used to demonstrate that the opponents fit the reconstruction" (82). The only real evidence of pneumatic prowess is Paul's description of his own ecstatic journey; nothing in Chapters 10–13 alludes to such claims for the super-apostles. Some (e.g., Ernst Käsemann, "Die Legitimität des Apostels: Eine Untersuchung zu 2 Korinther 10–13," *Zeitschrift fur die neutesmentliche Wissenschaft und die Kunde der älteren Kirche* 41 (1942), 33–71; and C. K. Barrett, *The Second Epistle to the Corinthians*, Harper's New Testament Commentaries (New York: Harper and Row, 1973), 274, cite the triad "another Jesus . . . a different spirit . . . a different gospel" (2 Cor 11:4) as evidence of pneumatic disputes. However, because these authors also take note of the emphasis on preaching in this verse, they tend not to see ecstatic behavior as the point of conflict. Only the circular reasoning of mirror exegesis allows one to claim both that in Chapter 12 Paul must be defending himself against accusations of being unspiritual and that the evidence of his opponents' spirituality is found in Chapter 12.

[91]   This appears to be the case with Bruce, *1 and 2 Corinthians*, 132; Hurd, *Origin of I Corinthians*, 188: "Thus although he said, 'Now I want you all to speak in tongues' (14.5), and, 'I thank God that I speak in tongues more than all of you' (14.8), the context in each case shows how little he valued this 'gift'"; Hays, *First Corinthians*, 237–38; and Roy A. Harrisville, *I Corinthians*, Augsburg Commentary on the New Testament (Minneapolis: Augsburg, 1987), 237.

[92]   Jerome Murphy-O'Connor, *The Theology of the Second Letter to the Corinthians* (Cambridge: Cambridge University Press, 1991), 118.

1.3.2 *Well, Maybe Once, But Only by Accident: Conversion as the Catchall for Paul's Ecstasy*

A second significant way in which Paul's ecstatic religious experience has been minimized derives from the view of Paul as a convert. Thanks in no small part to the dramatically compelling narratives in Acts (and their perpetuation in centuries of Christian art, homiletics, and even personal histories), the notion of an extraordinary, moment-in-time conversion is the one category of religious experience that most people will readily permit Paul. Consequently, the idea of a single extraordinary experience provides an acceptable, and even attractive, event into which a number of Pauline texts can be absorbed. So, most typically, where Paul speaks of a vision of the risen Christ, it is interpreted as another account of the one and only vision he ever had. But the aggregation also absorbs many of the other sorts of allusions to ecstatic religious experience. This snowballing of texts creates a lopsided (and potentially pitiable) portrait of Paul. He becomes, in effect, someone who had one initiatory ecstatic religious experience on which he then reflected for the rest of his career.[93]

Some qualification of the term "conversion" is in order because it is a notoriously imprecise term, a fact that will be examined in more detail. In my opinion, it is most useful and meaningful when used to describe the movement out of one (religious) community or social grouping and assimilation into another.[94] If an ecstatic (or otherwise exceptional) experience is part of the impetus for such a transfer of affiliation, then it is best to identify two events – the ecstatic experience and the conversion. If it is a moment of insight, then it is better to trace the thought processes that led into and out of the insight. These approaches provide clearer and more crisply defined categories than the amorphous, malleable notion of "conversion." In doing so, they also provide the means by which each element in the individual's history can be tested, described, and

---

[93] The one experience that is not usually lumped in with the rest is Paul's account of an ascent to heaven in 2 Corinthians 12, although there are exceptions. John Knox, *Chapters in a Life of Paul* (New York: Abingdon, 1950), 77–78, described it as Paul's conversion but later changed his mind. See also Morton Scott Enslin, *Reapproaching Paul* (Nashville, Tenn.: Abingdon, 1962), 53–55; and Charles Buck and Greer Taylor, *Saint Paul: A Study of the Development* (New York: Scribner, 1969), 219–26.

[94] On this understanding of conversion (i.e., as a social phenomenon), see, for example, Peter L. Berger and Thomas Luckmann, *The Social Construction of Reality: A Treatise in the Sociology of Knowledge* (Garden City, N.Y.: Doubleday, 1966). Alan Segal discusses this problem at length in *Paul the Convert*.

interpreted with the potential for greater precision. That said, in the discussion that follows, I will allow the term in the many ways it is used in Pauline scholarship. I do so because all the authors whose views I discuss use the term, and the looseness of its fit is precisely the point of the analysis that follows.

As mentioned, the prevalence of this ill-defined use is due in no small part to the influence of the accounts in Acts. The simple fact that the phrase "the Damascus road experience," or others like it, can be used of Paul with such easy currency speaks to the extent of the influence. Therefore, it is necessary to discuss Acts; though there is nothing to be gained by it, I will go on to visions and revelations described by Luke.[95] There are many difficulties in using Acts as a source of historical information about the life of Paul. Several standard principles guide my own evaluation in this discussion. First, the historical value of details in Acts must be assessed on a case-by-case basis because sources of various kinds seem to lie behind some parts of the book. A second, related principle is that the burden of proof lies equally with those who would accept and those who would reject the historical value of any given account in Acts.[96] Third, the evidence from Acts is most reliable when it is confirmed by Paul's own writings (although this point would be moot if in fact Acts is dependent on some of the letters of Paul[97]).

When we apply these principles to Paul's conversion, Acts would appear to be of limited biographical value for this question. With regard to the first principle, the fact that the author of Acts presents three distinct – and, in part, mutually exclusive – accounts of the same event (Acts 9:1–19, 22:3–16, 26:9–18) suggests that factual representation is not Luke's primary

---

[95] The style of this sentence is in imitation of 2 Cor 12:1.

[96] This is contra Martin Hengel and Anna Marie Schwemer, who simply assert that "there are no reasonable grounds for rejecting [Luke's account] as legendary" in *Paul between Damascus and Antioch: The Unknown Years* (Louisville, Ky.: Westminster/John Knox, 1997), 38. The grounds that they give for accepting the historical authenticity of the details of Damascus road accounts are perhaps less reasonable because they gloss over the significant differences among the accounts in Acts, stating that only "in the last narration Luke brings together what he considers to be essential." Their discussion is moderated with words like "evidently," "presumably," "somewhat varying," "not so clearly," and "we may assume." Their observations indicate *reasonableness*, but do not demonstrate evidence. The burden of proof rests equally on either position.

[97] Such dependence is advocated by Benz, *Paulus als Visionär*; Hans Joachim Schoeps, *Paul: The Theology of the Apostle in the Light of Jewish Religious History* (Philadelphia: Westminster, 1961), 54; and Charles W. Hendrick, "Paul's Conversion/Call: A Comparative Analysis of the Three Reports in Acts," *Journal of Biblical Literature* 100 (1981), 415–32.

objective.[98] This multiform event is therefore reasonably understood as an interpretation beyond the normal levels of interpretation entailed in historical accounts. In fact, all of Luke's "conversion" accounts bear the same dramatic, instantaneous, and supernatural character (cf. the accounts of the disciples from Emmaus in Luke 24:13–35, the Ethiopian courtier in Acts 8:26–39, and perhaps especially Peter in Acts 10:9–23). Furthermore, it has long been noted that Luke's characterization of Paul, in these passages in particular, owes a great deal to the evangelist's own redactional purposes.[99]

The next step is to compare Acts with Paul's own testimony. In Paul's writings, the closest parallels to the three accounts in Acts are Gal 1:13–17 and, to a lesser extent, 1 Cor 15:8–9. The Galatians account, no less than those in Acts, is also recounted as the narrative means to persuasive ends. In the face of Galatian resistance, Paul interjects it as support for his authority as an apostle. In that context, his call serves as evidence of a direct divine commissioning like that of Isaiah and Jeremiah. The polemical intent of the letter requires that we understand this account similarly as an interpretation of the

---

[98] I follow the convention of using the traditional name attributed to the author of the third Gospel and Acts.

[99] Authors who describe various redactional purposes in the conversion accounts include David M. Stanley, "Paul's Conversion in Acts: Why Three Accounts?" *Catholic Biblical Quarterly* 15 (1953), 315–38; Howard Clark Kee, "The Conversion of Paul: Confrontation or Interiority?" in *The Other Side of God: A Polarity in World Religions*, ed. Peter L. Berger (Garden City, N.Y.: Anchor/Doubleday, 1981), 48–60; William Long, "The *Paulusbild* in the Trial of Paul in Acts," *Society of Biblical Literature Seminar Papers* 22 (1983), 87–105; Abraham J. Malherbe, "'Not in a Corner': Early Christian Apologetic in Acts 26:26," *The Second Century* 5 (1985–1986), 193–210; Robert L. Brawley, "Paul in Acts: Aspects of Structure and Characterization," *Society of Biblical Literature Seminar Papers* 27 (1988), 90–105; John T. Carroll, "Literary and Social Dimensions of Luke's Apology for Paul," *Society of Biblical Literature Seminar Papers* 27 (1988), 106–18; John Townsend, "Acts 9:1–29 and Early Church Tradition," *Society of Biblical Literature Seminar Papers* 27 (1988), 119–31; Dennis Hamm, "Paul's Blindness and Its Healing: Clues to Symbolic Intent," *Biblica* 71 (1990), 63–72; Ronald D. Witherup, "Functional Redundancy in the Acts of the Apostles: A Case Study," *Journal for the Study of the New Testament* 48 (1992), 67–86; Daniel Marguerat, "Saul's Conversion (Acts 9, 22, 26) and the Multiplication of Narrative in Acts," in *Luke's Literary Achievement: Collected Essays*, ed. C. M. Tuckett, *Journal for the Study of the New Testament Supplement Series* 116 (Sheffield: Sheffield Academic Press, 1995), 127–55; Willy Rordorf, "Paul's Conversion in the Canonical Acts and in the Acts of Paul," *Semeia: Social-Scientific Criticism of the New Testament and Its Social Work* 80 (1997), 137–44; Ira J. Jolivet, Jr., "The Lukan Account of Paul's Conversion and Hermagorean Stasis Theory," in *The Rhetorical Interpretation of Scripture: Essays from the 1996 Malibu Conference*, ed. Stanley E. Porter and Dennis L. Stamps, *Journal for the Study of the New Testament Supplement Series* 180 (Sheffield: Sheffield Academic Press, 1999), 210–20. Although some of the explanations for the details of the Acts accounts are competing, the authors agree in their sense of the indelible effects of Lukan redaction on the accounts.

original event (again, perhaps beyond the normal extent to which all history is innately interpretative).[100] In the final tally, the accounts from Acts agree with Paul's own only in (1) the notion of some sort of apprehension of the divine and (2) the association of this apprehension with a change in Paul's social identity. So, Paul's description and the accounts in Acts correspond only in the general thrust of the passages. In the end, the only significant historical information provided by the Lukan accounts is the fact that some sectors of early christianity told a story of Paul's dramatic conversion as a means of validating his role and to address concerns about the nature of the movement. They do not inform us about Paul's experience. Nonetheless, when the two sets of data are pressed together, the heavier (i.e., more detailed) accounts from Acts inevitably mold the less substantial descriptions from Galatians and 1 Corinthians into their own image. This is especially true outside of the field of biblical studies, where many are content to assume Paul's moment-in-time conversion and to take Acts as the only evidence necessary.[101]

Within biblical studies, among the various Pauline texts promoted as descriptions of or allusions to a moment-in-time conversion, the trio of 1 Cor 9:1, 1 Cor 15:8, and Gal 1:12–16 is the most secure.[102] The three texts coincide in their mention of an apprehension of the risen Christ and in their interest in Paul's identity as an apostle. In the two passages from 1

---

[100] The fact that Paul has tailored the form of his account according to the pattern of prophetic vocation has been noted for some time, perhaps in its most cited form by Krister Stendahl, *Paul among Jews and Gentiles* (Philadelphia: Fortress, 1976), but before him by E. Lohmeyer, *Grundlagen paulinischer Theologie* (Tübingen: Mohr, 1929), 210–12; Hans Windisch, *Paulus und Christus: Ein biblisch-religionsgeschichtlicher Vergleich*, Untersuchungen zur Neuen Testament 24 (Leipzig: J. C. Hinrichs, 1934–37); and Johannes Munck, *Paul and the Salvation of Mankind*, trans. Frank Clarke (Atlanta: John Knox, 1977), 11–35. On the broader question of whether first-person accounts of conversion experiences are reliable, see the discussion by Paula Fredriksen, "Paul and Augustine: Conversion Narratives, Orthodox Traditions and the Retrospective Self," *Journal of Theological Studies* 37 (1986), 3–34.

[101] So, one book on conversion (to Christianity) can optimistically proclaim, "by examining the three accounts of Paul's conversion we will find the core elements that define his conversion and hence those elements that define how conversion was understood in the New Testament." See Richard V. Peace, *Conversion in the New Testament: Paul and the Twelve* (Grand Rapids, Mich.: Eerdmans, 1999), 17.

[102] For the purposes of the discussion here, I will not distinguish between those who argue that the experience at hand must be conceived exclusively as a call (see footnote 100, this chapter) and those who describe it as a conversion. Although the category of "call" is sometimes used as a buffer against ecstatic connotations, as I think it is with Stendahl, that distinction does not bear up under scrutiny. Furthermore, the important difference that the terminology highlights is not the difference that is the focus of this discussion.

Corinthians, the verb of perception is ὁράω (to see, notice), perhaps the most ordinary of the available options for sight. In Galatians, it is "to reveal,"ἀποκαλύπτω. The Galatians text connects the encounter with the beginning of Paul's apostolic identity. The text in 1 Cor 15:8–9 places it in sequence with other sightings. In its own way, each of these texts is interested in representing a chronology. In 1 Cor 9, the sighting and apostleship are related merely by juxtaposition ("Am I not an apostle? Have I not seen the Lord?") rather than an explicit statement of cause and effect, or even neces-sarily before and after. The evidence, as far as it goes, does not preclude the possibility that the three all refer to a single initiatory experience, and vir-tually all authors who entertain the category of conversion for Paul cite these three references in that context.[103] Thus, it is possible, and certainly com-mon, to say that near the beginning of Paul's changed understanding of his apostolic status, he experienced a vision of the risen figure of Jesus.

This modest observation has become an exegetical black hole into which dozens of other texts are sucked. The next text most commonly pulled in this direction is Phil 3:4ff.[104] Paul's description of his former sources of honor and his current contrasting values speaks unequivocally to change in his life. However, only a few commentators are willing to argue that the comprehensive reorientation of worth that Paul describes here could have occurred instantly, somewhere between the horse and the road, if you will.[105] The fact that many are nevertheless willing to describe this as a

---

[103] 1 Cor 9:1 is rarely central in these arguments and sometimes omitted from the list, but I found no examples of anyone arguing explicitly against its inclusion.

[104] Wikenhauser (*Pauline Mysticism*, 146ff), on the basis of the present tense (ἡγοῦμαι) in verse 8, argues that Philippians 3 cannot describe Paul's conversion. However, such an argument erases the distinction between textual purposes and underlying historical events.

[105] Those who imply instantaneous reevaluation are typically of an earlier generation of schol-ars: Marvin Richardson Vincent, *A Critical and Exegetical Commentary on the Epistles to the Philippians and to Philemon* (Edinburgh: T. and T. Clark, 1902), 99; J. Hugh Michael, *The Epistle of Paul to the Philippians* (London: Hodder and Stoughton, 1946), 144, who claims that the wording of verse 7 "points to some moment at which the old standard of values passed away and the new took its place . . . from that moment on the Damascus road he has never wavered in his fidelity to the decision then made"; C. H. Dodd, *New Testament Studies* (Manchester: Manchester University Press, 1953), 80–82, who argues that this is a second conversion; Jacobus Johannes Müller, *The Epistles of Paul to the Philippians and to Philemon*, New International Commentary on the New Testament (Grand Rapids, Mich.: Eerdmans, 1955), 113; Karl Barth, *The Epistle to the Philippians* (London: SCM Press, 1962), 97, who states, "in point of fact it did happen 'all at once'"; and Ralph P. Martin, *Philippians*, New Century Bible Commentary (Grand Rapids, Mich.: Eerdmans, 1980), 129–30. For purposes of the conversation here, the debate regarding conversion versus call makes little difference because most of those who advocate strongly for the call paradigm imagine that event also to have been instantaneous. Johannes Munck (*Paul and the Salvation of Mankind*, 11–35; 22–23 discuss Phil 3) more or less sets the pattern for this position.

conversion text[106] speaks to the convenient and/or obfuscating elasticity of the term. What Paul describes here is not itself an ecstatic religious experience; as Beverly Gaventa puts it, one "can conclude merely that behind the statement 'I count everything as loss' stands something that produced a powerful cognitive shift."[107] However, the fact that both the "cognitive shift" and the "something" that produced it are called "conversion" by others suggests that in this case keener taxonomy is in order.[108]

Thus, the passage from Philippians illustrates the slipperiness of the category of conversion and the sloppiness with which it is applied to the life of Paul. Clearly, Paul's tally of gains and losses pertains to change and, in that broad sense, can be called "conversion" with equal breadth and imprecision. That an ecstatic vision, which occurred on a particular day in a particular place, can also be called conversion – by many of the same commentators – tells us more about the lexical flexibility of the term than it does about the character of the experience. "Conversion" can expand and recontract to take in at one point and eliminate at another a variety of phenomena, from social to psychological to historical. The single pliable term allows the

---

[106] Those who describe it as a conversion text without a sense of instantaneous change include Günther Bornkamm (*Paul*, 16–17), who calls it "conversion" but in so doing distinguishes it from "the hour when Christ appeared to him"; F. F. Bruce and W. Ward Gasque, *Philippians*, New International Biblical Commentary 11 (Peabody, Mass.: Hendrickson, 1989), 114; Martin Dibelius and Werner Georg Kümmel, *Paul* (Philadelphia: Westminster, 1953), 50; Beverly R. Gaventa, *From Darkness to Light: Aspects of Conversion in the New Testament* (Philadelphia: Fortress, 1986), 29–33, although she defines Paul's conversion as a cognitive "transformation"; Seyoon Kim, *Paul and the New Perspective: Second Thoughts on the Origin of Paul's Gospel* (Grand Rapids, Mich.: Eerdmans, 2002), 13; Richard Longenecker, ed., *The Road from Damascus: The Impact of Paul's Conversion on His Life, Thought, and Ministry*, McMaster New Testament Studies (Grand Rapids, Mich.: Eerdmans, 1997), xiii; Stanley B. Marrow, *Paul, His Letters and His Theology: An Introduction to Paul's Epistles* (New York: Paulist, 1986), 30–37; Carolyn Osiek, *Philippians, Philemon*, Abingdon New Testament Commentaries (Nashville, Tenn.: Abingdon, 2000), 90, who declares that "[t]his change of orientation was . . . forced on him by his experience of encounter with the Risen Christ"; Raymond V. Schoder, *Paul Wrote from the Heart: Philippians, Galatians in Straightforward English* (Oak Park, Ill.: Bolchazy-Carducci, 1987), 32; Thomas R. Schreiner, *Paul, Apostle of God's Glory in Christ: A Pauline Theology* (Downers Grove, Ill.: InterVarsity, 2001), 472; Mark Strom, *Reframing Paul: Conversations in Grace & Community* (Downers Grove, Il.: InterVarsity, 2000), 95–97; Ben Witherington III, *Paul's Narrative Thought World: The Tapestry of Tragedy and Triumph* (Louisville, Ky.: Westminster/John Knox, 1994), 227.

[107] Gaventa, *From Darkness to Light*, 33.

[108] That taxonomy is available and has been deployed in Pauline studies, but this greater concern for precision remains the exception. Gaventa's categories of conversion, alternation, and transformation are now sometimes taken up by other Paul scholars. Alan Segal's summary of available models and taxonomies, "Paul's Conversion; Psychological Study" (285–300 in *Paul the Convert*), provides a convenient survey of models.

commentator to forego methodological precision that more exacting terminology would require. So, "conversion" inevitably begins as the term that
indicates an event in Paul's life, a moment in time. Next, it expands to
include all sorts of discussions about what Paul's life was like in the past
and what defines it at whatever moment he happens to be writing the
particular letter under discussion. Then it contracts again to protect the
notion of a single religious experience and to exclude additional ecstatic
encounters at other points in time. So, the term expands to include all sorts
of textual details and contracts again to reduce them to a simplified dichotomy of then and now.

The case of 2 Cor 4:6 is an example of the even greater latitude with which
conversion is sometimes extended. In this verse, Paul writes intriguingly
about light shining in the hearts of himself and his co-ministers, bringing
"knowledge of the glory of God in the face of Christ." The comment is
frequently discussed as Paul's reflection on his sole ecstatic experience.[109]
So, for example, Alfred Wikenhauser can assert unequivocally that, "This
passage can have only one meaning. Hitherto Paul had hated Jesus bitterly,
and had savagely persecuted him in his followers. But he suddenly saw Jesus
in heavenly glory, and simultaneously realised that this Jesus was truly the
divinely sent Messias and that he had risen from the dead."[110]

Note the model of moment-in-time conversion that informs his
description. Jerome Murphy-O'Connor's more tepid appraisal seems
far more accurate. He observes that Paul's image of the "knowledge of

---

[109] Bornkamm, *Paul*, 23; Donald Coggan, *Paul: Portrait of a Revolutionary* (New York: Crossroad, 1985), 102; Deissmann (*Paul*, 129–30), who describes it as "hinting" at Paul's conversion; Dibelius and Kümmel (*Paul*, 60), who call it "the most expressive witness of what
took place inwardly" at conversion; James D. G. Dunn allows the possibility in "'A Light to
the Gentiles': The Significance of the Damascus Road Christophany for Paul," in *The Glory
of Christ in the New Testament: Studies in Christology in Memory of George Bradford Caird*,
ed. L. D. Hurst and N. T. Wright (Oxford: Clarendon, 1987), 259–60; J. Dupont, "The
Conversion of Paul and Its Influence on His Understanding of Salvation by Faith," in
Apostolic History and the Gospel, ed. W. W. Gasque and R. P. Martin (Grand Rapids, Mich.:
Eerdmans, 1970), 192; Michael Grant, *Saint Paul* (London: Weidenfeld and Nicolson, 1976),
107; Martin Hengel and Roland Deines,*The Pre-Christian Paul* (London: SCM Press, 1991),
79; Werner Georg Kümmel, *Kirchenbegriff und Geschichtsbewusstsein in der Urgemeinde und
bei Christus* (Uppsala: Niehans, 1943), 147; Jan Lambrecht and Daniel J. Harrington, *Second
Corinthians*, Sacra Pagina 8 (Collegeville, Minn.: Liturgical Press, 1999), 69; Giuseppe Ricciotti, *Paul, the Apostle*, trans. Alba I. Zizzamia (Milwaukee, Wis.: Bruce, 1953), 209, n. 3;
Schoeps, *Paul*, 54; David Wenham (with some hesitation), *Paul, Follower of Jesus or Founder
of Christianity?* (Grand Rapids, Mich.: Eerdmans, 1995), 359, n. 62; Witherington, *Paul's
Narrative Thought World*, 233; and Munck (*Paul and the Salvation of Mankind*, 34), who is
otherwise enthusiastic about a dramatic conversion, explicitly rejects this verse as referring
to that event.

[110] Wikenhauser, *Pauline Mysticism*, 134.

the glory of God in the face of Christ" is "neither explicitly nor exclusively concerned with Paul's conversion."[111] Instead, the "light of the knowledge of the glory of God in the face of Christ" is a phrase that was included by the history of religions school, particularly Wilhelm Bousset and Adolf Deissmann, as part of Paul's mysticism and established his "in-Christ" language as a significant category of Pauline studies.[112] Still, even according to Deissmann, not only 2 Cor 4:6 but "everything which can be called Christ-Mysticism in Paul comes from his reaction to this initiatory experience."[113] In other words, it may not be a direct description of the sole conversion event, but neither is it related to a separate occasion.

Others have followed this pattern of agglomeration.[114] A full tally of examples is well beyond the scope of documentation possible here, but the views of Seyoon Kim deserve mention if only to illustrate an end point in the spectrum. Not only does Kim include the trio of usual suspects (i.e., 1 Cor 9:1, 15:8–9; Gal 1:13–17), as well as the runners-up (2 Cor 4:4, 6; Phil 3:4–11),[115] but he also claims allusions to the conversion in a number of other places.[116] In fact, Kim sees many of the most interesting bits of Pauline ideology as deriving directly from a singular conversion moment. For example, he asserts that all Pauline transformation language[117] derives from the moment of conversion and, related to this, all those Pauline passages that contain "[eikōn] and related terms."[118] Among these, Kim treats 2 Cor 5:11–21 and Rom 11:25 at greatest length.[119] The former, in

---

[111] Jerome Murphy-O'Connor, *Paul: A Critical Life* (Oxford: Clarendon, 1996), 78, n. 20.

[112] Wilhelm Bousset, *Kyrios Christos: Geschichte des Christusglaubens von den Anfängen des Christentums bis Irenaeus*, 6th ed. (Göttingen: Vandenhoeck and Ruprecht, 1967); and Deissmann, *Paul*. In the generation before Schweitzer, they coined the term "Christ-mysticism" and introduced the category into discussions of Paul's life. See the helpful, if statistically oriented, discussion of the breadth of "in-Christ" language in Dunn, *Theology of Paul the Apostle*, 396–408.

[113] Deissmann, *Paul*, 105.

[114] For example, Richard Longenecker (*Road from Damascus*, 27) includes all the odds and ends from Rom 16:25; 2 Cor 11:32; Eph 3:1–13; Phil 3:20–21; Col 1:23c–29; and even 1 Tim 1:11–14 as remnants of Paul's Damascus road ravishment.

[115] Seyoon Kim, *The Origin of Paul's Gospel* (Grand Rapids, Mich.: Eerdmans, 1981), 3.

[116] Ibid., 3–31. These include Rom 10:2–4; 1 Cor 9:16–17; 2 Cor 3:4–4:6, 5:16; Eph 3:1–13; Col 1:23c–29; and even 1 Tim 1:11–14.

[117] Kim (*Paul and the New Perspective*, 166) lists Rom 8:29; 1 Cor 15:49; 2 Cor 3:18; Phil 3:21; and also 1 Cor 15:52; Gal 4:19; Phil 3:10; Col 3:9-10; Eph 4:24; and Rom 12:2.

[118] Kim, *Paul and the New Perspective*, 167. In this case, he includes Gal 1:16; 1 Thess 1:10; Col 1:15, 2:9; Phil 3:20–21; 1 Cor 2:8, 15:44–49; and 2 Cor 3:1–4:6. He finds 2 Cor 3:1–4:6 in particular "to be conclusive evidence that Paul derived his conception of Christ as the Εἰκών of God from the Damacus Christophany."

[119] Kim, *Paul and the New Perspective*, 214–38 and 239–57, respectively.

particular, he feels "is full of allusions to Paul's Damascus experience of conversion/call: what he is talking about in that passage is *what happened to him on the Damascus road.*"[120] Kim is also at pains to show that Paul might well have used scripture to inspire his further reflection on that one experience,[121] but the effect of that single, and singular, experience on Paul's comments is nonetheless direct and immutable. In a footnote, Kim does allow that "Paul may have had several visions" subsequent to his conversion encounter but that those later occasions would only "have confirmed and deepened the insights that he obtained from the first vision."[122]

The ideological implications of such a strong position are clear. If, as Kim argues, Paul's first vision of Jesus was an "objective external event,"[123] then one can argue that Paul's theology is equally objective and directly and divinely transmitted. Thus, the category of "conversion" can provide the means by which Paul – and thereby the Christianity to which he converts – can be seen to supersede whatever came before. Paul's dramatic experience is sufficient proof of the superiority of the "after." Furthermore, in this approach, whatever claims are attached to conversion are rendered unfalsifiable. There is no way to test the validity of one proposal against another because the experience itself is opaque. So, for example, Kim asserts that "[t]he revelation of the crucified Jesus as the embodiment of God's righteousness and the endowment of the Spirit at his conversion/call led him to see the structural weakness of the law, its association with the flesh and sin."[124]

Frequently, scholars who coordinate Paul's comments around a single ecstatic religious experience are also invested in discerning a coherent Pauline theology even though they might not agree on its core. Bruce Corley has sorted various assertions about the theological core of Paul's purported conversion into four categories. He includes Kim in the "doxological" group because of Kim's sense that conversion "revealed

---

[120] Ibid., 236 (emphasis original).

[121] Ibid., 239. For example, he suggests that "Paul obtained the 'mystery' of Rom 11:25–26 from an interpretation of his Damascus revelation chiefly in the light of Isa 6 and 49."

[122] Kim, *Paul and the New Perspective*, 186, n. 69.

[123] Kim, *Origin of Paul's Gospel*, 56. In his subsequent recapitulation and elaboration of his thesis, Kim speaks of the "Damascus experience" without specifying its objective, external nature. However, he does add the notion of "the Jesus tradition" as the second parent (he specifies the mother) of "Paul's gospel." See Kim, *Paul and the New Perspective*, 297. In either case, the purity of Paul's thought is the point being made. Kim's later presentation, with its eugenic overtones, introduces new difficulties.

[124] Kim, *Paul and the New Perspective*, 163.

Jesus as the Lord of glory (2 Cor 4:6), whose radiance intimated the very presence of God and the eschatological glory to come."[125] However, by the time Kim published his second take on the subject, his reconstruction of the essence of Paul's experience had grown to include four elements. These are: 1) "the revelation of the gospel of Jesus," which really concerns the identity of Jesus but cannot be narrowed down to any single aspect or role;[126] 2) Paul's call to go to the Gentiles; 3) the endowment of the Holy Spirit; and 4) the revelation of God's plan for salvation as summarized in Rom 11:25–26.[127]

Corley's other categories are soteriological, christological, and missiological. The soteriological interpretations place Paul's rejection of the law at the center of Paul's conversion. It was the change in the mechanism of salvation, with Christ as the end of the law (Rom 10:4), that was revealed to Paul. The missiological approach tends to focus on the call component of Paul's experience and suggests that "Damascus revealed Jesus as the Messiah of Israel (Gal 1:12), whose death and resurrection inaugurated the 'Age to Come' and fulfilled the covenant promises of the Old Testament Scriptures."[128] These are arguably the major categories, but many other theological odds and sods have been similarly attributed to the single experience of conversion.[129]

Such grounding of Paul's theology unmitigatedly in a moment of revelation participates in a version of cognicentrism. Paul is not an ecstatic; he is the recipient of an unsolicited, divine (read: objective) interference. In this line of argument, the many texts that might speak to ecstatic awareness become de facto rational reflections on a single experience. Furthermore, that experience is safely opaque – and

---

[125] Bruce Corley, "Interpreting Paul's Conversion – Then and Now," in *The Road from Damascus: The Impact of Paul's Conversion on His Life, Thought, and Ministry,* ed. Richard N. Longenecker (Grand Rapids, Mich.: Eerdmans, 1997), 16.

[126] Kim (*Paul and the New Perspective,* 81) includes each element of Jesus' identity as "Christ, Lord, Son of God, and Image of God" as being revealed equally in the "Damascus event."

[127] Kim has virtually abandoned the effort to find a coherent theological core that can account for all the variation. Instead, he finds a malleable experience that is shaped by theological content.

[128] Corley, "Interpreting Paul's Conversion," 16. He suggests that J. Dupont, U. Wilckens, and P. Stuhlmacher were early proponents of the soteriological interpretation. The missiological is held by P. H. Menoud, R. B. Hays, and N. T. Wright.

[129] For example, David Wenham (*Paul, Follower of Jesus or Founder of Christianity?* 122) attributes all Paul's lordship language to the "Damascus road experience." F. F. Bruce, *Paul: Apostle of the Free Spirit* (Exeter: Paternoster, 1980), 421, claims the conversion as the source of Paul's "body of Christ" imagery.

therefore a kind of tabula rasa on which the central Pauline tenets might be written. Recent sympathetic sociological studies of conversion have helped to rehabilitate this category of experience. But many New Testament scholars who take it up do not apply the critical parameters of that sociological category.[130] For them, there is no going back behind the moment of conversion to causes, ingredients, or elements that can be studied or parsed or, most importantly, attributed to Paul's imagination (in either the most frivolous and idiosyncratic or the most productive and disciplined sense of the word). The rich theological reflection in Paul's letters is derived directly from the divine as Paul apprehended it that day at the beginning of his career. The problem I want to highlight here is not a debate about the nature of conversion (how to describe it, whether or not it took place, etc.) or the content of Paul's theology but the way in which the assertion of a conversion experience allows one to lump all sorts of ecstatic experience into a single event and some derivative thought about it.[131]

1.3.3 *Through the Reading Glasses*

There is one final approach to Paul's ecstatic language that warrants consideration here. One of the most intriguing perspectives is that of those authors who do not doubt "that Paul had a number of ecstatic experiences in his life"[132] yet still despair about the barriers to assessing them precisely because they recognize them as *experience*. Other of these contributors place ecstatic experience – the means by which it is achieved, the content of what is apprehended, and the interpretation after the fact – completely within the purview of the host culture. In broad terms, this perspective assumes that there is no experience apart from linguistic construction of it,

---

[130] Notable exceptions are Gaventa, *From Darkness to Light*, and Segal, *Paul the Convert.*

[131] Beverly Gaventa (*From Darkness to Light*, 39–40) and others who emphasize cognitive shift are able to avoid the sense of any significant religious experience in Paul's life. Gaventa also claims that all we can say is that behind Paul's words "stands something that produced a powerful cognitive shift" (*From Darkness to Light*, 33).

[132] Segal, *Paul the Convert*, 37. Segal (*Paul the Convert*, 12) recognizes the ecstatic implications of a number of texts (the standard trio of "conversion" texts, as well as Phil 3:4–11; Rom 10:2–4; and 2 Cor 3–5) and even attributes "the scholarly reticence" on the topic to "embarrassment with the nonrational aspects of the human soul." He also suggests that Paul's experience of ecstatic transformation informs his thought about the resurrection (*Paul the Convert*, 22). These unelaborated insights of Segal were part of the original impetus for my own examination.

and hence that culture is both necessary and more or less sufficient for the description of ecstatic experience.[133]

In Pauline studies, Alan Segal might be counted among the most important in that number.[134] In fact, Segal's *Paul the Convert* has become a standard work on Paul's "mysticism" despite his hesitation to tackle Paul's experience directly. Part of the crux for Segal and others like him is their methodological conviction that one cannot get to *experience* via a *text*. In part, furthermore, Segal is also contesting arguments like those of Seyoon Kim (discussed earlier) that would make Paul's revelation(s) unique. Against this, Segal tries to show the ways in which Paul's ecstatic experience is in keeping with the cultural norms of Jewish mysticism.[135] He argues that Paul was influenced by the sorts of Jewish mystical traditions that eventually developed into Merkabah mysticism. In order to place Paul as one among many, Segal points to the well-established later evidence for Merkabah at the one end of the line of practitioners and the early seeds

---

[133] Steven Katz, though not interested in Paul, has been among the most vigorous proponents of this view, as, for example, in the following quotation: "[T]he Hindu mystic does not have an experience of x which he then describes in the, to him, familiar language and symbols of Hinduism, but rather he has a Hindu experience, i.e. his experience is not an unmediated experience of x but is itself the, at least partially, pre-formed anticipated Hindu experience of Brahman"; see Katz, "Conservative Character of Mystical Experience," 4.

[134] Anticipating Segal, James D. Tabor had earlier taken a similar comparative approach in his *Things Unutterable*, in which he includes Hellenistic sources and parallels along with Jewish material. Like Segal, Tabor recognizes the fundamental importance of the ecstatic experience behind 2 Cor 12:1–4, and, like Segal, he addresses it only in passing. In fact, Tabor goes to great lengths both to emphasize that Paul does not disparage such experience and that Paul is not speaking of visions and revelations simply because his opponents have forced him to do so (as in the argument of those who practice mirror exegesis). Rather, Tabor thinks that Paul has raised the issue because he values such an experience and assumes that his audience does, too; see Tabor, *Things Unutterable*, 29–38.

[135] Segal relies on a kind of post hoc ergo propter hoc evidence to establish the relevance of Jewish mysticism for Paul's experience. For example, he notes that "the traditions concerning the son of man are centuries older than Christianity" (Segal, *Paul the Convert*, 42), that "[o]ne apocalyptic mediator, Enoch, predates Paul" (4), and that "[t]echniques of theurgy and heavenly ascent were secret lore in rabbinic literature (see b. Hagiga 13a–15b), which dates from the third century" (36). B. Hagiga 13a–15b relates a lengthy dispute between rival rabbinical groups, one studying the "Work of Creation" (Gen 1 and 2) and the other the "Work of the Chariot" (Eze 1). Although there is good evidence in b. Hagiga for the esoteric nature of the mystical speculation on these biblical texts (e.g., minimum age requirements for those who will be instructed [13a], perhaps 50 years old [14a]), I am unable to find in it any mention of technique. Again, if we fill in Segal's implicit argument, it must be that (1) the account represents a remnant of a real visionary experience, and (2) if there was ecstatic experience, then there must have been techniques by which the rabbis could achieve it. But this is hardly secure footing on which to establish the idea that Paul had been taught techniques of mystical transformation. Segal acknowledges that Paul would provide the only first-century evidence for such traditions.

from which it grew at the other. He then places Paul as a midpoint in the genealogical trajectory.

Segal is not the first to associate Merkabah mysticism with Paul's vision in 2 Cor 12:1–4. As early as 1901, Wilhelm Bousset identified Paul's journey to paradise as an example of Merkabah,[136] and since then many others have noted points of contact between the two.[137] The designation "Merkabah mysticism" encompasses a broader range of activity than that circumscribed by ecstatic religious experience. It includes, for example, meditation on texts for exegetical purposes and, in particular, on Ezekiel's visions of the divine throne-chariot and the representation of YHWH seated there (cf. Ezek 1:1–3:13 and 10). *Merkabah* is in fact the word for the throne-chariot on which a figure is seated. Ezekiel speaks of "the likeness of a throne, in appearance like sapphire, and seated above the likeness of a throne was a likeness as it were of a human form.... Such was the appearance of the likeness of the glory of the Lord" (Ezek 1:26, 28b). However, in the later full-blown mysticism of Merkabah, it is assumed that the adept not only meditated on that form in the texts but also on occasion experienced an ecstatic journey to heaven where he[138]

---

[136] Wilhelm Bousset, "Die Himmelsreise der Seele," *Archiv für Religionswissenschaft* 4 (1901), 139–69, 229–73.

[137] Among those who place Paul within the trajectory of Merkabah mysticism are Gershom G. Scholem, *Jewish Gnosticism, Merkabah Mysticism and Talmudic Tradition*, 2nd ed. (New York: Jewish Theological Seminary, 1965); J. M. Bowker, "'Merkabah' Visions and the Visions of Paul," *Journal of Semitic Studies* 16 (1971), 57–73; Martin Hengel, "'Setze dich zu meiner Rechten!' Die Inthronisation Christi zur Rechten Gottes und Psalm 110:1," in *Le Trône de Dieu*, ed. M. Philonenko, *Wissenschaftliche Untersuchungen zum Neuen Testament* 69 (Tübingen: Mohr-Siebeck, 1993), 108–94; C. R. A. Morray-Jones, "Paradise Revisited (2 Cor 12:1–12): The Jewish Mystical Background of Paul's Apostolate. Part 1: The Jewish Sources," *Harvard Theological Review* 86 (1993), 177–217; C. R. A Morray-Jones, "Paradise Revisited (2 Cor 12:1–12): The Jewish Mystical Background of Paul's Apostolate. Part 2: Paul's Heavenly Ascent and Its Significance," *Harvard Theological Review* 86 (1993), 256–92; Alan F. Segal, "Paul and Ecstasy," *Society of Biblical Literature Seminar Papers* 25 (1986), 555–80; Segal, *Paul the Convert*; Alan F. Segal, "Paul and the Beginning of Jewish Mysticism," in *Death, Ecstasy and Other Worldly Journeys*, ed. John Collins and Michael Fishbane (Albany: State University of New York Press, 1995), 93–120; Tabor, *Things Unutterable*; James M. Scott, "The Triumph of God in 2 Cor 2:14: Additional Evidence of Merkabah Mysticism in Paul," *New Testament Studies* 42 (1996), 260–81; M. E. Thrall, "Paul's Journey to Paradise," in *The Corinthian Correspondence*, ed. R. Bieringer, Bibliotheca ephemeridum theologicarum lovaniensium (Leuven: Leuven University Press, 1996), 347–63.

[138] I use the masculine pronoun advisedly because, among its other particularities, Merkabah mysticism appears to have been the exclusive realm of male mystics; see Scholem, *Jewish Gnosticism, Merkabah Mysticism and Talmudic Tradition*, 37–38. Elliot R. Wolfson, "Woman – The Feminine as Other in Theosophic Kabbalah: Some Philosophical Observations on the Divine Androgyne," in *The Other in Jewish Thought and History: Constructions of Jewish Culture and Identity*, ed. Laurence J. Silberstein and Robert L. Cohn (New York: New York University Press, 1994), 166–204, has observed more broadly that "the circles of Jewish mystics through the ages ... were exclusively male fraternities" (169).

encountered the physical glory of the throne and/or the figure of the human representation of God.

Paul's language of the glory of God in the face of Christ (2 Cor 4:6) and his claims to have seen a risen, heavenly figure (1 Cor 9:1, 15:8) have also been compared to elements of the Merkabah traditions. However, some of the parallels between Paul's views and those of Merkabah are part of the general culture of first-century Judaism and not specific to a mystical tradition. One of these cultural constructs is belief in the assumption and sometimes the transformation of certain exemplary figures at the end of their lives. Elijah, Moses, and Enoch, in particular, were subjects of such speculation because scripture was suggestive regarding their ultimate disposition – Elijah most dramatically because he was carried off to heaven before his death (2 Kings 2); Moses because his burial site was unknown (Deut 34:6); and Enoch because the text claimed enigmatically that he "walked with God and was no more, for God took him" (Gen 5:24). Philo, for one, demonstrates a lively interest in the assumption of Moses and even speculates on his apotheosis (e.g., *Sacrifices of Cain and Abel* 1–10; *Moses* 1.155–58). Another document singled out by Segal is a fragment of *Moses*, dating from the second century BCE, which depicts Moses experiencing a vision of a figure seated on the throne of God.[139] The speculation regarding Enoch's ascent also circulated by Paul's time in the book of 1 Enoch, which was found among the Dead Sea Scrolls and in several manuscripts of an Ethiopic version. In several scenes in this book, Enoch tours the heavens and views an enthroned figure called the Son of Man and finally, in 1 Enoch 71, Enoch himself is transformed into that figure.[140]

If these textual remnants nourished the gestation of Merkabah, the mysticism itself appears to have been born in scholarly circles where scribal meditation grew into the experience of mystical revelations. J. M. Bowker observes

---

[139] The figure is called "*phos gennaios*" (a venerable man). As Segal points out, the description "is a double entendre in Greek, since *phos* can mean either 'light' or 'man' depending on the gender of the noun." See Segal, "Paul and the Beginning of Jewish Mysticism," 102.

[140] The date of Chapters 32–71 is disputed in part because this section of 1 Enoch is missing from the manuscripts found among the Dead Sea Scrolls. It seems clear, however, that the Gospel of Matthew reflects familiarity with the text (Matt 19:28, 25:31) and that its ideas, if not the text itself, were current during Paul's life. Among those who support Matthew's familiarity with the Similitudes is J. C. Hindley, "Towards a Date for the Similitudes of Enoch: An Historical Approach," *New Testament Studies* 14 (1967–68), 551–65; John J. Collins, "The Heavenly Representative: The 'Son of Man' in the Similitudes of Enoch," in *Ideal Figures in Ancient Judaism: Profiles and Paradigms*, ed. John J. Collins and George W. E. Nickelsburg, Society of Biblical Literature Septuagint and Cognate Studies (Chico, Calif.: Scholars Press, 1980), 111–34 at 125; John J. Collins, "The Son of Man in First-Century Judaism," *New Testament Studies* 38 (1992), 448–66 at 452; and J. Theisohn, *Der auserwählte Richter*, Studien zur Umwelt des Neuen Testaments 12 (Göttingen: Vandenhoeck and Ruprecht, 1975).

that by the end of the first century, "certain highly respected rabbis had practiced Merkabah contemplation and seen visions, not least Johanan b. Zakkai (one of the greatest scholars at the time of the fall of Jerusalem), who had taught Merkabah contemplation to some of his most favored pupils."[141] The stylized account of the four rabbis who entered paradise preserves one tradition about such ascents. It is found with small differences in t. Hag 2:3–4, y. Hag 77, b. Hag 14– 15, and a manuscript fragment of the Mekilta de R. Simeon b. Johai.[142] The tradition recounts the fates that befell the four mystical travelers because of their vision in paradise: One "looked and died," another "looked and suffered harm," the third "looked and cut down the shoots," and only Rabbi Akiba "ascended and descended in peace."

Segal's efforts to understand and describe Paul's comments as an example of a larger phenomenon are theoretically preferable to the views he opposes; however, Segal's own case may be slightly overstated or insufficiently nuanced. This use of the label "mysticism" is clearly distinct from those discussed in the preceding sections. It identifies primarily a body of secondary reflection that likely developed in relation to ecstatic experience and now includes traditions for interpreting it, imaginative cosmological elaborations of it, and possibly techniques for attaining such experience as well. Segal's claim of a genealogical link to Paul depends in particular on the understanding that, in 2 Cor 12:4, Paul demonstrates that he is part of an esoteric tradition. The two words *harrētos rhēmata* and their nuances are at the heart of these claims. Specifically, does the wording that Paul heard "unutterable" things amount to an esoteric prohibition of the sort applied in the so-called mystery religions of the time? Segal finds parallels in the Talmudic passage that suggests certain esoteric prohibitions or commitments concerning the teaching of the creation story and the account of Ezekiel's vision of the heavens (b. Hag 13ff) and, closer in time, in the Mishnah directive to teach the texts one-on-one (m. Hag. 2.1). In order to draw such conclusions for Paul's use, Segal must highlight Paul's limited reference to Pharisaic connections (Phil 3:5) so that he can link Paul's experience with later rabbinic writings. Segal repeatedly describes Paul's former identity as Pharisaic[143] and Paul's

---

[141] Bowker, "'Merkabah' Visions and the Visions of Paul," 57. Bowker assesses accounts of Johanan's vision in t. Hag. 2:1, y. Hag. 77a, b. Hag. 14b, and a fragment of Mekilta de R. Simeon b. Johai.

[142] S. Schechter, "Genizah Fragments," *Jewish Quarterly Review* 16 (1904), 446–52, originally published the fragment. It is reprinted in parallel with the other accounts in the article by Bowker.

[143] Segal, *Paul the Convert*, 26, 128, 146, 209, 227, 283.

use of "received" and "passed on" (1 Cor 15) as indications of knowledge of Pharisaic oral conventions.[144] For Segal, Pharisaic training may also account for how Paul learned techniques of trance and esoteric prohibitions about the content of such revelations.[145] He even goes so far as to posit Paul's awkward use of third-person speech in this account as a kind of missing link in the development of mystical traditions: "[R]abbinic rules also forbid public discussion of mystic phenomena. A first-century date for this rule would explain why Paul could not divulge his experience *in his own name* at that place. It also suggests why Jewish mystics consistently picked pseudepigraphical literary conventions to discuss their religious experience, unlocking the mystery behind the entire phenomenon of pseudepigraphical writing."[146]

If we can imagine so early a date for well-developed mystical traditions and if we can imagine a context in which Paul would have engaged in this degree of training, then Segal's scenario is indeed possible. However, to grant this understanding of Paul's intentions and their root would create problematic implications. The hypothesis requires either that Paul be expressing a predetermined position or that something in the revelation itself indicates to him that secrecy is required. Esoteric prohibitions are a way of distinguishing the inside from the outside, of demarcating who is an initiate and who does not belong. If Paul's silence regarding what he heard is in honor of a commitment to maintaining esoteric prohibitions, then what does that say about his affiliations, particularly if, as Segal seems to suggest, he learned these prohibitions in his early (Pharisaic) training?

Two social configurations are possible in this case: Paul belonged to either (1) a group within early christianity that met apart from and to the exclusion of the full assemblies[147] or (2) a strictly Jewish/Judean circle to which he was initiated (fourteen years ago?) and whose prohibitions he still honored despite his reinterpretation of his mysticism as a revelation of Christ for the sake of the Gentiles. Although either of these sets of

---

[144] Ibid., 27.

[145] In a footnote, Segal (*Paul the Convert*, 320, n. 64) allows that Paul may have had "previous instruction in mystical and apocalyptic Judaism, either as a Pharisee or a Hellenistic Jew, or because he has been taught to do so by another Christian in his community" but concludes that a determination is beyond the nature of the evidence.

[146] Ibid., 58. The suggestion of literary anonymity was made previously by J. Baumgarten, *Paulus und die Apokalyptik* (Neukirchen-Vluyn: Neukirchen Verlag, 1975), 143–44.

[147] In fact, this option seems to be Segal's choice: "When Paul speaks of the person who has heard unutterable things (2 Corinthians 12), he may equally be admitting to the existence of secret traditions in Christianity" (*Paul the Convert*, 24).

circumstances is possible, they create in the first case a significantly more complicated picture of the social organization of earliest christianity than is generally entertained or in the second case a far more nuanced sense of Paul's loyalties than has been recognized – and, I think, than the texts will bear.[148] In other words, although the context of an esoteric association is regularly raised, no attention has been given to the social-historical implications of such a claim.

A third possibility would be the more moderate idea of silence out of respect for the sacredness of the heavenly revelation. However, this suggestion does not fit with Paul's sense of purpose as he outlines it in his letters. First of all, nothing in what Paul says otherwise about his visions and revelations suggests a commitment to secrecy, let alone an order against divulgence. For example, in the context of relating this very vision, he voluntarily recounts what he perceives as the words of the risen Christ (2 Cor 12:9). Furthermore, elsewhere when Paul does use the language of secrecy and mystery, he does so only in order to claim that what had once been concealed is now meant to be proclaimed: "For I do not want you to be ignorant, brothers [and sisters], about this mystery" (Rom 11:25);[149] "but we speak the wisdom of God in a mystery which had been hidden" (1 Cor 2:7a); and "Behold, I tell you a mystery!" (1 Cor 15:51).[150] Even his claim to be one of the stewards of the mysteries of God (1 Cor 4:1) does not counter this direction.

Given these implications, it is difficult to support the notion that *harrēta rhēmata* is an expression of esoteric prohibition. It is possible that Paul encountered the language through its use by initiate to the mysteries, but if so the influence on his own thought is of the most insipid kind. In fact, its use even in the mysteries sometimes means simply "inexpressible." Rather, for Paul, the mysteries of God's workings have become εὐαγγέλιον, but the ῥήματα of ecstasy remain ineffable. Segal's contention that Paul can be read as part of the history of what might be called mystical speculation is an important contribution to the

---

[148] The timing of the second scenario would also be difficult to coordinate with what is otherwise known about Pauline chronology because, in most reconstructions, fourteen years before the writing of 2 Corinthians 10–13, Paul would have already been affiliated with the christian sect. However, if we attempt to grant the scenario the greatest scope for possibility, it could be that fourteen years before his letter Paul was still practicing a tradition he had learned in another setting.

[149] Likewise in the disputed Rom 16:25–26.

[150] The disputed letters also contain several references to Paul's sense of commission to reveal divine mysteries to all believers and even potential believers. See Eph 1:9, 3:1–9 (5:32), 6:19–20; and Col 1:25–27, 2:2–3, and 4:3.

conversation. But the notion that this history is a single continuous developmental trajectory with Paul as the only necessary midpoint between biblical narratives and the Talmud goes beyond, and perhaps misreads, the evidence. Segal has done a great service in bringing this set of texts into conversation with Paul's experience and thought. I will return to some of these issues in the next chapter. For now I note only that the concern is not whether the general background of Judaism is relevant to Paul's religious ecstasy; it clearly is. It provides a general cultural context in which religiously construed ecstasy is meaningful, and it offers some of the representations through which it can be interpreted. That granted, however, Jewish mystical guilds cannot be claimed as the source of Paul's ecstasy, nor could their influence account for the fullness of his ecstasy. Thus, explanations must lie elsewhere.

1.4 CONCLUSION

To a significant extent, the problem of accounting for Paul's ecstasy is a problem of seeing. Several cultural features and bits of historical happenstance have placed most (Western) readers of Paul's letters in a perspective from which experience in general sits in shadow; ecstatic experience, in particular, is sometimes wholly obscured from view. In this chapter, I have sketched first the relationship between some colonial circumstances and the attitudes toward ecstatic practitioners. In some cases, the complex politics of Otherness have found leverage in descriptions of shamans and occasions of spirit possession. This dynamic has been repeated in the power struggles of religious identity, in which "mysticism" – that peculiarly religious subset of ecstatic practice – has had the sort of vilifying power that accusations of "impurity" also sometimes carry. The label in itself is often sufficient to malign one's opponents. Thus, to see in Paul's letters the references to ecstatic experiences of the divine requires that one somehow dig through that mound of attitudes that has become more or less part of the cultural landscape. That work of sifting has not been of interest to most Western interpreters because we are the heirs of those who heaped up the layers in the first place.

Those broader cultural tendencies are not the only cause of neglect of this question. In addition, something in the nature of biblical exegesis itself has expanded the blind spots in which Paul's ecstasy sits. In other words, some of the methods and widespread presuppositions of Pauline studies have limited how we see the letters. In this chapter's quick tour through some of the oversights, I have predominantly attended to commentary literature. That choice is determined in no small part by the fact that so few monographs address questions of Paul's religious experience but also in part because the commentary literature frequently illustrates the status quo of how and what we see in biblical studies. Furthermore, as James Smith asks in the introduction to his study of Philippians, "Does not the commentary seek to isolate difficulties and smooth them over so as to represent, or 'manifest,' the text as comprehensible and coherent? Does not the commentary seek to precede the text, to displace and eventually replace the text in favor of itself?"[151] Smith argues that these interpretive tendencies are further connected to the pervasive notions about the nature of Paul's thought and communication. The widespread assumption that Romans is a more characteristic and fuller example of Paul's communication than the shorter, less carefully structured letters is exemplary of these tendencies in the scholarship. In a sense, the privileging of Romans shows how these methodological choices place Paul in the same position as the commentary writer. In the standard ordering, Paul is elevated over the original readers as knowing more – quantitatively and qualitatively – than they do. Furthermore, he is presented as knowing only in cognicentric categories. Certain aspects of this positioning make perfect sense, perhaps especially for the letter to the Romans, which was written prior to anything but a formal relationship between Paul and its recipients. But, in other ways, such a construction blurs the process by which the letter does more than elucidate propositions and clarify coherent principles. In short, as I have tried to show here, it is all too easy to slide into explanations of passages that interpret them as *corrections* of the readers' views and as emotionally transcending (e.g., ironic or sarcastic) the relationship with the recipients. Moreover, our methods tend to demand that we treat the letters as sufficient (if read with the right historical information) rather than, by their very nature, insufficient substitutes for something else that is actually more vital to the writer.

Both of these spheres – the general cultural and the specific exegetical – share a sensibility about words that we would do well to adjust or at least supplement. For a time, culminating perhaps in the 1980s, language was taken as the primary, and nearly sole, means of knowing. This view had significant effect on debates about religious experience, with authors

[151] James A. Smith, *Marks of an Apostle: Deconstruction, Philippians, and Problematizing Pauline Theology*, ed. Gale A. Yee, Semeia Studies (Atlanta: Society of Biblical Literature, 2005), 11.

such as Steven Katz arguing that no experience exists without language.[152] In response to that helpfully emphatic formulation, others began to argue for a more tempered recognition of the significance of language and culture in coloring the interpretation of experience. In her own context, Margaret Miles is among those who have offered a penetrating critique of the predominant focus on language. For instance, she questions some of the premises that inform the hermeneutical theory of authors such as Wittgenstein, Dilthey, and Gadamer. In Miles's estimation, their way of reading

> . . . gives an absolute advantage to language users, those whose primary tool for relating to the world is trained linguistic skill. It renders inaudible and invisible those whose primary mode of understanding and relating to the world is not verbal. Not only does this view of reality as verbally constituted unjustly exclude all people some of the time, and some people all of the time, but it also forces discourse to entertain and respond only to itself – to discourse – rather than to perceptive, affective, and intellectual experience.[153]

In other words, sometimes language is a blind guide pointing the way to a land in which it does not live.[154]

When "what Paul said" is placed so centrally, when it is both the means and the end of the study, what we see is indeed determined by how we look. The historical happenstance of cultural documentation, the convenient strangeness of ecstatic states in describing Otherness, and the political needs of the groups doing the describing have all pushed the text into a certain

---

[152] See Katz, "Conservative Character of Mystical Experience," 3–60. Katz's argument sounds outrageously reductionist now, but that limit is largely due to the fact that he was refuting other claims that have also lost their currency. In particular, he took issue with the claims of "perennial philosophy" that a certain kind of religious experience provided direct access to the divine. For example, see Huston Smith, "Is There a Perennial Philosophy?" 553–66, esp. 560–4. Katz's opinion is shared by Proudfoot, *Religious Experience*, esp. 123; and Scholem, *Major Trends in Jewish Mysticism*. See also Holm, "Ecstasy Research in the 20th Century." A more moderate course is argued in King, "Two Epistemological Models for the Interpretation of Mysticism." King counters Katz's view with the criticism that it reduces experience to language – that language is in fact inextricable from culture, but that religious ecstasy, like all experience, cannot be reduced to the attempt to describe it. In other words, the whole of the mystical experience cannot be contained in the adept's description of that experience. In fact, there are many who find that mystical experience is in its very nature a nonlinguistic experience. Thus, as Proudfoot argues, terms like "ineffable" and "paradoxical," which are often applied to religious ecstasy, are not vague efforts to describe the experience but in fact quite precise descriptions of what it is. See Proudfoot, *Religious Experience*, 125.

[153] Miles, *Image as Insight*, xi.

[154] The inescapably referential essence of all language has been argued most thoroughly by George Lakoff and Mark Johnson, *Philosophy in the Flesh: The Embodied Mind and Its Challenge to Western Thought* (New York: Basic Books, 1999).

light. Most interestingly of all, however, the (discipline-specific) focus on language has sometimes distorted the vision of much that informs the text. It becomes too easy to forget, as Miles has put it, that language is often not the "primary mode of understanding and relating to the world" but is in fact sometimes a poor substitute for something else, a floundering attempt to do justice to referents that actually matter more than the words themselves. The next chapter examines one of Paul's experiences that both existed apart from words and demanded attention. From this point, we begin the exploration of some of the referents of Paul's letters that have not been well served by our habits of seeing. If Paul came to certain views through his ecstatic experience, then we might ask not only "What does Paul know?" but also "How did Paul come to know this?" and "What kind of knowledge is it that arises out of (bodily) experience?"

2

◌

Paul's Brain: The Cognitive Neurology of Ecstasy

God guard me from those thoughts men think in the mind alone.
— W. B. Yeats

When the Canadian psychologist Dr. Michael Persinger got hold of a similar device a few years ago, he chose instead to stimulate parts of his temporal lobes. And he found to his amazement that he experienced God for the first time in his life.
— V. S. Ramachandran

G IVEN THE DIFFICULTIES WITH REPRESENTATIVE TREATMENTS OF Paul's ecstatic religious experience, a fresh assessment seems warranted. In this chapter, I will consider Paul's ecstatic religious experience as a thing in itself, and in particular as an experience of an ASC. This approach commends itself for a number of reasons. First of all, it seems prudent to begin with the assumption that Paul's ecstatic religious experience shares some of the character of the religious ecstasy of others; although his experience may well be distinctive, it is fallacious to begin by assuming that it is unique. So, if Paul did *not* "journey" to heaven and speak in tongues in an altered state of consciousness, he would be unique, at least among those whose testimonies are accessible to critical scrutiny. Second, this approach offers an exploratory perspective through which experience can be described as more than second-order reflection and conscious thought. Finally, and relatedly, it takes seriously the fact that Paul was a contributing participant in his own experience, not merely in later reflection on it. For these three reasons, the discipline of medical – and, in particular, neurological – science provides a perspective that might appropriately help to flesh out (quite literally) the ecstatic details in Paul's letters.

67

Among those details in Paul's letters that may be considered to parallel the ecstatic experiences of others are: (1) speaking in tongues (1 Cor 14:18); (2) visions and/or revelations (2 Cor 12:1–4; Gal 1:12, 2:2);[1] (3) ecstatic prayer (Rom 8:23, 26); (4) "signs and wonders" and acts of power (Rom 15:18–19; 2 Cor 12:12; and possibly Gal 3:5 – cf. 1 Cor 1:22); and (5) perhaps some of the other *pneumatika* in 1 Corinthians 14.[2] Of these experiences, Paul's ascent account in 2 Corinthians 12[3] will serve in this chapter as the test case for neurological approaches, primarily because it presents the fullest description and perhaps the most powerful of the experiences that Paul discusses. In this chapter, I will not present a full exegesis of the passage but will limit my comments to 2 Cor 12:1–4. These verses are typically given quite short shrift in exegeses of this chapter. More often, Paul's "thorn in the flesh" dominates the exegetical agenda,[4] or, as outlined in

[1] See also Eph 3:3. Throughout, I will relegate parallels from disputed letters to footnotes.
[2] Also 2 Thess 2:9. In his list of Paul's practices, David Edward Aune, *Prophecy in Early Christianity and the Ancient Mediterranean World* (Grand Rapids, Mich.: Eerdmans, 1983), 248, adds prophetic, oracular speech, as evidenced by comments such as 1 Cor 2:13 and 7:40.
[3] It is not clear whether Paul would describe his heavenly journey as a "vision" or a "revelation" because he uses both words, in the plural, in his introduction to the account. ἀποκάλυψις (*Apocalypsis*) makes some sense here because of the connection between Paul's ascent to paradise and the genre of intertestamental literature of tours of the cosmos, as well as the repetition of the word in v. 7. However, based on the scant evidence of his use of the two words (Gal 1:12, 2:2), "revelation" is Paul's favored term and also may be related to occasions that involve intellectual insight. ὀπτασίας (*Optasias*) is used only here. For these reasons, the use of "visions" in this passage may be worth noting. Still, what little indication there is one way or another suggests that the distinction was not vitally important to Paul and that the pairing here may well be a formula.
[4] See, for example, T. J. Leary, "'A Thorn in the Flesh' – 2 Corinthians 12:7: Was Paul Visually Impaired?" *Journal of Theological Studies* (n.s.) 43 (1992), 520–22; Ralph P. Martin, "The Opponents of Paul in 2 Corinthians: An Old Issue Revisited," in *Tradition and Interpretation in the New Testament: Essays in Honor of E. Earle Ellis for His 60th Birthday*, ed. Gerald F. Hawthorne and Otto Betz (Grand Rapids, Mich.: Eerdmans, 1987), 279–89; Herbert R. Minn, *The Thorn that Remained: Materials for the Study of St. Paul's Thorn in the Flesh: 2 Corinthians XII. vv. 1–10* (Auckland: Institute Press, 1972); J. C. Thomas, "'An Angel from Satan': Paul's Thorn in the Flesh (2 Corinthians 12:7–10)," *Journal of Pentecostal Theology* 9 (1996), 39–52; L. Woods, "Opposition to a Man and His Message: Paul's 'Thorn in the Flesh' (2 Cor 12:7)," *Australian Biblical Review* 39 (1991), 44–53; D. L. Akin, "Triumphalism, Suffering, and Spiritual Maturity: An Exposition of 2 Corinthians 12:1–10 in Its Literary, Theological, and Historical Context," *Criswell Theological Review* 4 (1989), 119–44; A. R. Brown, "The Gospel Takes Place: Paul's Theology of Power-in-Weakness in 2 Corinthians," *Interpretation* 52 (1998), 271–85; J. A. Loubser, "Winning the Struggle (Or, How to Treat Heretics): 2 Corinthians 12:1–10," *Journal of Theology for Southern Africa* 75 (1991), 75–83; and Johan Janse van Rensburg, "Die Betekenis van Lukas 13:10–17 en 2 Korintiers 12:1–10 vir die Okkultism-Diskoers," *In Die Skriflig* 32 (1998), 37–52. Robert M. Price "Punished in Paradise (An Exegetical Theory of II Corinthians 12:1–10)," *Journal for the Study of the New Testament* 7 (1980), 33–40, provides a summary of some of the many speculations about the exact nature of the "thorn."

the previous chapter, the passage is assessed for what it says about the claims of Paul's opponents rather than Paul's comments about his own ecstatic experience. In the analysis that follows, I will focus instead on the more neglected details of the ascent itself and, in particular, on Paul's comments about what he felt and perceived. This approach is not unlike a social-scientific reading in which the text is "mined" for details about the social world, but, in this case, I explore the text for details about the world of religious experience. Furthermore, that focus is guided by attention to what has typically escaped the scan of scholars, as discussed in the preceding chapter. But before moving either to Paul's account of his religious ecstasy or to the neurological description of ecstatic states, I offer an apology for the use of recent medical findings in the exegesis of ancient texts.

2.1 ECSTATIC RELIGIOUS EXPERIENCE AND HUMAN NEUROLOGY

If "conversion" was the problematic designation in traditional treatments of Paul, then one might reasonably object that "consciousness" is its difficult partner in this discussion. Like conversion, consciousness is broadly understood to describe concisely a real and important phenomenon; like conversion, its very convenience limits its precision; "consciousness," like some senses of "conversion," is also difficult to measure. Nonetheless, important distinctions exist between the two. For example, the inaccessibility of conversion typically relates to the wholly subjective interiority of its purported nature, whereas the inaccessibility of consciousness relates to the complexity of the human nervous system. That complexity can be quantified in part by the fact that there are more than 10 billion neurons in the body and more than 10 trillion synapses (that is, the connections between neurons). According to the neuroscientist Antonio Damasio, "on the average, every neuron forms about 1,000 synapses, although some can have as many as 5,000 or 6,000." Still, he argues, considering the grand neurological perspective of billions of potential neighbors, "we realize that each neuron is nothing if not modestly connected."[5] So, despite the breadth of the task of mapping all the connections of consciousness, there are those who feel confident that it will eventually be accomplished. That claim may seem extraordinary, and it is frequently worded with a kind of blithe optimism; yet, however enormous the undertaking might be, given enough time and resources, this documentation project

---

[5] Antonio R. Damasio, *Descartes' Error: Emotion, Reason, and the Human Brain* (New York: Quill, 2000), 29.

is exactly the sort of brute force collection of data that science does very well. Indeed, over the last decade, surprising strides have been made to that end.[6] Furthermore, although the mapping is far from complete, much can be said in broad strokes about brain functioning even now.

Still, there are others who contest scientific confidence, and I want to flag some of those cautions. For one thing, it must be emphasized that even after (and if) this mapping is completed, it will trace so complex a set of interconnections that it will never have significant predictive power; the possible paths and interrelationships will be so myriad as to prevent much generalizable prediction of how an individual might respond to a given stimulus. However, it does seem likely that the mapping could enable informed description of a neural response after the fact. A second sort of objection comes from people such as Bruce Wexler, a psychiatrist and clinician, who has argued that brain functioning is shaped enormously by environmental factors, and indeed that the brain requires environmental stimulation in order to develop at all. According to Wexler, some animal testing has shown that very early environmental influences can affect the brain even at the level of DNA structure and functioning.[7] Thus, he is among those who wager that nurture has nature in something of a headlock. Taking these cautions into account, one should expect that a degree of individual difference affects the patterning of neurological experience. At the same time, such variation does not negate the usefulness and even necessity of generalizations about neurological functioning. They are still instructive and very likely necessary to allow refinements according to individual differences. My own wager is that, in some aspects of religious experience, what we all bear in common is significantly greater than our individual variation. Either way, it is worthy of examination.

That examination has been assisted by a number of developments that have allowed neurologists to feel their way along the dimly lit paths of the brain, mapping what they encounter. Primarily because of advancements in technology that use computer imaging to interpret magnetic (magnetic resonance imaging, MRI), x-ray (computerized tomography, CT, scans), electrical (electroencephalogram, EEG), and nuclear (single photon emission

---

[6]   For example, the U.S. government is sponsoring a brain documentation project like that of the Human Genome Project. See Stephen H. Koslow, *The Human Brain Project* home page, National Institute of Mental Health, online at http://www.nimh.nih.gov/neuroinformatics/index.cfm. Technology is also advancing in its ability to examine deep brain tissue. See, for example, Michael J. Levene et al., "In Vivo Multiphoton Microscopy of Deep Brain Tissue," *Journal of Neurophysiology* 91 (2004), 1908–12.

[7]   Bruce E. Wexler, *Brain and Culture: Neurobiology, Ideology, and Social Change* (Cambridge, Mass.: MIT Press, 2006), 92–93.

tomography, SPECT, and positron-emission tomography, P
living brains during normal functioning, much clearer pic·
anatomy and the functioning of the brains of living subje·
able. Furthermore, there now exists a substantial body of '
the effects of lesions and injuries in specific regions of the ··
allow neurologists to correlate normal behavior with the specific regions ··
the brain that correspond to the impaired behavior of brain-damaged subjects. One of the benefits of this growing database is a greater ability to
describe the processes and systems of human consciousness. Note that the
ability to *predict* with great precision the results of brain functioning still lies
outside the grasp of science and will likely remain so; yet it does allow general
predictive force and significant descriptive potential after the fact.

Of course, ancient brains were not studied neurologically in any state of
consciousness, ecstatic or otherwise; still, two categories of evidence suggest
that it is appropriate to apply contemporary neurological findings to the
experience of ancient ecstatics as well. The first of these categories is the
common set of characteristics reported by ecstatic practitioners across cultures and times: The experience of religious ecstasy bears virtually universal
characteristics that undergird the culturally determined differences in interpretation. These include disturbance of bodily awareness, often experienced
as disembodiment; ineffability; a sense of timelessness; and blurred boundaries of the self – or, to put it positively if somewhat vaguely, a sense of
participation in a greater category of being.

The second category of evidence is the universality of the human brain.
Describing that cerebral consistency, Damasio clarifies that, both at the level
of morphology and the level of control circuits and neural pathways, there is
little variety: "On the contrary, as is always the case in the brain, they are
arranged in consistent anatomical patterns which can be found in all
humans, in exactly the same arrangement, and can be found in many other
species in almost the same position."[8] As with the human face, there are
differences in size and absolute placement of features in the brain, but,
barring injury and congenital defect, the same features appear universally
and perform the same functions.

2.1.1 *Cross-Cultural Ecstatic Experience*

Anyone who has had this experience will know what I am talking about. He
will know that the soul lives another life as it advances toward the One,

---

[8]   Antonio R. Damasio, *The Feeling of What Happens: Body and Emotion in the Making of
Consciousness* (New York: Harcourt Brace, 1999), 239.

reaches it and shares in it. . . . It needs nothing more. On the contrary, it must renounce everything else and rest in it alone, become it alone, all earthliness gone, eager to be free, impatient of every fetter that binds below in order so to embrace the real object of its love with its entire being that no part of it does not touch the One.[9]

[A]t that time, I began to keep silence with the greatest joy, and especially in the night before Shrove Tuesday I was in a great grace. And then it happened on Shrove Tuesday that I was alone in the choir after matins and knelt before the altar, and a great fear came upon me, and there in the fear I was surrounded by a grace beyond measure. . . . An immeasurable sweetness was given to me, so that I felt as if my soul was separated from my body. And the sweetest of all names, the name of Jesus Christ, was given to me then with such a great fervor of his love, that I could pray nothing but a continuous saying that was instilled in me by the divine power of God and that I could not resist and of which I can write nothing, except to say that the name Jesus Christ was in it continually.[10]

> The one who explains, lies.
> How can you describe the true form of Something
> In whose presence you are blotted out?
> And in whose being you still exist?[11]

> Neither thinking nor imagination
> can ever reach this state.
> This Ultimate reality
> retains neither self nor other.
> In this non-dual world
> all is one, nothing is left out.
> In this unmeasurable truth
> one instant is ten thousand years.
> One thing is everything
> all things are one.
> . . . Words fail to describe it
> for it is neither of the past, present, nor future.[12]

[9] Plotinus, *Enneads*, 6.9:8–11, in *The Essential Plotinus*, trans. Elmer O'Brien (New York: Mentor, 1964), 86.

[10] Sister Margaret Ebner, as cited in David A. Cooper, *Silence, Simplicity, and Solitude* (New York: Bell Tower, 1992), 186.

[11] Rabi'a al-Adawiyya, *Doorkeeper of the Heart: Versions of Rabia*, trans. Charles Upton (Put-
   Threshold, 1988), 36.
   n ming, "freely rendered" by James H. Austin, *Zen and the Brain* (Cambridge, Mass.:
   :ss, 1998), 700–1.

The preceding authors include a third-century Greco-Roman philosopher, a thirteenth-century German nun, an eighth-century Mesopotamian
Sufi freedwoman, and a seventh-century anonymous Chinese poet. Across
traditions, ethnographic descriptions and the reports of practitioners of
culturally sanctioned ASCs circumscribe a consistent set of characteristics.
The preceding quotations illustrate ineffability, a sense of unity or absolute-
ness, disruption of temporal awareness, and feelings of euphoria and awe. All
of the authors cited were also members of religious traditions (theistic and
nontheistic) that provided each of them with a distinctive interpretative
framework in which they could reflect on what happened to them, and
the ways in which they describe their experiences show the influence of these
traditions. Given these competing realities, it has been rightfully asked: What
is the balance between apparent universal characteristics of ecstatic religious
experience and obvious signs of cultural influence? Is the very experience
(not simply its later interpretation) the product of the informing culture? Is
the ecstasy subsumed by the culture in which it is practiced?

Japanese Zen provides a good test case for this debate. Its core cultural
goal is attainment of "insight-wisdom" rather than an encounter with the
divine, and this feature alone distinguishes it from a great many other
traditions of ecstasy. Given this important distinction, is it, in fact, a different experience? In this regard, it is instructive to consider the teaching about
and training for Zen states of consciousness. Japanese Zen teaching specifically discourages the following ecstatic phenomena:

> (1) the sensation of being lifted up in the air like a cloud; (2) the feeling of
> the presence of some indescribable luminosity; (3) the experience of super-
> natural joy; (4) the clarification and transparency of mind such that it
> appears to reflect all the world like a very brilliant mirror; (5) the feeling
> as though the soul had escaped the bodily confinement and had expanded
> itself out into the immensity of space; (6) a return toward that definite state
> of conscious awareness in which all mental functions are present . . . ; (7) a
> feeling of nothingness in which no mentation is present; (8) a state neither
> of loss of consciousness nor of consciousness of anything in particular . . .[13]

The list is no random collection of prohibitions but touches on phenomena that are reported widely by practitioners of ecstatic states in various
times and places. The fact that such experience is forbidden by Zen teaching
speaks to its prevalence in the very midst of cultural difference. Apparently,
with training and aptitude, these phenomena can be unlearned or managed,

---

[13] Austin, *Zen and the Brain*, 373.

but they are native even to cultures that do not value them. In the case of Japanese Zen, culture is imposed on this experience.

This cross-cultural similarity is further supported by the comparison of studies of trance states across cultures. Measurements taken during the practice of transcendental meditation,[14] tantric yoga,[15] and a variety of other forms, including even untrained meditation,[16] all demonstrate the same changes in autonomic nervous functioning of their practitioners. In addition, the neurological studies that have been conducted have included participants from distinct traditions, so that the model is not biased toward any one cultural practice or experience. Culture is no barrier; although it introduces differences to be contended with, by no means do they negate the possibility of cross-cultural comparison. Furthermore, the fullness of experience is not laid bare by culture alone, and culture alone cannot do justice to its impact. That more complete picture depends on other perspectives.

2.1.2 *A Brief History of the Human Brain*

The second potential barrier to examining Paul's experience in the way proposed here concerns the evolution of the brain. What checks and balances are necessary to responsibly apply contemporary findings to ancient brains? Here the answer is even more straightforward. The human brain as it now exists is really quite an ancient organ – it is quite as old as recorded history itself because the ability to record history depends on brain developments that are present in moderns. Its history of development can be told in five acts: the neuron, the brainstem and midbrain, the limbic system, the neocortex, and the development of specialization and lateralization. I recount this development at some length at this point because these details will help to clarify the information in subsequent sections.

The brain's story begins quite humbly some 650 to 700 million years ago, when the first neurons developed.[17] Neurons respond to stimuli by producing electrical current that is carried by and triggers chemical messengers in

---

[14] C. R. K. MacLean, K. G. Walton, S. R. Wenneberg, et al., "Altered Responses to Cortisol, GH, TSH and Testosterone to Acute Stress after Four Months' Practice of Transcendental Meditation (TM)," *Annals of the New York Academy of Sciences* 746 (1994), 381–84.

[15] J. C. Corby, W. T. Roth, V. P. Zarcone, and B. S. Kopell, "Psychophysiological Correlates of the Practice of Tantric Yoga Meditation," *Archives of General Psychiatry* 35 (1978), 571–77.

[16] R. Jevning, R. K. Wallace, and M. Beidebach, "The Physiology of Meditation: A Review. A Wakeful Hypometabolic Integrated Response," *Neuroscience and Biobehavioral Reviews* 16 (1992), 415–24, reviews the scientific literature on many forms of meditation.

[17] Rhawn Joseph, *Neuropsychiatry, Neuropsychology, and Clinical Neurology: Emotion, Evolution, Cognition, Language, Memory, Brain Damage, and Abnormal Behavior*, 2nd ed. (Baltimore: Williams and Wilkins, 1996), 7.

the body (so-called neurotransmitters). Individual neurons, in turn, gradu-
ally developed interconnections across which information was shared. This
arrangement is the extent of the central nervous system that still exists in
freshwater flatworms, one of the most primitive organisms in existence.[18]
When a neuron fires, a muscle may contract in response, thus moving the
organism away from an aversion stimulus or toward a positive one. We have
inherited neurons – virtually unchanged, though far more abundant – from
these, our oldest neurological ancestors.

A mere 150–200 million years later, these neural fibers had become
increasingly organized and interconnected, eventually developing into the
brainstem and midbrain, the second neurological layer. This region is com-
posed of the (euphonically named) medulla oblongata, the pons, and the
cerebellum. In the fully evolved brain, the brainstem gathers together the
neural fibers from the body and distributes them again into the cerebral
hemispheres. The evolution of the neural network of the brainstem allowed
for more sophisticated exchange of information and hence the coordinated
control of some physiological systems. So, for example, the brainstem mon-
itors heart and breathing rates, sensory filtering, and motor reflexes. It also
sets "the trigger for motor reactions to visual, vestibular, painful, sexual and
edible stimuli."[19] From the beginning of its evolutionary development, the
brainstem has mediated the transmission of tactile stimuli, which necessarily
originate from a source that is in immediate contact with the organism. That
proximity requires an immediate, and hence reflexive, response from the
sensing organism. For these reasons, the brainstem has not evolved beyond
reflexive "thought."[20] Although the work of the brainstem takes place apart
from conscious thought, injury to a small portion of this area nevertheless
makes even basic consciousness impossible.[21]

The third development is the limbic system, a kind of medial stratum of
the brain. It includes a number of structures that began to develop about 500
million years ago and continued to do so for about 100 million years.[22] The
most important parts of the limbic system for ecstatic states are the hippocampus, the hypothalamus, and the amygdala. These structures are vital in
what medical students memorize as "the four m's" and "the three f's"; that is,

[18] E. H. Colbert, *Evolution of Vertebrates* (New York: Wiley, 1980).
[19] Joseph, *Neuropsychiatry, Neuropsychology, and Clinical Neurology*, 10; Eric R. Kandel and
      James H. Schwartz, *Principles of Neural Science*, 4th ed. (Stamford, Conn.: Appleton and
      Lange, 2000), 320.
[20] Joseph, *Neuropsychiatry, Neuropsychology, and Clinical Neurology*, 16.
[21] Damasio, *Feeling of What Happens*, 238.
[22] Joseph, *Neuropsychiatry, Neuropsychology, and Clinical Neurology*, 11.

mating, memory, mood, and motivation and fighting, feeding, and fear. Described broadly, the limbic system functions as a kind of cerebral switchboard, determining which impulses will move between other regions of the brain and the body and brainstem. It controls autonomic processes and organic balance, details that are discussed more fully in Section 2.2.1. It is also fundamental to the emotional meaning of thought and experience. More specifically, the hippocampus plays a major role in orienting the organism in the face of novel stimuli[23] and then in encoding new memories based on that information.[24] For its part, the hypothalamus is largely responsible for maintaining of equilibrium between the body's quiescent functions (basically rest, cell repair, and nourishment) and its arousal functions (so-called fight-or-flight mechanisms). It is also essential to the motivational system of the organism, "initiating and maintaining behaviors the organism finds rewarding."[25] Finally, the amygdala "controls and mediates virtually all high-order emotional functions,"[26] both pleasurable and fearful,[27] and thereby contributes an essential ingredient in the successful encoding of new knowledge.[28] Individuals with amygdaloid damage, who are therefore working without this emotional content, fail to make effective decisions and choices.[29] Thus, emotion is essential to cognitive functions that are normally thought to be singularly rational. The combined effects of these characteristics also give the amygdala a significant role in determining the social and emotional nuances of speech.[30] There are those who claim further that all religious experience is dependent on the functioning of the amygdala.[31] In these various ways, the evolution of the limbic system provided the means for more complex

[23] Robert T. Knight and Marcia Grabowecky, "Prefrontal Cortex, Time, and Consciousness," in *The New Cognitive Neurosciences*, ed. Michael S. Gazzaniga (Cambridge, Mass.: Bradford, 2000), 1325–28; and I. Fried, K. A. MacDonald, and C. L. Wilson, "Single Neuron Activity in Human Hippocampus and Amygdala during Recognition of Faces and Objects," *Neuron* 18 (1997), 753–65.

[24] Larry R. Squire and Barbara J. Knowlton, "The Medial Temporal Lobe, the Hippocampus, and the Memory Systems of the Brain," in Gazzaniga, *New Cognitive Neurosciences*, 765–76.

[25] Kandel and Schwartz, *Principles of Neural Science*, 322.

[26] Newberg et al., *Why God Won't Go Away*, 44.

[27] Kandel and Schwartz, *Principles of Neural Science*, 992. Both of these emotions require the coordination of a number of details in order to effectively assess the value of stimuli.

[28] Hans J. Markowitsch, "The Anatomical Bases of Memory," in Gazzaniga, *New Cognitive Neurosciences*, 785.

[29] On the importance of emotion to successful decision making (an essential survival skill), see Daniel Tranel, Antoine Bechara, and Antonio R. Damasio, "Decision Making and the Somatic Marker Hypothesis," in Gazzaniga, *New Cognitive Neurosciences*, 1047–61.

[30] Joseph, *Neuropsychiatry, Neuropsychology, and Clinical Neurology*, 240.

[31] Rhawn Joseph, "The Limbic System and the Soul: Evolution and the Neuroanatomy of Religious Experience," *Zygon* 36 (2001), 112; and Joseph, *Neuropsychiatry, Neuropsychology, and Clinical Neurology*, 273–80.

interaction with the environment, including a role in generating ecstatic states of consciousness.

The neocortex, the fourth layer of neurological development, is most commonly identified by its four pairs of lobes: the left and right frontal, parietal, temporal, and occipital. These designations, however, derive more from descriptions of morphological features (the first means by which the brain was studied) than from studies of brain functioning. However, neo-cortical function pertains far more to phylogeny than to physiognomy. For example, the amygdala gave rise to most of the temporal and portions of the frontal lobes, whereas the hippocampus developed into the occipital lobe and the superior portion of the parietal lobe. Therefore, these two sets of areas are closely related in function. From the beginning of its development, the forebrain (the limbic system and neocortex) was associated with olfac-tory processors. That fact allowed for evolutionary developments in the forebrain that were not possible in the brainstem. Olfactory stimuli can be sensed at some distance and therefore allow the time necessary to consider possible reactions to the information before a response is required. As Rhawn Joseph explains, because of this distance, "the forebrain was given time to 'think.' . . . Moreover, because the source of this information might be far away and hidden, the forebrain had to retain this information in 'memory.'"[32] So it was that the forebrain continued to develop refinements of cognition, a fact that is reflected in part by the percentage of cranial space it now occupies.

The final neurological layer to be outlined here is precisely these refine-ments. They include both cognitive systems and specializations, some of which are significant factors in ecstatic states. Handedness and language are the most convenient indicators of the evolution of brain lateralization and specialization. Handedness seems to have become pronounced around 2–3 million years ago. It is estimated that 60–70 percent of Australopithe-cines were right-handed. The estimates for 150,000 years ago are that 90 percent of archaic humans were right-handed, approximately the same per-centage as today. Hand dominance requires the ability of the right and left brain hemispheres to divide their attention and work independently from one another. Still, it appears that the left-hemisphere specialization for speech was established only 50,000 years ago, culminating in the evolution of writing and reading around 10,000 years ago.[33]

---

[32] Joseph, *Neuropsychiatry, Neuropsychology, and Clinical Neurology,* 16.
[33] Ibid., 121–22.

Other forms of specialization are more complex, but apparently equally old. For example, the region of the brain known as Broca's area was one of the first areas of specialization to be identified and examined in detail. It is located in the lower posterior left frontal lobe and is directly connected to other cortical areas and secondarily to limbic structures. From these connected regions, it receives auditory, visual, and somaesthetic (i.e., the interrelations of touch and body position) impulses and sequences them in ways that enable "the expression of thought in linguistic form," resulting in speech and writing.[34] Injury to this small area of the brain deprives the patient of the ability to produce fluent speech even though all the necessary individual cognitive and motor components for speech are functioning. Thus, this region and others like it are described as areas of executive control because they are responsible for directing, monitoring, and coordinating disparate functions into seamless, synchronized action.

Two areas of specialization of more relevance to ASCs are the attention association area and the (spatial) orientation association area. The former is located in the prefrontal cortex and is "richly interconnected with the limbic system . . . and all secondary and tertiary sensory association cortices," but not primary areas.[35] The latter is located in the posterior superior parietal lobe (i.e., the upper back portion) and is responsible for the synthesis of a three-dimensional image of one's own body in space and in relation to objects.[36] It exercises control based on processing of somaesthetic, visual, auditory, and verbal-conceptual information channeled to it from other brain areas. Although it processes information from many parts of the brain, in itself the association area appears to be discretely bounded and contained. In this way, a great many independent functions are transparently blended. Thus, Damasio notes that, in many cases, the sense we have of a single fluid thought is really something of an illusion.[37] One decision can require the input of numerous systems that are relatively isolated from one another. For example, to register a single image as "sight" appears to require thirty

---

[34] Ibid., 409–10. For the fuller description of interconnections, see Colin M. Brown, Peter Hagoort, and Marta Kutas, "Postlexical Integration Processes in Language Comprehension: Evidence from Brain-Imaging Research," in Gazzaniga, *New Cognitive Neurosciences*, 890–92.

[35] D'Aquili and Newberg, *Mystical Mind*, 34–35. See also David LaBerge, "Networks of Attention," in Gazzaniga, *New Cognitive Neurosciences*, 718.

[36] Paul W. Brazis, Joseph C. Masdeu, and José Biller, *Localization in Clinical Neurology*, 3rd ed. (Boston: Little, Brown, 1996), 496–98; and d'Aquili and Newberg, *Mystical Mind*, 33–34.

[37] As Damasio (*Descartes' Error*, 84) says, in some cases "we have the illusion that everything comes together in a single anatomical theatre . . . [because of] the relative simultaneity of activity at different sites."

distinct brain activities. Still, the attention and orien hold together a great deal of interconnected infor level of processing that such information is gener scious awareness.

These five sets of features are the basic engines states of consciousness. Although they are quite evolutionary development, the most recent are sands of years old. Their antiquity makes it possible to use the last century to understand the workings of the human mind 2,000 years ag

2.2 THE NEUROLOGICAL AND CEREBRAL BASIS FOR ECSTATIC EXPERIENCE

The next two major sections of this discussion appear in order from greatest abstraction to least. I will present the neurological model of religiously altered states of consciousness before I present some of the evidence for the model on which it is based. Although, as I have said, the model represents the greatest degree of abstraction from the findings, it also provides a manageable frame of reference to hold the many details that inform it.

In the past few decades, some neurologists have turned their attention more directly to religious experience and begun to theorize about and test the functioning of the brain related to religiously altered states of consciousness. It is difficult to gather data on religious ecstasy directly. Whereas one can measure the cerebral blood flow of a meditating Buddhist practitioner, for example, it is significantly more difficult to carry out more accurate – and inevitably more invasive – tests and impossible to carry out even these less invasive measures on other kinds of ecstatics who practice active methods. In extraordinary medical circumstances, the neocortex itself has been directly stimulated electrically,[38] but nothing below the cortical surface (for example, all the limbic structures) has been available for direct manipulation. Because of these limits, comprehensive models of brain functioning in religious ecstasy are especially valuable. They allow theorists to use the information

[38] The effects of localized stimulation of the brain's surface were first documented by the brain surgeon Wilder Penfield, who was performing surgery on patients with intractable epilepsy in the 1950s. See Wilder Penfield and P. Perot, "The Brain's Record of Auditory and Visual Experience," *Brain* 86 (1963), 595–696. Most recently, observations of the effects of direct stimulation were published in Olaf Blanke, Stéphanie Ortigue, Theodor Landis, and Margitta Seeck, "Stimulating Illusory Own-Body Perceptions," *Nature* 419 (2002), 269–70, and reported widely in the popular press (e.g., *Toronto Star*, September 19, 2002).

e from other contexts (e.g., records of brain injuries, lesions, surgical
ulation) more intelligently and even to construct tests that can appro-
ately target particular aspects of the larger model. Among those who have
pursued the relationship between neurology and religious experience are
Charles Laughlin and John McManus, Barbara Lex, Carol Rausch Albright
and James Ashbrook, Roger Sperry, Colwyn Trevarthen, Rhawn Joseph, and
James Austin.[39] Still others are involved in parallel neurological modeling of
emotion[40] and attention.[41]

One neuropsychiatrist in particular, Eugene d'Aquili, has led this modeling, and since his death Andrew Newberg, a clinician in nuclear medicine,
has taken over the direction of their research.[42] D'Aquili's work with Newberg represents the most comprehensive attempt to model the neurocognitive phenomena of ecstatic religious experience. This comprehensiveness is
reflected in part by the broadly interdisciplinary character of their work. In
the words of one reviewer, "[u]nderstanding d'Aquili requires one to com-
prehend Husserl and Merleau-Ponty, to have a working knowledge of modern neuroscience, to have familiarity with contemporary theology, to
develop an anthropology and non-Marxist sociology, and quite possibly
to have had a mystical experience."[43]

The model has received corresponding attention and critical review by
both scientists and philosophers of religion. Scientific review has, as would

[39] Robert A. Rubinstein, Charles D. Laughlin, and John McManus, *Science as Cognitive Process: Toward an Empirical Philosophy of Science* (Philadelphia: University of Pennsylvania Press, 1984); Barbara Lex, "Neurological Bases of Revitalization Movements," *Zygon* 13 (1978), 276–312; Barbara Lex, "The Neurobiology of Ritual Trance," in *The Spectrum of Ritual: A Biogenetic Structural Analysis*, ed. Eugene G. d'Aquili, Charles D. Laughlin, and John McManus (New York: Columbia University Press, 1979), 117–51; Ashbrook and Albright, *Humanizing Brain*; Roger W. Sperry, "Consciousness, Personal Identity and the Divided Brain," in *The Dual Brain: Hemispheric Specialization in Humans*, ed. D. Frank Benson and Eran Zaidel (New York: Guilford, 1985); Colwyn Trevarthen, *Brain Circuits and Functions of the Mind: Essays in Honor of Roger W. Sperry* (Cambridge: Cambridge University Press, 1990); Joseph, "Limbic System and the Soul"; Austin, *Zen and the Brain*.
[40] Damasio, *Feeling of What Happens*.
[41] Michael I. Posner and Marcus E. Raichle, *Images of Mind* (New York: Scientific American Library, 1994).
[42] Up until his death, d'Aquili was clinical associate professor of psychiatry at the University of Pennsylvania Medical School and an M.D. He died just before the publication of his book *Mystical Mind* in 1999, co-written with Andrew Newberg. D'Aquili's work began at the conceptual level along with Charles Laughlin, professor of anthropology at Carleton University. See Charles D. Laughlin and Eugene G. d'Aquili, *Biogenetic Structuralism* (New York: Columbia University Press, 1974); and Charles D. Laughlin, John McManus, and Eugene G. d'Aquili, *Brain, Symbol and Experience: Toward a Neurophenomenology of Human Consciousness* (Boston: New Science Library, 1990).
[43] H. Rodney Holmes, "Thinking about Religion and Experiencing the Brain: Eugene d'Aquili's Biogenetic Structural Theory of Absolute Unitary Being," *Zygon* 28 (1993), 203.

be hoped, raised issues for further exploration and refinement,
the need to analyze more fully the evidence that has infc
theorizing. D'Aquili's last presentation of the model, *The My*
profited from that critique.[44] Despite the need for continued
work is praised for its "tremendous heuristic value."[46] Furth<
remaining critique of the model is at the level of clinical detail, not primary or foundational components. With those provisos in mind, I summarize their model in Section 2.2.1, setting aside some of the more
speculative and philosophical elements[47] to focus on the core neurological
insights.

2.2.1 *The Model of Neurological Tuning*

According to the neurological model of trance, religious ecstasy is made
possible in part by the normal functioning of the nervous system. The
experience is not exhausted by scientific description, but certain of its features are shaped distinctively by human neurology. According to the model,
trance may follow the path of either one of two neurological complexes:
either the sympathetic nervous system along with its related brain centers,

[44] For example, he has done away with the implication, present in his work with McLaughlin
and McManus (*Brain, Symbol and Experience*, 37–38), that neurons act like organisms and
are "goal-seeking."

[45] For example, Michael Spezio, a neuroscientist at the Institute of Neuroscience at the University of Oregon, has raised the need for a greater degree of precision in some measurements and more clarity about whether certain brain systems are partially or fully inhibited
during trance. See Michael Spezio, "Understanding Biology in Religious Experience: The
Biogenetic Structuralist Approach of Eugene d'Aquili and Andrew Newberg," *Zygon* 36
(2001), 477–84.

[46] Holmes, "Thinking about Religion and Experiencing the Brain," 207. D'Aquili's work is
similarly evaluated in Watts, "Cognitive Neuroscience and Religious Consciousness." The
work of James Austin (*Zen and the Brain*), who has undertaken a comprehensive neurological description of Zen experience, is complementary to that of d'Aquili and Newberg.
Quite independently of d'Aquili et al., Austin has also posited that "different patterns of
excitation and inhibition developed in certain regions inside [the] brain during ecstatic
states including absorption and kensho" (*Zen and the Brain*, 589). The states of internal
absorption and kensho, or "insight-wisdom," are the working categories of Zen meditation.
This combination of shared interests and distinct approaches makes Austin's contributions
a helpful supplement to those of d'Aquili. See Austin's discussion in *Zen and the Brain*,
589–621.

[47] D'Aquili's hope was to promote and refine a metatheology (i.e., "the overall principles
underlying any and all religions or ultimate belief systems and their theologies," *Mystical
Mind*, 195) and a megatheology (i.e., "contain[ing] content of such a universal nature that it
could be adopted by most, if not all, of the world's great religions as a basic element without
any serious violation of their essential doctrines," *Mystical Mind*, 198). The portions of their
work that I present here do not depend on these larger agendas.

glands, and the limbic system, together known as the arousal system,[48] or the parasympathetic nervous system and its corresponding neocortical and limbic components, together designated the quiescent system.[49] The former system, when sufficiently stimulated, results in what is commonly known as the "fight-or-flight" reaction in the body. This state typically includes increases in heart rate, blood pressure, and breathing rate, as well as sweating, dilated pupils, and increased blood flow to skeletal muscles in reaction to some stimulus in the environment. In effect, it prepares the body for action. When the arousal system is active during normal consciousness, we often interpret such sensations to be the result of imminent danger or intense infatuation (or, particularly in adolescence, some indecipherable combination of the two). In any case, the sympathetic system is dominant in circumstances of survival, either in its procreative aspects or as protection from threat. The quiescent system, for its part, normally ensures maintenance of the body through functions such as digestion, cell growth and repair, and reduction in heart rate. It is associated with sleep and other states of rest and generally acts to keep the basic bodily functions in balance.

These systems interact continuously to maintain appropriate responses to changing conditions. Typically, when one is activated, the other is inhibited, and in that sense they have traditionally been described as antagonistic. Human beings and other mammals experience the push and pull of arousal–quiescence interaction daily. One of the most common forms of this interaction is the cycle of sleep and wakefulness. Other ordinary examples involve interruption of one system by a stimulus that triggers the other, "such as ergotropically orienting to a sound while falling asleep or trophotropically salivating at the smell of food preparations while one is hard at work."[50] The pattern of interaction between systems is distinct for each person, and evidence suggests that these levels are determined before birth.[51] This base level of focusing on one or the other system, either in established cycles or in response to stimuli, is the most common mode in which the autonomic nervous system functions.

Yet these common patterns can also be interrupted and modified. For example, many people in a variety of cultures have learned to control their autonomic nervous functions through disciplines as disparate as athletic

---

[48] The arousal system is also sometimes called the "ergotropic" system because of its regulation of the organism's active states.

[49] The quiescent system is also sometimes called the "trophotropic" system because it governs rest.

[50] Lex, "Neurological Bases of Revitalization Movements," 286.

[51] Ibid., 283–84.

training, religious meditation, and pain-management techniques. Furthermore, according to d'Aquili and Newberg, trance or ecstatic states are experiences of just this sort of unusual interplay between autonomic systems.[52] Recent research is creating a more complex picture of how the two systems interact. It is no longer thought that they are simply reciprocal; that is, that one decreases its influence while the other increases proportionately.[53] Rather, they exhibit a more flexible interaction, which helps to describe the rich mix of neurological phenomena that result in ecstatic states. According to the model, as someone enters meditation, they can "tune" their parasympathetic nervous system to a significantly greater degree than normal. Such states are known as hyperquiescence because of the extraordinary predominance of rest functions. Hyperquiescent tuning is controlled by activity with slow ritual behavior.[54] Through acts as simple as prolonged intentional relaxation of muscles, lowering of breathing rates, concentration on a limited visual field, or chanting, the practitioner can activate the quiescent system beyond its normal levels. In contrast, someone whose "output of motor activity is continuous and rhythmical"[55] (e.g., ritual drumming, Sufi or Voudon dancing, or even marathon sports) tunes the sympathetic system to the point of hyperarousal. This "low-grade" ecstasy, if you will, is experienced differently in its two forms: Hyperquiescence is perceived as a sense of "tranquillity and bliss in which no thoughts, feelings or bodily sensations intrude," whereas in hyperarousal people feel as though they can channel vast quantities of energy and sensory information related to a narrow field of attention with "keen alertness and concentration."[56] In Austin's explanation, absorption is an experience that neurologically "mimics extreme attention" colored by "enchantment."[57]

---

[52] Here d'Aquili and Newberg are building on the work of E. Gellhorn and W. F. Kiely, "Mystical States of Consciousness: Neurophysiological and Clinical Aspects," *Journal of Nervous and Mental Disease* 154 (1972), 399–405; Lex, "Neurobiology of Ritual Trance," 117–51; Lex, "Neurological Bases of Revitalization Movements"; and d'Aquili and Newberg, "Liminality, Trance, and Unitary States in Ritual and Meditation," 2–34.

[53] Kenneth Hugdahl, "Cognitive Influences on Human Autonomic Nervous System Function," *Current Biology* 6 (1996), 252–58.

[54] D'Aquili and Newberg, *Mystical Mind*, 99.

[55] D'Aquili and Newberg, "Liminality, Trance, and Unitary States in Ritual and Meditation," 29. Wedenoja, "Ritual Trance and Catharsis," 275–307, has also documented this avenue of entry to trance states in the ritual dances used by Jamaican Revivalists.

[56] D'Aquili and Newberg, "Liminality, Trance, and Unitary States in Ritual and Meditation," 8. See also Newberg et al., *Why God Won't Go Away*, 40–41.

[57] Austin, *Zen and the Brain*, 591. He also posits the importance of the association regions "and their counterpart nuclei within the thalamus and the limbic system."

In this way, one's consciousness is altered in large part by an intensification of particular brain activity. In addition, it is further altered by "tuning out" other aspects of the brain's normal functioning. The flow of impulses between cerebral regions is identified as either afferent (stimuli *entering* a given structure or area) or efferent (stimuli *proceeding from* a structure or area). Thus, ecstatic states of consciousness are marked by pronounced deafferentation in some cerebral regions even while normal or increased levels of efferent activity continue.[58] By these means, the cerebral components of the central nervous system are active, but the sensory, vascular, and muscular inputs that they would normally be processing are largely blocked from their attention. The narrowed cerebral focus allows for far greater levels of "attention" to the stimuli that are received. That higher degree of attention may well account for the fact that many people who experience religious ecstasy find the event to be "more real" and certainly more intense than normal experience;[59] the more limited field of input receives proportionately more of the mind's attention and is felt to be known more fully.

Neurological stimulation is a physical, electrochemical phenomenon in the brain. So, in circumstances such as grand mal seizures, electrical impulses can spread indiscriminately to adjacent cerebral structures. However, in regular functioning, the neurotransmitters that carry the impulses between neurons ensure a more selective targeting of regions. A single neuron is typically responsive to more than one neurotransmitter, thus creating the potential for communication that is far more complex in tone than the binary opposites of on and off would allow. So, in the case of ecstatic states of consciousness, electrochemical stimulation appears to begin quite selectively – less a contagion than a targeted recruitment. According to the model, as the ritual action continues successfully, a kind of self-reinforcing loop, or "reverberating circuit,"[60] of brain structures is established that involves much of the limbic system and some specialized brain areas, especially the *orientation* association area and the *attention* association area.[61] As this process proceeds to its (neuro)logical conclusion, what began as the intense stimulation of one half of the autonomic nervous system ends as the maximal stimulation of both. D'Aquili and Newberg describe the process of mutual maximal stimulation as the result

---

[58] D'Aquili and Newberg, *Mystical Mind*, 110.
[59] Ibid., 113.
[60] Ibid., 111.
[61] Ibid., *Mystical Mind*, 100–16.

of "spill-over" of excitation from either the sympathetic to the parasympathetic system or vice versa.

The experience of maximal stimulation varies according to the direction
of "spill-over." Quiescent (i.e., parasympathetic) entry to trance, the *via
negativa*, might typically begin with the practitioner's attempt to clear the
mind of all thought, which is the intentional, behavioral face of the hidden,
neural experience of deafferentation. This effort, when successful, is focused
in the right orientation association area in particular.[62] As already mentioned, the orientation association area is a brain *system*; that is, it is
informed by other brain structures, each of which contributes particular
sensory or processing capacity to an integrated task. In this case, that task
is the creation of a sense of one's body in space. It requires somaesthetic
input and visual, auditory, and even verbal-conceptual processing, all of
which are tuned out of the ecstatic loop. When the input to the system is
blocked while the system remains active, such widespread deafferentation
can result in an absolute subjective sensation of pure space, "which is experienced subjectively as absolute unity or wholeness."[63] According to the
model, that is why so many people report an experience of oneness or
limitlessness as part of their ASC.

The process and effects of active methods, the *via positiva*, differ in a few
respects. First, the arousal (sympathetic) entry into trance is unlocked by
intense focus on a mental image or external object or through vigorous,
repetitive activity,[64] and so, to begin with, the right attention association
area is stimulated by afferent impulses related to the external focus of
attention.[65] Second, the early phases of trance are accompanied by pleasant sensations emanating from stimulation of the hypothalamus. Finally,
the trance culminates in total deafferentation of the left attention and
association systems but (among trained practitioners) strong continued
engagement of the right attention association area. It is the trained meditator's effort to focus on a particular object or image that keeps the
attention system engaged, which in turn affects the subjective nature of
the experience. In this case, as the input to the orientation areas is
inhibited, there is again an experience of pure space, except that this time
something else – the focus of the meditation – is in that space. Hence, in

---

[62] The right hemisphere is especially important in ecstatic states. I will discuss its significance
in more detail in Section 3.3.2.
[63] D'Aquili and Newberg, *Mystical Mind*, 112.
[64] Ibid., 114.
[65] Ibid., 99.

the *via positiva*, the practitioner experiences not simply pure space but a sense of union.[66]

Obviously, then, the competence and training of the meditator are essential elements in determining the character of the experience. One set of contingencies that the successful practitioner must manage is tied to control of the hypothalamus. This limbic structure is deeply implicated in the culmination of these experiences. Because the hypothalamus helps to control both arousal and quiescence, the culmination of the *via negativa* can be either a persistent bliss or a moment of peak ecstasy followed by stabilization in "a deep quiescent void."[67] In fact, it takes a great deal of practice to restrict the hypothalamus consistently to one tendency or the other. A different set of challenges concerns maintenance of the focal image in the *via positiva*. This focus is very difficult to maintain against a system that generally is working toward deafferentation. It takes a great meditative determination to maintain the input to the right attention area. Eventually, say the modelers, either the meditators surrender or the inhibitory stimuli overpower their abilities and "the end point of the *via positiva* then becomes the end point of the *via negativa*."[68] Thus, the character of the experience hinges to some degree on the aptitude of the practitioner. D'Aquili and Newberg summarize the two ways as follows:

> It seems to be the case that most mature meditators who practice the *via negativa* tend to end up in the quiescent state. Likewise, it is true that those who practice the *via positiva* . . . tend to end up with the ecstatic experience of AUB [i.e., absolute unitary being], which we would suggest is an arousal state. So it may be that one ends up more or less according to the general mode in which one starts out. . . . Perhaps the socioculturally determined belief system of the meditator has something to do with the outcome as well.[69]

Separate work regarding the religious nature of some brain activity has been conducted by neuroscientist V. S. Ramachandran and his colleagues. Ramachandran has specialized in the study of epilepsy and found it noteworthy that patients with left temporal lobe seizures often experienced, in seizure, "deeply moving spiritual experiences including a feeling of divine presence and the sense that they are in direct communion with God.

---

[66] Ibid., 116.
[67] Ibid., 113.
[68] Ibid., 116.
[69] Ibid., 113.

Everything around them is imbued with cosmic significance. They may say, 'I finally understand what it's all about. This is the moment I've been waiting for all my life. Suddenly it all makes sense.' "[70]

Furthermore, patients with such seizure-related experiences demonstrate ongoing effects related to their sense of religious significance. Religious behavior and commitments become far more important to them or in some cases begin to matter for the first time in their lives.[71] Ramachandran hypothesizes four possible explanations for these phenomena and their unusual and lasting effects: (1) it is divine communication, (2) it is due to mental health problems, (3) it is a reasonable and even healthy response to the set of abnormal neural phenomena, (4) humans have "evolved special neural circuitry for the sole purpose of mediating religious experience."[72] He concludes provocatively that religious experience might be due solely to temporal lobe activity and he christens the relevant cerebral area the "God module."[73] I will return to this work in Chapter 4.

2.3 PAUL'S ECSTASY: TEXTUAL AND SOMATIC

What then are the implications of this research for Paul's account of his heavenly journey? The answer to this question will be clearer when placed in contrast with more typical readings of 2 Cor 12:1–4. In the previous chapter, I mentioned that some students of Paul's letters do recognize his account as an example of a real religious experience. For those who do, their analyses tend to fall into three groups. First, some, such as Seyoon Kim, see the experience(s) as "objective" and external. Second, many authors suggest that, although Paul's ecstatic religious experience was authentic, it cannot be discussed precisely because there is no access to another person's ecstatic experience. Third, there are those who would describe Paul's ecstasy solely as an expression of Jewish and/or Hellenistic mysticism. Here I set aside the first option as unresolvable, the second

---

[70] V. S. Ramachandran and Sandra Blakeslee, *Phantoms in the Brain: Probing the Mysteries of the Human Mind* (New York: William Morrow, 1998), 179.

[71] Ibid., 180. A clinical report of similar findings is also available in M. R. Trimble, "The Gastout-Geschwind Syndrome," in *The Temporal Lobes and the Limbic System*, ed. M. R. Trimble and T. G. Bolwig (Petersfield: Wrightson Biomedical, 1992).

[72] Ramachandran and Blakeslee, *Phantoms in the Brain*, 185.

[73] Ibid., 183. Ramachandran and Blakeslee ask further, and provocatively, what would happen if a chunk of the temporal lobe were surgically removed: "Would we have performed a Godectomy?" (187).

option as incomplete, and the third for its tendency toward unnecessary reduction.[74]

Growing out of the second option, one of the main objections to examining Paul's experience is that such readings amount to psychologizing Paul. Although this accusation is frequent, there are rather fewer examples of its practice.[75] What qualifies as "psychologizing" is rarely defined in these contexts, but it appears to be an accusation of attributing Paul's experience to factors such as emotional stress or a crisis of conscience pertaining to his persecution of the fledgling christian movement. Inasmuch as some such accusations attempt to cloister Paul's theology from the influence of his life experience, they are expressions of cognicentrism or other ideological bias. However, in its strongest form, the accusation of "psychologizing" Paul appropriately criticizes unsubstantiated claims.[76] Alfred Plummer has suggested that Paul's contemporaries – without the benefit of modern psychological theories – may nonetheless have thought Paul "was a deluded enthusiast, if not actually crazy" and cites the *Clementine Homilies* as a possible example of this view.[77] John Cheek has suggested that drug use might best account for Paul's experience.[78]

---

[74] Among those who approach the topic through a comparison of texts, even those who are sympathetic to the idea of Paul's experience are unable to address it. They are forced instead to focus on peripheral and idealized issues. For example, there is a great deal of discussion of whether Paul's mention of the third heaven and paradise refer to the same location and of what that fact might indicate about Paul's cosmology. See Lincoln, *Paradise Now and Not Yet*, 77–81; Alfred Plummer, *A Critical and Exegetical Commentary on the Second Epistle of St. Paul to the Corinthians*, International Critical Commentary on the Holy Scriptures of the Old and New Testaments (Edinburgh: T. and T. Clark, 1915), 344; Adolf Schlatter, *Paulus der Bote Jesu: Eine Deutung seiner Briefe an die Korinther* (Stuttgart: Calwer, 1969), 663; and Hans Dieter Betz, *Der Apostel Paulus und die sokratische Tradition; eine exegetische Untersuchung zu seiner Apologie 2 Korinther 10–13*, Beiträge zur historischen Theologie 45 (Tübingen: Mohr, 1972), 91.

[75] Such accusations may well have been true at the beginning of the last century, when psychoanalysis was finding a broader audience. At that time, William James (*Varieties of Religious Experience*, 450) could accurately write that: "To the medical mind these ecstasies signify nothing but suggested and imitated hypnoid states, on an intellectual basis of superstition, and a corporeal one of degeneration and hysteria" (450).

[76] For example, John Ashton's unsupported comment illustrates this tendency: "In all probability [Paul] will have been contending for some time against an uneasy and growing conviction that the persecution in which he was engaged could not really be justified; and what the earliest Christian missionaries were saying about Christ had already begun to cast its spell on him." See Ashton, *Religion of Paul the Apostle*, 40. The hypothesis is appropriate but requires some substantiation.

[77] Plummer, *Critical Exegetical Commentary on the Second Epistle of St. Paul to the Corinthians* , 338–39.

[78] John L. Cheek, "Paul's Mysticism in the Light of Psychedelic Experience," *Journal of the American Academy of Religion* 38 (1970): 381–89. The theory has not been well received but still should not be dismissed out of hand. Psychotropic drugs were certainly available and used in antiquity, and do produce these sorts of phenomena. However, it is hard to construct a context for such drug use in Paul's life because it was not a part of any cultic environment in which he is likely to have participated.

Two quotations exemplify the end points in the spectrum of concern about psychological explanations of Paul's experience:

> Discussions have taken place as to how far it was psychologically prepared. . . . If we adopt this approach and explain away the vision on a psychological basis, so that it becomes but the subjective vision of an ecstatic in a state of tension, then to be consistent we should have to adopt the same method of easy explanation – which is only an explaining away – for Moses' vision of God at the burning bush, while the divine voice to the patriarchs and prophets would have to be similarly explained as subjective and fanciful. If we wish to understand what happened at this point in the life of the apostle, and what were its consequences, then we must accept fully the real objectivity of the encounter as it is testified in the letters and in Acts.[79]
>
> Whenever anyone tries to explain an event like the encounter with the risen Jesus to me, I turn skeptical: not because no one can have such an experience, nor because of a reluctance on my part to believe anyone who does, but simply because anyone pretending to explain it could not have had the same kind of experience, consequently lacks the means to comprehend it, and, therefore, could not be talking about the same thing that Paul writes about. Paul's experience, like any genuine experience of the kind, is literally ineffable; it cannot be put into words.[80]

In its best forms, this resistance to psychological explanations appears to be an effort to protect Paul's experience from reductionism or dismissal. In its less robust expressions, it precludes the text from critical examination. For example, the first quotation, from Hans-Joachim Schoeps, rejects all claims that the life or thought of Paul may have in any way prepared him for an ecstatic experience. Schoeps is not making a general argument against reductionist invocations of psychology, nor is he mustering a specific argument against applications of culturally specific psychological studies across cultures. Instead, he is using the term "psychology" to disallow any part for Paul in perceiving or interpreting the event. Schoeps claims, in effect, that one cannot consider Paul's subjective experience because there was none; there was only an objective external event to which Paul was witness. His is the extreme case both in its position against subjective contributions and in its uncritical use of the texts. However, given its extremity, it is all the more interesting that his assessment shares some features with more moderate positions like that of Stanley Marrow, the author of the second quotation. For his part, Marrow is quite ready to entertain the category of religious

---

[79] Schoeps, *Paul*, 54–55.
[80] Marrow, *Paul, His Letters and His Theology*, 36.

experience, but he uses it nonetheless to fence off Paul's experience as being out of bounds for any critical inquiry or examination – precisely because it is experience, it cannot be critically accessed.

2.3.1 *Critical Issues in the Interpretation of 2 Cor 12:1–4*

So, I continue the movement toward Paul's experience from the grounding that is best established in the scholarship. Although there are questions about critical access to Paul's experience, there is confidence about access to the *text* of Paul's description of ascent, and the wording of that text raises three significant issues that have attracted scholarly attention. The first question has already been discussed in the previous chapter: Paul's introduction to the account ("I know a man . . .") poses the possibility that the account is not his own. Because this view has won few supporters, I will set it aside here. The two remaining issues deserve greater consideration and in fact lead directly into the relevance of a neurological reading of the passage. The text raises, first, a significant question about Paul's sense of the status of his own body during the experience of ascent and, second, the question of whether his comments are shaped largely by a prohibition against divulging an esoteric event.

Two explanations have been offered for Paul's repeated uncertainty, "whether in the body I do not know, or out of the body I do not know" (2 Cor 12:2b, 3b). In one case, those who favor mirror exegesis (as discussed in Section 2.3.1) of this section of 2 Corinthians take this comment as a part of the polemic against Paul's opponents. According to this argument, the opponents must have boasted about their own bodily status in one way or another, thus prompting Paul to address that aspect of his own ascent. For example, Andrew Lincoln suggests that:

> Since the opponents placed great weight on external and visible claims to the Spirit and charged Paul with bodily weakness . . . it would have been consistent if some had felt it necessary to boast that in their visionary experiences their bodies had come into contact with the fullness of divine power. . . . Paul again is content to rest his claim with God alone.[81]

In the alternative position, Alan Segal posits not the influence of outsiders but the absence of insider guidance. For Segal, Paul is wholly reliant on the

---

[81] Lincoln (*Paradise Now and Not Yet*, 81). Others who assess this phrase as part of Paul's strategy with his opponents include Tabor, *Things Unutterable*, 121; Schmithals, *Gnosticism in Corinth*, 211–12; Baumgarten, *Paulus und die Apokalyptik*, 142–3; and Robert Jewett, *Paul's Anthropological Terms: A Study of Their Use in Conflict Settings*, Arbeiten zur Geschichte des antiken Judentums und des Urchristentums 10 (Leiden: E. J. Brill, 1971).

teaching of an interpretative community to inform him about his bodily status. Thus, since Paul does not know whether he was in the body or out of it, it must be because the mystical guild has not yet established a position on the matter. Says Segal, "Paul's confusion over the nature of his ecstatic journey to heaven provides a rare insight into first-century thinking, since it demonstrates either a disagreement in the community or more likely a first-century mystic's inability to distinguish between bodily and spiritual journeys."[82]

These hypotheses suggest reasonable explanations for Paul's decision to include the comment in his letter. However, they do not adequately account for the fact that Paul is even able to report that he does not know whether his vision was "in the body" or "out of the body." He is genuinely unsure, and clearly that fact warrants consideration in itself. It may well be the circumstances of the Corinthian community or the evolution of mystical doctrine in his context that prompts him to report it in this letter at this time, but, in the first place, there is something in the character of the experience itself that must precede the repeated uncertainty.

The remaining critical issue in this passage concerns the proposition that Paul feels he is prohibited from discussing the event at hand. This argument hangs on the interpretation of the phrases "unutterable utterances" ($\ἄρρητα\ ῥήματα$) and "which are not proper or possible for human speech" ($\ἃ\ οὐκ\ ἐξὸν\ ἀνθρώπῳ\ λαλῆσαι$). The second phrase is read frequently not as a modification of $ῥήματα$ but as if it were in apposition, restating the same thought. Furthermore, both $ἄρρητα$ and ν are taken as references to authorization to speak rather than the ability to do so. These decisions often affect not only the interpretation of the passage but even its translation. This is certainly true of Bible translations:

> "heard things that are not to be told, that no mortal is permitted to repeat" (New Revised Standard Version, NRSV; New International Version, NIV)
> "heard secret words, which it is not granted to man to utter" (Douay-Rheims)
> "heard words so secret that human lips may not repeat them" (New English Bible, NEB)
> "heard secret words that man may not repeat" (Confraternity)

However, some versions translate one clause with reference to possibility and the other to reflect esoteric connotations:

---

[82] Segal, *Paul the Convert*, 38–39. See also Segal, "Paul and the Beginning of Jewish Mysticism," 109.

"heard things which cannot be put into words, things that human lips
    may not speak" (Good News)
"heard words not to be spoken, which no man can utter" (Tyndale)
"heard things which must not and cannot be put into human language"
    (Jerusalem Bible, JB)
"heard inexpressible words which a man is not permitted to speak" (New
    American Standard, NAS)

The same approaches are reflected in the translations of many commentaries, which often render both parts of the sentence as esoteric prohibitions:[83]

"things that cannot be told, which man may not utter"[84]
"heard unutterable words, which human lips may not speak"[85]
"What Paul heard in Paradise is too sacred to relate... cf. Rev 10:2–4
    where the seer has such a prohibition laid on him"[86]
"heard things that cannot be told, which man may not utter"[87]
"heard unutterable words, which it is not permitted a man to speak"[88]
"heard things that cannot be told, which man may not utter"[89]

Others translate one half or the other in this manner.[90]
A number of authors build a more sustained argument around the notion
that Paul is claiming an esoteric injunction. For the most part, they account

---

[83] This choice is also that of BAGD: "words too sacred to tell."
[84] Lincoln, *Paradise Now and Not Yet*, 76.
[85] Karl Schelkle, *The Second Epistle to the Corinthians*, trans. Kevin Smyth (New York: Herder
and Herder, 1969), 187. Schelkle contrasts Paul's approach with "contemporary Jewish
narratives" that were profuse and unrestrained in their comments. By his restraint, Paul,
of course, shows the greater virtue (188).
[86] Talbert, *Reading Corinthians*, 124.
[87] Francis T. Fallon, *2 Corinthians*, New Testament Message 11 (Wilmington, Del.: Glazier,
1980), 103.
[88] C. K. Barrett, *A Commentary on the Second Epistle to the Corinthians, Black's New Testament
Commentaries* (London: Black, 1976), 305. Barrett goes on to specify that it is the innate
character of the words as "divine secrets" that signals to Paul that they cannot be uttered.
[89] Colin G. Kruse, *The Second Epistle of Paul to the Corinthians: An Introduction and Commentary*, The Tyndale New Testament Commentaries 8 (Grand Rapids, Mich.: Eerdmans,
1987), 203. He states further that the wording comes from the mysteries, although every-
where else in his writings, Paul explicitly countermands secrecy (204).
[90] Lambrecht and Harrington (*Second Corinthians*, 201) render it as "ineffable words which a
human being is not permitted to tell." Some try to have it both ways, as in the case of Héring
(*Second Epistle of Saint Paul to the Corinthians*, 89, 91), who translates the verse as "heard
ineffable words which it is not permitted to repeat" but qualifies that choice with the
proviso that "[i]t can be seen that arrātos does not necessarily mean 'inexpressible in human
language,' but at all events *forbidden to divulge*. The same applies in 12:4 where a ouk exon
anthrōpō lalāsai can only mean: *it is forbidden* for a man *to utter them*."

for Paul's statement by appealing to Hellenistic influences. In the first place, this was the position of those of the history of religions school, Deissmann, Bousset, and others, but it has been carried on since then.[91] It is noteworthy that even those who are uncomfortable with comparisons with the mystery religions still cling to this interpretation. For example, C. K. Barrett says the "words" that Paul heard "were *unutterable* in the sense that they conveyed divine secrets which were not to be communicated to men at large. The language is that of the mystery religions." Yet, he then goes on to assert that "[i]t would be wrong, however, to suppose that Paul was directly dependent on the mysteries."[92] It is noteworthy that interpreters are willing to use evidence to which they are hostile, especially when an alternative and quite ordinary meaning is readily available. Perhaps the notion of ineffability, with its connotations of an "irrational" element, in Paul's experience is even less attractive than reliance on awkward claims of dependence. This seems to be the case especially among those who explicitly argue against interpreting ἄρρητος as ineffable, often simply by asserting this fact to be self-evident.[93] Alan Segal's more recent effort to lodge the comments in rabbinic literature rather than the mysteries creates another set of difficulties, which I have discussed in the preceding chapter (Section 1.3.3).

2.3.2 *A Neurological Rereading of 2 Cor 12:1–4*

So, although comparisons with Jewish and Hellenistic religious writings provide a broad context in which experience like Paul's makes sense, they fail to account for a number of features; in particular, why Paul is perplexed about his body and conflicted about how to describe his experience. What happens if instead we place Paul among the cross-cultural list of those who have spoken about their ecstatic experiences (Section 2.1.1)? He shares a number of features with those writers of various times and places. For example, like Plotinus, Rabi'a al-Adawiyya, and *Hsin hsin ming*, Paul

---

[91] Tabor (*Things Unutterable*, 122) says it is "drawn from the vocabulary of the mystery cults" and reflects "the motif of secrecy found in most Hellenistic religions." See also Hans Windisch, *Der Zweite Korintherbrief*, Kritisch-exegetischer Kommentar über Neue Testament 6 (Göttingen: Vandenhoeck and Ruprecht, 1924), 377–78.

[92] Barrett, *Second Epistle to the Corinthians*, 311. Others simply take up the concepts of the mystery religions without indicating the connection. For example, Schelkle (*Second Epistle to the Corinthians*, 188) says Paul "only says that he heard words, but that he can't impart them, since they are forbidden to human lips; they are mysteries of God which may not be revealed before the due time. But to have been initiated into them is a supreme moment in the life of the Apostle."

[93] As in the case of Jean Héring, cited in note 90, this chapter.

ιe blurring of his own somatic awareness. In Paul's case, the
xpressed as confusion regarding the status of his body during
Like Margaret Ebner and *Hsin hsin ming*, part of what he per-
:arly audible but nonetheless ineffable, literally ἄρρητα ῥήματα.

In this section, I will detail some of the medical literature that informed
the model of d'Aquili and Newberg, particularly as it relates to the details of
Paul's account in 2 Cor 12:1–4. The medical findings derive, in part, from
direct measurements of the neurological activity of religious ecstatics. But, in
greater part, they are available from the study of people with diseased or
injured brains. As I have mentioned, many of the brain structures implicated
in religiously altered states of consciousness are buried deep within the
cranium and therefore are not available to more direct measurement, let
alone manipulation. However, this seclusion is offset somewhat by the combination of a growing database of information about patients with localized
brain lesions along with developments in functional neurological imaging.
These developments make it possible to observe changes in behavior and
perception related to ever more specific regions of the brain.

In large part, the relevant literature is invested in disease treatment, pre-
vention, and intervention. Given this orientation toward morbidity and
clinical treatment, one might ask how useful the medical information is to
the distinct phenomena of religious ecstasy. One example of the overlap is
the relationship between research related to stroke treatment or brain injury
and implications for philosophical questions such as the construction of a
sense of self. The curious point of intersection of these concerns is object
sense and manipulation. At the clinical level, work in this field is directed to
helping people compensate for impaired physical abilities due to strokes or
other forms of brain damage.[94] Yet, given these goals, when scientists consider how it is that a person conceptualizes an object, they have necessarily
been forced to consider the corresponding question of how it is that a person
can conceptualize the self. "Object" is possible only when there is "subject"
against which to distinguish it. Thus, scientists encounter the neurology of

[94] In addition to a dominant concern for basic quality of life, the direction of neurological
research is further impacted by circumstantial and evolutionary factors. In the case under
discussion, because of the shared evolution of human brains and those of other primates,
the study of object manipulation is one of the more experimentally accessible aspects of
brain functioning. In short, it remains socially acceptable to damage the brains of monkeys.
Clinicians can make meaningful comparisons between the neurology of the two species in
some manipulation tasks. However, others – impairments of language, for instance – must
be conducted without the benefit of laboratory-controlled, culturally sanctioned destruc-
tion of subjects' brains. One cannot read the medical studies without thinking of the cost to
other creatures.

what might normally be considered a philosophical or even religious category – how do we construct a notion of self?

For some of the reasons that have already been outlined, as well as a habitual antipathy between disciplines, less study has been devoted to this question. Nonetheless, some of what has been measured of the architecture of the brain has significant implications for the construction of self. The neurology of object manipulation includes a region of the parietal lobe known prosaically as "area 7." Neurologists have demonstrated that when we are manipulating objects with our hands, area 7 becomes stimulated as an object moves close enough to the subject to be reached, and it returns to rest as soon as the object is grasped. On its own, this brain center makes a small contribution, but in combination with other spatial and visual neural activity it forms a system that allows, for instance, for optimal attention during problem-solving tasks that involve the manipulation of objects in one's environment. But area 7 might also play other roles. It is hypothesized that area 7, in combination with other body-related processing centers, might contribute some of the data necessary for the higher-order distinction between self and other.[95] In brief, it helps us define where we end and an external object begins. So, the same center functions in more than one system, and one neuron within it can connect with multiple neurons in nearby sets of centers. It is precisely this road less taken that enables religious ecstasy: "[N]eural impulses normally follow certain pathways to produce the perceptions associated with our five senses and the movements of our muscles associated with the motor systems of the brain. But neural impulses can also travel a fundamentally different path through the same labyrinth of neural circuits. In this rare mode, senses, time, and movement lose their usual perceptual boundaries."[96]

THE BODY AND ECSTASY. In customary approaches to 2 Cor 12:1–4, Paul's comments about his own body are thought to be inscrutable. So, despite the fact that Paul's repeated somatic bewilderment plays a prominent role in these verses, it plays next to no role in most exegesis. For example, Tabor comments blandly that Paul merely "wants to separate what he knows – that he was taken into Paradise and received secret revelation – from what he

---

[95] V. B. Montcastle, B. C. Motter, and R. A. Andersen, "Some Further Observations on the Functional Properties of Neurons in the Parietal Lobe of the Waking Monkey," *Brain Behavioral Sciences* 3 (1980), 520–29; and E. T. Rolls, D. Perret, S. J. Thorpe, et al., "Responses of Neurons in Area 7 of the Parietal Cortex to Objects of Different Significance," *Brain Research* 169 (1979), 194–98.

[96] Holmes, "Thinking about Religion and Experiencing the Brain," 204.

does not know, just how this took place."[97] The absurdity of such a situation seems to strike very few people, but what an odd state of affairs it would be that anyone should be certain that they were located precisely in the third heaven but simultaneously have no clear sense of the whereabouts of their own torso. This confusion is replicated when one compares Paul's comments about the body in other passages as well. On the one hand, in some texts, the body is a significant element in Paul's ruminations about the resurrection of the dead (1 Cor 15:35–57; Phil 3:21; Rom 8:23?), and in these cases he seems to expect a bodily transformation. On the other hand, at other points, even within the same letter, he seems to expect not that the body will be transformed but that it will be left behind (Phil 1:20–24; 2 Cor 5:1–10). Segal observes that Paul's thoughts on transformation are the earliest extant in Judaism[98] but tries to account for this fact by locating the idea in even earlier Jewish mystical speculation. Whatever traditions Paul may have inherited from Jewish literature or Hellenistic practice, he seems to be of two minds/bodies. These two notions – transformation of the body and elimination of the body – are both reasonable responses to the bodily experience of ecstasy.

An ecstatic experience of the body is most clearly elucidated in contrast to normal bodily consciousness. During normal consciousness, a stable sense of the body is reinforced by a number of means. We all bear on the surface of our cortices, particularly in the right cerebral hemisphere, a neural depiction of our own bodies. In fact, we bear two – one, a motor depiction in our frontal lobes, and the other, a set of sensory correlates in our parietal lobes.[99] Thus, the bodily coordinates from tongue to toes are plotted out on our brains, and neurologists have deciphered those maps based on numerous records of patients' responses to cortical stimulation and localized brain lesions. The reconfigured whole created by these neural maps is sometimes referred to as the homunculus, the little human we carry around in our heads.

These neural maps are responsible for what Damasio calls "as if" experiences, in which the somatosensory cortex repeats the same basic activity pattern that was triggered in it when an event was first experienced but repeats it in the absence of the equivalent inputs from the body. Damasio clarifies that the "as if" activity pattern will not be exactly the same as that of a real bodily state[100] but, still, "[t]he consciousness of apprehending

---

[97] Tabor, *Things Unutterable*, 121.
[98] Segal, *Paul the Convert*, 48.
[99] Kandel and Schwartz, *Principles of Neural Science*, 387.
[100] Damasio, *Descartes' Error*, 184.

something is the same, whether perceived or recalled."[101] When we remember something, we (re)experience bodily knowledge without the normal external stimuli.[102] In addition to these neural representations of the body, the brain also includes a secondary area of processing, the orientation or somaesthetic association area, which, as described in Section 2.2.1, is located in the parietal lobes. The right parietal lobe plays a dominant role in this regard.[103]

Various types of impairments, known as agnosias, are associated with damage to somatosensory areas in the brain, particularly the association area in the parietal lobes. In some cases, subjects with localized brain damage have limbs that are perfectly healthy and capable of normal performance but are nonetheless functionally paralyzed. Even more tragically, these same people sometimes deny that the affected limbs even exist. They may fail to wash, dress, or groom one whole side of their body. When clinicians confront them with the existence of their limbs, they have been known to claim that the limb actually belongs to the doctor or even to someone in the next room.[104] The phenomenon of "phantom limbs" is also associated with the persistence (and plasticity) of somatic neural imprinting, even in the absence of actual bodily parts.[105] In this case, sensations continue to be experienced (remembered) with all the force and reality of the original event, as if the limb continued to exist.

---

[101] Damasio (*Feeling of What Happens*, 183) specifies further that: "We store in memory not just aspects of an object's physical structure . . . but also aspects of our organism's [i.e., the self] motor involvement in the process of apprehending such relevant aspects: our emotional reactions to an object; our broader physical and mental state at the time of apprehending the object. As a consequence, recall of an object and deployment of its image in mind is accompanied by the reconstruction of at least some of the images which represent those pertinent aspects."

[102] It is also interesting in this regard to note Paul's wording in 1 Cor 7:29–31. There, Paul encourages his auditors to live "as if " they were not in the various physical circumstances that characterize their lives.

[103] The right somaesthetic association area is thought to coordinate information from both sides of the brain and body. Thus, when injury is sustained to the left association area, subjects are able to compensate somewhat based on the right hemisphere's continued capacity. However, when the right parietal lobe is injured, the effects on the left side of the body are unmitigated. See Brazis et al., *Localization in Clinical Neurology*, 497. For the original clinical report, see D. N. Levine, R. Calvanio, and W. E. Rinn, "The Pathogenesis of Anosognosia for Hemiplegia," *Neurology* 41 (1991), 1770.

[104] Joseph, *Neuropsychiatry, Neuropsychology, and Clinical Neurology*, 94–95; Brazis et al., *Localization in Clinical Neurology*, 496–97. Early work in this area was published in M. Nathanson, P. S. Bergman, and G. G. Gordon, "Denial of Illness," *Archive of Neurological Psychiatry*, 68 (1952), 380–87. More recently, see K. M. Heilman, E. Valenstein, and R. T. Watson, "Neglect," in *Diseases of the Nervous System: Clinical Neurobiology*, ed. A. K. Asbury, G. M. McKhann, and W. I. McDonald, 2nd ed. (Philadelphia: Saunders, 1992), 768–79.

[105] Jon H. Kaas, "The Reorganization of Sensory and Motor Maps after Injury in Adult Mammals," in Gazzaniga, *New Cognitive Neurosciences*, 230–31.

Identification of the impaired cortical regions in these sorts of patients has helped to define brain specialization. The resulting compendium of information on healthy and impaired functioning circumscribes the experience of trance, which lies somewhere between the two. During intense phases of religious ecstasy, the combined effects of deafferentation of some impulses and increased efferent transmission of others provide an odd set of phenomena to be interpreted. On the one hand, bodily sensation (from both the "homunculus" and the body proper) is blocked from consciousness. On the other hand, the efferent activity of the orientation association area is more intense than usual. The human mind[106] is left to interpret this strange combination of neurological silence and noise in an intelligible way. Thus, the body is perceived as present, but its sensations – its weight, boundaries, pain, or voluntary motion – are all absent from consciousness. In an attempt to interpret these phenomena as coherently as possible, ecstatics frequently report the sensation of floating or flying without physical boundaries between themselves and the people and objects in their awareness. Not surprisingly, descriptions of ascent are also common in interpretations of ecstatic experiences. Paul's ascent is among them. Like other ecstatic thinkers, Paul genuinely could not know the status of his body by using the sensate signals that would normally inform him. The question of whether he was in the body or outside it is not simply a rhetorical means of dismissing the issue; it is rather an account of one of the phenomena of trance.

Another phenomenon of intense ecstatic experience is the release of a number of body chemicals that have analgesic and euphoric effects. Together they leave the mystic with a profound sense of wellness and pleasure lasting for as long as days or even weeks.[107] In this way, the cognitive experience is amplified by somatic, chemical phenomena. Within the brain, neurotransmitters both enable impulses to cross some nerve synapses (excitatory transmitters) and block passage at others (inhibitory transmitters), thus managing which parts of the brain and nervous system

---

[106] "Mind" is frequently used to distinguish the holistic and opaque functioning of the nervous system, whereas "brain" is the term that distinguishes the same entity as an organ, divisible into component parts. Then again, "mind" is used in a related way to distinguish the subjective, "first-person" phenomena of consciousness from the externally measurable, investigatable functioning of our neurology.

[107] Wedenoja, "Ritual Trance and Catharsis," 288. The same effects mutatis mutandis can result from orgasm. The parallels between mystical and sexual trances have been modeled most thoroughly in Donald L. Mosher, "Three Dimensions of Depth of Involvement in Human Sexual Response," *The Journal of Sex Research* 16 (1980), 1–42; and Louis H. Swartz, "Absorbed States Play Different Roles in Female and Male Sexual Response: Hypotheses for Testing," *Journal of Sex and Marital Therapy* 20 (1994), 244–53.

communicate with one another at any given moment. Still others are modulatory; that is, they act more slowly on synapses and set the "tone" of the network. Thus, they "enable it to function in many different ways according to the general state or conditions under which it operates."[108] In this way, neurotransmitters change our perceived experience by facilitating which parts of the system are active and which are inhibited and the degree of change. Neuromodulators frequently affect the body more directly by synchronizing the activity of the peripheral nervous system with the prevailing brain state. For example, they trigger an increase in heart rates to correspond with the stimulation of arousal states in the brain. A number of neurotransmitters are also opiates that, as they are released, cause the relaxation of skeletal muscles. The combined effect of these endogenous chemicals is to reduce not only the experience of bodily pain but the emotional states that accompany it.[109]

James Austin summarizes in four categories the effects of the endogenous chemicals associated with trance. The first, as already mentioned, is pain reduction. For example, serotonin and norepinephrin both have analgesic and sedative effects.[110] Second, some of these chemicals regulate mood and, in particular, are responsible for the polar ends of depression and euphoria. Experiments with distance runners have correlated feelings of euphoria with the release of these natural opioids.[111] Euphoria, in particular, is a consequence of the large quantities of enkephalins being released and the high concentrations of opiate receptors located throughout the amygdala.[112] Conversely, low levels of serotonin and norepinephrin are both associated with depression and even affect an organism's ability to avoid unrewarding stimuli.[113] A third set of

[108] Trevor Robbins, "The Pharmacology of Thought and Emotion," in *From Brains to Consciousness,* ed. Steven Rose (New York: Allen Lane, 1998), 37.

[109] Joseph, *Neuropsychiatry, Neuropsychology, and Clinical Neurology,* 369. Initial studies in which endorphins are injected into spinal fluid (i.e., away from the targeted brain centers where they are naturally released) and thereby dispersed more rapidly throughout the body suggest that pain is relieved without some of the usual accompanying emotional effects. See J. Lipman, B. Miller, K. Mays, et al., "Peak ß-endorphin Concentration in Cerebrospinal Fluid: Reduced in Chronic Pain Patients and Increased during the Placebo Response," *Psychopharmacology* 102 (1990), 112–16.

[110] Austin, *Zen and the Brain,* 217; Kandel and Schwartz, *Principles of Neural Science,* 442. During "highly stressful, fearful, or painful stimuli," the body naturally begins to produce more serotonin, "which results in numbing, analgesia and a loss of pain perception" (Joseph, *Neuropsychiatry, Neuropsychology, and Clinical Neurplogy,* 369).

[111] Austin, *Zen and the Brain,* 218–19.

[112] Joseph, "Limbic System and the Soul," 177.

[113] Joseph, *Neuropsychiatry, Neuropsychology, and Clinical Neurology,* 370. For example, primates with abnormally low serotonin levels will repeatedly put bad-tasting or nonfood items in their mouths when they are hungry.

effects are physiological. Endogenous opioids slow breathing as well as overall brain metabolism and motor responses.[114] A final effect of these brain chemicals can be broadly described as behavioral. The neurotransmitters in question act both to reduce fear and anxiety[115] and to activate attention to novel stimuli.[116] Abnormally high levels of serotonin are also associated with obsessive-compulsive disorder, a fact that evidences the importance of serotonin in the reward and encoding of behaviors.[117] In the grand scheme of evolution, these chemicals are widely thought to contribute to survival. Their association with pain management as well as with sex and hence procreation has obvious survival implications, as does their role in encoding behaviors. But coupled with these circumstances is the fact that the presence of the body's own opioids is self-rewarding – survival behaviors are reinforced by the release of the catalysts to such pleasant (and at least in the case of exogenous opiates) addictive sensations.[118]

One ubiquitous characteristic of religious ecstasy that is not expressed in Paul's brief account of his ascent in 2 Corinthians is the experience of absorption or union. However, as is widely recognized, union with Christ is an aspect of Paul's thought that appears elsewhere in his letters (e.g., Gal 2:19b–20a; Phil 3:8b–11).[119] I have already discussed the fact that during ASCs bodily sensations are chemically numbed and neurologically ignored. At the peak of neuropsychological tuning, this change in bodily perceptions extends to "a decreased sense or awareness of the boundaries between the subject and other individuals, between the subject and external inanimate objects, between the subject and putative supernatural beings, and indeed, at the extreme, the diminution and abolition of all boundaries of discrete being."[120] This state results in a profound sense of unity that is nuanced by the enculturation of the mystic. The ecstatic experiences a certainty of

[114] Austin, *Zen and the Brain*, 216.
[115] Ibid., 216–17.
[116] Joseph, *Neuropsychiatry, Neuropsychology, and Clinical Neurology*, 367.
[117] Kandel and Schwartz, *Principles of Neural Science*, 1224.
[118] Austin (*Zen and the Brain*, 220) reports the amazing persistence of operant-conditioning behavior in an experiment in which opiates were the reward. In order to get shots of morphine, one experimental monkey continued to repeat a trained motor behavior 12,800 times after the shots ceased to be administered; reported in T. Yanigita, "Self-administration Studies on Psychological Dependence," *Trends in Pharmacological Sciences* 2 (1980), 161–64. Joseph (*Neuropsychiatry, Neuropsychology, and Clinical Neurology*, 367) describes this part of the role as "the mediation of pleasure and reward."
[119] The simple phrase ἐν Χριστῷ (*en christō*) appears some 164 times in Paul's letters. The secondary literature on Paul's "Christ mysticism" is extensive but is conveniently summarized by James Dunn in his chapter on "participation in Christ" in *Theology of Paul the Apostle*, 390–412.
[120] D'Aquili, "Liminality, Trance, and Unitary States in Ritual and Meditation," 3.

oneness with a particular divine being or with all being, a certainty that endures long after the trance ends. D'Aquili and Newberg describe this unitary consciousness as "[a]n extremely strong sense of reality, to the point of its being absolutely compelling under almost all circumstances."[121]

LANGUAGE AND ECSTASY. The second main interpretive issue from the text of 2 Corinthians 12 concerns speech, or lack thereof. Although more textual parallels to Paul's use of ἄρρητα ῥήματα can be marshaled than in the case of his bodily status, it is not any clearer that they explain Paul's own use of the phrase. Instead of looking in that direction for an explanation, here we will consider the fact that Paul's comment corresponds to those of many, many other mystics who describe their experience as ineffable.[122] In this case, the normal and abnormal mechanisms of language and hemisphere specialization are central in understanding ecstatic ineffability. The major language center is in the left hemisphere. The right hemisphere language center supplements communication by interpreting and generating the emotional nuances of language.[123] This division of labor is especially noteworthy because researchers have observed during ASCs the shift from brain activity dominated by the left cerebral hemisphere to right hemisphere activity. Measurements of electrical and metabolic activity of subjects during dream states,[124] drug-induced hallucination,[125] meditation, and glossolalia[126] have all shown the same shift in brain activity. Furthermore, mystics' reports of their experiences bear significant correspondence to some of the specialization of the right brain in normal consciousness.

Observations of brain hemisphere specialization first became possible in the 1950s, when surgeons began to sever the corpus callosa of patients with intractable epilepsy in order to reduce the damage caused by the severity of their seizures. The corpus callosum is the dense set of neural fibers

---

[121] Ibid., 33.
[122] On ineffability as a characteristic of ecstatic states, see Nora Ahlberg, "Some Psycho-physiological Aspects of Ecstasy in Recent Research," in *Religious Ecstasy*, ed. Nils G. Holm, Scripta Instituti Donneriani Aboensis (Uppsala: Almqvist and Wiksells, 1982), 63–73.
[123] The right hemisphere also appears to generate stereotypic and patterned utterances, especially speech triggered or influenced by emotions, particularly expletives. See Brazis et al., *Localization in Clinical Neurology*, 514.
[124] Joseph, *Neuropsychiatry, Neuropsychology, and Clinical Neurology*, 112; and L. Goldstein and N. Stoltzfus, "Changes in Interhemispheric Amplitude Relationships in the EEG during Sleep," *Physiology and Behavior* 8 (1972), 811–16.
[125] L. Goldstein and N. Stoltzfus, "Psychoactive Drug-Induced Changes of Interhemispheric EEG Amplitude Relationships in Man," *Agents and Actions* 3 (1972), 124–32.
[126] Krista Björkqvist, "Ecstasy from a Physiological Point of View," in Holm, *Religious Ecstasy*, 74–86.

connecting the right and left halves of the brain, and when it is severed, the two hemispheres exercise a much higher degree of independent control than previously. In fact, each hemisphere is described as having its own consciousness.[127] Following this surgery, patients and their caregivers observed changes in patient behavior that have led to new understandings of the brain. Since the 1960s, the distinct functioning of the brain's two hemispheres has been studied in humans,[128] and the findings have bred insights in educational theory, gender research, linguistics, schizophrenia, and a host of clinical concerns.

Two classic studies offer compelling illustrations of hemispheric functioning with implications for language. In the first, Jerre Levy and her colleagues observed a group of so-called split-brain patients who were instructed to memorize a set of facial photographs and the names corresponding to each picture.[129] These photographs were then reconfigured into split or chimeric figures in which the right half of one face and the left half of another were joined, as shown in part A of Figure 2.1. A screen was placed in front of the participants, and these composite images were flashed onto it for so short a time that each eye was able to register only the half of the image directly in front of it. In this way, the design of the experiment ensured that only half the picture was available to each brain hemisphere. Finally, subjects were then asked to identify who they saw either by giving the corresponding name or by pointing to the corresponding picture. When subjects were asked for the *name*, they always identified the individual who was projected to their right eye, the eye connected to the left hemisphere. When they were asked to point to the *picture*, they always identified the individual projected to their left eye, the eye connected to the right hemisphere, and they could not tell the experimenters the name of that individual. The experiment illustrates both the separate consciousness of each hemisphere and their differing

---

[127] Kathleen Baynes and Michael S. Gazzaniga, "Consciousness, Introspection, and the Split-Brain: The Two Minds/One Body Problem," in Gazzaniga, *New Cognitive Neurosciences*, 1351.

[128] Notable among researchers of split-brain phenomena is Nobel laureate Roger Sperry. Some of his foundational research can be found in Roger Sperry, "Cerebral Organization and Behavior," *Science* 133 (1961), 1749–57; and Roger W. Sperry, Michael S. Gazzaniga, and J. E. Bogen, "Interhemispheric Relationships: The Neocortical Commisures; Syndromes of Hemispheric Disconnection," in *Handbook of Clinical Neurology*, vol. 4, ed. P. J. Vinken and G. W. Bruyn (New York: Wiley, 1969), 273–90. For a more readable overview of some of the methods and findings of brain hemisphere research, see Sally P. Springer and Georg Deutsch, *Left Brain, Right Brain: Perspectives on Cognitive Neuroscience,* 5th ed., Books in Psychology (New York: Freeman, 1998).

[129] Jerre Levy, Colwyn Trevarthen, and Roger W. Sperry, "Perception of Bilateral Chimeric Figures following Hemispheric Disconnection," *Brain* 95 (1972), 61–78.

Figure 2.1. Chemeric-stimuli test. From Jerre Levy, Colwyn Trevarthen, and Roger W. Sperry "Perception of Bilateral Chimeric Figures following Hemispheric Disconnection," *Brain* 95, no. 1 (1972), 68. Reprinted by kind permission of Oxford Universtiy Press.

linguistic and visual-patterning capacities,[130] the left specializing in language, the right in imaging.

In the second experiment, similar in design, subjects were presented with bilateral pictures – that is, a different and complete picture was flashed to the visual field of each eye. The subjects also had an array of smaller images displayed in front of them for the duration of the experiment. After each bilateral picture was flashed, subjects were instructed to point with both hands to the smaller image that related most to what they had seen. Not surprisingly, the left side chose a different picture than the right side. But what is surprising is that these subjects were not confused by their conflicting choices. Instead, they were instantly able to create a coherent explanation of their behavior based on the dominance of the left hemisphere. For example, in the case illustrated in Figure 2.2, the subject explained that the shovel selected by his left hand (and right hemisphere) was needed to clean up after the chicken illustrated in the choice of his right hand (and left hemisphere).[131] In addition to confirming the independence of hemispheric consciousness, the experiment points to ways in which this independence is managed; it illustrates the dominance of the left hemisphere in tasks that require conscious interpretation of hemisphere-specific knowledge. In this case, when a logical and narrative account is required, the significance of the image of the shovel becomes subordinated to the dominant (left hemisphere) consciousness of the chicken.

Complementary findings regarding the exchange of information and compensation for impaired exchange between brain regions have been demonstrated by patients with localized injuries to brain regions. For example, in contrast to patients with a commissurectomy, patients with lesions affecting only part of their corpus callosum will not explain their own split behavior but will be baffled and upset by the phenomenon. This is because enough information continues to be exchanged between their hemispheres that there

---

[130] Although the right hemisphere is "mute," it is not without specialization. It knows, for example, how to dance, how to find the way in the dark, how to read Braille, how to construct a metaphor, how to play music by ear, how to be infuriated, and how to be ecstatic – in both senses of the word. For a summary of the functional organization of the brain hemispheres and the studies that have demonstrated these findings, see the Appendix in M. K. Raina, *Education of the Left and the Right: Implications of Hemispheric Specialization* (New Delhi: Allied, 1984), 83–103.

[131] Reported in Baynes and Gazzaniga, "Consciousness, Introspection, and the Split-Brain," 1358, based on the earlier work of Michael S. Gazzaniga, J. E. LeDoux, and D. H. Wilson, "Language Praxis and the Right Hemisphere: Clues to Some Mechanisms of Consciousness," *Neurology* 27 (1977), 1144–47.

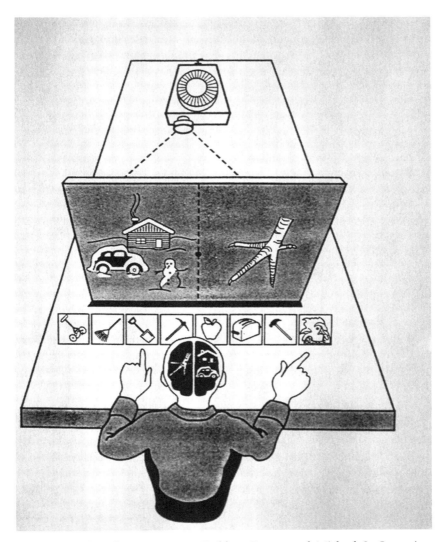

Figure 2.2. Bilateral Images. From Kathleen Baynes and Michael S. Gazzaniga, "Consciousness, Introspection, and the Split-Brain: The Two Minds/One Body Problem," in *The New Cognitive Neurosciences*, ed. Michael S. Gazzaniga (Cambridge, Mass.: MIT Press, 2000), 1359. Originally printed in Michael S. Gazzaniga and Joseph E. LeDoux, *The Integrated Mind* (New York: Plenum, 1978). Copyright 1978 Plenum Press, New York, with the kind permission of Springer Science and Business Media.

is a battle for interpretation; they are partially aware of two simultaneous yet distinct sets of reasoning and cannot fully subordinate one to the other.[132]

This automatic attempt to make sense of partial or conflicting information is known as confabulation (illustrated by the patient in Figure 2.2). In the case of split-brain patients, emotional knowledge in particular continues to pass through the limbic system, which connects the hemispheres beneath the neocortex and "below" consciousness, but the awareness of the left hemisphere does not necessarily take in the source of the feeling. In the case of ASCs, a modified confabulation takes place after the fact when intense deafferentation ends. At that point, the dominant language processors are called on to describe what they did not experience. In normal consciousness, much of this specialized information is continuously shared across hemispheres, and the strengths of each side appear to be integrated fluidly. But quite often the knowledge of nondominant centers is simply not brought to consciousness at all.

Four findings from these studies are particularly significant to the neuropsychological description of religiously interpreted ecstasy.[133] The first is that each hemisphere can have knowledge that the other hemisphere does not possess. The second concerns the "gestalt" nature of the right brain; that is, its ability to see things as wholes and the corollary inability to separate things into their component parts. This specialization dictates, for example, that the *left* hemisphere can describe a cube whereas the *right* hemisphere can draw it. The right hemisphere recognizes people and objects by sight; the left hemisphere knows their names. This division of labor is related to a third characteristic of the hemispheres: The left brain exercises master control over most aspects of language and interpretation, whereas the right hemisphere, by contrast, functions mainly to color language, particularly with regard to emotion. Speech and literacy require sequencing, and sequencing, in turn, permits temporal awareness. Not surprisingly, then, marking time is also a function of the left hemisphere. In contrast, the right brain is characterized by simultaneity rather than progression.

This is a fourth characteristic of the right. In summary, right-brain activity is distinguished in part by its ineffable, nonchronological, emotional, and holistic perception.

[132] Reported by Baynes and Gazzaniga, "Conciousness, Introspection, and the Split-Brain," 1358, based on the work of Kathleen Baynes, M. J. Tramo, A. G. Reeves, and M. S. Gazzaniga, "Isolation of a Right Hemisphere Cognitive System in a Patient with Anarchic (Alien) Hand Sign," *Neuropsychologia* 35 (1997), 1159–73.

[133] For an overview of some of the findings from a fascinating field of research, see Springer and Deutsch, *Left Brain, Right Brain,* 25–59.

These details make immediate sense of the fact that ecstatics often describe their experiences as ineffable apprehensions of unity or oneness. The neurology of trance also wields significant explanatory power in Paul's case. His use of ἄρρητος can be seen as another consequence of his trance experience, in this case the ineffability of right-brain knowledge and selective deafferentation. In this light, ἄρρητος should be understood in 2 Cor 12:4 with its more common connotation. Even in the literature of mystery religions, and most frequently in its other occurrences, ἄρρητος straightforwardly denotes the quality of being *inexpressible*. It is used in that sense, for example, even in one passage of the Greek Magical Papyrii (PGM, XIII, 763, with exact clarification of the nuance "not able to be spoken by human mouths"), where it might more accurately be translated as "ineffable." That signification makes complete sense in the context of Paul's comment as well. There were no words for what Paul heard or saw while he was in ecstasy.[134]

But that fact does not stop Paul from "confabulating"; in fact, it requires ― NO that he do so. Like the translation of *harrētos* the ensuing clause (ἃ οὐκ ἐξὸν ἀνθρώπῳ λαλῆσαι) also involves an interpretative choice because *exesti* can denote either "permissible" or "possible."[135] But in practice the distinction need not be rigidly fixed. For Paul, and for ancient theists in general, the created order comprised the will of God, and the appropriateness of an activity had as much to do with the nature of the universe as it did with explicit divine sanction. For example, Paul makes just such a claim in Rom 1:18–32, in which he asserts that everyone should know right behavior because what can be known of God (*to gnōston tou theou*) has been revealed equally to all people (v. 19). So the unutterable nature of what Paul heard might just as well be the effect of God's ordering of the cosmos as it is Paul's obedience to a directive. Thus, the modifying clause is Paul's effort to interpret his trance experience in cultural terms and, in particular, to make sense of the experience of ineffability. In that effort, Paul interprets the ineffable character of his auditions as being due to the fact that they are not within human capabilities – they are delegated to the celestial. Like the "tongues of angels," they are purely for the benefit of those who experience them. On the basis of these considerations, then,

---

[134] This interpretation is supported by Tabor (*Things Unutterable*, 122), who claims that the ensuing clause would not be necessary if Paul understood ἄρρητος to mean something limited to initiates.

[135] Paul's only other use of ἔξεστιν is of limited help in interpreting his use here because the comment πάντα μοι ἔξεστιν (1 Cor 6:12) also permits both meanings. Furthermore, the use in this latter case may be a quotation of a letter from Corinth rather than Paul's own words. In my opinion, it is Paul's paraphrasing and slight exaggeration of the Corinthian position, but either way it seems prudent to set it aside in the current discussion.

I would propose that a more sympathetic interpretation of Paul's comment might well be: "and heard inexpressible things that it is not possible for a human being to speak."

2.4 CONCLUSION

In this chapter, I have presented the neurological understanding of religious ecstasy. I have outlined in broad strokes the evolutionary foundation that allows comparison of ancient brains like Paul's, which were not directly studied, with modern ones, which have been probed and cataloged in normal, injured, and surgical conditions. Finally, I have described the ways in which an understanding of the neurocognitive aspects of ecstasy illumines Paul's abstruse account in 2 Cor 12:2–4.

The neurology of ecstatic experience provides a more cogent framework for Paul's ascent account than do conventional readings of the text. For one thing, neuroscience explains two generally neglected but important features of Paul's report – namely his confusion about his bodily status and his assertion of unutterable auditions. Attempts to account for these features through comparisons with various mystical traditions have not succeeded. For example, Tabor and Segal both acknowledge that their textual parallels cannot account for Paul's confusion about his own body. What remains for them an anomalous feature of the text is illuminated in the light of neurological findings; the disturbance of bodily perception is a telltale sign of ecstasy. Likewise, the detail of ineffability is far more intelligibly understood as the result of neural tuning than it has been as an awkward remnant of esotericism. The comments regarding ἄρρητα ῥήματα have long betrayed an undercurrent of ambivalence about the term. By interpreting it as Paul's commitment to an esoteric prohibition, commentators seem to have been choosing the lesser of two evils – better to ignore the problems with that picture of influence than to admit the apparent irrationality, and perhaps logical meaninglessness, of ineffability.

Two additional contributions of the neurological sciences are also implicit in this chapter. First, the science of the brain and central nervous system provides a disciplined and testable means to examine "subjective" experience. Thus, it opens a door for those who have recognized something real and vital in Paul's account but have had no way to speak about it. Second, it begins to expose a fuller picture of the conversation and the real lives that occasioned Paul's letter to the Corinthians in the first place. In particular, it opens up the personal investments behind Paul's side of the conversation. It offers a taste of the cognitive, chemical, neural, and emotional richness that informed his moment of halting boastfulness. With this taste of Paul's inner life in mind, in the next chapter we shift to considering how it was expressed in Paul's letters and his secondary theological reflection.

3

◈

Paul's Voice: Parsing Paul's Ecstatic Discourse

*And how totally wrong those are who refuse to admit that Paul was a logical
thinker, and proclaim as the highest outcome of their wisdom the discovery
that he has no system! For he is a logical thinker and his mysticism is a
complete system.*

— Albert Schweitzer

For that's the way you ought to write—
Without a trace of trouble;
Be super-charged with high delight
And let the words out-bubble

— Robert Service

SOMEWHERE BETWEEN THE POLES OF ALBERT SCHWIETZER'S
description and Robert Service's prescription lies the bulk of Paul's
discourse. Although few would hold as firmly as Schweitzer to the claim
that every aspect of Paul's theology contributes to a complete system, there is
still a general effort to coherently interconnect Paul's various theological
assertions. Given this general effort, it is especially interesting to note that
some aspects of Paul's thought do not fit easily into the major theological
categories as traditionally defined. This is true perhaps especially for Paul's
language of being in Christ. That theme, as Schweitzer put it, is the "prime
enigma" of Paul's thought.[1] Schweitzer tried to reconstruct a system with
this theme at its center, and although many have been respectful of his effort
and the intuition behind it, virtually no one has been fully convinced by it.[2]

---

[1] Schweitzer, *Mysticism of Paul Apostle*, 3. "Das große Rätsel" translates as "prime enigma."
[2] See, for example, E. P. Sanders, *Paul and Palestinian Judaism: A Comparison of Patterns of
Religion* (Philadelphia: Fortress, 1977), 434–41. Sanders is especially sympathetic to Schweitzer's efforts, foremost the latter's observation of the "realism" of incorporation into Christ.

So, decades later, in a massive survey of Pauline theology, James Dunn can still introduce his chapter on "participation in Christ" by characterizing the concept as something of an anomaly in New Testament scholarship. Dunn's comments are instructive both for their clear indication of a persistent intuition about the importance of this theme and for their frank admission of failure to deal with it adequately, so I quote them at some length:

> In comparison with the amazingly vigorous contemporary debate on justification by faith, interest in our present theme, even the thoroughly and distinctively Pauline "in Christ" and "with Christ" motifs, has been modest and marginal.
>
> . . . Not least of importance is it to reintegrate into Paul's larger theology the dimension of Christ mysticism (or whatever we call it) and the experience of the Spirit and to find the best way to correlate his relatively brief teaching on baptism and the body of Christ with these major emphases. . . . For, in fact, study of participation in Christ leads more directly into the rest of Paul's theology than justification [does].[3]

However, in the end, even Dunn contents himself with merely flagging the importance of Paul's in-Christ language because the "depths and resonances" of the theme are beyond the scope of a chapter.

The difficulties of accounting coherently for this aspect of Paul's writing run parallel to another, methodological problem in Pauline studies. That is, many authors would like to address their sense that Paul's experience contributed to his theology but have no means of exploring the connection in a disciplined manner.[4] For example, in 1888, Hermann Gunkel suggested that "[t]o the apostle, his life was an enigma whose solution lay for him in his teaching regarding the *pneuma*: to us the apostle's teaching regarding the *pneuma* is an enigma whose solution is to be found in his life and only in his life."[5] But lacking the disciplined means by which to pursue such insights, most authors are forced merely to touch on them as interesting asides. For example, in discussing Paul's vision of paradise, Andrew Lincoln suggests that "[w]hile Paul did not receive any revelation about the future which he could communicate to others, it could well be that his

---

[3] Dunn, *Theology of Paul the Apostle*, 395.

[4] The examination of Paul's "convictional world" in Terence Donaldson, *Paul and the Gentiles: Remapping the Apostle's Convictional World* (Minneapolis: Fortress, 1997), approaches Paul's experience with a breathtaking degree of discipline but as a result is forced to restrict its examination to primarily cognicentric categories.

[5] Hermann Gunkel, *Die Wirkungen des heiligen Geistes nach der populären Anschauung der apostolischen Zeit und der Lehre des Apostels Paulus; eine biblisch-theologische Studies* (Göttingen: Vanderhoeck, 1888), 84, as cited in Ashton, *Religion of Paul the Apostle*, 31.

anticipatory experience of Paradise is reflected in his perspective on the state of the believer after death."[6] Indeed, it could well be. In the same manner, Tabor says, "there is every reason to conclude that this experience [of Paul's ascent], along with that of his initial conversion, would have closely tied in with his gospel message," particularly in regard to Paul's idea of glorification of the faithful.[7] Likewise, Segal entertains the possibility that Paul's idea of a glorious body arises from his encounter with Jesus in a glorious, resurrected form, and that based on that vision, Paul posits a similar form for those who die "in Christ."[8] This supposition is also surely correct as far as it goes. Part of the purpose of this chapter is to test its limits further.

A related problem, particularly among more conservative scholars, is that the understanding of experience is often not very robust or sometimes even very realistic. This tendency is exemplified most thoroughly by Seyoon Kim, who finds unparalleled significance in the event of Paul's conversion. In fact, Kim imagines Paul's conversion as the source of virtually all of Paul's theology. For example, he claims that Paul's "soteriology of justification and reconciliation originated from his experience of his own justification and reconciliation through God's grace on the Damascus road while persecuting Christians." Not only that, but his "Adam- and Wisdom-christology" also originated at that point, as did his reception of the "mystery" (Rom 11:25–26) of God's eschatological and soteriological master plan.[9] However, in Kim's reconstruction, Paul's conversion feels more like a chapter from a commentary than a religious experience of any kind for, as he would have it, this collection of themes is simply presented to Paul at conversion and then made meaningful and given content through the process of reflection on a great many passages of scripture. This picture is possible only with a rather thin understanding of experience and knowing. For example, what precisely an "experience of justification" might be is never explained. Thus, in the form in which Kim's argument stands, experience is de facto cognicentric – it is the amassing of theological constructs and their expansion through reflection on scripture.

In contrast, the examination that follows will begin from the phenomena of religious trance. Thus, having considered the account of one of Paul's ecstatic experiences in 2 Cor 12:1–4 in some detail (and 1 Cor 14:18 to a lesser

---

[6]   Lincoln, *Paradise Now and Not Yet*, 81.
[7]   Tabor, *Things Unutterable*, 21.
[8]   Alan F. Segal, "Paul's Thinking about Resurrection in Its Jewish Context," *New Testament Studies* 44 (1998), 417.
[9]   Kim, *Paul and the New Perspective*, 293.

extent), the discussion will now shift to consider what difference an under-standing of such experience makes to a broader reading of Paul's letters and circumstances. The focus on Paul's religious ecstasy – by its very nature – moves experience to a more central place in exegetical reconstruction. Thus, it provides a means by which one can begin to address the repeated intuitions about the significance of Paul's comments. Neurocognitive research describes some of the specific somatic features of ASC – changes in sensory perceptions, alterations of language processing, neurochemical effects, emotional impact, and the like. It also accounts for some of the religious valuation that attaches to ecstatic experience – a profound sense of union, a sharing of self, and a conviction about the absolutely compel-ling nature of the religious experience. Through these means, a neuro-cognitive approach provides clues to decipher some of Paul's distinctive language and theology. However, the focus on Paul's ecstatic experience should not be made to explain more than it can sustain, and the discipline of neurology (in all its hyphenated subsets) also provides controls on what can be claimed as experience and what can be asserted about its influence. In an examination that is conducted within neurocognitive limits, sugges-tions that Paul had an "experience of justification" are meaningless with-out further elaboration. In short, neurocognitive research does *not* predict how a practitioner will "confabulate" about the experience after the fact. With those factors in mind, this chapter offers a partial solution to the dilemmas outlined above; the very themes that have been noted as "cen-tral" and "primary" yet enigmatic in Paul's discourse begin to make greater sense when (ecstatic) experience is seen to precede (Pauline) speech. Furthermore, the unsystematic nature of some of what Paul says is also understandable when Paul is seen to be speaking out of ecstatic experience.

I will begin this shift to the experiential bases of Paul's speech by describ-ing a fuller picture of religious ecstasy, including its less dramatic effects. These details provide a template that will guide my reading and choice of particular texts. A more complete picture of religious ecstasy includes both a larger set of sensory-cognitive phenomena and a more detailed considera-tion of the contexts and triggers for ecstatic states. I will then consider a number of other places in which Paul reflects on ecstatic experiences. Scattered throughout Paul's letters are comments that suggest, in light of this model, that ecstatic speech was more prevalent in his daily affairs than much scholarship tends to acknowledge and, furthermore, that ecstatic experience informed his thought even at times when he was not directly describing a particular ecstatic event. The fuller catalog of the bioneurological phenomena of ecstatic experience helps to identify some publicly observable features of ecstatic states as well as the features of low-level ecstasy.

3.1 OTHER FEATURES OF ECSTASY

The analysis of Paul's brief description of his ascent to paradise (2 Cor 12:1–4) introduced some of the private cognitive and somatic features of ecstatic states. First, Paul mentions that his ascent included auditory phenomena, and his introductory category of "visions and revelations" (2 Cor 12:1) also suggests that he counted visual/visionary features among his ecstatic experiences. In fact, cross-culturally, practitioners more commonly report visions than auditions. Second, the emotional tone of ecstatic experience is also distinctive. In general, religious experience is marked by numinosity, or awe, which is a particular complex of more basic emotions and cognitive states. Religious emotion is characterized by a feeling of euphoria or elation combined with "mild to moderate fear."[10] These are limbic emotions and, given the significant involvement of the limbic system in driving and controlling ecstatic states, their generation would be expected. The feeling of awe is very likely compounded by the intense and narrowed neurocognitive focus during trance.

Dreams offer the closest observable parallels to the waking phenomenon of visions and lucid hallucination,[11] for the visual wealth of dreams suggests that such images are always available but blocked from our attention during normal consciousness. Clinical studies have established that the inferior temporal lobe and amygdala, a combined region also associated with religious ecstasy, are especially active during REM (rapid eye movement), or dream, sleep.[12] Furthermore, the information available both from people with brain injuries and through exceptional stimulation of primary optical cortical regions confirms the conclusions of dream study. For example, patients with small lesions in their primary visual cortex are frequently left with a blind spot, or scotoma, in their visual field. These scotomas vary in their size and location within the visual field according to the nature of the injury. Typically, the scotoma is experienced as a black spot, but for some

---

[10] D'Aquili and Newberg, *Mystical Mind*, 102.
[11] In fact, in cultures that value other modes of consciousness, the distinction between dreams and visions is not always clearly delineated. See, for example, the accounts in Felicitas Goodman, *Speaking in Tongues: A Cross-cultural Study of Glossolalia* (Chicago: University of Chicago Press, 1972), 61–62.
[12] J. Allan Hobson, Edward F. Pace-Schott, and Robert Stickgold, "Consciousness: Its Vicissitudes in Waking and Sleep," in Gazzaniga, *New Cognitive Neurosciences*, 1350–51. See also Joseph, *Neuropsychiatry, Neuropsychology, and Clinical Neurology*, 301–4.

individuals it is filled in with images – hallucinations, really. If the scotoma is quite small, these images can provide compensation for the missing visual data;[13] however, in more severe cases, the images inserted are sometimes bizarre intrusions in the visual field. So, for example, one man who was trying to put on his shoes saw dozens of additional pairs in his large blind spot and was unable to distinguish the real shoes from the hallucinated ones. One woman typically saw two-dimensional cartoon images filling in her blind-spot.[14] What these cases demonstrate is that a range of visual imagery is always available to us but only attended to when permitted by circumstances such as dream states or when required, for example, as compensation for injury. Michael Winkelman describes visions as "a natural phenomenon of the central nervous system, resulting from disinhibition of the regulation of the visual cortex."[15] In the normal brain, ecstatic visions are like a trip into the brain's visual archives made possible when their door is shut against the external world. Trance states are one way to shut that door. Furthermore, although visions can occur spontaneously in altered states of consciousness (ASCs), in some cultures certain practitioners of ecstatic states are trained in their cultivation.[16] However, the spontaneous and untrained generation of visual phenomena also often includes the sensation of bright and intense light, sometimes perceived as glowing figures.[17]

Along with the subjective phenomena of trance, certain social or physical settings and observable behaviors can also be suggestive of religious experience. These circumstances include ritually structured events, ascetic practices, occasions of severe pain and/or danger, and meditative practices such

---

[13] In fact, the normal optics of the human eye includes a small blind spot relative to objects at close range. However, in everyday circumstances, we are unaware of it because the brain habitually fills it in with visual information that corresponds to surrounding patterns. In other words, as in the case of confabulation, this is another of the brain's "habits" of making seamless sense of the world. All other things being equal, cerebral mechanisms appear to favor an intelligible universe. In fact, one experiment shows that this normal visual compensation mechanism even corrects small imperfections in the pattern of the substituted image. See Jerome Lettvin, "A Sidelong Glance at Seeing," *Sciences* 16 (1976), 1–20.

[14] Ramachandran and Blakeslee describe some of the more unusual examples of scotoma-related hallucinations in *Phantoms in the Brain*, 105–12. See also Joseph, *Neuropsychiatry, Neuropsychology, and Clinical Neurology*, 509–10. For a fuller presentation of the research, see V. S. Ramachandran, "Filling in Gaps in Perception: Part II. Scotomas and Phantom Limbs," *Current Directions in Psychological Science* 2 (1993), 56–65.

[15] Michael Winkelman, *Shamanism: The Neural Ecology of Consciousness and Healing* (Westport, Conn.: Bergin and Garvey, 2000), 85. To put it in terms of d'Aquili's neurobiological model, visions are the result of the deafferentated visual association area interacting with the amygdala and hippocampus (see d'Aquili and Newberg, *Mystical Mind*, 102).

[16] Winkelman, *Shamanism*, 85–88.

[17] Joseph, *Neuropsychiatry, Neuropsychology, and Clinical Neurology*, 283–86. The perception of brilliant light is likely related to intense stimulation of the amygdala and hippocampus.

as focused periods of prayer.[18] All of these occasions are connected by the way
such stimuli act on the autonomic nervous system. D'Aquili and Newberg have
been especially interested in the efficacy of ritual for central nervous system
tuning. They conclude that the rhythmic and repetitive patterning of some
ritual acts is especially effective in generating religious experience. Such patterning synchronizes "affective, perceptual-cognitive, and motor processes within
the central nervous system."[19] Thus, one enters a trance state "from the bottom
up," using the body to tune the brain and central nervous system. D'Aquili also
highlights the significance of a participating community in ritual stimulation of
religious experience because the activities of other members of the group provide a stronger driving stimulus than solitary activity can.[20] Particularly
dominant and socially appealing leaders are especially effective in driving group
experience.[21]

Deprivation and asceticism are the other "bottom-up" means of ecstatic
tuning.[22] Both lack of food and elimination of sensory input can activate limbic
structures beyond their normal patterns. Whenever the normal signs of health
in the body (satiation, regular arousal-quiescent interchange, etc.) are disrupted,
the limbic system adjusts its control over the functioning of the central nervous
system, even affecting higher cognitive activity. In this way, and in contrast to
meditation, one enters second-stage tuning through the body. In addition,
severe, dangerous, or painful stimuli (e.g., extensive burns, extreme cold, injury,
and toxic substances) or extreme emotional stimulation "leads to sympathetic
activation, which, when prolonged, can then lead to a rebound parasympathetic
collapse."[23] So, in their intense forms, both asceticism and accident can stimulate some degree of alteration in consciousness.

It is worth noting that, even when a trance state has ended, ecstatic
experience continues to have measurable effects, often in a generalized
way, throughout the lifetime of the practitioner. So, if Paul's religious experience is like that of others, then its impact cannot be limited to the moments
of ecstasy alone. I have already discussed the lasting euphoria of some

[18] These occasions of ecstasy are discussed, respectively, by d'Aquili and Newberg, *Mystical Mind*, 89–93 (ritual); Winkelman, *Shamanism*, 92, 150–51 (austerities); Joseph, *Neuropsychiatry, Neuropsychology, and Clinical Neurology*, 280–84 (injury and extreme stress); and d'Aquili and Newberg, *Mystical Mind*, 109–16 (meditation).
[19] D'Aquili and Newberg, *Mystical Mind*, 89.
[20] Ibid., 89. Wedenoja ("Ritual Trance and Catharsis," 306) notes the importance of communal settings as well.
[21] Goodman, *Speaking in Tongues*, 60.
[22] Another bottom-up means is to use psychotropic drugs. It is interesting to note that Plotinus (*Enneads*, I.9:14–16) cautions against taking drugs as a means to allow the soul to escape the body because it is not good for the soul.
[23] Winkelman, *Shamanism*, 150.

endogenous chemicals, but other effects have been known to be even more enduring. In an article that summarizes the findings of multiple investigations, Jevning and colleagues review a number of longitudinal studies of the health effects of low-level ecstatic practice. A number of these studies show the persistence of "markedly lower" blood pressure levels as well as cholesterol levels, alleviation of insomnia and asthma, and even reduction in addictive behaviors such as nonprescription drug use and smoking.[24] Thus, there is evidence that continued practice of even low-level ecstatic tuning can enduringly reset metabolic rates and other aspects of the body's functioning. The extensive involvement of the limbic system in meditation and effective ritual makes that conclusion immediately intelligible.

The firsthand reports of some people suggest that instances of profound insight also sometimes accompany ecstatic states. To some degree, comparable moments of insight often accompany dream states. This phenomenon is on a different plane than those discussed so far because it is in no way independently verifiable, and even the possibility of measuring it in healthy brains is unlikely in the foreseeable future. Still, the experience of those who come to such insight is often one of the most subjectively compelling features of their ecstatic state. The phenomenon is common enough, and indeed valued enough, that Zen even has a technical term, *prajna*, for the flashes of understanding that come during meditation.[25] This insight often takes the form of resolution of tensions or opposites.[26] Frequently the one who is treated to such a moment of resolution has been pondering the problem for some time. This phenomenon has been attributed to the reduction in left hemisphere executive control during sleep and ecstasy. Because the brain as a whole is primarily focused on the external environment, conscious thought is typically taken up with information related to the outside world. In ASCs, this control of attention is relaxed, and other ways of knowing can come into play, particularly the knowledge of the right brain.[27]

---

[24] Jevning et al., "Physiology of Meditation," 415–24.

[25] James H. Austin, "Consciousness Evolves when Self Dissolves," *Journal of Consciousness Studies* 7 (2000), 209–30, at 211.

[26] See d'Aquili and Newberg, *Mystical Mind*, 91–93, for further discussion of resolution of opposites and tensions during meditation.

[27] Ibid., 70–71. The phenomenon of "blindsight" is one of the most fascinating illustrations of how much we know, and even act on, without attending to it consciously. People with blindsight are blind because of damage to executive visual areas. Nonetheless, they are able to respond to objects around them in ways that are possible only through perception of the physical attributes of the object. For instance, they can accurately grasp objects that are placed somewhere in front of them, even spacing their fingers to the appropriate width for each article. Some can even navigate successfully through a furnished room. See the original documentation of the phenomenon in Lawrence Weiskrantz, *Blindsight: A Case Study and Implications*, Oxford Psychology Series 12 (Oxford: Clarendon, 1986).

The right hemisphere, as discussed previously, tends to generate holistic cognition.

Albert Einstein's accounts may be the most famous records of ecstatic insight outside of a religious context – certainly his thought and thought processes have been tracked with more than passing interest. By his own reports, Einstein was someone who thought in bursts of insight, in fully formed pictures, rather than in linear, cause-and-effect units of logic. He described his own cognitive process as one of turmoil in which he experienced "psychic tension . . . visited by all sorts of nervous conflicts. . . . I used to go away for weeks in a state of confusion, as one who at that time had yet to overcome the stage of stupefaction in his first encounter with such questions."[28] Most of Einstein's theories were not the result of laboratory work but rather the fruits of thought experiments. For example, he described his theory of relativity coming to him in a fully formed picture as he imagined himself riding a beam of light through space. In fact, he said, "I rarely think in words at all. A thought comes, and I may try to express it in words *afterwards*."[29] The prominence of his thought pictures and the holistic and nonlinguistic character of Einstein's insight suggest that the importance of the right brain – unfettered by customary dominance of the left – was an important feature of his "state of mind." In one of his many interviews, Einstein commented that "[i]magination is more important than knowledge. For knowledge is limited, whereas imagination embraces the entire world, stimulating progress, giving birth to evolution."[30]

Despite his public agnosticism, Einstein spoke almost equally famously of soaring religious feeling and awareness of the divine (though not a personal God) in ways that also testify to low-level ecstatic states. He understood his drive for scientific insight to be the same dynamic that was at work in religiosity:

> The scientist is possessed by a sense of universal causation. . . . His religious feeling takes the form of a rapturous amazement at the harmony of natural law, which reveals an intelligence of such superiority that, compared with it, all the systematic thinking and acting of human beings is an utterly

[28] Einstein, as cited in Carolyn Abraham, *Possessing Genius: The Bizarre Odyssey of Einstein's Brain* (Toronto: Penguin, 2002), 14.

[29] Spoken to his longtime friend Max Wertheimer and cited in Max Wertheimer, *Productive Thinking* (New York: Harper, 1959), 213. A group of scientists who, under the supervision of an indigenous Peruvian shaman, took the narcotic ayahuasca experienced similar flashes of insight related to their research. See the report in Narby and Huxley, *Shamans through Time*, 301–5.

[30] Albert Einstein, *Cosmic Religion with Other Opinions and Aphorisms* (New York: Covici-Friede, 1931), 97.

insignificant reflection. . . . It is beyond question closely akin to that which has possessed the religious geniuses of all ages.[31]

These more general perceptions of religious feeling as well as extraordinary moments of insight can result from lower levels of neurological tuning. Nonetheless, d'Aquili and Newberg describe them as part of the same trajectory of experience that ends in peak ecstasy.

So, according to the neurobiological model of religious trance, most ecstatic experience is low-grade ecstasy, or "lesser mystical states" in d'Aquili and Newberg's terminology, and not the surpassing experience of what they call "absolute unitary being" (AUB). These lesser states are also ASCs, including alterations in the functioning of the nervous system, but do not necessarily include all the attendant features most often associated with peak ecstatic states. In particular, d'Aquili and Newberg conclude that such lesser states will not progress all the way to total deafferentation of both the left and right association areas; therefore, they will not include the profound experience of oneness that characterizes AUB.[32] Still, lesser states will include the release of some endogenous chemicals and the generation of limbic emotions (particularly the combination of mild fear and elation), and they will include some disruption of self-perception, the passage of time, and the processing of peripheral conscious thought. They will also include observable behaviors that point to the internal processes of the ecstatic state.

In addition, even low-grade ecstasy has a number of lasting effects. Furthermore, the deep involvement of the limbic system in trance and its several mechanisms for imprinting behavior (e.g., its significance in the creation of memories, motivational drives, and generation of emotion) tend to favor reinforcement of ecstatic practice. Given these long-lasting effects, perhaps it is not surprising to discover that Paul, in a way, marks time by an event from fourteen years ago (2 Cor 12:2).

3.2 BEYOND PARADISE

It is now possible to assess how these additional phenomena of religiously interpreted ASCs correlate with what Paul says outside of the account in 2 Corinthians 12. The category of visions figures significantly in this tally because it was omitted in the previous chapter. Because Paul can take the authenticity and significance of these events for granted in his

---

[31] Albert Einstein, "The Religious Spirit of Science," in *Mein Weltbild* (Amsterdam: Querido, 1934), 18.

[32] See their summary discussion in d'Aquili and Newberg, *Mystical Mind*, 102–3, 116–18.

correspondence, he tends not to describe the occasions of his visions. Indeed, it is quite likely that such conversations were part of his visits to the various communities. But in his letters, they are identifiable by allusions to some of the phenomena of trance: sensations of light; awareness of transformed states, especially somatic transformation (including reduced voluntary control of the body); and, where discernible, signs of the characteristically religious combination of emotions. Ritual contexts may also serve as markers for low-grade ecstatic experience because, as described earlier, the setting and practices of ritual facilitate central nervous system tuning. The surest examples will obviously be those that combine a number of these characteristics. As it turns out, when these criteria are applied to the Pauline corpus, the resulting list of relevant passages is not especially unique. A number of other authors, although for other reasons, have also identified these texts as being informed in one way or another by Paul's own religious experience.[33] Thus, some of Paul's comments have on occasion been recognized as echoes of extraordinary experience – they simply have not been seen to cohere with one another as a result of that fact.

3.2.1 *Visions and Revelations*

The first of these passages concerns the fact that, at the most fundamental level, in the Corinthian correspondence, Paul twice assumes the audience's knowledge of his direct apprehension of the risen Jesus (1 Cor 9:1, 15:8). I assume, along with others, that this vision, like his vision of the third heaven, took place in trance.[34] Paul describes it with the straightforward verb of seeing, ὁράω. His use of that ordinary language puts him on a par with those apostles who saw Jesus both before and after his death. Although Paul describes only his ascent with any detail, he also states that he had other visions and revelations (2 Cor 12:1, 7), and Lincoln suggests that he may have intended to discuss a number of these occasions when he first turned to the

---

[33] So, Ashton (*Religion of Paul the Apostle*), Kim (*Paul and the New Perspective*), Schweitzer (*Mysticism of Paul and the Apostle*), and Segal (*Paul the Convert*), for example, have all, for their own reasons, identified some portion of Rom 6:1–11, Rom 8, and 2 Cor 3–5 as being relevant to Paul's religious experience. However, they do so in varying ways. As discussed in Chapter 2, Kim speaks as though there was a single religious experience, "the Damascus Christophany," and Schweitzer, although he recognizes the fact of Paul's visions, has sealed off Paul's "mystical" thought as a more or less self-contained phenomenon.

[34] For example, Tabor (*Things Unutterable*, 21) and Segal (*Paul the Convert*, 12) understand them as occasions of "spiritual experience." John Dominic Crossan, *Jesus: A Revolutionary Biography* (San Francisco: HarperSanFrancisco, 1994), 167–68, comments that "[t]here can be no doubt that Paul's experience involved trance."

topic of *visions and revelations* (ὀπτασίας καὶ ἀποκαλύψεις).[35] Sorting out other allusions to visions of Christ is complicated by Paul's use of the genitive construction. The enduring and perhaps irresolvable debate is whether, for example, in his reference in 2 Cor 12:1 and 7 to multiple visions and revelations "of the Lord,"[36] he meant that Christ was revealed to him (the objective genitive) or that Christ gave him a revelation (the subjective genitive).[37] My own feeling is that the objective genitive is quite likely intended but that a definitive determination is beyond the evidence. However, as a number of authors have argued, the distinction between the two need not be drawn too sharply.[38] The ambiguity between the two senses may be more reflective of Paul's mind, at any rate. Even if some of these occasions did not include visions, the language of "revelation" is significant, as is Paul's interpretation of their supernatural source. So, Paul goes to Jerusalem according to a revelation (Gal 2:2), and the gospel he preaches came through revelation (Gal 1:11–12), in direct contrast to human agency or teaching. In both cases, low-level ecstatic tuning would account for Paul's interpretation of the divine source of his knowledge.

Paul's language of glory is an especially interesting datum in the context of visions because among some rather pedestrian uses he has also given it a specialized sense like that anticipated in the Septuagint (LXX). Apart from the Septuagint, as far back as Homer and Herodotus, *doxa* most often means "what one thinks" or "opinion."[39] Other common meanings include reputation or renown and sometimes, more specifically, the material evidence of honorable status.[40] As in the rest of the New Testament, Paul does

---

[35] Lincoln, *Paradise Now and Not Yet*, 72.

[36] The comment is complicated further by Paul's use of "Lord" – is the source or content of the visions God or the risen Jesus? On this ambiguity of usage, see Dunn, *Theology of Paul the Apostle*, 249–52.

[37] The meaning, in Gal 1:12, of a "revelation of Jesus Christ" is clear because Paul clarifies that God "was pleased to reveal his son in me" (Gal 1:15–16). Thus, in this case at least, Paul must have intended the Christ as the object of the revelation.

[38] Lincoln, *Paradise Now and Not Yet*, 73; Windisch, *Zweite Korintherbrief*, 377; Philip Edgcumbe Hughes, *Commentary on the Second Epistle to the Corinthians* (Grand Rapids, Mich.: Eerdmans, 1962), 428, n. 97; C. K. Barrett, *Commentary on the Second Epistle to the Corinthians*, 307; and James D. G. Dunn, *Jesus and the Spirit: A Study of the Religious and Charismatic Experience of Jesus and the First Christians as Reflected in the New Testament* (Grand Rapids, Mich.: Eerdmans, 1997), 414, n. 88.

[39] Gerhard Kittel and Gerhard von Rad, "δοκέω, δόξα" *Theological Dictionary of the New Testament*, vol. 2, ed. Gerhard Kittel, trans. Geoffrey Bromiley (Grand Rapids, Mich.: Eerdmans, 1964)., 236.

[40] In the latter context, *doxa* is often translated into English as "splendor." See, for example, common translations of Qumran 4:6 referring to geopolitical entities, Qumran 12:27 in reference to Solomon, and Josephus, *Ant.* 8.166, referring to the queen of Sheba.

sometimes use *doxa* (including δοξάζω) in this pedestrian sense to refer to reputation or honor,[41] but neither he nor any other New Testament writer uses it to mean opinion.[42] Much more often, Paul reserves its use for God's honor or reputation[43] and, growing from that use, for the status that God confers on people.[44] That Paul should make God the sole source of *doxa* in these contexts is in keeping with notions of honor and its dynamics. In all of these uses, *doxa* is ultimately an attribute flowing from God.

However, in others of Paul's uses, *doxa* is nearly a technical term that combines first its root sense of appearance or manifestation and second the superlative connotations connected with its use for the splendor of God. Through this combination, it can at times function almost synonymously with brilliance or light. Notably, the authors of the Septuagint use *doxa* almost exclusively as the rendering of God's *kavod* (the Hebrew word that is usually translated as "glory"), and Paul's use reflects this innovation at several points. In a few passages, he speaks of *doxa* as a substance or dynamic force in ways that move well beyond normal Greek usage.[45] For example, in Rom 6:4 (a passage in which he is also discussing the transformation of the baptized and participation in Christ), Paul speaks of God's glory as the force by which Christ was raised: Christ was raised from the dead by the glory (*doxa*) of the father. *Doxa* is virtually a location in Rom 15:7, into which Christ welcomed members of the assemblies. Paul uses *doxa* in 1 Cor 15:40–41 as the point of comparison between cosmic bodies (the sun, moon, and stars) and the resurrection body. In this case, the connotations of radiance, light, splendor, and elevated status are all fluidly at play in the passage, and Paul's vocabulary is more provocative than precise. Most importantly, in Paul's usage, the glory that is almost exclusively a divine property slides into his descriptions of Christ. For example, in Phil 3:21, Christ has a glorious body, and in Phil 4:19 clear distinctions of whose glory is at hand are impossible. In 1 Cor 2:8, he is simply the lord of glory.

---

[41] Rom 2:7, 10, 9:4, 11:13; 1 Cor 12:26; 2 Cor 6:8; Phil 3:18; 1 Thess 2:6.

[42] That idea is represented throughout the New Testament (and even in the writings of post-apostolic authors) by the words *gnōmē* and others (Kittel and von Rad, *Theological Dictionary of the New Testament*, vol. 2, 237). Kittel and von Rad specify that, in the Septuagint, a variety of Hebrew words that connote "opinion" are translated with *boulē* ("doxa," 2:242). In fact, in the Septuagint, *timē* typically substitutes for occurrences in which *kavod* is used in the sense of human reputation (2:243).

[43] Reference to an attribute of God accounts for the bulk of Paul's usage: Rom 1:21, 23, 3:7, 23, 4:20, 5:2, 11:36, 15:6, 9, 16:27; 1 Cor 6:20, 10:31; 2 Cor 1:20, 8:19, 9:13; Gal 1:5, 24; Phil 1:11, 2:11.

[44] Examples of this usage are found in Rom 8:30, 9:23; 1 Cor 2:7, and 11:7. In the latter, assemblies are God's glory.

[45] Alan Segal (*Paul the Convert*, 39–44) has discussed the "mystical" connotations of Paul's use of *doxa* as God's self-representation.

3.2.2 *2 Corinthians 3–5*

The fullest example of this change in meaning is Paul's use of *doxa* as a recurring theme in 2 Corinthians 3–5. In 2 Cor 3:7–18, Paul presents his own interpretive elaboration of Moses' encounter with the presence of God and the residual glory that was reflected in his face.[46] This *doxa* is obviously light and radiance (not status or reputation) both in its original narrative context and in Paul's interpretation. The language has some metaphorical valences, but it is not merely metaphorical. Furthermore, Moses is not simply an analogy but a parallel – Paul, too, saw God's glory. In introducing the comparison between "the ministry of death" and "the ministry of the spirit," Paul's assertion of physical radiance passing from one to the other seems to be the only proof of superiority that he requires (2 Cor 3:10–11): "For indeed, the thing having been glorified in this respect/case ($\mu\acute{\epsilon}\rho os$) is no longer glorified, on account of the surpassing glory. For if the thing that is being neutralized ($\kappa\alpha\tau\alpha\rho\gamma o\acute{\nu}\mu\epsilon\nu o\nu$) [was] through glory, how much more the remaining thing [is] in glory." The wording is awkward, as is the logic, but as most commentators suggest, it is quite likely a version of greater-to-lesser reasoning. Still, it is difficult to understand how *doxa* can carry the rhetorical weight that Paul is loading on it unless it is understood as something approaching the physical representation of the divine or the residue of direct contact with God. He concludes the comparison with Moses by attaching this new *doxa* specifically to "the Lord" into whose image ($\epsilon i\kappa\acute{\omega}\nu$) we are being transformed "from glory to glory" (2 Cor 3:18). The present tense of that assertion again suggests something more on Paul's part than intellectual assent to the idea of transformation – transformation is occurring now, and Paul has felt its effects in his own person. Such a statement stands in contradiction to what he says about

---

[46] Whether the elaboration is of Paul's own creation has been debated but is most often resolved in favor of Paul's reworking of an existing tradition. In the case of a story like that of Moses' encounter with God, one need hardly posit direct contact with other traditions to imagine similar adaptations. The importance of the narrative in salvation history combined with its captivating and concrete details is certainly sufficient to account for more than one person elaborating on it in similar directions. Still, parallel texts are not irrelevant to understanding Paul's comments. For a discussion of the possible influences and sources of the passage, see Margaret E. Thrall, *Introduction and Commentary on II Corinthians I–VII, Vol. 1: A Critical and Exegetical Commentary on the Second Epistle to the Corinthians* (Edinburgh: T. and T. Clark, 1994), 238–39. For a detailed comparison of Paul's use with that of other midrashim on Moses' glory and a corresponding argument in favor of Paul's independent adaptation, see Linda L. Belleville, *Reflections of Glory: Paul's Polemical Use of the Moses-Doxa Tradition in 2 Corinthians 3.1–18*, Journal for the Study of the New Testament Supplement Series 52 (Sheffield: Sheffield Academic Press, 1991).

resurrection transformation when he is providing a more careful response, even prior to his comments in 2 Corinthians 3 (i.e., 1 Cor 15:20–26).[47] But that contrast makes this unfiltered comment all the more instructive.

As Paul continues to construct the passage, he picks up the thread a number of other times before the end of Chapter 5. The most significant occurrence is in 2 Cor 4:4–6, especially the evocative phrases "the illumination of the good news of the glory of Christ, who is the image ($\epsilon\grave{\iota}\kappa\acute{\omega}\nu$) of God" (v. 4b) and "who shone in our hearts for an illumination of the glory of God in the face of Christ" (v. 6). The theological significance of Paul's language has been well documented elsewhere,[48] and virtually all those who are willing to entertain some form of ecstatic religious experience include this passage as an instance of Paul's reflection on it. Of greatest significance is Paul's description of Christ as the image of God.[49]

But lest we assume that Paul has left the tangible territory of body and religious experience behind and is (merely) elaborating textual traditions in light of the idea of the resurrection of Jesus, two additional details in this section bring us back to earth, so to speak. The first is the repeated mention of groaning ($\sigma\tau\epsilon\nu\acute{\alpha}\zeta\omega$ 2 Cor 5:2, 4) in connection with bodily transformation, and the second is Paul's fervent desire ($\grave{\epsilon}\pi\iota\pi o\theta\acute{\epsilon}\omega$) for such a transformation. These details, I would suggest, are some of the contextual and emotional indications of ecstatic experience. Here Paul's thought draws closer to the experience of ecstasy than in other texts in which he reflects on transformation

---

[47] Segal also notes this difference in the ways Paul speaks about transformation and tries to resolve the tension between the two views (Segal, "Paul's Thinking about the Resurrection in Its Jewish Context, 413): "Paul speaks of the transformation being partly experienced by believers already in their pre-parousia existence. His use of the present tense in Rom 12:2 and 2 Cor 3:18 underscores that transformation as an ongoing event. However in 1 Cor 15:49 and Rom 8 it culminates at Christ's return, the parousia. This suggests that for Paul transformation is both a single, definitive event yet also a process that continues until the second coming."

[48] For example, David J. Halperin, *Faces of the Chariot* (Tübingen: Mohr [Siebeck], 1988), 231–38; Kim, *Origin of Paul's Gospel,* Chapter 6; Segal, *Paul the Convert,* Chapter 2; C. C. Newman, *Paul's Glory-Christology: Tradition and Rhetoric,* Novum Testamentum Supplement 69 (Leiden: E. J. Brill, 1992); James M. Scott, "Throne-Chariot Mysticism in Qumran and in Paul," in *Eschatology, Messianism, and the Dead Sea Scrolls,* ed. Craig A. Evans and Peter W. Flint (Grand Rapids, Mich.: Eerdmans, 1997), 101–19, esp. 113, 118; Dunn, *Theology of Paul the Apostle,* 290–92.

[49] Kim (*Paul and the New Perspective,* 176–84) discusses the significance of "$\epsilon\grave{\iota}\kappa\acute{\omega}\nu$-Christology" at some length as part of his defense against Dunn's critique of his position. Although many recognize the ecstatic implications of that statement, they do so only in passing and are unable, or unwilling, to integrate that fact into their interpretations of the passage. As they analyze the passage in detail, their attention shifts away from experience toward the comparison of texts and elaboration of traditional material.

(e.g., 1 Cor 15:35–57). For example, we find (1) implications of visionary experience expressed as radiance and an apprehension of a divinized Jesus; (2) reflections of Paul's changed perception of his own body expressed as knowledge of transformation and subarticulate speech (i.e., groaning); and (3) intensified emotional experience.

A great deal is revealed in Paul's use of στενάζω *(stenazō)* throughout this passage. Johannes Schneider, author of the entry on *stenazō* in the *Theological Dictionary of the New Testament,* offer "sigh" *(seufzen)* as the translation and suggests that the Greek tragic poets employed the word to describe characters who sigh "at destiny or individual blows of fate."[50] One has the sense of the ennui of the idle classes. Yet, when Schneider goes on to document the biblical texts that use *stenazō,* he lists such "existential predicaments" as mortal combat (Exod 26:15; Isa 59:10), women "sighing" during childbirth (Jer 4:31), mourners during funeral rituals (Ezek 24:17), and couples in sexual embrace (Sir 30:20). "Sighing" hardly does justice to the nature of the noise one might encounter in any of these contexts, including funerals in Mediterranean cultures. Clearly, groaning, moaning, wailing, or some other form of guttural vocalization is closer to the sense of the word.

Noteworthy, too, is the number of times that *stenazō* is used in cultic or ritual contexts. It is sometimes the form that the deep longing of prayer takes, as in the cases of the prisoners and the condemned whose *stenagmoi* reach God (Ps 78:11 LXX), the anguished prayer of Tobit (3:1), or overwrought supplications of eleventh-hour penance (Isa 30:15 LXX; Mal 2:13). So, too, *stenazō* accompanies ecstatic states when the prophet receives a particularly powerful vision (Isa 21:2).[51] The same combination of ecstatic prophecy and an alarming message is also the context in Ezekiel 21. In this case, the translation resulting from Schneider's choice of sigh is almost absurd: "But thou, son of man, sigh! With broken thighs and in bitter grief, sigh! When they ask thee why thou sighest, then answer them: Because of a message of terror" (Ezek 21:14). Again, the scriptural examples suggest something more primal in *stenazō* than groaning in resignation with one's lot in life. Rather, the examples speak to a lack of control of vocalization and

50 Johannes Schneider, "στενάζω, στεναγμός, συστενάζω," in *Theological Dictionary of the New Testament,* vol. 5, ed. Gerhard Kittel, trans. Geoffrey Bromley (Grand Rapids, Mich.: Eerdmans, 1971), 600. Elsewhere, he states: "Sighing takes place by reason of a condition of oppression under which man suffers and from which he longs to be free because it is not in accord with his nature, expectations, or hopes" (601).
51 The Septuagint differs here from the Hebrew recension in which Babylon has caused generalized groaning. In the Septuagint, the prophet groans under the weight of the vision and the pain of receiving it, which is compared to labor pains.

the sort of circumstances in which central nervous system tuning is triggered.[52]

So, a number of details coincide in Paul's thought throughout this section. In 2 Corinthians 5 he labors with metaphors of nomadic ($\sigma\kappa\eta\nu\dot{\eta}$) and permanent dwellings to describe the transformation of the body (2 Cor 5:1) and lumps those images together with verbs of dressing and undressing (2 Cor 5:4). The clumsy construction of the metaphor suggests that Paul is struggling to express something that here is more vital to him than the images with which he is forced to express it. In other words, experience lies closer to the surface of his comments than either scriptural exegesis or doctrinal proposition. He talks about being with the Lord by being out of or away from the body (2 Cor 5:8), and he speaks of groaning with the longing for that transformation (2 Cor 5:2–4). I would suggest that the groaning in this case is not the "burden of mortality"[53] but the recollection of ecstatic prayer in which one actually attains some degree of transformation. In fact, Paul caps the discussion with the recognition that such talk – such experience – gives him the appearance of being mad, $\dot{\epsilon}\xi\dot{\iota}\sigma\tau\eta\mu\iota$, in contrast to $\sigma\omega\phi\rho\text{ον}\dot{\epsilon}\omega$,[54] because, he explains, he is not in control of himself but "the love of Christ has hold ($\sigma\upsilon\nu\dot{\epsilon}\chi\epsilon\iota$) of us" (2 Cor 5:14). It is remarkable language, driven more by ecstatic knowledge than by the systematic exposition of two covenants. As John Ashton puts it, "these are all, surely, characteristically fumbling attempts of the genuine mystic to give expression to the ineffable."[55]

---

[52] A related context is Mark 7:34, in which Jesus healed the blind man by looking up to heaven, groaning, and using a foreign "magic" word that Mark preserves and explains: "Ephphatha, that is, Be opened." This is also likely an ecstatic context. Commenting on this text, Schneider says "$\sigma\tau\epsilon\nu\dot{\alpha}\zeta\omega$ here undoubtedly denotes a prayer-sigh." The two other New Testament examples of its use are Heb 13:17 and James 5:9, where a translation of grumble or mutter might be more appropriate because both are in the context of complaint.

[53] Victor Paul Furnish, *II Corinthians*, Anchor Bible 32A (Garden City, N.Y.: Doubleday, 1984), 296, uses the phrase in the same way as Schneider and also invokes Hellenistic usage. However, he is not completely comfortable with the implications because he qualifies this suggestion of borrowing with the proviso that "it is not because [Paul] shares the dualistic anthropology that notion involves."

[54] The suggestion that $\dot{\epsilon}\xi\dot{\iota}\sigma\tau\eta\mu\iota$ refers to ecstatic behavior has been made before. See Bousset, *Kyrios Christos*, 187; Windisch, *Zweite Korintherbrief*, 179; Bruce, *1 and 2 Corinthians*, 207; Furnish, *II Corinthians*, 324; Thrall, *Introduction and Commentary on II Corinthians I–VII*, 405–6; and Lambrecht, and Harrington, *Second Corinthians*, 93–94. See Moyer Hubbard, "Was Paul Out of His Mind? Re-reading 2 Corinthians 5:13," *Journal for the Study of the New Testament* 70 (1998), 40–42, for an overview of the history of the discussion. Hubbard himself presents a contrary thesis, arguing that the contrast between $\dot{\epsilon}\xi\dot{\iota}\sigma\tau\eta\mu\iota$ and $\sigma\omega\phi\rho\text{ον}\dot{\epsilon}\omega$ addresses the shortcomings of Paul's rhetorical style.

[55] Ashton, *Religion of Paul the Apostle*, 149. In this quotation, Ashton is not referring to 2 Corinthians 3–5 in particular but rather to the breadth of Paul's language of participation in Christ.

In summary, a number of ecstatic phenomena appear in this passage. In 1 Corinthians 3–5, *doxa* is associated with the immediate presence of God, or of Christ as the image ($\epsilon\grave{\iota}\kappa\acute{\omega}\nu$) of God (see also Rom 8:29; 1 Cor 15:49), which is in turn apprehended as radiance or light. Thus, the "seeing" of the risen Jesus, of which Paul speaks directly elsewhere (1 Cor 9:1, 15:8), resonates in these texts as well and is further elaborated with details of light which is a known component of religious ecstasy.[56] However, in 2 Corinthians 3–5, these details are not necessarily discrete components of a particular event or occasion. It is just as instructive that Paul slides into a fluid mingling of all these notions because they are neurologically connected in all of us. But Paul, as someone who has used those neural circuits and strengthened them, is alive to those interconnections in ways that others are not. When he begins to work with the comparison with Moses in 3:7, a range of associated details arise. As Paul completes that comparison in 4:16, the experience of somatic transformation is already on his mind and comes to the surface of the discourse. In the neural logic of ecstatic experience, this conglomeration of features belongs together, and ecstatic knowledge provides the core content of this whole section.

3.2.3 *Romans 8*

Similar observations apply to Paul's comments in Romans 8, and indeed the two passages have many affinities. Once again, commentators are not indifferent to the distinctive content and even tone in Romans 8. Still, for the most part, they discuss it under the *topos* of eschatology, or perhaps pneumatology, which, as it is used in New Testament scholarship, is not at all the same thing as religious experience. As in the case of Schweitzer's category of "mysticism," eschatology and pneumatology are cognicentric constructs that allow one to imagine that here Paul is delineating (albeit with some poetic finesse) categories of systematic theology. I do not argue that either category is irrelevant to the passage but that both are secondary academic derivatives of experience and are typically discussed at its expense. In Romans 8, Paul is largely contrasting two modes of life: the one, according to flesh ($\kappa\alpha\tau\acute{\alpha}$

---

[56] It is interesting to note the coincidence of the same context and vocabulary in Luke's version of the transfiguration (Luke 9:29–32), a connection also noted by Segal (*Paul the Convert*, 111–12). Attempts to connect the Lukan text with ecstatic states have been made. See John Pilch, "The Transfiguration of Jesus: An Experience of Alternate Reality," in *Modeling Early Christianity: Social-Scientific Studies of the New Testament in Its Context*, ed. Philip R. Esler (London: Routledge, 1995), 47–64; and Ashton, *Religion of Paul the Apostle*, 70–71. My own position is not unlike that of Morton Smith, *Jesus the Magician* (New York: Harper and Row, 1978), 122, when he suggests that the prevalence of the theme of a heavenly journey is more likely due to the nature of ecstatic states (he calls them "hallucinative rites") than a direct sharing of traditions.

σάρκα) and the other according to spirit (κατά πνευμα) (Rom 8:4–5). The contrast follows on Paul's argument about the inability of the law to accomplish the good that is latent in it. Along these lines, most commentators (at least since the advent of the "new perspective") emphasize that Paul's point is not that the law is flawed but that it was without the power to enable people to keep it. In Romans 8, Paul's primary point is that the Spirit, in contrast, makes it possible to do the good encoded in the law. But what brings Paul to such a conclusion about the Spirit? Sanders reconstructs Paul's logic in this section of Romans as follows:

> It was not *from* the analysis of the weakness of the flesh and the challenge of the commandment that Paul actually came to the conclusion that all men are enslaved to sin. This is a view which springs from the conviction that God has provided for universal salvation in Christ; thus it follows that all men must need salvation. . . .
>
> Paul's logic seems to run like this: in Christ God has acted to save the world; therefore the world is in need of salvation; but God also gave the law; if Christ is given for salvation, it must follow that the law could not have been.[57]

In Sanders's reconstruction, the Spirit is of little utility to Paul's logic despite its prominence in the explanation that follows in Romans 8. Indeed, measured by occurrence alone, the Spirit is the emphatic crescendo of this whole section of the letter.[58] Where, then, does it fit in the logic?

When one considers Romans 8 as the discourse of someone for whom ecstatic religious experience is a significant biographical element, the talk of spirit becomes far more central to its interpretation. Paul alternates between claims about the believer being "in the Spirit" and statements that locate the spirit within human beings. He combines both uses in Rom 8:9a: "But you are not in flesh but *in spirit* since God's spirit *dwells in you.*" If Romans were anything other than a Christian document, such a statement would easily be recognized as a declaration of spirit possession. Paul asserts the possibility of a new mode of life (in spirit) because the Spirit has taken up permanent residence (οἰκέω) in the faithful. Here Paul speaks as someone whose neurological tuning has been reset by repeated ecstatic events. A kind of integrated devotion is possible for him because of the lasting effects of such experience and he, in turn, assumes it to be available to the whole Christian community.

---

[57] E. P. Sanders, *Paul and Palestinian Judaism*, 475.

[58] The word occurs twenty-two times, three of which refer to an aspect of human anthropology. The remaining nineteen references make up more than half the total occurrences in the letter.

Although it is not incorrect to see here the account of an individual "caught between the ages," neither is it especially illuminating of the investments of the text. It is far more profitable to read it as an expression of the tension of someone who has experienced two distinct bioneurological states. Paul is caught between the somatic transformation that he has experienced in trance and the more common bioneurological apprehension of his own body. Thus, the "now" of Rom 8:1 is, at least in part, Paul's attempt to account for his own change in being. His categories for these two experiences of the body are "spirit" and "flesh." So, in verse 18, when Paul sets out to describe God's ultimate disposition toward the community, he ends up describing his own ecstatic knowledge of it: The sufferings of the present, which he knows intimately, do not compare with the glory, which he also knows in part through ecstasy. The language in Rom 8:18 of the glory that will be revealed "in us" is reminiscent of Paul's comment in Gal 1:16, in which Christ was revealed "in him." He makes the same assertion in 2 Cor 4:16–17: "if our outer person is being decayed, yet our inward is being renewed." Is this eschatology?

If there were hope for attention to ecstatic experience, one might expect to find it in the category of pneumatology. But pneumatology has been used in a static way, often wedded to eschatology, to describe the current state of affairs, in which the spirit is working automatically, as it were, without the immediate knowledge of the individual. So, for example, in a kind of stilted literalism, commentators fret over whether the spirit functions in Rom 8:15 as "the Spirit which actually effects adoption" or "the Spirit which anticipates adoption"; as the symbol of "humans in their receptivity to God"; or as the thing that "pledges" a future status.[59] Frequently the spirit is simply glossed over as being incidental to the understanding of the text.[60]

However, much of the ample talk of the spirit in this chapter is manifestly ecstatic. In the first place the use of $\kappa\rho\acute{\alpha}\zeta\omega$ (to cry out) in Rom 8:15 is conspicuously ecstatic (see also Gal 6:6). Dunn has noticed that fact

[59] The three views belong respectively to C. K. Barrett, *A Commentary on the Epistle to the Romans* (London: A. and C. Black, 1971), 163; Robert Morgan, *Romans,* New Testament Guides (Sheffield: Sheffield Academic Press, 1995), 48; and Brendan Byrne, '*Sons of God' – 'Seed of Abraham': A Study of the Idea of Sonship of God of all Christians in Paul against the Jewish Background,* Analecta Biblica 83 (Rome: Pontificio Instituto Biblico, 1979), 100.

[60] This is the strategy in Brendan Byrne, ed. Daniel J. Harrington, *Romans,* Sacra Pagina 6 (Collegeville, Minn.: Liturgical Press, 1996), 250, emphasis added: "*Whatever believers have received* is a spirit that goes with or attests to the fact that they enjoy the filial privilege pertaining to the eschatological people of God."

and understands κράζω as the obvious "enthusiastic context" of Paul's prayer.[61] The emotional and exuberant character of the worship that includes participants shouting "Abba! Father!" is self-evident. In fact, a number of commentators recognize that reality but are nonetheless quick to deny its importance to the "real point" of the passage. For example, Brendan Byrne describes the Abba prayer as an authentic practice within early Christian liturgy that was "characteristic and distinctive" and even "precious" to those who practiced it. However, he insists, "Paul's chief point" is that "the divine Spirit is bearing clear witness along with 'our spirit' that we here and now enjoy a filial status."[62] Byrne is using "enjoy" in its secondary sense – certainly what he describes says little of either pleasure in particular or emotion in general; it expresses instead the mono-phasic knowing[63] characterized by a rational distinction of categories. In contrast, Paul's own evidence for the adoptive status of those who are led by the spirit is phenomenological – shouting barbarisms and shared testi-mony of spirits. As I have said, if such a statement were made in the text of a non-Christian culture, it would be easily recognized as indicative of spirit possession.

There are several other signs of ecstatic religious experience in Rom 8:22–27. The ecstatic groaning found in 2 Corinthians 5 is repeated here and is combined again with fervent expectation.[64] Likewise, in Rom 8:26, Paul uses the prefixed action of the Spirit interceding on behalf of the person (ὑπερεντυγχάνω) to describe the level of pneumatic participation that he has in mind. Here Paul describes the Spirit's participation in noncognizant prayer ("how we should pray...we do not know") and inarticulate groanings (στεναγμοῖς ἀλαλήτοις). But rather than taking these details at face value as phenomena of ecstatic prayer, many commentaries wax

---

[61] James D. G. Dunn, *Romans 1–8*, Word Biblical Commentary 38 (Milton Keynes: Word, 1971) 453; see also Dunn, *Jesus and the Spirit*, 240.

[62] Byrne and Harrington, *Romans*, 250. They do add that the Spirit supports "the sometimes faltering conviction of the individual believer" (251).

[63] "Monophasic" is a term coined by Laughlin, McManus, and d'Aquili that serves in much the same way as "cognicentric." The authors prefer to speak of phases of consciousness rather than states because "phase" connotes some of the dynamic process of thinking and knowing. Where I have been using the terminology of "neural circuits" to describe the physiological grounds for ASC, they use the notion of phases to communicate something of both the physiology and the higher cognitive functioning that is functionally inseparable anyway. Thus, monophasic cultures are those that typically value only a single kind of cognitive functioning – the same sort that Harner calls cognicentric.

[64] One finds a similar combination of details in Phil 3:20–21: "For our citizenship exists in heaven from whence we also eagerly await (ἀπεκδεχόμεθα) a saviour, Lord Jesus Christ, who will transfigure our abject body into conformity with his body of glory."

catechetical at this point.[65] Dunn's determination that the phrase refers instead to "a more inarticulate mode" of speech is far more salutary.[66] Paul is simply describing ecstatic prayer, the mode in which he experienced his transformation from a human being with a fleshly body destined for death to a son of God with a spiritual body of glory (8:12–14; paralleling the transformation of Jesus that he describes in Rom 1:3–4).

The number of σύν compounds in Romans 8 is another of its remarkable features. As in 2 Corinthians, the prevalence of this expression of shared experience is indicative of ecstatic union. The examples include the spirit bearing witness *with* our spirit (v. 16); being heirs together *with* Christ (v. 17); suffering *with* Christ (v. 17); being glorified *with* Christ (v. 17); groaning *with* and suffering *with* creation (v. 22); the Spirit that takes our part *with* us in our weakness (συναντιλαμβάνομαι. 26); and being conformed to the image of the risen Christ (v. 29). The combination of groaning in prayer and language so weighted with participation creates a passage that is saturated with knowledge of ecstatic religious experience. Whether the Roman audience would have heard it that way is difficult to say – Paul at least seems to assume their understanding of the patterned "Abba" prayer and cites it as convincing evidence. Either way, the connections in Paul's mind are many and flowing. As Dunn says, "the tremendous sense of 'togetherness'" in this passage "can hardly be reduced to a merely literary motif, a feature of Pauline style," or to "simply a description of ... membership in the believing community."[67]

3.2.4 *Ecstasy and Suffering*

In addition to the features outlined previously, some of these passages also contain a significant coincidence of ecstasy and suffering. It is especially

---

[65] The strain in exegeses that try to determine just what it is that the Spirit had to "teach" early Christians about the nature of prayer (was it the content? was it the form?) is perhaps evidence enough that those questions miss the point of Paul's comment. C. K. Barrett suggests that in Rom 8:26 Paul uses the gnostic idea that "man does not know the secret prayers which alone can give him access to God; when he is initiated the divine spirit speaks through his mouth the correct formula." Still, Barrett clarifies, "[i]t is certain that Paul does not mean what the gnostics meant; for him, prayer is no formula, nor are men saved by repeating unintelligible words" (Barrett, *Commentary on the Epistle to the Romans*, 168). Byrne uses ἀλάλητος as evidence that no actual sound is made in this wholly interior "groaning" (Byrne and Harrington, *Romans*, 271). Perhaps recognizing the ecstatic implications in the text, Ernst Käsemann, *Commentary on Romans,* trans. G. W. Bromiley, 4th ed. (Tübingen: Mohr, 1980), argued that Paul was referring to glossolalia.

[66] Dunn, *Romans 1–8*, 479. Although he, too, seems to hedge that comment with the suggestion that Paul's language is metaphoric and chosen in order to express "more clearly his solidarity with nonhuman creation."

[67] Dunn, *Theology of Paul the Apostle*, 404.

interesting that Paul introduces his vision of paradise in the immediate context of his *peristasis* catalog (2 Cor 11:16–33). He creates similar combinations of details in 2 Corinthians 3–5 and Romans 8. Into the middle of the extended discussion in 2 Corinthians, which as I have argued is marked by ecstatic knowledge, Paul introduces a statement on suffering (2 Cor 4:7–12). Furthermore, at its end, he places a full-blown *peristasis* catalog (2 Cor 6:3–10). Although 2 Cor 4:7–12 is typically identified as a peristasis catalogue as well,[68] unlike those lists Paul provides elsewhere, this one lacks mention of any specific incident. Rather, here Paul focuses more generally on bodily ($\sigma\hat{\omega}\mu\alpha$, v. 10, and $\sigma\acute{\alpha}\rho\xi$, v. 11) participation in the experience of Jesus. In a similar pattern, as Paul ends his allusions to ecstatic prayer in Romans 8, he places those thoughts in contrast to experiences of suffering (Rom 8:35–39).

This conjunction of suffering and ecstasy has two immediate implications in the context of this study. At the most pragmatic level, Paul's several circumstances of severe pain through injury and accident provide a probable occasion for alterations in consciousness. In the first section of this chapter, I described the efficacy of physical extremes – fasting, sensory deprivation, prolonged activity, and the like – in inducing both low-level and peak ecstatic experiences.[69] With that fact in mind, Paul's frequent references to occasions of suffering bear consideration. Any of the punishments Paul mentions in his list of hardships (beating with rods,[70] flogging, stoning, imprisonment[71]) was capable of inflicting the sort of bodily response that triggers the ascendancy of limbic functions and a more focused tuning of nervous system activity. He does not say that the experience of suffering was the direct cause of ecstasy – in fact, in his interpretation of events (2 Cor 12:7–10), he suggests the opposite dynamic – but still he holds them together.

---

[68] See especially John T. Fitzgerald, *Cracks in an Earthen Vessel: An Examination of the Catalogues of Hardships in the Corinthian Correspondence,* Society of Biblical Literature Dissertation Series 99 (Atlanta: Scholars Press, 1988), 166–80.

[69] In addition to details already outlined, Joseph (*Neuropsychiatry, Neuropsychology, and Clinical Neurology,* 280–82) reports the personal accounts of a number of documented out-of-body experiences that occurred spontaneously during traumatic and life-threatening events. Furthermore, a number of societies that have established traditions of mediums or other ecstatic practitioners use austerities and even toxic levels of botanical extracts to induce and teach control of ASC; for examples, see Narby and Huxley, *Shamans through Time,* 67–68, 170–74, 253–54.

[70] Cicero's account (*Against Verres* II.5.140–42) of Gaius Servilius's death from injuries inflicted during his beating with rods bears graphic witness to the severity of this Roman punishment.

[71] Cassidy's study of incarceration in the Roman empire provides the concrete details of various sorts of deprivation. See Richard J. Cassidy, *Paul in Chains: Roman Imprisonment and the Letters of St. Paul* (New York: Crossroad, 2001).

The significance of the combination is furthered by the fact that Paul seems to have practiced voluntary austerities as well (1 Cor 9:24–27).

On another level, some of Paul's comments suggest that he had pondered the coincidence of suffering and ecstasy at some depth. It is true that Paul's reports of his own suffering can be accounted for in part by conventions of self-presentation. John Fitzgerald convincingly demonstrates the coherence of Paul's comments with the general tenor of Greco-Roman philosophical commitments to strength of character. That apologetic purpose is very likely sufficient to account for Paul's choice to speak about his occasions of suffering (θλῖψις). Nonetheless, it remains a significant curiosity that the two sets of experiences – suffering and ecstasy – are brought together repeatedly in his discourse. That Paul should adopt a common pattern of self-commendation is not unexpected, but nothing predicts that he should regularly pair it with statements of ecstatic knowledge. The force of the connection is especially evident in 2 Cor 4:10–11. In that passage, Paul asserts that he is always "bearing about" the death of Jesus in order that the life of Jesus might be manifested in his body and flesh. The statement implies more than mere coincidence of circumstances; rather it suggests an intimate, almost causal, connection in Paul's thinking. The sections that follow suggest similar points of contact.

3.3 PAUL'S BODY OF KNOWLEDGE

Another set of texts deals more specifically with the body as the literal site of Paul's religious ecstasy. These texts also speak more directly to the issues of transformation and participation raised at the beginning of the chapter. However, before examining them, it will be helpful to consider briefly Paul's anthropology of the body per se.[72] The parameters of Paul's understanding of the human body are typically defined as the Hebraic and Hellenistic. The danger in discussing ancient anthropological concepts is that they are easily overstated and overcircumscribed, as if the ancient understanding of "body" was just one thing for each group, which in turn could easily be set against that group's similarly singular view of "soul" or "spirit." Furthermore, in

---

[72] The literature on this topic is vast, as are the primary sources that are available for comparison, but in the present context I can only summarize some of the most fundamental features. Some classic works that deal with Pauline anthropology are Rudolf Bultmann, *Theology of the New Testament*, vol. 1 (New York: Scribner, 1951), 191–246; John A. T. Robinson, *The Body: A Study in Pauline Theology*, Studies in Biblical Theology 5 (London: SCM Press, 1952); and Robert Horton. Gundry, *Sōma in Biblical Theology: With Emphasis on Pauline Anthropology*, Society for New Testament Studies Monograph Series 29 (Cambridge: Cambridge University Press, 1976).

discussions of Pauline literature, the temptation is to set Jewish views and Hellenistic views over and against one another as discretely bounded options – the wheat and the chaff (or vice versa) of the Pauline harvest.[73]

Against this tendency, Mary Douglas cautions that "[p]erhaps all social systems are built on contradiction, in some sense at war with themselves."[74] In other words, in most social discourse, the real conversation is conducted somewhere in the messy middle of idealized parameters. For example, Howard Eilberg-Schwartz fills in his sense of the fundamental tension that infused the ancient Jewish culture of the body. On the one hand, there existed the strong affirmation that the embodied human being was created in the image of God, the divine injunction to be sexually active, and the permanent marking of the (male) body with a sign of membership among the people of God. On the other hand was the persistent (though not sole) view that God actually had no body, the inherently polluting nature of sexual contact and female physical maturity, and the Levitical preoccupation with regulating the body.[75] Dale Martin provides a similarly complex picture of the available options within Greco-Roman discourse about the body. The messy middle of Greco-Roman conversations was bounded by the Platonic opposition of body and soul; the Aristotelian sense that the body is the form that the soul takes; and the Stoic distinction between different types of substances, one bodily and another spiritual.[76]

Yet even within this range of options and mixture of tensions, a number of commentators have determined that Paul's "somatology" is distinctive. For example, Daniel Boyarin describes Paul's comments as an "astonishing combination" of "a biblical 'positive' sensibility toward the *body*, combined with a Hellenistic/platonistic devaluation of the *physical*." According to Boyarin, Paul resolves these tensions by positing a spiritual body in addition to a physical one. Furthermore, Boyarin observes that the resulting "dyadic conjunctures are so necessary or so obvious in Paul's thought that he can use

---

[73] The extremities of Jewish anthropology are marked by the purported absence of any single word for the body in Hebrew because it is frequently noted that Hebrew lacks any real word for human anatomy as an integral, living whole. See, for example, Robinson, *Body*, 11–16. In the Septuagint, *sōma* translates thirteen different terms. Typically, *sōma* substitutes for words that indicate the body in the sense of machine or tool, especially as a reference to slaves (e.g., Gen 47:18; Neh 9:37). It is also used for corpse or carcass (e.g., Judg 14:8, 9; 1 Sam 31:10, 12; Nah 3:3; Ps 110:6).

[74] Mary Douglas, *Purity and Danger: An Analysis of Concepts of Pollution and Taboo* (London: Routledge and Kegan Paul, 1976), 141.

[75] Howard Eilberg-Schwartz, "The Problem of the Body for the People of the Book," in *Reading Bibles, Writing Bodies*, ed. Timothy K. Beal and David M. Gunn (London: Routledge, 1997), 34–55.

[76] Dale B. Martin, *The Corinthian Body* (New Haven, Conn.: Yale University Press, 1955), 3–37.

them as a logical argument. He says: If there is a physical body, there must be a spiritual body as well."[77] Segal characterizes Paul's language of the resurrection body, in particular, as "entirely unique." He elaborates:

> The term for physical body is not exactly what one might expect. Neither the term [*sōma sarkikon*] nor the term [*sōma physikon*] occurs; rather the term which occurs is [*sōma psychikon*], a word which can mean *natural body* but is not the most obvious term, since it is a combination of the term for soul and the term for body . . . [*psychē*] could be taken to mean life in the physical sense.[78]

Indeed, what seems most surprising about Paul's anthropology is his effort to retain "body" as a positive, or at least neutral, aspect of the human condition.[79] Paul protects the positive valences of *sōma* by introducing *sarx* as a counterpoint in many statements. When he distinguishes various aspects of humanness, the spiritual and the fleshly mark out the end points. Still, in either case – in the flesh or in the spirit – there is, for Paul, a body. Whether the influences for this Pauline pattern are due to Hebraic[80] or Hellenistic influences,[81] it is clear that Paul had options and that from among them he has chosen to emphasize quite consistently the relatively positive value of the body and the persistent embodiment of the individual, whether according to the flesh or the spirit. That state of affairs is perhaps most apparent in 1 Corinthians 6:12–20. The passage is part of a larger section of paraenesis that includes Paul's judgment on the case of incest (1 Cor 5:1–13), advice against lawsuits (1 Cor 6:1–8), and a list of vices (1 Cor 6:9–11). Paul then begins a short discourse on the body that outlines the orientation that will guide the Corinthians in all their deliberations. In this section, he contrasts sexual ecstasy and religious ecstasy as analogous forms of bodily union.[82] In either case, the ecstatic is joined, bodily, to the object of

---

[77] Boyarin, *A Radical Jew: Paul and the Politics of Identity* (Berkeley: University of California Press, 1994) 61.

[78] Segal, "Paul's Thinking about Resurrection and Its Jewish Context," 417.

[79] Here I refer not to Paul's appropriation of the political trope of the body as society (1 Cor 12:12–27), a borrowing that is thoroughly explored in, among others, M. Mitchell, *Paul and the Rhetoric of Reconciliation.*

[80] Robinson, *Body*, 14–16, on the basis of the observation that Hebrew has no real word for body but only for flesh.

[81] For example, Segal ("Paul's Thinking about Resurrection and Its Jewish Context," 418) suggests that Paul's position is like that of "a very sophisticated minority opinion in Greek culture, thinking that everything, even the soul, is a kind of body."

[82] For a description of the trance phenomena related to orgasm but paralleled in religious ecstasy (including the experience of union and euphoria), see Mosher, "Three Dimensions of Depth of Involvement in Human Sexual Response"; and L. Swartz, "Absorbed State Play Different Roles in Female and Male Sexual Response."

his (or her) attentions – but sex creates one flesh (1 Cor 6:16), and union with Christ creates one spirit (1 Cor 6:17). Paul describes sexual immorality as a sin against one's own body and therefore different from every other sin (1 Cor 6:18), and he concludes with the claim that one's body is the temple of the holy spirit (1 Cor 6:19).

Of course, the body is not always only positive for Paul. Like many people who are aged or suffering, from time to time he can imagine, and even relish, escaping it (Phil 1:21–24). But more often he continues to assert it in the conversation, especially in relation to transformation and life after death. That pattern, even in the face of some deviation, deserves attention in itself.

3.3.1 Transformation and Union

Paul speaks often of his knowledge of and hope for the transformation of the faithful. The strong claim of bodily transformation is present in both Romans 8 and 2 Corinthians 3–5, discussed earlier. I have already described Paul's depiction of an unfiltered vision of the glorious Christ in the latter text. He says further that all the faithful are being transformed into that image "from one degree of glory to another" (2 Cor 3:18). That passage includes other indications that the body is the site of the knowledge Paul is discussing. The evocative metaphor of a clay vessel containing treasure draws attention primarily to the contrast between the two states – one common and cheap, the other rare and valued. But the metaphor also communicates the understanding that the body, the "innerness" of it, is the locale of revelation. It is within the vessel of the body that the glorious Christ is known. In Rom 8:18–23, Paul characterizes that somatic transformation by describing the present bondage to decay (v. 21) and the eventual liberation of bodies (v. 23). In the end, this bodily redemption will conform to the image of the risen Christ, the "firstborn among many siblings" (v. 29). Thus, the somatic transformation releases bodies from degeneration and renders them "incorruptible." That understanding is thoroughly elaborated in 1 Corinthians 15.

Transformation is also closely related to intimacy with Christ. Paul speaks of that intimacy in various ways. Most commonly he does so simply through his habitual reference to being "in Christ" or "with Christ." Not every one of his uses of the phrase is indicative of significant reflection on his relationship to Christ; as mentioned, this language often appears to be habitual rather than volitional. Still, that habit of speech in itself suggests "how much the language and the perspective it embodied had become an integral part of the warp and woof" of Paul's thought.[83] Paul can also talk about "putting on Christ" (Gal 3:27) and longing for Christ to be "formed within" the people (Gal 4:19).

A number of explanations have been offered for Paul's conviction regarding transformation and union with Christ. Frequently, his understanding is thought to be compelled by his conviction of the dawning of the eschaton.[84] Others see the image of the corporate Christ as originative and argue that all other uses of participation language are derived from the social metaphor.[85] For John A. T. Robinson, the varied and realistic language of union that Paul coins is necessitated by "the painful inadequacy of language to convey the unique 'withness' that Christians have in Christ."[86] With his usual eye for a cultural parallel, Segal argues that Paul is using "an established ancient language of transformation" to describe the conversion from his former, preconversion life to his present circumstances.[87] A final example of the restriction of this language comes from Douglas Moo, who illustrates the persistence of Protestant misrepresentations of ecstatic experience: "Even though it has been popular to call this union a 'mystical' one, this language is best avoided as suggesting an ontological or natural union. In the case of both Adam and Christ, the union between them and those whom they represent is primarily – and in Christ's case perhaps exclusively – forensic."[88]

As an alternative to these positions, I would argue that Paul felt himself to be "gloriously" transformed through his religious ecstasy and that those experiences inspired his thinking about a corporate body of Christ. Paul's transformation is based on the distinctive pattern of religious ecstasy during which signals from the body are neurologically blocked (deafferentation) while, simultaneously, higher-level somatic processing centers remain active. The combination facilitates a general awareness of having a body, but it eliminates the perception of the body's weight, pressure, strain, and aching. The analgesia and euphoria of trance along with the numbing of normal

---

[83] Dunn, *Theology of Paul the Apostle*, 398.

[84] Douglas J. Moo, *The Epistle to the Romans*, New International Commentary on the New Testament (Grand Rapids, Mich.: Eerdmans, 1996), 392, summarizing the opinion of several authors.

[85] Robert C. Tannehill, *Dying and Rising with Christ: A Study in Pauline Theology*, Beiheft zur Zeitschrift für die neutestamentliche Wissenschaft und die Kunde der älteren Kirche 32 (Berlin: Töpelmann, 1967), 24. Tannehill combines eschatology and the notion of a corporate Christ. He writes that "Christ, as inclusive person, represents and embodies the new dominion in himself."

[86] Robinson, *Body*, 63.

[87] Segal, *Paul the Convert*, 28 (also 22). In this case, the similarity in language is quite loose and hardly indicative of dependence, as Segal admits (23).

[88] Moo, *Epistle to the Romans*, 395.

neurological information about the body offer physical confirmation of this altered sense of the self and the possibility of somatic transformation. The stripping away of the body is one component of the transformation. The expression of union with Christ is another. Furthermore, because these experiences are vital and compelling, and because they linger even after the ASC has ended, Paul can speak about a transformation that is already under way but not yet completed. What has taken conceptual form in Paul's reflections is what is *experienced* in religious ecstasy. These are some of the epistemological correlates of Paul's ecstasy.

One final example will serve to illustrate another level of knowing that can accompany ecstatic religious experience. The letter to the Philippians contains a number of comments related to bodily knowledge of transformation. In his reflections regarding his imprisonment and possible death, Paul speaks of his hopes in bodily terms: "It is my eager anticipation and hope that I will be put to shame in nothing, but in all boldness – as always even now – Christ will be magnified/greatly manifested ($\mu\epsilon\gamma\alpha\lambda\nu\nu\theta\dot\eta\sigma\epsilon\tau\alpha\iota$) *in my body* whether through life or through death" (Phil 1:20). The concreteness of the statement is inescapable; Paul's body is the site within which Christ is presented. Notwithstanding that clear implication, biblical translations demonstrate various attempts to make the statement meaningful in a context where such experience is too alien to be taken literally. The NRSV glosses $\pi\alpha\rho\rho\eta\sigma\dot\iota\alpha$ with the phrase "by my speaking in all boldness." Because $\pi\alpha\rho\rho\eta\sigma\dot\iota\alpha$ often refers to speech, the gloss is not unreasonable. However, it also has the effect of transforming Paul's statement into a metaphor. In the reworded form, it is Paul's speech that magnifies Christ, not his body.[89] Paul goes on to claim that to live is Christ and to die even more so (Phil 1:21). At this point, he abandons talk of the body to refer to continuing on "in the flesh" because now his attention is also shifting away from ecstatic knowledge to his ordinary work among the Philippians (Phil 1:22–25).

In Philippians 1, Paul expresses some of the adaptive value of ecstatic experience. As he anticipates a possible death sentence and his own execution, he draws on his experience of union with Christ. The neurocognitive

---

[89] Other translations subvert the somatic investment of the statement by substituting some other word for body. So, the NEB not only glosses $\pi\alpha\rho\rho\eta\sigma\dot\iota\alpha$ but also transforms the rest of the verse to say that Paul hopes "the greatness of Christ will shine out clearly in my *person*." The REB avoids the problem more subtly by substituting "in me" for "in my body," and Today's English Version uses "my whole self." Both of these options obscure the concrete, somatic context of Paul's statement by substituting vocabulary that refers to abstracted identity.

experience of temporarily sharing the identity of the exalted Christ is now "written" on Paul's person. Michael Winkelman, whose work will be discussed in greater detail in the next chapter, has considered some of the epistemological benefits of occasions of mystical union and spirit possession. He suggests that these experiences offer "a mechanism for the incorporation of various 'others' in the development of self."[90] Janice Boddy details similar effects in her essay on spirit possession. She describes spirit possession as a means for drawing on ways of knowing that are "quite different from the infinitely differentiating, rationalizing, and reifying thrust" of most of our thinking.[91] Boddy further emphasizes that in ecstatic experience "the body is the ground for legitimating objective knowledge, internalizing it, and making it experientially real."[92] Thus, through religious experience, Paul's very body came to contain the perception that he was not alone and that the strength of others – in particular, the strength of Christ, to whom he was joined in trance – was available to him. It is one thing for Paul to assent to the idea that he has divine protection and quite another for him to have experienced the nearness and tangibility of that idea through the transformation of his own body. Paul has, quite literally within himself, the resources on which he can draw if the time comes to face execution. As he contemplates that possibility from prison, the fear that accompanies these possibilities is a natural stimulus to (and sign of) limbic system tuning that would help to trigger the somatic memory of union.[93]

Later in the letter to the Philippians,[94] in a section commonly taken as reflection on his conversion, Paul addresses the ledger of his life. As he accounts for it, the various goods of his life have been handed over in trade

[90]   Winkelman, *Shamanism*, 162.
[91]   Janice Boddy, "Spirit Possession Revisited: Beyond Instrumentality," *Annual Review of Anthropology* 23 (1994), 407.
[92]   Boddy, "Spirit Possession Revisited," 425.
[93]   Paul may be drawing on similar resources at the end of his letter to the Galatians. Throughout, Paul has been pleading with the Galatians not to abandon the gospel as he had originally delivered it. He heaps one appeal on top of another and even resorts to taking up the pen in his own maladroit hand (Gal 6:11). But in the end, it seems he is not at all confident of his success in turning them back to the original preaching. He despairs of convincing them, wishes peace to those who follow his standard of new creation (6:15), and commands no more trouble from the rest (Gal 6:17a). Finally, he declares that he bears the *stigmata* of Jesus in his body (Gal 6:17b). That last declaration has the tone of self-consolation about it. Paul's own resources may have failed, but he is reassured in the face of such strong opposition (and failure in his task) by his bodily knowledge of communion with Jesus.
[94]   For the purposes of my examination, theories of partition need not be settled definitively. The fact that Paul's ecstatic comments to the Philippians appear in what may have originally been separate letters does not change their meaning in their immediate context.

for "the surpassing value of knowing Christ Jesus my Lord" (Phil 3:7–8).
Paul goes on to describe the nature of that knowledge in participatory terms.
He uses the startling phrases "participation of his sufferings" and "being
conformed to his death" (Phil 3:10). Generations of interpretation have
tempered the force of the second phrase in particular. With these words,
Paul speaks of a union that is not comfortably idealized but rather is rooted
in unexpected combinations of participation and sensation. Perhaps the
forcefulness of the statement strikes Paul, too, because he immediately soft-
ens its impact by insisting that he has not yet been perfected in this way but
that he is able to continue because "Christ Jesus has made me his own" (Phil
3:12). After encouraging the Philippians to imitate his perseverance, Paul
ends the section with a claim that combines somatic transformation with
a sense of union with Christ (Phil 3:21): Christ "will transfigure the body of
our humiliation to conformity with the body of his glory."

3.3.2 Embodying Death

As in his letter to the Philippians, a number of Paul's other comments about
union with Christ focus on sharing Christ's death. Some of these comments
are second-order reflections, but others suggest a more immediate translation of experience into words. For example, in Gal 2:19–20, Paul says that
he has been crucified with Christ and their identities are now intermingled;
Paul no longer lives, but Christ lives in him. I have already discussed this
imagery as it appears in Phil 3:10. Foremost, though, among these texts is
Paul's description of baptism as "being buried with Christ through baptism
into death" (Rom 6:4).[95] The context of the passage is that of ritual initiation
by baptism, and the practice of baptism on behalf of the dead in Corinth
(1 Cor 15:29) suggests a powerful sense of ritual efficacy within that community at least. The imagery of crucifixion is secondary, but through it Paul
communicates the same sense of participation and union described in the
preceding section. For example, Paul strings together a chain of σύν
compounds: buried with (Rom 6:4), grown with (Rom 6:5), crucified with
(Rom 6:6), and live with (Rom 6:8). The passage also speaks of being baptized "into (εἰς) Christ Jesus." Because of this emphasis, the conceptualiza-
tion of baptism is different in this passage than elsewhere in Paul's letters.[96]
That difference is characterized especially by the association with death.

---

[95] See also Col 1:24.
[96] Hans Dieter Betz, "Transferring a Ritual: Paul's Interpretation of Baptism in Romans 6," in
Paul in His Hellenistic Context, ed. Troels Endberg-Pederson (Minneapolis: Fortress, 1995),
85–86.

The connection between death and union with Christ has been accounted for in various ways. As with Paul's language of transformation, the most common suggestion is that Paul has a compelling sense of the beginning of a new age and that a change in eras demands a dramatic break with the past, a break that is described as a death.[97] But another explanation is possible. In some cultures, practitioners of ASC interpret some of their ecstatic experiences as a process of death and reconstitution. This "death" is sometimes experienced as dismemberment or the unhinging of body parts or sometimes the stripping away of flesh. Common, too, is the sensation that one is viewing the scene of "self-destruction" from above.[98] These interpretations are closely paralleled by the phenomena of near-death and so-called out-of-body experiences, which are being treated with increasing seriousness in neuroscientific studies.[99] According to Winkelman, the perception of dismemberment is an intelligible attempt to interpret the rearrangement of ego structures that occurs during trance. That is to say, our sense of ourselves as stable and discrete beings depends on all those neurognostic means of creating and maintaining an enduring image of self within the changing environment around us. This sense of self is built from elements like "area 7" of the parietal lobe as well as the cortical maps of motor and sensory modalities (discussed in Chapter 2). Typically we are aware of this self-generating process only when it is interrupted by extraordinary circumstances.

The fact that we exist unaware, for the most part, of much of the information available to us from our bodies is really a survival mechanism. Damasio suggests that our selective, externally focused "consciousness has succeeded in evolution precisely because it supports life most beautifully."[100] Our visual system and other parts of our brain and central nervous system are occupied with mapping the world around us, taking in a wide scope of information and ranging broadly in their attention. This external focus allows the organism to respond to unexpected threats and opportunities, but the cost of this outward attention is a lack of conscious awareness of our own bodies. In contrast to this wide field of interest of the conscious mind, the neurological circuits that map our own "organism" are tuned to a very narrow and discretely bounded "object." Survival of any individual also

---

[97] See, for example, Dunn, *Theology of Paul the Apostle*, 403.
[98] Winkelman, *Shamanism*, 82. Some traditions teach that the eyes of the adept have been removed and placed above the scene. These death experiences, as they relate to shamanism, will be discussed further in Chapter 5.
[99] See, for example, the discussion in Joseph, *Neuropsychiatry, Neuropsychology, and Clinical Neurology*, 280–86.
[100] Damasio, *Feeling of What Happens*, 135.

depends on the maintenance of quite a narrow range of internal fluctuation (e.g., blood sugar levels, core temperature, tissue regeneration, hydration), but organisms have evolved so that this range can usually be maintained automatically, without our attention. Damasio describes the limitedness of these internal circuits. They are, he says, "the body's captive audience, and they are at the mercy of the body's dynamic sameness."[101] I discussed some aspects of this mapping of the self as object in the previous chapter. Here I would emphasize again that the knowledge of this mapping is mainly invisible to us. That this knowledge can function at a nonconscious level shows that "the brain knows more than the conscious mind reveals."[102] Only when the change in the map of the self is critically altered is that hidden information brought to consciousness. The knowledge of the body exists unobserved until the stability of the self-image is dismantled in circumstances such as ASC.

Thus, a number of factors have come together to inspire Paul's comments about dying with Christ. The dramatic circumstances of Jesus' death are one of these factors, as is Paul's own circumstantial suffering, documented in his catalogs of hardships. Through the various neurophysiological effects of ecstasy, he experienced his own bodily transformation, including the deafferentation of the orientation association area, which permitted his profound sense of union with Christ. However, it may very well be that his experience of neurocognitive "self-destruction" encouraged the combination of these details in a rich and adaptive synthesis. The death of Christ was repeated in Paul's own person, and Christ's new spiritual existence was temporarily made tangible within Paul as well.

3.4 CONCLUSION

The discussion in the previous chapter was necessarily limited to a single event in order to assess it thoroughly in some neurological detail. Here the scope has been wider, both in terms of the number and sorts of texts under consideration and in the move from the intimacy of a single, essentially private, perhaps superlative event to multiple conversations and public occasions reflected in Paul's correspondence. Talk of ecstatic experience – including Paul's visions of the risen Jesus and his practice of ecstatic prayer – was part of a public discourse between Paul and the christian assemblies to which he wrote. That he shares these details as a matter of course in his letters is of more than passing interest. Paul's ecstasy is part of his public

[101] Ibid., 22.
[102] Ibid., 92.

persona. In Romans 8 and 2 Corinthians 3–5, he uses it as evidence of his claims about the gospel in ways that suggest he is appealing to shared knowledge. This public character is evidenced nowhere more than in the correspondence with the Corinthians, the community with whom Paul had the most written contact (at least based on the extant evidence). But that fact makes it all the more noteworthy that ecstatic talk also registers in Paul's letter to the Romans – a community with which he has no personal history.

In this chapter, I have also discussed the ways in which such experiences are incorporated into human knowing. The neurocognitive phenomena of ecstatic religious experience generate a sense of shared identity. That experience creates in Paul the "inner" resources that make the death of Jesus a transformative force in Paul's own life. In other words, Paul's own neural networks have been imprinted with his apprehension of the risen Jesus. In these cases, by placing experience before discourse, the resulting exegesis explains some of the unusual features of Paul's thought – especially his so-called Christ-mysticism – more satisfactorily than traditional theological readings can. It also provides a more satisfactory picture of Paul's process of coming to know and his speech about that knowledge. For example, when one privileges established doctrinal categories as the hermeneutical key for Paul's discourse, the text is read as a fait accompli, as if there were no process in Paul's understanding but only conclusion. Most often, epistemology is simply ignored. Because the texts themselves are normative, there is no coming to know but only knowledge.

By now, the importance of the body in ecstatic states should be clear – both the physical body that experiences the lasting effects of neurochemical transformation and the neurocognitive "as if"[103] body, whose boundaries are dissolved during trance. The body so understood is a significant background to Paul's comments about the transformation of his own *sōma* and the future somatic transformation of all Christians. His delineation of the two ways (spirit and flesh) coheres with the experience of someone for whom religious experience is a significant neurological reality. Further, his persistent language of union with Christ ceases to be so puzzling when it is understood not as the synthetic product of Paul's heroic reasoning[104] but as a reflection of the physical experience of religious ecstasy.

---

[103] As I have mentioned, this descriptor (i.e., "as-if"), discussed in Chapter 2, is Damasio's shorthand for the neurocognitive representation of the whole body in the cortex, which stores and recreates much of the fullness of original bodily experience as if it were actually happening again (Damasio, *Descartes' Error*, 184).

[104] Albert Schweitzer, who, as I have said, popularized the term Christ-mysticism, also argued that Paul developed it out of the application of "ruthless logic" (*gewalttätig*) to the circumstances of history (*Mysticism of Paul the Apostle*, 111). Schweitzer goes so far as to beatify Paul as "the patron saint of thought in Christianity" (ibid., 377).

The fact that ecstasy is a prevalent part of Paul's conversations leads naturally to the question of its role in community life. Therefore, in the next chapter, I turn to considering the social circumstances in which ecstatic practice might be possible and meaningful in the christian communities. The Corinthian correspondence offers the clearest example of such practice. It also offers the greatest potential challenge to the positive details I have been amassing so far.

4

ॐ

Paul's Practice: Discerning Ecstasies in Practice

Revival services are not simply theatre or variety shows; Revivalists are "making a joyful noise unto the Lord." Ritual art takes place in a cosmic or sacred context. It is used to express beliefs that give meaning and purpose to existence, and it also makes existence seem beautiful.

– William Wedenoja

Do not confuse your finger with the moon.

– Zen proverb

IN THE LAST CHAPTER, I DISCUSSED A NUMBER OF POINTS AT which Paul speaks of ecstasy (and out of ecstasy) as a matter of course, without elaboration or qualification. At these times, ecstatic knowledge and practice are something he takes for granted and even invokes in the service of other – disputed – topics (for example, his apostleship). At other times, however, Paul raises the issue of religious ecstasy in order to clarify its practice or significance in a particular context (for example, glossolalia in Corinth). When this full range of talk of ecstasy is considered, the resulting discourse is complex and nuanced. For that reason, this chapter will seek an alternative to the common procedure of assigning Paul to one side or the other in an artificial binary assessment of religious ecstasy. Instead, this chapter strives to place Paul's comments within a coherent sense of the social dynamics of this public practice. What social logic might undergird Paul's statements? What kind of social power does this sort of religious experience wield in Christian origins? How is religious ecstasy controlled and interpreted within communities? What place does it have in Paul's understanding of himself and his authority as an apostle of Christ?

In Chapter 2, I used the findings of neurological science to illuminate the inner world of experience. In this chapter, the anthropological descriptions of groups that accommodate particular types of ASCs will serve as the template with which to organize the disparate details of these neurological phenomena and practices into patterns of social dynamics. Despite the fact that many forms of ASC appear to be possible in any given population, only some modes are accommodated by any given social group. Practices such as shamanism, spirit possession, and mediumship (to use the most common taxonomies) are welcomed in some groups and not in others. Some expressions are normalized, and their practitioners hold a specific role in the community. Others, although they may be normalized, are occasional and are understood as expressions of specific kinds of social problems or remedies. In still other cases, if someone shows particular signs of dissociation, they are considered more or less deviant; in other words, there is no socially established category to which they are seen to belong. Thus, although ASC may be a universal human capacity, not every society has accepted patterns of behavior or social roles for those who express it. Necessarily, then, one must consider the connection between the circumstances of the society and the accepted form of ASC.

Nonetheless, even in the midst of such variation, many societies explicitly distinguish between two general types of socially relevant ASCs: one that is the result of the spirit(s) possessing the individual and one that is the result of the individual "mastering" the spirit(s). Furthermore, these societies tend to assign distinct roles or statuses to practitioners according to which option they exercise. These distinctions are not unlike those that Paul makes, for he, too, imagines different kinds of spiritual experiences and also distinguishes them from one another on the basis of control or mastery of the experience. In short, although much exegesis of 1 Corinthians 12–14 characterizes Paul's instructions as the rejection of an ecstatic and irrational practice and promotion of an ordinary and rational one, that dichotomy represents an unhelpful narrowing of the question. For one thing, Paul does not make such a distinction. For another, the rational–irrational dichotomy depends on a narrow (logocentric) understanding of ecstatic religious experience as well as a lack of attention to the fact that it is typically practiced in a socially defined setting that can be generalized.[1] For these reasons, the social anthropology of altered states of

---

[1]   Here I do not refer to the very specific social circumstances of Corinth in the mid-50s CE, which have received an excellent level of attention and description. Instead, I mean to highlight the way in which the peculiar circumstances of this community might reflect patterns that can be generalized across social groupings.

consciousness provides a useful approach to begin to sort Paul's multifold talk of ecstasy.

This chapter compares the variety of ecstatic practices in Corinth with the social anthropological categories of shamanism, spirit possession, and mediumship. The comparison serves heuristic purposes; it is not intended to be some kind of species identification. This is so particularly because (as should already be clear from earlier chapters) I consider shamanism to be a quite specific social and neurological phenomenon that is most useful when its boundaries are kept firmly in mind. Paul was not a shaman. Nonetheless, a clear sense of the social and phenomenological patterns of shamanism help to highlight the distinctive profile of Paul's practice. The picture we have of Corinth from Paul's letters is little more than a snapshot of a moving target. Certainly this is the case with regard to the ecstatic practices of the assembly. Such activities are still being negotiated, and the community appears to have written to Paul partly in the hopes of getting them sorted.[2] Given that state of flux, the more firmly defined categories of possession, mediumship, and shamanism provide some comparative clarity of focus. These points of comparison show both what could come to be in Corinth and why the practices as they existed at the time may have been contentious.

In this discussion, then, I will assess "Pauline pneumatology" as a form of spirit possession. Likewise, some of Paul's own practices of ASC will be assessed for their fit within the category of soul journey, which includes shamanism.[3] For example, how does he invoke his visions in his communications with Christian assemblies? Does he interpret his own experience as

---

[2]   The uncertainty of the Corinthian community is signaled by the fact that this section of the letter begins with another of the $\pi\epsilon\rho\grave{\iota}$ $\delta\acute{\epsilon}$ ("now concerning . . .") clauses (1 Cor 12:1). As is widely recognized, this phrase serves as Paul's formal transition to each of the topics in the letter he received from the Corinthian assembly and therefore indicates their desire for his counsel about *pneumatika*, or "spiritual things."

[3]   The terminology for this mode of consciousness is diverse and unsystematized. Townsend and others use the phrase "shamanic states of consciousness" (SSC) to distinguish the neurological conditions that allow an experience of soul journey from those that are interpreted as spirit possession. See also Harner, *Way of the Shaman*, 20–30, 46–56. Although shamanism is often used as a designation for this category, the term is so tangled up in the politics of its misuse (I have discussed its history in Chapter 1) that it has become nearly impossible to use it helpfully. The term also tends to highlight social role over phenomenology. Bourguignon uses "trance," but this term likewise seems too generally applied in popular culture to escape those many associations. Although "soul journey" is also imperfect, it has the advantage of relatively few associations and holds together some balance of both cultural interpretation and neurological phenomena. I will use it throughout this chapter to refer to a phase of consciousness and reserve the term shaman(ism) for a particular social role that uses soul journey.

being different from theirs? Finally, I will provide an account for the other *pneumatika* that Paul highlights, especially prophecy. Throughout the ensuing discussion, I attend both to the apparent neurological differences between the various forms of ASC and to the way they are typically deployed in communities in order to explore with additional depth and nuance the customary observation that Paul is promoting the communal good in Corinth.

One of the milestones in the study of the anthropology of ecstatic practice is the thorough documentation project conducted by Erika Bourguignon in the 1960s. Bourguignon headed a five-year study of ethnographic records of societies distributed throughout the major ethnographic regions of the world. The study established that 90 percent of the societies for which relevant information was available practiced some form of culturally or socially acknowledged trance. Based on cultural interpretation of the ecstatic behavior, the study further distinguished between forms of ASC that involve possession trance and those that do not. The practitioners who were understood to be under control of the spirits were routinely identified as practicing spirit possession and, for the purposes of the Bourguignon study, those who were identified as controlling the spirits were grouped together in the category of trance.[4]

The data cataloged in that original study also permitted recognition of a number of other factors relevant to the use of ASC that have since been studied more carefully. First, the available data allowed the observation that the type of ecstatic practice varies with the degree of stratification in the host society. This link between social structure on the one hand and religious practice on the other opened the way for more richly contextual assessments of ASC in religious contexts. Second, the project helped to expand the focus of the study of ASC beyond the emphasis on the individual practitioner to its role as a dynamic within community life. As Bourguignon put it:

> When we consider the relationship of religion to change, its double role as a bulwark against change on the one hand and as a mediator or even initiator

---

[4]   The findings and fruits of this study are presented in Erika Bourguignon, *Cross-cultural Study of Dissociational States* (Columbus: Ohio State University Press, 1968); Bourguignon, "World Distribution and Patterns of Possession States," in *Trance and Possession States,* ed. Raymond Prince (Montreal: R. M. Bucke Memorial Society, 1968), 39–60; Bourguignon, "Introduction"; and Bourguignon, *Possession,* Chandler and Sharp Series in Cross-cultural Themes (San Francisco: Chandler and Sharp, 1976). In the years since Bourguignon's study, trance practices have been further distinguished by their use in mediumship, healing, shamanism, and, to some degree, witchcraft.

of change on the other, we often find that key individuals in this process experience altered states of consciousness. It is on this point of juncture – between religious institutions (beliefs, practices, and personnel) and the processes of sociocultural change, where altered states of consciousness may play a critical role.[5]

So it is that two major categories of influence, the neurological and the social, come into play in the experiences in question.

One more preliminary matter requires attention before addressing 1 Corinthians. There is a fourth state (in addition to possession, soul journey, and mediumship) that is sometimes considered to be of religious significance. For some authors, the spectrum of religious experience extends to phenomena resulting from epileptic seizures. The possible connections between epileptic phenomena and others deserve some discussion, especially in light of the fact that, since as early as Albert Schweitzer, people have suggested seizures as the cause of Paul's visions.[6] In Chapter 2, I touched on the work of V. S. Ramachandran with patients who have religious experiences as a result of temporal lobe seizures.[7] Ramachandran's category of "temporal lobe syndrome," or "interictal personality," pertains to rare maladaptive personality effects that seem to result from chronic, pathological stimulation of this region of the brain. For example, in one very small experiment, he measured the galvanic skin response (GSR, a simple indication of arousal levels) of these patients while he showed them a series of words and images. In control groups, all sexual and violent stimuli trigger increased GSR, while most other images produce no change in GSR readings. However, among patients with "temporal lobe personality," religious imagery triggers arousal to the exclusion of all other types of imagery.[8] It may be that the sensitivities of these individuals have been permanently altered in ways that are similar to the changes in some mystics and holy people who have developed their

---

[5] Bourguignon, "Introduction," 4.

[6] Schweitzer, *Mysticism of Paul the Apostle*, 154.

[7] Ramachandran and Blakeslee, *Phantoms in the Brain*, 180–88. Although Ramachandran and Blakeslee's discussion in this book is thin and the authors are clear about their bias against religion, many others are also working in this area. A review of some of the relevant studies is available in David Bear, "Temporal Lobe Epilepsy – A Syndrome of Sensory-Limbic Hyperconnection," *Cortex* 15 (1979), 357–84; and G. W. Fenton, "Psychiatric Disorders of Epilepsy: Classification and Phenomenology," in *Epilepsy and Psychiatry*, ed. E. Reynolds and M. Trimble (New York: Churchill Livingstone, 1981), 12–26.

[8] Ramachandran and Blakeslee, *Phantoms in the Brain*, 188. Although the experiment produced strong results, it included only two patients with temporal lobe seizures. The authors are appropriately insistent on the limitations of its findings. It is suggestive rather than demonstrative.

sensibilities in interaction with a religious or philosophical tradition of interpretation. For his own provocative purposes, Ramachandran suggests that this epileptic form of religious imagery and interest is the same mechanism that produces the other forms.[9]

Setting aside Ramachandran's polemics, these rare epileptic events do help to define distinguishing features of other sorts of religious ecstasy, but largely by way of contrast. Both seizure-related and certain other forms of religious experiences result in long-term changes to the individual's belief system and personality, but the changes are generally very different in character. Wesley Wildman and Leslie Brothers have attempted to distinguish the seizure-related form from what they call "authentic" religious experience. In the pathological form:

> The salient feature is not discrete experiences . . . but an ongoing interest in religious and philosophical matters together with a moralistic attitude, intensified emotions, and a "viscous" interpersonal style. What is notable, as regards the elements of that category (existential potency, social embedding, transformation of behaviour and personality, and transformation of beliefs), is a dissociation of beliefs (which are pronounced in these individuals) from behaviour and character changes of a moral and ethical nature.[10]

By contrast, they report that religious ecstasy that is not the result of disease or injury is associated with behaviors that are integrated more fully into a more coherent pattern of belief and behavior. Whereas the epileptic patients so afflicted become noticeably self-absorbed, ecstatic practitioners, in contrast, typically become more deeply engaged in the world.[11] Whereas the former may display isolated behaviors associated with religion, the latter

---

[9]   There are several other differences between religious states and the effects of seizures. The latter are restricted to the temporal lobe, which has not generated measurable arousal during clinical investigations of religious practitioners, whereas the neural activity of meditators and ecstatics has intensified in the posterior parietal lobe. Findings are reported in Newberg et al., "The Measurement of Regional Cerebral Blood Flow during the Complex Cognitive Task of Meditation: A Preliminary SPECT Study," *Psychiatry Research: Neuroimaging* 106 (2001), 113–22; and Newberg et al., "Cerebral Blood Flow during Meditative Prayer: Preliminary Findings and Methodological Issues," *Perceptual and Motor Skills* 97 (2003), 625–30. Second, the electrical activity of seizures is indiscriminate in its force and distribution, whereas in religious practice, it appears to be dynamically controlled and regionally selective.

[10]   Wildman and Brothers, "Religious Experience," 391.

[11]   Ibid.," 406–7. Although the distinction may be too rigidly drawn, their comments nonetheless highlight real and meaningful differences in experience and its lasting effects.

display full religiosity.[12] Fraser Watts makes a more basic observation about the differences in the emotional character of the two experiences: "The emotional tone of seizure experiences is often disturbing, being associated with an element of anxiety, whereas it is a fairly standard feature of powerful religious experiences occurring in other contexts that they result in a positive emotional tone, even when people have been severely stressed before the experience."[13]

These observations raise many issues, and the factors that may contribute to such differences are myriad and require further study. For example, whereas the behavior patterns that Wildman and Brothers summarized as "full religiosity" could be fueled largely by cultural forces, other characteristics are neurologically dependent. Still, one point is most salient to this discussion: There appear to be a range of neurologically distinct patterns that include powerful religious experience. Perhaps the most distinctive of these patterns is the wholly involuntary nature of temporal lobe seizures. These neurological storms are centered in the temporal lobe but are relatively indiscriminate in their stimulation of the brain, whereas other patterns are voluntary (in varying ways) and seem to entail more discrete stimulation of particular brain centers that are not necessarily proximately located. Furthermore, the evidence suggests that despite the fact that the whole range of experiences can be called "religious," they display important differences in character. Voluntary, ecstatic patterns appear to enhance the personality of the practitioner and sometimes seem to function as a catalyst for the integration of belief and behavior for the long term. In other words, some ecstatic experience affects higher-order cognitive functioning. In the case of epileptic patients, this is not always the case, and in fact some of the most strongly patterned religious behaviors are strikingly isolated from otherwise associated thoughts and actions. Thus, the religious elements of their seizures appear to remain neurologically isolated from other cognitive processes. For these reasons, the suggestion that Paul's visions were caused by epileptic seizures should be laid aside or, at the very least, bracketed as an insufficient explanation. In fact, all of the three types of

[12] David M. Tucker, R. A. Novelly, and P. J. Walker, "Hyperreligiosity in Temporal Lobe Epilepsy: Redefining the Relationship," *Journal of Nervous and Mental Diseases* 175 (1987), 181–84. Very likely cultural influence comes to bear in these circumstances as well, but such influence seems insufficient to account for the distinctions.
[13] Watts, "Cognitive Neuroscience and Religious Consciousness," 333.

religious experience mentioned can be distinguished categorically from such seizures.[14]

So then, in the following discussion, these three remain: glossolalia, Paul's own ecstatic practices, and the category of *pneumatika*. Each section that follows will first outline the phenomenological and anthropological features of the practice before discussing the specifics of Paul's comments in the letter to the Corinthians.

4.1 SPIRIT POSSESSION

4.1.1 *Neurological and Social Anthropological Features*

If we begin again with the interplay between phenomenology and cultural interpretation, the most telling point is that those who are culturally identified as possessed consistently experience their trance possession behavior as outside of their own control.[15] But other, more intriguing phenomena also attend possession. For example, frequently the spirit-possessed do not later remember their own actions while they were in trance. Bourguignon describes the experience as one of "radical discontinuity of personal identity."[16] In addition, possession trance "generally involves the impersonation of spirits – the acting out of their speech or behavior. It does not involve hallucinations, and it is typically followed by amnesia."[17] Etically, this disruption of personality combined with post-trance amnesia is suggestive of a distinct neural experience. Emically, it is also in keeping with the understanding that the individual has been taken over by another being.

---

[14] Possession trance appears to fall somewhere between the peak state I outlined in Chapter 3 and the wholly uncontrolled and sometimes maladaptive experience of temporal lobe seizures. (I assess the maladaptive nature of the latter partly by the fact that the severe and indiscriminate stimulation of seizures damages brain tissues.) The overlap lies in the fact that although the spirit-possessed persons might well control the behaviors that induce their ASCs, they do not seem to exercise as much voluntary control over the pattern of the trance itself.

[15] This pair of characteristics distinguishes spirit possession from circumstances in which an individual is labeled by others in the community as possessed but does not experience ASC or any other possession phenomena. Such "nontrance possession" is really a form of social deviance labeling (or at most is related to witchcraft) and will not be taken up further in this discussion. See Bourguignon, *Possession*, 46, for a description.

[16] Bourguignon, "Introduction," 13. She discusses the phenomenon of amnesia in more detail in Erika Bourguignon, "The Self, the Behavioral Environment and the Theory of Spirit Possession," in *Context and Meaning in Cultural Anthropology*, ed. Milford E. Spiro (New York: Glencoe, 1965).

[17] Bourguignon, "Introduction," 12.

Therefore, it is quite likely that the actual ecstatic experience and its cultural interpretation are mutually influential. The challenge in describing such mutuality is to avoid reductionism – to resist resolving one aspect into the other.

The characteristic neurological nature of possession trance can be elaborated further because possession trance seems to involve a set of neural circuits that are distinct enough to constitute a discrete state of consciousness. The independent cross-cultural study of Michael Winkelman, director of the Ethnographic Field School at Arizona State University, supports this hypothesis. Using a new, smaller, and more thorough set of data than was available to Bourguignon, Winkelman has carried out a level of assessment that was not possible in the earlier study.[18] His results include the finding that possession trance correlates strongly to a characteristic set of neurological factors. In the first place, he corroborates the experience of amnesia.[19] Second, he finds quite consistent occurrence of "tremors or convulsions, and compulsive motor behavior,"[20] indicative of somewhat indiscriminate neural stimulation. It is not difficult to see how this is an experience of the body outside of one's control and thus how the label of possession is not an arbitrary designation of any given society.

Moving from the individual experience to its social context, another feature that correlates strongly with possession trance is political integration and population density. This connection was already identified by Bourguignon and was verified again by Winkelman's research. Bourguignon's study permitted comparison of three types of societies: those with only

[18] The original study of thirty societies selected from G. P. Murdock and D. White, "Standard Cross-Cultural Sample," *Ethnology* 8 (1969), 329–69, is reported in Michael James Winkelman, *Shamans, Priests and Witches: A Cross-cultural Study of Magico-Religious Practitioners*, Anthropological Research Papers 44 (Tempe: Arizona State University Press, 1992).

[19] Memory does sometimes occur in ASCs that are interpreted as possession trances, but amnesia never occurs in other ASC practices (such as soul journey).

[20] Michael Winkelman, "Altered States of Consciousness and Religious Behavior," in *Anthropology of Religion: A Handbook*, ed. Stephen D. Glazier (Westport, Conn.: Praeger, 1999), 413. Such phenomena do appear to place possession trance in a position somewhere between the extreme temporal lobe stimulation and the neurological characteristics of soul journey. Winkelman ("Altered States of Consciousness and Religious Behavior," 414) has found further that societies in which women make up the majority of the spirit-possessed are also those in which women receive inadequate nutrition because of cultural norms. In other words, there could exist a neurophysiological link between their living conditions and the nature of their ASC. I. M. Lewis has famously interpreted this link as one means that women, as a relatively powerless subgroup in most societies, have of influencing the distribution of goods; however, that interpretation seems driven by logo-, ethno-, and egocentric biases. At least it is insufficient to fully account for the experience.

possession trance, those with only nonpossession ASC, and those that
include both. The comparison demonstrated that societies with only possession trance fit a distinctive profile marked most notably by a high degree
of social stratification and complexity, including factors such as slavery,
polygynous marriage, and marriage by bride price.[21] Also significant is the
degree to which economic, subsistence, and settlement patterns predict
possession trance. Possession societies tend to be sedentary and often agri-
culturally dependent. Compared with societies that include belief in (and/
or accusations of) possession but no actual practice of ASC, full-blown
spirit-possession societies are larger, with greater "jurisdictional hierarchy
above the local level."[22] Thus, all other things being equal, the degree of
possession trance in a society increases with the complexity of the society's
organization.

Bourguignon has pursued the link between ASC type and food produc-
tion. Perhaps surprisingly, the two factors correlate with child-rearing practices. As mentioned, possession ASC is commonly normalized in agricultural
societies. In contrast, shamanistic/soul journey ASC is accommodated in
hunter-gatherer societies. Studies of agricultural societies show that "independence, experimentation, and innovation will be discouraged" and
"responsibility, obedience, and nurturance" reinforced because such behaviors are vital to the maintenance of a food supply that requires activity to
conform to the patterns of seasons and weather. In contrast, in hunter-
gatherer societies the nature of food provision requires "self-reliance, independence, initiative."[23] This statistic provides a meaningful link between
subsistence type and ASC type because in spirit possession "the individual
enhances his power and his status by total abdication and self-effacement
before the spirits," whereas "a shaman's chances for achievement are
enhanced by the acquisition of spirit power."[24] This correspondence is supported by William Wedenoja's study of Jamaican Revival groups, for whom

---

[21] Bourguignon, "Introduction," 19, 22–23. The study did not distinguish between occurrences
of positive (cultivated, voluntary, valued) and negative (feared, spontaneous, negatively
evaluated) possession, due in part to the complexity of some cultural interpretations that
tolerated high levels of ambivalence about the benefits of possession (Bourguignon, "Introduction," 28).

[22] Bourguignon, *Possession*, 43; also Winkelman, "Altered States of Consciousness and Religious Behavior," 413.

[23] Bourguignon, *Possession*, 47, discussing the studies in H. Barry III, M. K. Bacon, and
I. L. Child, "Relations of Child Training to Subsistence Economy," in *Cross-cultural
Approaches: Readings in Comparative Research*, ed. C. S. Ford (New Haven, Conn.:
HRAF, 1967).

[24] Bourguignon, *Possession*, 48.

dissociative possession trance and "strong pressure for compliance in Jamaican child rearing" coincide.[25]

4.1.2 Spirit Possession in Corinth

Given that stratification and complexity are correlated with spirit possession, it is not surprising that the letter to the Corinthians should be the one in which spirit possession is of greatest concern because a number of factors combined in that city to heighten the dynamics of social stratification that already marked Roman culture. According to Lee Johnson, these social tensions were born out of the extraordinary political history of the city as well as its economic and geographic circumstances.[26] Corinth's peculiarities distinguish it not only from other cities with which Paul had contact but even those within the empire itself. Chief among these distinctions is the fact that in 44 BCE it was recolonized – predominantly by freedpersons and veterans[27]– after a period of near desertion. Donald Engels suggests that these *liberti* were relocated from Rome partly in an effort to remove a "politically disaffected and volatile" group from the city.[28] Thus, from the beginning, the city was set apart in that a significant portion of its population was socially and politically volatile and of low social status. At the same time, all the new citizens of Corinth had been given an unparalleled opportunity to change their circumstances both by the fact of their resettlement and because of the distinctive economic profile of the city.

The *liberti* in Corinth shared some of the chief conditions of other freedpersons but also differed from that norm in significant ways. Despite having attained manumission, all *liberti* normally remained disadvantaged in a number of ways. Their past continued to be asserted through the requirement that they take their patron's name and wear distinctive dress.

---

[25] Wedenoja, "Ritual Trance and Catharsis," 296. Wedenoja's study further tested for this division of traits in a small sample of adults of the cult and found that those who had experienced possession trance scored much higher on measurements of compliance than did those who belonged to the cult but had not experienced trance.

[26] Lee A. Johnson, "The Epistolary Apostle: Paul's Response to the Challenge of the Corinthian Community" (PhD dissertation, University of St. Michael's College, 2002), 88–132. The following comments draw largely on Johnson's analysis.

[27] Corinth was further distinguished as the only city in the Roman empire apart from Carthage, that was settled by a mostly new population. Other colonies had more substantial indigenous populations to which colonists were added. See A. H. M. Jones, *The Roman Economy: Studies in Ancient Economic and Administrative History* (Oxford: Basil Blackwell, 1974), 3.

[28] Donald W. Engels, *Roman Corinth: An Alternate Model for the Classical City* (Chicago: University of Chicago Press, 1990), 16–17.

Their future was limited by ineligibility for certain positions (praetorian guard, priesthood, and knighthood), by social sanctions against marriage above their own station, and by the persistence of such restrictions to the next generation. However, in Corinth some of the other burdens of freedperson status were removed. First, the resettlement at some distance from Rome meant that the former slaves were, for all intents and purposes, freed of the labor obligations to their former owners. Second, two factors allowed for the economic advancement of these newly minted citizens. For one, all the Corinthian colonists were provided with a parcel of land, and the coastal plain was an excellent generator of agricultural surpluses.[29] For another, the entrepreneurial potential of a trade city as important as Corinth provided further opportunities for economic advancement to all its citizens,[30] and those of low status in particular had nothing to lose in taking up the sorts of trades that were available. The Isthmian Games, the passage provided across the relatively calm Aegean Sea, and the religious activity of the city all offered access to wealth and its use in increasing social standing. So, all the new citizens had correspondingly new potential to improve their living conditions and some to use wealth to earn social influence.

For a time, the Corinthian *liberti* also had the potential to improve their social status beyond the normal limits of freedperson status. When Julius Caesar established the colony, he allowed the *liberti* the possibility of serving in the local senate.[31] Thus, they could use their new wealth to gain social positions normally beyond their reach. However, that possibility came to an end during the reign of Tiberius, shortly before Paul's first visit to the city. Tiberius revoked the law that allowed access to the senate to *liberti*. Meanwhile, all the reminders of Roman domination remained in Corinth, and a number of details suggest the ways in which it was operative there. For example, archaeological evidence indicates the

---

[29] Johnson, "Epistolary Apostle," 90. These parcels amounted to between seven and thirty acres. Engels (*Roman Corinth*, 27–33) makes a convincing argument for the (often underestimated) economic significance of agriculture in the region.

[30] Strabo describes the city as the "master of two harbors" and outlines the cargos that moved through it between Asia and Italy (*Geography*, 8.6.20–23), and the related services generated a good deal of income for inhabitants; see M. I. Finley, *The Ancient Economy*, Sather Classical Lectures 43 (Berkeley: University of California, 1973), 138–39. The city also supported a number of temples, was the major banking center for the region, and manufactured and sold bronze, pottery, and marble sculpture.

[31] E. T. Salmon, *Roman Colonization under the Republic* (London: Thames and Hudson, 1969), 132–45. Eligibility for the senate was otherwise available to freedpersons only in Carthage.

popularity of a great many cults in Corinth,[32] but when it came to public demonstrations of support, the imperial cult received the attention. Latin inscriptions predominated, with the highest percentage of these devoted to the imperial cult.[33] Furthermore, both the architecture of Corinth and the plan of the city were distinctively Italian.[34] Given the evidence favoring Roman culture and politics, it is instructive to note that Greek appears to be the lingua franca of the christian assembly. Together, these factors place Corinth within a complex and layered political arrangement that was further heightened by the social-historical circumstances of the city, all of which create the kind of profile typical of possession societies.

GLOSSOLALIA. In Corinth, glossolalia appears to be the predominant form of that spirit possession. In fact, glossolalia continues today as a common phenomenon of possession trance in Christian groups. Felicitas Goodman, who was a student of Bourguignon, continued the work of the original cross-cultural study by documenting groups in which speaking in tongues is the predominant form of spirit possession,[35] and her observations support significant cross-cultural similarities and have important implications for understanding the early Christian practice. In particular, she has demonstrated that specific phenomena of ASC accompany and enable glossolalia. She describes the state as "hyperarousal dissociation" and, like Winkelman, has identified involuntary trembling and twitching as accompanying phenomena.[36] Her observations also confirm curtailed awareness of surroundings and the practitioner's own bodily state as well as the absence of any memory of the behavior during trance even among those who behave in extraordinary ways (such as leaping and somersaulting during the episode).[37] At the same time, she has shown that communities differ in their expectations for trance behavior and

[32] On the cult of Demeter and Kore, see Peter D. Gooch, *Dangerous Food: 1 Corinthians 8–10 in Its Context*, Studies in Christianity and Judaism 5 (Waterloo: Wilfrid Laurier University Press, 1993).

[33] Engels, *Roman Corinth*, 71. Engels reports that 101 of the 104 inscriptions prior to Hadrian were in Latin, and 63 percent of these were devoted to the imperial cult.

[34] Johnson, "Epistolary Apostle," 92.

[35] Goodman's study of glossolalia in Mexico City, the Yucatán, and the United States is documented in *Speaking in Tongues*. See also Felicitas D. Goodman, *How about Demons? Possession and Exorcism in the Modern World* (Bloomington: Indiana University Press, 1988); and Felicitas D. Goodman, *Ecstasy, Ritual and Alternate Reality: Religion in a Pluralistic World* (Bloomington: Indiana University Press, 1988).

[36] Goodman, *Speaking in Tongues*, 126–34.

[37] Ibid., 128.

that these expectations are learned and enacted by participants.[38] Because Goodman followed the same group over a few years, she was also able to observe changes over time. The most significant of these was the general trend toward attenuation of the individual's experience over time. One practitioner in particular, Emilio, found that speaking in tongues greatly reduced his otherwise persistent state of anxiety. For that reason, when his experience began to taper, naturally he was desperate to regain his earlier ecstasy and tried (unsuccessfully) to physically induce some of the preliminary phenomena that had once arisen spontaneously.[39] One final relevant observation from Goodman's studies concerns the corporate character of glossolalia. She observed the importance of the group leader(s) in exercising a "driving" function that spread the ASC among the individuals gathered for worship.[40] Close, intense, and rhythmic interaction of the leader, in effect, drives others to enter ecstatic states.

These findings have important implications for an understanding of the situation in Corinth. First, it is immediately obvious that the conditions in Corinth match the various indicators and predictors of spirit possession. For one, glossolalia is manifestly an altered state of consciousness. Studies of the nature of these utterances confirm this fact. Based on both her own tapes and those available from other ethnographers, Goodman analyzed the cross-cultural patterning of vowel and consonant arrangements, of intonation, stress, and pacing.[41] She concluded not only that glossolalia is "uttered while in dissociation but is an artifact of the mental state, or rather of its neurophysiological processes."[42] The other indicator of spirit possession is also demonstrated in the case of Corinth: Glossolalia is understood by Paul and most certainly by the Corinthians themselves to be a result of spirit

---

[38] Ibid., 156–59.

[39] Goodman (*Speaking in Tongues*, 132) describes Emilio eighteen months after his first experience: "[I]n low-level dissociation, he presses his arms against his chest to produce the sensation of pressure on the rib cage characteristic of his former, more intense, altered state. He tries to impel himself by richer and richer kinetic patterns. All the while, his glossolalia slips away from him."

[40] Ibid., 90–92.

[41] It is interesting to note that earlier studies conducted by linguists focused narrowly on predeterminations of what constituted language. See William T. Samarin, "The Linguisticality of Glossolalia," *Hartford Quarterly* 8 (1968), 74. Because of this narrowness, these studies explicitly eliminated speech factors such as intonation, which they considered to be "emotional" and therefore not a "linguistic factor." Although early studies established the fact that no known practice of glossolalia qualified as a language, they did much less to determine what, in fact, it was. Goodman's more inclusive documentation allowed assessment of glossolalia as a neurological phenomenon.

[42] Goodman, *Speaking in Tongues*, 123–24.

possession. All of Corinthians 12–14 is set in that context (*"now about spiritual things..."* 1 Cor 12:1), and speaking, in particular, is also explicitly identified in this way (ἐν πνεύματι, 1 Cor 12:3). Paul's statements that *"everyone"* speaks in tongues (1 Cor 14:23) and *"everyone"* has some vocalization to add to the worship (a hymn, instruction, a revelation, a tongue, an interpretation; 1 Cor 14:26) are likely exaggerations for the sake of argument. Still, the comments evidence the prevalence of these expressions in Corinthian worship. Goodman's description of driving behaviors is echoed in Antoinette Clark Wire's reconstruction of Corinth, where "[o]ne person's speaking inspired others to speak until voices overlapped and became extended into periods of communal prophecy. People were inspired less by what they heard than what they spoke."[43]

The watershed work of anthropologist I. M. Lewis continues to influence much thought on spirit possession. In his book *Ecstatic Religion,* Lewis distinguishes between central and peripheral possession cults on the basis of the part they play "in upholding the moral code of the societies in which they receive so much attention."[44] In peripheral cults, the spirits are typically thought to arise from other groups and to exert hostile influence on those they possess. Lewis argues further that the victims of peripheral possession (for it is interpreted as negative possession) are usually individuals from "downtrodden categories" of the society "who are subject to strong discrimination" in situations of fixed stratification.

A number of authors have applied Lewis's description in their analyses of the circumstances in the Corinthian assembly. The prevalence of glossolalia as the mode of spirit possession in Corinth is clearly an example of positive spirit possession within the assembly; that is, the effects of the spirit are sought and positively valued. Within the christian group, the possessing spirit is central in maintaining the moral code. However, from the perspective of nonmembers, and perhaps especially the "unbelieving" spouses (1 Cor 7:12–16) of members of the assembly, the opposite is likely true. They are bound to see the new christian possession cult as negative possession, dominated by an unknown spirit and resulting in destructive or malevolent intent and unwanted changes to the behavior of their family members or

---

[43] Antoinette Clark Wire, "Prophecy and Women Prophets in Corinth," in *Gospel Origins & Christian Beginnings: In Honor of James M. Robinson,* ed. James E. Goehring (Sonoma, Calif.: Polebridge, 1990), 149. In this quotation, Wire does not distinguish sharply between the occasions of speaking in tongues and those of prophecy. In her later, fuller treatment, she proposes instead that the "movement into tongues could occur as the climax of prophecy" (*Corinthian Women Prophets,* 140–46).

[44] I. M. Lewis, *Ecstatic Religion,* 27.

neighbors. Thus, the in-group dynamics of the possession and its out-group dynamics will be quite distinct.

Mary Douglas's observations about group control and spirit possession are apropos of this difference. Douglas has argued that where social stratification is rigidly enforced, a society is more likely to include negative possession, and, alternatively, where the grid is weak, positive possession beliefs are far more common.[45] In general, ancient Mediterranean societies were high grid (and high group), certainly much more than contemporary Western ones. In Corinth, however, group controls were softened somewhat by its social history. Jerome Neyrey has picked up on Douglas's observation in his analysis of the apparent problems in Corinth. He argues that the Corinth assembly (the in-group) favors weak social controls over their eating, gender roles, and worship patterns (especially ecstatic speech). The positive and inclusive possession trance of glossolalia participates in this weak social control. Neyrey contends that Paul, in contrast, is attempting to assert a higher "grid" and tighter "group" for the in-group of the assembly.[46] Outside of the christian assembly, a strong sense of grid continues to function in the highly status-conscious city of Corinth, with its imperial sensitivities. For the members of the assembly, the contrasting social freedom offered within the community and especially through the invigorating activity of glossolalia may well have been one of the major attractions of membership. Thus, in the case of the Corinth assembly, two distinct sets of social circumstances apply.

However, this dual set of factors is not often identified in Corinth. More typically, and under the influence of approaches like that of Lewis,[47] the practice of glossolalia in Corinth has been read exclusively as an in-group dynamic of power struggle. There are some widely recognized signs of status sensitivity in the letters to the Corinthians, but they do not apply to glossolalia to the degree that is sometimes supposed. For example, a number of commentators have noted the way issues of gender difference correlate with the practice of tongues in Corinth. Building on that observation, they have tended to interpret glossolalia as the way in which female members of the community had achieved social change and an increased measure of power

---

[45] Mary Douglas, *Natural Symbols: Explorations in Cosmology*, 2nd ed. (London: Routledge, 1996 [1970]), 84.

[46] Jerome Neyrey, "Body Language in 1 Corinthians: The Use of Anthropological Models for Understanding Paul and His Opponents," *Semeia: Social-Scientific Criticism of the New Testament and Its Social World* 35 (1985), 127–70.

[47] Lewis's categories of "central moral" and "peripheral amoral" cults may have made his work especially amenable to theological frameworks.

vis-à-vis their fellow members. These arguments are in keeping with Lewis's Weberian interpretation of spirit possession as a means of effecting social change. Indeed, he has championed the line of inquiry that assesses the benefits that some disenfranchised women attain through their possession by peripheral spirits. Lewis describes his sense "that we are dealing with a widespread strategy employed by women to achieve ends which they cannot readily obtain more directly."[48] Indeed, the phenomenon of spirit possession does have higher incidence among women cross-culturally. Furthermore, there are a number of examples of societies in which the possessed person has received benefits (e.g., temporary relief from work, some material goods, social attention) because of the possession.[49] Whether or not biblical scholars draw directly on Lewis, his understanding of the use of spirit possession colors much related discussion in New Testament studies.

The problem with this perspective is twofold: First, Lewis's descriptions of particular examples do not in themselves constitute a model, and the pattern he describes is perhaps less pervasive than sometimes assumed; and second, care must be taken in applying his observations to the circumstances in early christian communities. I will first assess the limits of Lewis's hypothesis. Mary Douglas has addressed the fact that possession cults are not always peripheral but sometimes central; nor is spirit possession always used to redress deprivation.[50] Bourguignon, too, has described the ways in which even so-called peripheral cults often participate quite smoothly with the central cult and are integrated into it.[51] She shows, furthermore, that whatever benefits accrue to the spirit-possessed often do nothing to change the structure of the society. In fact, frequently possession tends to relieve the social pressure that is present in the group and thereby facilitates the survival of the status quo. Bourguignon identifies this relief of interpersonal pressure microchange and clarifies that, rather

---

[48] I. M. Lewis (*Ecstatic Religion*, 85–86) says further that: "Women are, in effect, making a special virtue of adversity and affliction, and, often quite literally, capitalizing on their distress. This cult of feminine frailty ... is admirably well adapted to the situation of those who employ it. By being overcome involuntarily by an arbitrary affliction for which they cannot be held accountable, these possessed women gain attention and consideration and, within variously defined limits, successfully manipulate their husbands and menfolk." See also Ioan M. Lewis, "Spirit Possession and Deprivation Cults," *Man* 1 (1966), 318.

[49] The muslim *zar* cults of Somalia were the primary source for Lewis's theory, and they are frequently raised as the paradigm in literature that is influenced by Lewis. See I. M. Lewis, *Ecstatic Religion*, 75–79.

[50] Douglas, *Natural Symbols*, 91–92, 97.

[51] Bourguignon, *Possession*, 35. Bourguignon ("Introduction," 26) mentions that in a conference paper delivered at a colloquium on possession cults, Lewis later revised his view to include a number of patterns of dynamics in addition to his thesis of social manipulation.

than leading to the macrochange of the structures that caused the social hardship, it frequently serves to maintain the social structure.[52] Often, where the so-called peripheral possession cults exist, they are no doubt tolerated by the system for this very reason.

So, social change is not the only reason that one might engage in possession practices. For example, based on his own fieldwork, primarily in Jamaica, William Wedenoja gives a far more multifaceted picture of the value of spirit possession for the practitioner, which begins to suggest the value of religious ecstasy as an end in itself. Wedenoja speaks, in essence, of the humanizing benefits of ecstatic states (and ritual practice in general) in social situations in which the pleasures of daily life are thin. I cite his summary statement at length because it offers a rich understanding of religious ecstasy and the complexities of human experience that are informed, in part, by neurological considerations. According to Wedenoja, possession trance

> is one of the oldest and most universal of the culturally constituted defence mechanisms. It is a response to psychological burdens imposed by human nature and the human way of life, a response to fears and anxieties stimulated by a cognitive ability to transcend the present and imagine the future, a response to intrapsychic conflicts resulting from the structure of the brain, a response to repressed and unconscious memories, feelings and drives, and a response to the inevitable frustrations involved in adherence to social rules. Periodic emotional discharge is functional for an individual and adaptive for society. . . . [It can] lessen the tensions of social life that might otherwise lead to rule-breaking or deviance.[53]

How then do these circumstances apply to Corinth? Inasmuch as spirit possession does effect some change in personal power, those gains are relative to the larger society, not the subculture of the possession cult. Thus, in 1 Corinthians, the meaningful frame of reference (with regard to power or influence) for the practice of glossolalia is the practitioner's status within the city of Corinth, not within the assembly itself. In Lewis's schema, the Christ cult is the peripheral one that contrasts with the official imperial cult and other Greco-Roman religions. Paul makes it clear that the possession of those who speak in tongues is not by a spirit that is peripheral to the assembly but the same central and in fact sole spirit

---

[52] Bourguignon, "Introduction," 31.
[53] Wedenoja, "Ritual Trance and Catharsis," 303–4.

of the cult. Thus, if benefits are afforded to the Corinthian glossolalists, they accrue relative to their fellow citizens rather than their fellow christians.

To demonstrate the difference that this approach can make to the text, I will use it to assess another study of 1 Corinthians 12–14 that is also interested in the social implications of glossolalia.[54] Dale Martin imagines the glossolalists to be people of relatively high status. More specifically, Martin's thesis is that the practice of tongues in Corinth participates in the same status struggle as other issues discussed in the letter and that glossolalia was practiced by those of higher status in order to assert that social currency over others in the community. He makes this point with three sets of evidence: (1) a general Greco-Roman background in which "esoteric speech" was highly valued;[55] (2) Paul's subtle reversals of hierarchy in his adaptation of the body topos (1 Cor 12:12–27); and (3) the parallel reversal of the standard cultural hierarchy of *pneuma* over *nous*. Martin sees these three features working together toward Paul's single aim of tempering the claims of the strong (i.e., those who practice the culturally privileged act of esoteric speech) for the sake of the weak. I am sympathetic to Martin's argument – it is well constructed, does not overreach the evidence, and offers an elegant proposal about the relationship between the various elements in this section of the letter. It also offers an account of why some Corinthians would want to practice glossolalia[56] and does so without assuming that either they or Paul were of inferior character or integrity, as is the case in some exegeses of this passage.

Still, there are difficulties with his analysis. Despite the fact that Martin wants to apply his findings to a social assessment of the Corinthian assembly,

---

[54] The discussion is that of Dale Martin and is available in article form (D. Martin, "Tongues of Angels and Other Status Indicators," 547–89) and as part of his larger study (D. Martin, *Corinthian Body*, Chapter 4, 87–103).

[55] Particularly in his first version of this study, Martin collected a broad range of evidence for the use of what he calls "esoteric speech acts." In order to illustrate that strange speech is not only a lower-class phenomenon, he has highlighted examples that cross class and status boundaries (D. Martin, "Tongues of Angels and Other Status Indicators," 551–56). In many ways, his body of evidence could function as a critique of the early, narrower view of Lewis regarding the sole use of possession as a tool of the disenfranchised, and that point is well taken.

[56] In some ways, the argument from status is simply the mirror opposite of the view that Martin opposes (that is, that only the underprivileged would participate in tongues). I have tried to show that external benefits are not the only ones available in ecstatic practice. Glossolalia can be an inherently rewarding experience. When we consider glossolalia as a function of possession ASC, we would find another set of reasons for participation: the religiously meaningful, bioneurologically rich experience of ecstasy in one of its more accessible forms.

he has characterized the phenomenon of glossolalia from a cultural perspective and not within the ecology of the group. In other words, he has successfully analyzed the cultural attitudes that might permit glossolalia, but I would argue that he has failed to assess how a particular society enacts the general cultural values by which it is informed. The most important social dynamic missing from his analysis is the difference between, on the one hand, one or two people speaking "esoterically" for the purposes of divine guidance for the community and, on the other hand, a whole subgroup exercising "esoteric speech" simply as an end in itself. The former circumstances are reflected in almost all of Martin's parallels, and the latter are in existence in Corinth. Paul makes this dynamic clear: "the one speaking in a tongue is not speaking to human beings but to God" (1 Cor 14:2); "the one speaking in a tongue edifies himself, but the one prophesying edifies an assembly" (1 Cor 14:4). As an alternative to glossolalia, Paul promotes prophecy (which is most like mediumship), which expresses different social dynamics than glossolalia or spirit possession. Thus, if Paul is trying to reverse status divisions, as Martin argues, he does so by ineptly asserting an arrangement with even greater potential for status distinctions. If prophecy is another deployment of ASC (as I will argue), then it is the more difficult of the two to attain and is necessarily practiced by fewer group members. Therefore, Paul's "solution" would not level the playing field but would in fact introduce an added layer of specialization into their worship. Furthermore, that distinction would be compounded by the fact that the social dynamics of prophecy are such that a community can only host a limited number of practitioners.[57] To emphasize that fact, Paul instructs the assembly to allow only two or three prophets to speak on any occasion (1 Cor 14:29–31). So, if Martin is correct in his theory that glossolalia was an assertion of superiority that Paul was trying to end, then Paul proceeded quite incompetently. It is certainly possible that Paul might have been that pastorally clumsy; he might have tried to end one stratifying practice by replacing it with another of even greater potential for distinction. But this is not Martin's position. Thus, his findings are limited in part by the fact that he assesses glossolalia simply as speech and not as a deployment of ASC within a social grouping.

---

[57] In fact, most of the ancient examples cited by Martin are either expressions of a general belief in divine language or cases of one or, at most, three people who speak ecstatically in a given community. The one exception is Irenaeus's hearsay report (*Against the Heresies* 5.6.1) of "many brethren" who exercise a variety of ecstatic gifts. No details of social arrangement are given in this example, and Irenaeus uses it as evidence of the ability of everyone to be "spiritual."

4.2 SOUL JOURNEY

The figure of the shaman stands in the way of access to the second form of ASC relevant to this study. In Chapter 2, I described the significance of shamanism in the history of attitudes about ecstatic practice and the way in which the term has recently expanded far enough for some to include Paul within its boundaries. Although the comparison is helpful in many instances, some aspects of the popularized shamanism complex distort or obstruct what is most relevant in understanding the experience of early christians, Paul in particular. The official history of the term shaman links the word to the practice of the Tungus-speaking people of eastern Siberia.[58] When, in the seventeenth century, the Russians began to colonize their territory, accounts of individuals who practiced altered states of consciousness along with other ritualized behaviors began to find their way to the rest of the world. Eventually, reports from "explorers, missionaries, colonists, military and other representatives of Western culture wove together a series of ideas that were loosely connected and observations that were typically rather poor and unsystematic"[59] yet came to define shamanism.

Some commentators, often in fields other than anthropology, make much of the so-called shamanic career, with the Arctic form often serving as the standard. Of chief interest is the shaman's initiation crisis, which is popularly portrayed as illness, and an associated death and rebirth experience. Although this pattern of transition to shamanism is common enough, it is far from the only one.[60] The interest in these features was fed, in part, by early assumptions about the mental health of shamans, a history that I outlined in Chapter 1. More recently, it has been exploited as fuel for various "spiritual" quests. In response to these misunderstandings and misuses, Joan Townsend emphasizes both the ordinariness of shamanism as an activity and the ordinariness of most shamans as individuals.[61] In addition, other anthropologists emphasize the fact that shamanism is not primarily a feature

---

[58] An alternate history would see the word arising earlier and ultimately deriving from the Vedic term *śramana*, "one who practices austerities." See Townsend, "Shamanism," 430–31.

[59] Winkelman, *Shamanism*, 59. For a detailed discussion of this period in the development of the discipline, see Gloria Flaherty, *Shamanism and the Eighteenth Century* (Princeton, N.J.: Princeton University Press, 1992).

[60] Peggy Ann Wright, "The Nature of the Shamanic State of Consciousness: A Review," *Journal of Psychoactive Drugs* 21 (1989), 25–33, in a survey of related literature, identified the following transitions to shamanic status: recovery from illness or injury, circumstantial signs, dreams and/or visions, a slow change in personality or a period of erratic behavior, inheritance, natural portents, and the purchase or theft of shamanic power.

[61] Says Townsend ("Shamanism," 456): "Shamans I have known seem quintessential 'normal, average' people when not engaged in shamanic activities."

of personality but a complex of behaviors and conditions that is embedded in a given society. It is not conducted primarily for the sake of personal enlightenment.

The role of shaman is not always delineated as carefully as it is by the authors I have cited. In fact, it has become something of a "spiritual" cipher. The term has now been applied to a wide variety of cross-cultural practitioners, and the nature of some comparisons has significantly blurred critical distinctions and therefore blunted the heuristic power of the comparison. In many ways, shamanism has become "beatified"[62] as a category of popular culture, finding its way into public speech and how-to weekend retreats.[63] The category has also been taken up in other academic disciplines as a kind of metaphor rather than a real point of comparison.[64] The result of this metaphorical use of shamanism is that the category loses its critical utility. Almost any "spiritual quest" can be described as shamanistic and almost any charismatic figure as a shaman, not only in popular culture but increasingly in academic settings as well.

Recently, John Ashton has applied the category to Paul in an effort to throw neglected features of his biography into sharper relief. Ashton's monograph *The Religion of Paul the Apostle* advances a number of important arguments – for example, that Paul's language is frequently better understood as the faltering attempt to express experiential knowledge than it is as systematic theology, that ecstatic experience is far more central in Paul's life than has been recognized, and that the anthropology of altered states of consciousness is a fruitful avenue for exploration. While recognizing that Paul was "not really" a shaman,[65] Ashton conducts the comparison particularly for biographical purposes. He focuses his analytical attention on the "career" of the shaman as a pattern to which Paul's life can be compared. Although he does acknowledge the "social aspect" of shamanism, he

---

[62] This is Roger Walsh's term ("Psychological Health of Shamans," 102) for the popular appropriation of shamanism, in contrast with the opposite extreme of labeling the role as deviant.

[63] A variety of psychological metaphors have been affixed to shamanism. The notion of the "wounded healer" is perhaps the most common, but other ideas of the inward journey of self-fulfillment abound. "The shaman" has become a kind of spiritual hero, virtually a noble savage, as Townsend ("Shamanism," 457) characterizes it: "The shaman becomes a model of a 'primitive,' more noble, pure existence than is now found in modern corrupt industrial society."

[64] Townsend ("Shamanism," 457) identifies the following fields (and points of comparison): literary studies (Walt Whitman), feminist studies (a seventeenth-century lesbian nun), and cultural studies (artists in general). In biblical studies, it has tended to be treated as a real anthropological category and has been applied to Jesus in particular.

[65] Ashton, *Religion of Paul the Apostle,* 29.

understands it to be necessitated by the fact that "the shaman's authority depends upon an ability to persuade other people of his or her exceptional gifts."[66] In this way, he treats shamanism broadly as a form of personal power. The breadth of this approach correspondingly weakens the connections it attempts to forge.[67]

That broad platform of inquiry also allows Ashton to choose his points of comparison somewhat uncritically.[68] In searching for parallels to Paul's life, his criterion of selection appears to be a biographical pattern of personal crisis followed by religious activity. Frequently he ignores the cultural specificity of a given shamanic practice. For example, the points of comparison that he adduces are "a not atypical picture" of shamanism from Japan; a sixth-century Turkish Christian hermit, Theodore of Skyeon; and Oral Roberts, the twentieth-century professional evangelist. In each of these cases, Ashton emphasizes a dramatic illness early in each man's life and, in the case of the latter two, their ability to exorcise demons. However, more precise descriptions are possible. The crisis of the Japanese shamans is an initiatory rite in which trance is deliberately induced through austerities. In the case of Theodore of Skyeon, the crisis may well have been a psychotic episode, and for Oral Roberts it was tuberculosis (although that "initiatory" illness occurred a full twelve years before he felt a call to his healing ministry, thus grossly extending the notion of initiation). Ashton emphasizes the same features in Paul's life, but to do so he must rely heavily on the three accounts

---

[66] Ibid., 33.

[67] In many ways, Ashton has made an important contribution by expressing some views that he was not in a position to support with sufficient evidence. Such intuitions can serve well to stimulate subsequent hypotheses. However, in this case, some intuitions are not founded on sufficiently rich ground. Among the difficulties with his method that I will not discuss in detail are (1) the uncritical use of Acts as a source of experiential detail, especially the naïve correlation of the bright light in Acts 22 with what "sounds for all the world like a lightning flash (or possibly sunstroke)" and hence a stereotyped shamanic initiation crisis (Ashton, *Religion of Paul the Apostle*, 41); (2) oversimplification of the data, especially in dividing a shaman's career into three stages – "first their early life; secondly their call and the experiences that accompany it, usually involving trance or ecstasy; thirdly, their subsequent career, in which they . . . control the spirits by which they themselves used to be dominated" (33, elaborated on 40–47) – that are almost meaningless in their generalization of cultural detail; (3) the suggestion that, contrary to the basic anthropological definitions, shamanism is a religion rather than a social role (47–48); and (4) reclaiming Romans 7 as "the anguished self-questioning which . . . preceded [Paul's] conversion" (56, elaborated on 224–29).

[68] In concluding his description of Oral Roberts, he simply says: "The career of this American evangelist has numerous parallels with that of the typical shaman, and much of what he says about his relationship with God echoes Paul's own words concerning his relation to the spirit of Jesus" (Ashton, *Religion of Paul the Apostle*, 37). In this case, the possibility that the purported similarities might be due to the fact that Roberts spent his life reading "Paul's own words" seems worth considering.

in Acts of Paul's encounter with the risen figure of Jesus. He takes the blindness of the first account as historical fact and suggests that this sickness was caused by a lightning strike or sunstroke.[69] He also implies that Paul is alluding to some sort of physical ailment when he describes himself as an ἔκτρωμα (a faulty birth) among those who have seen the Lord (1 Cor 15:8).[70] These assumptions are fraught with difficulties related to the nature of the texts but also to an understanding of shamanism.

In many cultures that maintain a shamanistic social role, initiation into it is indeed accompanied by a crisis, but a crisis of a very different sort than depicted by Ashton. What Ashton interprets as spontaneous illness is better understood in many cases as part of the much more complex psychosocial phenomena of other rites of initiation. For the purposes of this examination, I will note only that many cultures expect that a shaman will experience physical crisis in the transition to the new social role, and in those societies shamans do experience a crisis.[71] Furthermore, the causal link can flow in either direction because ecstatic states themselves can produce the physical effects that are sometimes associated with the transition to shamanic status. Ecstatic states are not always positive experiences. They can be accompanied by nausea, limb pain, and uncomfortable neural

[69] Ibid., 45. Furthermore, inexplicably undermining the seriousness with which one might like to take his argument, he cites as relevant to his hypothesis the tendency among the Dinka people to honor cows that survive a lightning strike.

[70] Ibid., 45.

[71] See especially the classic work of Victor Witter Turner, *The Ritual Process: Structure and Antistructure*, Lewis Henry Morgan Lectures, 1966 (Chicago: Aldine 1969); and Mircea Eliade, *Birth and Rebirth: The Religious Meanings of Initiation in Human Culture*, trans. Willard R. Trask (New York: Harper, 1958). In a minority of societies, spontaneous illness is a legitimate means of transformation to shamanic status. Most often the crisis and illness that sometimes accompany the transition from undistinguished membership in the group to the role of shaman are related first by the social and personal drama accompanying any significant change in social identity and second by the exacerbating fact that many shamans are required to live in partial social isolation or are otherwise distanced within their society. The historical survey of ethnographic accounts of shamanism compiled by Jeremy Narby and Francis Huxley (*Shamans through Time*) includes several examples of "illness" accompanying resistance to a socially identified call to shamanism. I cite them here with the page number in Narby and Huxley rather than their original publications because some of the latter are quite rare: the Siberian Chukchee people, documented by Waldemar Bogoras, 1904 (53–57); a number of North American aboriginal groups, documented by Roland B. Dixon, 1908 (65–67); and the Saora people of India, documented by Verrier Elwin, 1955 (116). The following groups offer examples of initiatory illnesses induced by traditional use of plants, austerities, or self-inflicted wounds: the Caribs of Guyana, as documented by Antoine Biet, 1664 (16–17); other North American aboriginal groups documented by Dixon, 1908 (67–68); a number of South American groups, summarized by Alfred Métraux, 1944 (99–101); Australian aboriginal people, documented by Ronald Rose, 1957 (121–23); and the Secoya Indians, documented by Fernando Payaguaje, 1990 (230–33).

sensations (e.g., painful tingling).[72] Those practitioners who are preparing for shamanic roles must learn to master the neurophysiological processes that comprise the negative experiences. Those who are, by contrast, thought to be possessed can find ways to eliminate them (exorcism) or control them (appeasing the spirits). As I have mentioned, societies often maintain traditional techniques to teach such control.

Finally, because Ashton uses only a partial description of shamanism and no organizing model for the social use of altered states of consciousness, his observations are likely to be insensitive to important points of cultural difference and to bypass some of the more significant points of comparison. For example, he has dislodged from the Japanese society mentioned previously the imagery of the shaman being dismembered and having his flesh scraped, and he uses this culturally specific detail to explain Paul's language of participating in the death and resurrection of Jesus.[73] Again the comparison is not irrelevant, and the book is immensely helpful in raising these questions at all. Still, because of the general nature of his comparison, its heuristic payback is minimized and possibly misplaced. In effect, the comparison would suggest that Paul thinks he participates in the death of Christ because he is a shaman and shamans experience death in their initiatory trance.[74] Ashton's analysis ends with an attempt to assess the possible genealogical connections between classical forms of shamanism and Paul's own experience, a link that he ultimately abandons for the more modest achievement of offering shamanism as a "sustained metaphor."[75] Rather than cultural influence, it seems far more tenable that the neurophysiological phenomena of a certain kind of ecstatic state are the mediating factor between cultures (see Section 4.3.2). In one cultural context, generations of reflection have produced and elaborated a particular interpretation that

---

[72] Paul's report of his thorn in the flesh (2 Cor 12:7) is interesting in this context. The passage is too oblique to make a definitive determination, but it is possible that this difficulty was a feature of the trance experience itself. For example, Wedenoja ("Ritual Trance and Catharsis," 281) notes that some among the Jamaican Revivalists describe a feeling of "fire and pain" when they are "in the Spirit."

[73] Ashton, *Religion of Paul the Apostle*, 45. By page 122, this culturally specific detail has become generalized even further to "the shaman's traumatic sense of being torn apart and reconstituted as a new person at the time he was established in his call."

[74] Or perhaps his point is that because (some) shamans experience death and rebirth and Paul talks about his sense of participating in Christ's death and rebirth, Paul is a shaman. The circularity of reasoning (or fuzziness of methodology) makes it difficult to tell which way the reasoning runs.

[75] Ashton, *Religion of Paul the Apostle*, 59. The genealogical argument is on 47–59. Most anthropologists also reject genealogical explanations; see, for example, Winkelman, *Shamanism*, 74–75.

promotes initiation into a new social status. In the other, a central and
founding historical event (the death of Jesus) has found its way into the
interpretation. For these reasons, I will use "shamanism" to refer only to the
specific socially recognized role and "soul journey" to distinguish the phase
of consciousness that is used by shamans and others.

4.2.1 *Social Anthropological Definitions*

More recently, anthropologists have worked to provide critical parameters
capable of distinguishing the contribution of cultural variation from core
characteristics that might attend soul journey practices cross-culturally. As a
result, many now agree that shamanism, like spirit possession, has both
individual (the use of ASC experienced in a particular way) and social
(dependent on particular cultural constructs and communal structures)
characteristic features. The individual features have received the most attention, and I will address them first. Mircea Eliade is the name most associated
with shamanism, especially through his classic work *Shamanism: Archaic
Techniques of Ecstasy.*[76] His work is now viewed as occasionally romantic
and uncritical in its methods,[77] but it has nevertheless established some of
the enduring boundaries of the discussion. Eliade focused primarily on
phenomena related to the use of ASC, although he did not necessarily
identify them all as such. In particular, the cross-cultural phenomena of this
sort of ASC are characterized by the peak ecstatic state that d'Aquili and
Newberg have described in greatest detail. In it, the practitioners retain a
degree of awareness of their experience that is marked by sensations of
floating apart from the body and transformation. For Eliade, this state
was, in effect, the required identifier of a shaman, and many others have
followed him in noting its centrality for the category.[78]

A second characteristic frequently identified in shaman societies is mastery of the spirits. Typically, those who practice soul journey are specialists
who can voluntarily control trance (in contrast to practitioners, who are

---

[76] Mircea Eliade, *Shamanism: Archaic Techniques of Ecstasy* (New York: Pantheon, 1964). The
book was originally published in French as *Le Chamanisme et les techniques archaïques de
l'extase*, 2nd ed., revised and augmented (Paris: Payot, 1951).

[77] Townsend, "Shamanism," 430.

[78] Eliade, *Shamanism*, 5. Although soul journey is not the primary ecstatic experience of the
shaman, it seems that only those who at least occasionally practice it are identified as
shamans. Others who share this view include Gilberg, "How to Recognize a Shaman among
Other Religious Specialists," part 1, 21–27; Townsend, "Shamanism," 432–33; and Winkelman, *Shamanism*, 61–63, 70. Even those who do not grant the singular importance of soul
journeying still specify that shamanism involves a different sort of experience than spirit
possession does.

involuntarily taken over by a spirit, who then controls their behavior).[79] Spirits are sometimes described as entering the adept, but they do not take control away from him and he does not lose track of himself during the experience.[80]

Eliade noted that the shaman interacts with the spirit world as a representative for the community, and he identified this characteristic as another of the anthropological universals regarding shamanism. Significant functions of such figures across cultures include communication with other realms for the sake of providing food, healing activity, and intervention in the proper disposition of the dead. In many societies, healing also ranks high on the list. Such work is often carried out through ritual action and considered quite "down-to-earth" in its host society. Townsend describes the role as a "practical method for the use of the supernatural to heal physical, psychological, and emotional illnesses, foretell the future, and improve the lot of the living," always for the sake of the society.[81]

As in the case of spirit possession, the cross-cultural study of Bourguignon and associates helped identify more incisive and complex social data correlated with this practice of ASC and, again, Michael Winkelman has further tested and refined those categories.[82] Among Winkelman's findings is the fact that societies that maintain a role for such use of ASC have been located throughout the world, except in the circum-Mediterranean and Insular Pacific regions. These regions also lack societies whose sustenance is based solely on hunting, gathering, and fishing to provide the primary food supply – a factor that is significantly correlated with shamans.[83] Finally, such

---

[79] Harner, *Way of the Shaman*, xvi, 20–30, 46–56; Sergei Mikhailovich Shirokogoroff, *Psychomental Complex of the Tungus*, new ed. (Berlin: R. Schletzer Verlag, 1999); Lewis, *Ecstatic Religion*, 51; Åke Hultkrantz, "A Definition of Shamanism," *Temenos* 9 (1973), 25–37 at 28; and Åke Hultkrantz, "Comments on Richard Noll: Mental Imagery Cultivation as a Cultural Phenomenon: The Role of Visions in Shamanism," *Current Anthropology* 26 (1985), 453; Walsh, "Psychological Health of Shamans," 103; and Larry G. Peters and Douglass Price-Williams, "Towards an Experiential Analysis of Shamanism," *American Ethnologist* 7 (1980), 397–413.

[80] I use the masculine pronouns advisedly because shamans, at least within the more precise taxonomy that I am using, are universally almost exclusively male.

[81] Townsend, "Shamanism," 438. See also Walsh, "Psychological Health of Shamans," 103.

[82] Michael Winkelman, "Shamans and Other 'Magico-Religious' Healers: A Cross-cultural Study of Their Origins, Nature and Social Transformations," *Ethnos* 18 (1990), 308–52; Winkelman, *Shamans, Priests and Witches*; and Winkelman, *Shamanism*. Other works in this area include Gilberg, "How to Recognize a Shaman among Other Religious Specialists"; and Lila Shaara, "A Preliminary Analysis of the Relationship between Altered States of Consciousness, Healing, and Social Structure," *American Anthropologist* 94 (1992), 145–60.

[83] There are a few instances of shamanism in pastoral societies with some agriculture, including North American aboriginal cultures.

societies lack formal classes and any significant administrative political integration beyond the local community. No shamans were found in sedentary societies because settled and permanent residency leads inevitably to more complex political arrangements and the adoption of agriculture.[84] As groups become more complex internally and in their political ties, mediums, priests,[85] and often sorcerers or witches begin to appear and the use of soul journey ceases.[86] These factors and others are summarized in the comparison of the roles in Table 4.1.

Winkelman argues that there is an ecological logic at work in the correlation of these social factors with a particular magico-religious practice. The function of the shaman is more directly tied to life and death issues than is the work of the other magico-religious practitioners. As agriculture is introduced in a society, it provides a number of behavioral controls over food provision (techniques such as crop rotation, storage, astute timing of planting and harvest, development of technology, etc.) that are not afforded to hunters. In hunter-gatherer societies, there are simply fewer elements of mediation between the individual and his or her next meal. Furthermore, the nature of the food source requires that hunter-gather societies live in relative isolation from other groups so that population levels do not surpass the food supply and can respond to its cyclical changes. This lack of political integration allows a single individual, through occasional intervention, to exercise meaningful political leadership that directly addresses the survival of the group. Some of the means of accessing extrahuman resources are as unroutinized as the food source itself. But the shaman is also a repository of traditional knowledge and cultural lore, and divination is sometimes conducted without the use of ASC. Thus, in some societies, this leader is more or less the group's sage.[87] In contrast, as societies gain greater degrees

---

[84] Winkelman, *Shamanism*, 73.

[85] Several anthropologists identify a dichotomy specifically between priests and shamans. Whereas the change from shaman to shaman/healer to healer is gradual and the boundaries between the roles somewhat fuzzy, the difference between shaman and priest is more clearly marked. See Gilberg, "How to Recognize a Shaman among Other Religious Specialists"; Victor Witter Turner, "Religious Specialists," *International Encyclopedia of the Social Sciences*, vol. 13 (New York: Macmillan, 1968), 437–44; William A. Lessa and Evon Z. Vogt, *Reader in Comparative Religion: An Anthropological Approach*, 4th ed. (New York: Harper and Row, 1979); and Robert H. Lowie, *Indians of the Plains* (New York: McGraw-Hill, 1954), 161–64.

[86] The disappearance is gradual. Winkelman notes that with increased social complexity the work of the shaman begins to center exclusively on healing and to taper from there (shaman/healer → healer → medium).

[87] For example, according to Stanley Krippner, "The Epistemology and Technologies of Shamanic States of Consciousness," *Journal of Consciousness Studies* 7 (2000), 93–118, the Mazatec Indian shamans in Oaxaca, Mexico, have maintained through their chants and rituals the centuries-old mythologies of their culture (97).

Table 4.1. Characteristics of magico-religious practitioners

Characteristics	Shaman	Medium	Priest
Societal conditions	hunting and gathering, nomadic, no political integration, little inner stratification	agricultural, sedentary community, political integration, highly stratified	agricultural, permanent residency, political integration
Magico-religious activity	divination, healing, protection from spirit world, hunting magic	divination, spirit protection, malevolent magic, informal power	protection and purification, propitiation, socioeconomic rites
Sociopolitical power	charismatic leader, war leader	judiciary influence	political, legislative, judicial, economic, military power
Social characteristics	predominantly male, high social status, ambiguous integration into community	predominantly female, low socioeconomic status, integrated into main cult	predominantly male, high socioeconomic status, fully integrated into main cult
Selection and training	precipitated by extraordinary event, period of training or mastery, status communally affirmed	spontaneous spirit possession, training in practitioner group, ceremonial recognition	social inheritance or succession, political appointment
Social context	at request or need of community or client, part-time, individual practice	public ceremonies, acts for clients, part-time, collective	public social functions, calendrical rites, full-time, hierarchically ranked

(continued)

Table 4.1 *(continued)*

Characteristics	Shaman	Medium	Priest
Special skills/techniques	use of visions, dreams, other ASC mastery of spirits enviro-cosmological control	channel for spirit activity dominated by possessing spirit	negligible ASC authorized by superior spirits or gods sacrifice and administration of rites

Source: Adapted from Michael Winkelman, *Shamanism: The Neural Ecology of Consciousness and Healing* (Westport, Conn.: Bergin and Garvey, 2000), 66–69.

of political integration, additional sources of specialized help are available to those that experience something like crop failure, for example. At the same time, access to the spirit world also becomes more specialized. A variety of practitioners begin to coexist, and the nature of the spiritual intervention becomes either more removed from the source (as in the case of the priest, who uses primarily ritual action to communicate) or less proficient in its manipulation (as in the case of the medium, who does not fully control the encounter).

A number of anthropologists and cognitive scientists detail more precisely the nature of the contribution of a shaman to his or her society. Winkelman describes the controlled use of altered states of consciousness as a biological contribution to knowing. It provides access to universal human potentials that bring a kind of knowledge that is marginalized in modernity. In Winkelman's words, these "neurognostic structures provide experiences that facilitate adaptation to the operational environment."[88] The use of soul journey contributes both to the transformation and skills of the person practicing it and to the knowledge base of the community. Harry Hunt distinguishes between "representational symbolism," which is linguistic, and "presentational symbolism," which is rooted in emotional and spatial intelligence.[89] Hunt is also convinced of the social value of this sort of knowledge as a means of accessing "presentational symbols" for understanding and coping with one's environment. Presentational symbols include physiognomies and geometric figures as well as other sensory-motor and image-based patterns.[90] These sorts of emotional and spatial knowledge, as we have seen, tend to fall victim to the executive control of the left hemisphere. Hunt describes presentational symbolism as a kind of universal "grammar" akin to the linguistic building blocks shared by all language groups. In short, the role of the shaman, with its particular combination of mastery of religious ecstasy and distinct social influence, allows hunter-gatherer societies to

---

[88] Winkelman, *Shamanism*, 77–78.
[89] See Harry T. Hunt, "The Linguistic Network of Signifiers and Imaginal Polysemy: An Essay in the Co-dependent Origination of Symbolic Forms," *The Journal of Mind and Behavior* 16 (1995), 405–20; Harry T. Hunt, *On the Nature of Consciousness: Cognitive, Phenomenological, and Transpersonal Perspectives* (New Haven, Conn.: Yale University Press, 1995); and Harry T. Hunt, "Relations between the Phenomenon of Religious Mysticism and the Psychology of Thought: A Cognitive Psychology of States of Consciousness and the Necessity of Subjective States for Cognitive Theory," *Perceptual and Motor Skills* 61 (1985), 911–61.
[90] Joseph (*Neuropsychiatry, Neuropsychology, and Clinical Neurology*, 277) relates the fact that crosses, triangles, and circles were scratched into cave walls by Cro-Magnon people 30,000 years ago. He further relates these shapes to the temporal lobe and amygdala, which specialize in the discernment of shapes and features and related emotions. He suggests that crosses would have been especially effective stimuli because "when gazing at a cross, all four quadrants of the visual field (and thus the right and left temporal-parietal lobes) are activated."

access additional forms of knowledge. This activity, in turn, allows a society to navigate its circumstances more effectively.

4.2.2 *Paul's Use of ASC*

Although it should be clear by now that I do not intend to promote Paul as a shaman, the anthropology of shamanism is still of critical use in understanding Paul's life and writings. Certainly many of the details outlined so far can be accounted for on the basis of the human capacity for religious experience outlined in the previous chapters; they do not need models of shamanism to make them intelligible. But when it comes to understanding some points of negotiation between the christian communities and Paul, and the nature of Paul's role in them, the use of the category of shamanism is quite instructive. If shamanism is used simply to identify the fact that a person experiences altered states of consciousness, then it actually obscures more than it clarifies because it blurs real distinctions in the ways altered states are deployed by individuals in distinct societal contexts.[91] However, when the category of shamanism is used to distinguish social roles, it can be a very helpful model because it provides a means to measure ecstatic states as a social commodity. In other words, it provides the means to consider the public face of ecstasy.

The category of "apostle" is the core of Paul's own public depiction of his role. In his functioning definition of apostleship, "seeing the Lord" appears to be the basic qualifying requirement for all who would attain that status. This fact is clearest in 1 Corinthians 15 ,where Paul is reciting the list of those to whom Christ appeared. In the penultimate spot, he names an otherwise indistinguishable group as "all the apostles" (1 Cor 15:7). He is of course the

[91] I have already described the way in which some of Paul's ecstatic experiences were occasions of soul journey ASC. The primary example of such a state and its distinctive phase of consciousness is 2 Cor 12:1–4. Other Pauline texts are harder to judge as experiences of one type of ASC or another (whether defined etically or emically). For example, Paul emphasizes a number of times that he received knowledge unmediated by human means (e.g., 1 Cor 15:8; 2 Cor 5:16, 12:7–9; Gal 1:11–12, 15–17), and he also describes his apostolic role as something that was divinely conferred (see Rom 1:15; 1 Cor 1:1; 2 Cor 1:1; Gal 1:1). Segal ("Paul's Thinking about Ressurrection in Its Jewish Context," 404) suggests that seeing the resurrected Jesus was fundamental to Paul's identity as an apostle, most importantly because through it Paul can "demonstrate that his vision of Christ was of the same type and order as that of the other apostles." Which of the widely recognized magico-religious practitioners offer the most useful point of comparison for Paul's practice? In themselves, the phenomena of Paul's ASCs do not necessarily privilege shamanism because typically mediums are also judged to be privy to supernatural knowledge through the "mind of the spirit." Furthermore, the role of mediums in consulting with the spirits is understood to be conferred because typically a spirit chooses them as host. In fact, this concept of selection seems close to Paul's own depiction of his call.

end member in the tally and is not worthy to be an apostle because of his past but nevertheless seems to be qualified simply on the basis of his vision (1 Cor 15:8–9). The same cause-and-effect relationship seems to be the point of the juxtaposition of details in 1 Cor 9:1: "Am I not an apostle? Have I not seen our Lord Jesus?" In Chapter 15, he describes this revelation as a χάρις, a benefaction,[92] that he has tried to honor through his efforts (1 Cor 15:10). I have argued that this vision of Christ was part of an ecstatic experience, but that fact appears to be wholly beside the point to Paul. That is to say, the means by which Paul received the benefaction is relevant in only one aspect – whatever the means of revelation, it had to be amenable to the understanding that God was its source. In other words, not just any experience counts as divine benefaction, but this sort of visionary experience apparently does for Paul and others in the early christian communities. Furthermore, this sort of divine communication seems not to have been expected for all christians, but neither was the group quite as select as the apostles alone. The fact that a gathering of 500 are counted among the beneficiaries yet not identified as apostles (they are simply ἀδελθοί, 1 Cor 15:6) makes an absolute link between vision and apostolic status impossible to maintain.

In a handful of other places, Paul does seem to offer a more decisive measure of apostleship. On two of the occasions in which he is justifying his claim to apostolic status, Paul uses a stereotyped phrase for the sort of evidence he can offer. In 2 Cor 12:12, near the climax of his extended self-defense, he declares that "indeed, the signs of the apostle were performed among you in all endurance by both *signs and wonders and works of power*." In the second case, at the close of his letter to the Romans, he attempts to temper his assertive – and potentially offensive – rhetorical stance by restating his apostolic credentials: "I have written boldly to you in part as a [way of] reminding you because of the grace given to me from God to be a servant of Jesus Christ to the gentiles. For I will not dare to speak of anything except the things that Christ did through me ... by *power of signs and wonders, by power of the spirit of God*" (Rom 15:15, 18–19).

Both of these comments use the Septuagintal formula "signs and wonders," which would be understood reflexively as miraculous feats of some kind.[93] Paul makes a similar, but less formulaic, claim in 1 Cor 2:4–5. In this case, he

---

[92] Zeba A. Crook, "Patronage, Loyalty, and Conversion in the Ancient Mediterranean" (PhD dissertation, University of St. Michael's College, 2003), argues that Paul's sense of duty in response to a benefaction (*charis*) is the more valid way to understand the traditional category of Paul's "conversion."

[93] Σεμεία and τεράτα occur together twenty-nine times in the Septuagint. Fifteen of those occurrences are in reference to the exodus event.

does not use the title apostle, but once again he is justifying the nature of his public performance – his leadership – in the community: "My speech and my proclamation were not in persuasive words of wisdom, but in demonstration of spirit and power, that your faith may not be in wisdom of human beings but in power of God." In at least these three texts, Paul speaks of spiritual power or "signs and wonders" as evidence of his claims about his social role. Each of these statements assumes that such evidence will be innately convincing to the communities – not just to the Corinthians, who are often portrayed as enthusiasts, but also to the Roman assembly, which Paul assumes will also take his claim as self-evidently valid.

The last of the three texts cited raises another possible point of contact between Paul's apostolic role and the use of specific states of consciousness. It appears that Paul may have established Christian communities at least partly through performing some sort of ecstatic feat. He makes a related claim in 1 Thess 1:5, where he reminds the Thessalonians that "the good news came to you not only in word but also in Holy Spirit and with very great assurance." In discussing these texts, especially Rom 15:19 and 2 Cor 12:12, most commentators remark only that Paul emphasizes that Christ was the source of these feats, whereas Paul himself was merely the conduit. The question of what in the world these publicly verified signs and wonders might be – not to mention how in the world Paul accomplished them – is not addressed.[94] There are, however, exceptions to this silence, and two are particularly notable.

---

[94] The following authors take this approach in their commentaries on Romans: Käsemann, *Commentary on Romans*, 389; Moo, *Epistle to the Romans*, 892; John R. W. Stott, *Romans: God's Good News for the World* (Downers Grove, Ill.: InterVarsity Press, 1994), 380, who cautions that it would be wrong to conclude that these signs were necessarily miraculous (381); Ernest Best, *The Letter of Paul to the Romans*, Cambridge Bible Commentary: New English Bible (Cambridge: Cambridge University Press, 1967), 165–66; Adolf von Schlatter, *Romans: The Righteousness of God* (Peabody, Mass.: Hendrickson, 1995), 265; and John Murray, *The Epistle to the Romans*, New International Commentary on the New Testament (Grand Rapids, Mich.: Eerdmans, 1959), 211. Some avoid discussing it altogether: Matthew Black, *Romans*, 2nd ed., New Century Bible Commentary (Grand Rapids, Mich.: Eerdmans, 1989), 203, who focuses solely on the purported chiastic structure of the section; Paul J. Achtemeier, *Romans*, Interpretation, a Bible Commentary for Teaching and Preaching (Atlanta: John Knox, 1985), 229; Anders Nygren, *Commentary on Romans* (Philadelphia: Fortress, 1972), 452–55; Christopher Bryan, *A Preface to Romans: Notes on the Epistle in Its Literary and Cultural Setting* (Oxford: Oxford University Press, 2000), 223–24, which comments only on the awkward Greek, suggesting that it is a sign of Paul's embarrassment regarding this topic; Karl Kertelge, *The Epistle to the Romans*, New Testament for Spiritual Reading 12 (New York: Herder and Herder, 1972), 141–42; and Roy A. Harrisville, *Romans*, Augsburg Commentary on the New Testament (Minneapolis: Augsburg, 1980), 240. One distinctive argument is staged in Stanislas Lyonnet, *Études sur l'epître aux Romans*, Analecta Biblica 120 (Rome: Editrice Pontificio Istituto Biblico, 1989), 39, who (quite uniquely among those I consulted) subsumes the phrase under the discussion of "un culte spirituel," which consisted of the spiritual offering of the Gentiles.

Troels Engberg-Pedersen and Philip Esler have each discussed evidence of dramatic events in Paul's own comments about the reception of the gospel by various communities. Engberg-Pedersen focuses on the founding of the church in Galatia. He draws attention to a number of details in the letter that suggest extraordinary events during Paul's first visit:

> In fact, just as Paul had had Christ revealed "in him" (1:16), when God called him through his grace (1:15), so the Galatians have had the crucified Christ drawn to their very eyes (3:1) when Paul proclaimed the gospel to them for the first time (4:13–14). Apparently, the Christ event was transmitted by God in the special way that the figure of the crucified Christ was revealed to human beings in a sort of *direct vision*.[95]

Furthermore, Engberg-Pedersen suggests that Paul himself brought this transmission about during his visit. It was directly through him that Christ was "brought to their eyes," and so they received him as "a messenger of God, as Christ Jesus" (Gal 4:14). Although Engberg-Pedersen leaves it as a question (and that in a footnote), he nonetheless asks, "Is Paul not intimating that they had, as it were, seen Christ Jesus 'in' *him*?"[96] In this way, he takes Paul's own language quite seriously.

For his part, Esler suggests that Paul animated the practice of glossolalia among the fledgling christian communities.[97] His proposal is based in part on accounts from Acts, but he treats that evidence in a critically refined manner. Esler points out that in the narrative world of Acts glossolalia plays an intriguing role in the spread of christianity. In parallel to the foreign speech that occurred at Pentecost (Acts 2:1–41), speaking in tongues at the conversion of Cornelius (Acts 10:44–48) "serves as the final and irrefutable legitimation for the acceptance of the Gentiles."[98] While the physical details of these two scenes cannot be taken as a factual record of historical events, it is nonetheless instructive to note that the author of Acts uses ecstatic speech as a focal dynamic in these two watershed scenes. As Esler suggests, Peter's question in Acts 10:47 ("Can anyone forbid water for baptizing these people who have received the Holy Spirit?") assumes that glossolalia was a widely recognized sign of authentication. The verisimilitude

---

[95] Troels Engberg-Pedersen, *Paul and the Stoics* (Louisville, Ky.: Westminster/John Knox, 2000), 144.

[96] Ibid., 332, n. 22. Paul's closing burst, "I bear the brands [στίγματα] of Christ in my body," in Gal 6:17 offers another intriguing statement about Paul's representation of Jesus.

[97] Esler devotes a chapter to this question in Philip Francis Esler, *The First Christians in Their Social Worlds: Social-Scientific Approaches to New Testament Interpretation* (New York: Routledge, 1994), 35–51.

[98] Esler, *First Christians in Their Social Worlds*, 38.

of the scene depends on the fact that the audience of Acts would have recognized it as such, too.[99]

A number of other details conform to this picture. The first is the term glossolalia itself, which Esler suggests may be a christian neologism.[100] Second, there are instances of incoherent ecstatic utterance that occur in other cultures, and the ability seems to be universal, but the *group* phenomenon of speaking in tongues (a nonlanguage, not simply a garbled form of an existing language) seems to be uniquely Christian throughout history.[101] The persistence of the group phenomenon is very likely due in part to the fact that the practice is authorized by the canonical texts. However, the original corporate phenomenon in Pauline communities (and perhaps at some point in Jerusalem) appears to be something of an innovation.[102] The practice requires both the human potential for it, which the cross-cultural studies of Goodman, in particular, suggest is universal, and the social approval and promotion of it, a circumstance that appears to be limited to Christianity. Esler argues further that the "contagious" nature of "dissociative states" suggests that, when nonmember Gentiles were present while others were speaking in tongues, they were likely to "have broken into ecstatic utterance" themselves.[103] Goodman reports the fact that she spontaneously entered a low-level ecstatic state while witnessing glossolalia and also relates occasions in which others with no previous exposure spoke spontaneously in tongues.[104] Esler concludes that glossolalia (but not xenoglossy)[105] played a real role in demonstrating the presence of the spirit of God to the first generation of christians. If this is correct, then the demonstration of apostolic power of which Paul speaks may have been the ability to kindle ecstatic experiences in the communities he visited.

---

[99] Esler's larger thesis is that, in the formative stages of the movement, glossolalia served for Jewish christians as a primary justification for the inclusion of Gentiles.

[100] Esler (*First Christians in Their Social Worlds*, 45) cites, for example, its absence from Julius Pollux's long list of terms related to possession and prophecy, *Onomastikon* 1.15–19.

[101] Esler, *First Christians in Their Social Worlds*, 49.

[102] Christopher Forbes, *Prophecy and Inspired Speech in Early Christianity and Its Hellenistic Environment*, Wissenschaftliche Untersuchungen zum Neuen Testament 2 (Tübingen: Mohr [Siebeck], 1995), concludes that "the Hellenistic period knew of several related, though differing traditions of inspired or charismatic speech" (168).

[103] Esler, *First Christians in Their Social Worlds*, 50–51.

[104] Goodman, *Speaking in Tongues*, 71–72 and 70–71, respectively.

[105] The ecstatic speech in Acts 2 is represented as real languages that are unknown to their speakers; that is, xenoglossy. There is no reliable evidence that such speech is possible or has ever occurred. Classic works on this topic are Theodor Spoerri, "Ekstatische Rede und Glossolalie," in *Beiträge zur Ekstase*, Bibliotheca Psychiatrica et Neurologica 134 (Basel: Karger, 1967); and Mansell E. Pattison, "Behavioral Science Research on the Nature of Glossolalia," *Journal of the American Scientific Affiliation* 20 (1968), 73–86.

Given the question at hand, there is no need for a final determination regarding the propositions of Esler and Engberg-Pedersen. Both authors make arguments for Paul's use of ecstatic power – whether he demonstrated it himself, inspired it in others, or both – as a founding gesture in the christian communities. Their arguments offer a reasonable explanation for the established expectation that an apostle would perform signs and wonders (Rom 15:19; 2 Cor 12:12) and for the fact that Paul can speak so routinely of the unequivocal experience of the spirit when these communities were founded (1 Cor 2:4–5; Gal 3:1–5; 1 Thess 1:4–5). Speaking in tongues seems a more likely form for this reception of the spirit than does a corporate visionary experience, but both are possible based on the evidence. Other details, too, such as the patterned Abba prayer and ecstatic groaning discussed in the last chapter, are suggestive of the nature of these initiatory events. In any case, Paul's probable use of ecstatic states in such circumstances does not align well with the behavior of a shaman. Paul's ecstatic practice differs from that of the other members only in that it precedes and sets the pattern for theirs and presumably in that he is adept and they are not (yet).

Other apostolic functions also seem to have a possible connection to the spirit world and Paul's ability to access it. The title apostle in and of itself points to the function of messenger as one part of the role. Paul's frequent use of the term εὐαγγέλιον is a further marker of the importance of a message.[106] So, Paul sees himself as one of those "approved by God to be entrusted with the gospel" (1 Thess 2:4; also Gal 2:7). As mentioned, Paul emphasizes the fact that the message he carries is not something that was transmitted to him by "human means." Segal outlines his view of the scope and source of Paul's gospel as follows: "It appears that Paul considers himself special in that the whole process of salvation has been revealed to him. Others have not had his visions, so his visions give him special powers to speak on the meaning of Christian life."[107] Using 1 Corinthians 15 in particular, Segal suggests that Paul's vision of Christ resurrected might have provided the message of the resurrection of the whole christian community. Other evidence of this sort is the fact that Paul describes himself as a revealer of mysteries (Rom 11:25; 1 Cor 2:7, 4:1, 15:51).[108] In these respects, Paul's ecstatic experience does have different social valences than that of other members of the christian communities.

---

[106] It appears some fifty-nine times in the undisputed letters.
[107] Segal, *Paul the Convert*, 67.
[108] See also the disputed Rom 16:25–26a.

Still, in other ways, Paul's social role in the Corinthian community begins to move toward the characteristic priestly tasks of protection and purification, propitiation, and socioeconomic and calendrical rites (Table 4.1). In the first letter to the Corinthians, Paul's instructions regarding the Lord's Supper are especially relevant to a priestly role. There he insists that the proper performance of ritual action is intimately tied to the physical health of the participants (1 Cor 11:29–30). This union of rite and well-being shows that in his "priestly" instructions to them Paul is still acting as a magico-religious practitioner. Paul's self-presentation also moves much closer to that of a priest when he seeks to purify the community of a deviant member and define its boundaries (1 Cor 5) and when he informally attempts to codify social behavior (1 Cor 7).

Given this mix of characteristics and functions, what does the category of shaman help us to understand about Paul? Commenting on the cross-cultural prevalence of shamanism, Winkelman notes that fundamentally its prevalence is due to the universal human potential for ASC practice. So, it is possible for shamanism to be reinvented or rediscovered in diverse places and times because religious ecstasy continues to occur even without a tradition that fosters it. However, those experiences crystallize into social roles only where they provide vital adaptive strategies for the given society.[109] Thus, the strong correlation of shamanism with unstratified, politically isolated hunter-gatherer societies suggests that it is just plain silly to call Paul a shaman in the context of his work in Corinth.

At the same time, the nature of Paul's spiritual power is such that the comparison is not wholly without merit. I would suggest that the point of contact is both Paul's aptitude and the temporary or partial conditions in Corinth that made it possible for him to function temporarily or partially in this manner. The first of these enabling factors concerns the nature of Paul's presence in the community. He was not resident in Corinth on a permanent basis (and may, later on, have avoided being present there).[110] This sporadic contact meant that his practices would not be subject to the same degree of routinized social pressure that permanent residency would entail. As a result, a mismatched magico-religious practice could endure longer than it would have if Paul had to find his place in the daily workings and leadership of the

[109] Winkelman, *Shamanism*, 77.
[110] See his comments in 1 Cor 16:5–9, 4:18–21; 2 Cor 1:15–17, 1:23, 2:1, 9:4–5, 12:14, 13:1–4. There is at least one example of shamans working both within a small group or clan and in a kind of territorial practice. See A. Siikala, *The Rite Technique of the Siberian Shaman*, Folklore Fellows Communication 220 (Helsinki: Academia Scientiarum Fennica, 1978).

community. The second factor concerns the survival challenges to a group like the assembly in Corinth. By and large, their life needs have less to do with provision of food and far more to do with the benefits described by Wedenoja in the epigraph to this chapter – a fact that speaks against the utility of shamanism. At the same time, however, certain life and death issues were part of the founding of the new christian cult because a new ideology of salvation was being introduced. Whatever one might say about Paul's purported Pharisaic membership and their ostensible belief in an afterlife, it is clear that for Paul himself life after death was possible only because it had happened to Christ (Rom 6:3–4; 1 Cor 15:12–20; Phil 3:10–11). In other words, Paul knew the resurrection to be true because he had encountered the resurrected Christ with all the bioneurological force and conviction that an ecstatic vision affords. This set of circumstances fits with the many reports of shamans navigating the spirit world in order to ensure that the dead reached their proper place and to protect the living from them. To the extent that Paul's use (and perhaps that of others as well) of soul journey was seen to provide access to realms beyond this life, it could function "shamanistically" in organizing a new society of christians that was founded partially on an ideology of afterlife.[111]

Finally, the temporary sense of community independence in Corinth would have made it possible for adaptive uses of soul journey as a form of power for a while because of the relative break from normal social integration. But already in the first extant letter to the Corinthians, it is clear that elements of this sort of magico-religious practice are starting to chafe. The apparent struggles between Paul and the Corinthians about the nature of his role may well reflect this rapid shifting of social needs and conditions. Paul seems to be as conflicted as the community about the nature of his religious leadership. Furthermore, the apparent conflicts about leadership may also owe something to the similarities between their ecstatic practices and those of shamans because any single community can support only one shaman at a time.

To summarize, in some ways, Paul's ecstasy relates positively to his apostleship. First, it is relevant because his superlative visions and journey to heaven presumably gave him some of the content (particularly his certainty that Christ was raised) – and much of the conviction – of the gospel with which he was entrusted as an apostle. Second, through it, Paul brings people

---

[111] Of course, formative christianity was not only a resurrection cult, and I am convinced that a whole range of benefits (some as ordinary as companionship and sharing food) accrued to the various Pauline communities in configurations that were peculiar to each group. Still, judging by the conversation in 1 Corinthians 15, understandings of afterlife held a significant place in the life of that assembly.

into contact with the spirit in ways that are seen to demonstrate their divine election.[112] At the same time, the bumpiness of Paul's discussion in 2 Corinthians 12 is noteworthy: Paul both asserts his superlative ecstatic feats (2 Cor 12:1–4, 7, and 12) and tries to offer weakness as the truer measure of his character. This is not to say that his ecstatic experience was unimportant to him or that ecstatic feats and knowledge played no role in his apostleship; rather it is to say that the complexity of the interplay between Paul's social role and his ecstatic abilities seems to have required negotiation from time to time. Yet, in other moments, it seems to have verified and validated his status, as 2 Corinthians 12 also demonstrates. And, as in the case of those who have socially mandated roles that include ecstatic practice, it does seem to have contributed to his personal transformation and development in ways that allowed him to better cope with the conditions of his own life and, in some cases, the lives of his communities. In short, the utility of the comparison of Paul's ecstatic practice with that of shamanism is that it accounts for the elements of Paul's mixed record of leadership, in Corinth at least. The partial fit between Paul's ecstatic practice and the social anthropology of shamanism helps to explain both how someone with Paul's *charismata* might have come to gain influence in founding christian communities and why his leadership might have been problematic after those communities were established.

4.3 *PNEUMATIKA*

Glossolalia and Paul's own superlative religious experiences are not the only forms of spiritual ecstasy that Paul recognizes. He introduces this section of 1 Corinthians with the comprehensive term "spiritual things," *pneumatika* (1 Cor 12:1). In the ensuing discussion, not only are several social roles listed, but more than one category of spiritual things is also at hand – all of the endowments are "of the spirit," but some are additionally by spirit possession, which includes the requisite phenomena of ASC. Given the rhetoric of the passage, prophecy deserves special attention for two obvious reasons. First, Paul ranks it among a group of three superlative functions, surpassed only by apostleship (1 Cor 12:28). Second, he proposes it as the direct alternative to glossolalia (1 Cor 14:5). Thus, he appears to offer it as a solution to the "problem" of tongues. Still, even though there is general agreement about the significance of prophecy in Paul's instructions, precisely what prophecy is remains a point of contention. This difference of opinion endures, in part, because of problems of method.

---

[112] In addition to the explicit example of 1 Thess 1:4–5, see also the combination of details in Romans 8.

The analysis undertaken here will part from others in focusing on the *activity* (rather than the message) of prophets as *members of communities* (not solely solitary, autonomous actors). These points of reference allow broader cross-cultural points of comparison. Not surprisingly, studies of prophecy in Christian origins have focused on the *ideas* that the prophets were transmitting, often collapsing the category of prophecy into that of preaching. This approach, I would argue, is in keeping with the tendency toward cognicentric interests. Certainly, the message resulting from prophetic activity is not irrelevant, but the singular focus on discourse in Corinth ignores other factors of relevance to the significance of prophecy. Instead, in 1 Corinthians, Paul – like members of many other societies that practice altered states – is using the social means at his disposal to refine the practice of ASC in ways that are in keeping with the needs, values, and structure of the community. These sorts of refinements are common across cultures, and communities use a variety of both positive methods (e.g., apprenticeship) and negative ones (e.g., social pressure) to teach the control of altered states.

4.3.1 *Prophecy in the Taxonomy of Social Anthropology*

When one attempts to place this sort of activity in the range of ASC use, the prophecy that Paul is promoting to the Corinthians appears to be most comparable to mediumship (see Table 4.1).[113] Like mediumship, this prophecy is seen to be driven by spirit possession. The prophets are to act as conduits for divine communication. In anthropological literature that does not make sharp taxonomic distinctions, some incidences of mediumship are routinely identified as shamanism. However, Winkelman distinguishes between the two in a number of characteristics that blend neurological and social contributions. Typically, the first possession experience of a medium is understood to be spontaneous and involuntary, whereas that of the shaman is thought to be intentionally sought, often at a later point in life than is the case for mediums. After these initial involuntary experiences, mediums are brought into a relationship with other mediums, who train them in the management of their ASC. Eventually, although they are not understood to be in control of their ecstatic experience, they do cultivate a greater range of methods for initiating the trance than in more general forms of spirit possession. Thus, after a period of apprenticeship, "the possession episodes ... occur only when there is a deliberate intention on the part of the medium to enter into trance."[114] In a further

---

[113] The description of mediumship that I provide here is taken from Winkelman, *Shamans, Priests and Witches*, 59–63.
[114] Ibid., 61.

distinction from more general and involuntary forms of spirit possession, mediums usually exercise their spiritual mediation on behalf of a client or client group. They also typically maintain a collective or group practice that is well integrated into the main cult. Mediums coexist comfortably with some other magico-religious practitioners, notably priests and healers but also witches or sorcerers. They are often found in agricultural societies; however, the only sociological factors that are "significantly correlated" with mediumship are political integration beyond the local level and social stratification, and of these two, only political integration is an independent predictor.[115] Thus, Winkelman identifies social evolution as one of the factors associated with the shift from shamanism to mediumship.

Not everyone would agree that Paul's concept of prophecy fits the profile of mediumship. Perhaps the major point of contention in the exegesis of 1 Corinthians 14 is whether or not prophecy is an *ecstatic* religious practice.[116] A number of contingent factors affect the position that people take: Is prophecy constituted by formal characteristics of the speech?[117] Is it the content?[118] Is the

---

[115] Winkelman, *Shamanism*, 74.

[116] A great deal has been written on New Testament prophecy, some of which, for the purposes of my examination, I group according to their rejection or acceptance of prophecy as an ecstatic experience. Some studies ultimately reject comparisons with Greco-Roman parallels because they see Christian prophecy as essentially non-ecstatic and therefore different from "pagan" forms. These include David Hill, *New Testament Prophecy* (London: Marshall Morgan and Scott, 1979); M. Eugene Boring, *The Continuing Voice: Christian Prophecy and the Gospel Tradition* (Louisville, Ky.: Westminster/John Knox, 1991); Thomas W. Gillespie, *The First Theologians: A Study in Early Christian Prophecy* (Grand Rapids, Mich.: Eerdmans, 1994); Wayne A. Grudem, *The Gift of Prophecy in 1 Corinthians* (Lanham, Md.: University Press of America, 1982); Forbes, *Prophecy and Inspired Speech in Early Christianity and Its Hellenistic Environment.* Those who entertain a comparison that includes a common grounding in ecstatic experience include N. I. J. Engelsen, "Glossolalia and Other Forms of Inspired Speech According to 1 Corinthians 12–14," (PhD dissertation, Yale University, 1970); Aune, *Prophecy in Early Christianity and the Ancient Mediterranean World;* Wire, *Corinthian Women Prophets;* D. Martin, *Corinthian Body;* and Max Turner, *The Holy Spirit and Spiritual Gifts: In New Testament Church and Today* (Carlisle: Paternoster, 1996; repr. Peabody, Mass.: Hendrickson, 1998).

[117] Although Aune is invested in broader social scientific questions, his major contribution lies in this area. He provides a predominantly literary and form critical template against which to measure various speech acts in early Christianity. The result is a thorough and very helpful determination of Christian oracular speech that has implications for other questions.

[118] For example, this is more or less the interest of Gerhard Friedrich ("προφήτης" in *Theological Dictionary of the New Testament*, vol. 6, ed. Gerhard Kittel, trans. Geoffrey Bromiley (Grand Rapids, Mich.: Eerdmans, 1967), 848), who conceives of early Christian prophets as those "through whom God's plan of salvation for the world and the community and His will for the life of individual Christians are made known." Even Hill (*New Testament Prophecy*, 5), who claims to be offering a functional assessment, defines the function in terms of delivering a particular content: The prophet is "a divinely called and divinely inspired speaker who receives intelligible and authoritative revelations or messages which he is impelled to deliver."

term itself a sufficient marker? Is it characterized by the social function of the speaker?[119] Here I will consider briefly three factors that are especially problematic in the discussion of whether or not the prophecy in Corinth is ecstatic. They are the determination of the points of comparison, the functioning definition of ecstasy, and especially the meaning of νοῦς (*nous*) throughout this passage.

Both Greco-Roman and Jewish cultures include practices that might be called mediumship. However, there are a number of reasons why many of the Hebrew prophets provide an unsuitable parallel for early Christian practice. Although the single designation of "prophet" was used for a variety of practitioners in ancient Israel and Judah, it is clear that the various prophets did not all exercise the same social role. Some performed their work within the cult, others in the court, and, using David Aune's category, still others were free prophets. For my purposes, these differences in setting and social conditions are far more relevant than the common use of the term *nabi'* to refer to the various practitioners.

In the model of ASC deployment, the free prophets would appear to be more akin to shamans than mediums. This suggestion is supported by the fact that they were frequently in conflict with the king. Aune notes the political roots of that tension (although without drawing any conclusions on that basis). He comments that "[t]he monarchy had pragmatically reinterpreted Israelite traditions in the light of changing conditions. These reinterpretations were in conflict with the theocratic ideals of the free prophets."[120] The monarchy constitutes an additional stratum of political hierarchy over the tribes and allows for the development of a relationship between the tribes themselves but especially between the Hebrew people and other groups in the region. Thus, the monarchy creates the sort of political atmosphere in which shamanistic leadership is no longer viable because of the changed social dynamics of power. A figure who has direct access to heavenly realms through ASC would wield a degree of social power too close to that of the king to exist in close quarters

---

[119] For the most part, the concept of function has been quite narrowly defined in the scholarship. Aune (*Prophecy in Early Christianity and the Ancient Mediterranean World*, 19) found that all the studies of early Christian prophecy that he reviewed emphasize that prophets function to "edify, exhort, and console." Although that may be true, it is a limited observation of the role. The social function of Hebrew prophets has been assessed more fully and fruitfully by some Old Testament scholars, including, most notably, Robert R. Wilson, *Prophecy and Society in Ancient Israel* (Philadelphia: Fortress, 1980). See also Thomas W. Overholt, *Channels of Prophecy: The Social Dynamics of Prophetic Activity* (Minneapolis: Fortress, 1989).

[120] Aune, *Prophecy*, 87.

with the monarch.[121] Furthermore, the socioeconomic identity of the group primarily served by the king and retainer prophets was mainly the elite and settled portion of the people. In contrast, the free prophets were often associated with the people of the land.[122] So, when the institutions of monarchy and shamanistic prophecy did operate side-by-side, they did so only with a significant degree of tension and competition. These social circumstances along with the pronounced use of soul journey among some of the free prophets align Old Testament prophecy – far more definitively than New Testament prophecy – with a pattern like that of shamanism.[123] In contrast, the temple and especially the court prophets functioned as mediums whose client was the monarch, and their practice also included ASC that appears to be of the dissociative sort (e.g., 1 Sam 19:18–24).

The Greco-Roman mantic oracles are among the clearest ancient examples of mediums who practice dissociation trance. Many ancient authors who described oracles did so with great flourish (a feature that has distracted some contemporary readers[124]). The frequent pairing of "mantic" with "frenzy" is testimony to that fact. Still, it is clear from some of these descriptions that the functioning notion of prophecy could include spirit possession as described in Section 4.1.[125] Plato's oft-cited comments are a good illustration:

---

[121] The occasions on which the free ecstatic prophets opposed the political decisions of the monarch are many, but the following are illustrative: Jeremiah's opposition to the prophecy of the temple prophet Hananiah (Jer 28); Isaiah's confrontation of Ahaz after receiving a vision (Isa 6 and 7); and especially the story of Micaiah's conflict with both the kings and the court prophets concerning his visionary oracle predicting military failure (1 Kgs 22).

[122] This is especially true of Micah but is also reflected in Jeremiah's allegiance with the nomadic group of kinsmen. Although this difference can be interpreted along Marxist lines as a reflection of class dynamics, it is also reflective of the differing subsistence conditions and political organization that are identifiers of shamanistic societies.

[123] Aune (*Prophecy in Early Christianity and the Ancient Mediterranean World*, 202–3) argues further that Old Testament prophecy is closer to New Testament apostleship than to New Testament prophecy.

[124] This approach eliminates the need for the special pleading sometimes implemented in the case of Christian prophecy. As is often the case when authors want to claim the "unique" character of a particular Christian view or practice, eschatology has been invoked as the explanatory dynamic. Such is the case with Gerhard Dautzenberg, *Urchristliche Prophetie: Ihre Erforschung ihre Voraussetzungen im Judentum und ihre Struktur im ersten Korintherbrief*, Beiträge zur Wissenschaft vom Alten und Neuen Testament 6 (Stuttgart: Kohlhammer, 1975), who connects prophecy directly to apocalyptic eschatology in which (1) someone has a vision and (2) receives an equally inspired interpretation of it. That process may well be the case, but if so, it need not be justified by any Christian innovation in worldview; prophecy of that nature was already taking place in the surrounding culture.

[125] Especially Aune, *Prophecy in Early Christianity and the Ancient Mediterranean World*, 23–48.

There are good grounds for believing that divination (μαντίκη) is heaven's gift to human thoughtlessness/unwisdom (ἀφρονυνη) for no man in his mind (ἐννοῦς) achieves true and inspired divination, but only when the power of understanding is fettered in sleep or he is distraught by some disorder or, perhaps, by divine possession. It is for a man in his ordinary thinking (φρονέω) to recall and interpret the utterances, in dream or in waking life, of divination or possession, and by reflection to discern in what manner and to whom all the seer's visions portend some good or evil.... When a man has been overtaken by frenzy and continues in that condition, it is not for him to decide the meaning of his own visions and utterances.... It is therefore the custom to appoint spokesmen to adjudge inspired divination. (*Timaeus*, 71e–72a)[126]

Plato goes on to say that although the appointed spokespeople are often called diviners, they are merely interpreters of the actual divination. This passage suggests altered but decipherable speech and even suggests that mantic speakers might be able to recall and interpret their own words but should not do so because they were displaced or overtaken by the god during the event. Thus, privileging of dissociation trance seems to have been an active part of prophetic activity within the major cultures of the Mediterranean.

It is this depiction of the extremes of prophetic behavior that has disqualified its comparison to Pauline prophecy in the eyes of many New Testament exegetes. The aversion to ecstatic prophecy is not unlike the early anthropological examination of shamanism in that discipline. Indeed, the definition of ecstasy is the second problematic factor in assessing 1 Corinthians 14 because not infrequently the argument against ecstatic prophecy is based on a skewed understanding of ecstatic religious experience. Wayne Grudem's rejection of ecstatic prophecy in Corinth illustrates many of these misappropriations. He identifies four core characteristics that define ecstatic experience: (1) being forced to speak against one's will; (2) losing self-control and beginning to "rave violently"; (3) saying things that the speaker herself does not understand; and (4) a

---

[126] Plato's Phaedrus also finds "being out of one's mind" to be a gift, both in sex and in prophecy: "There's no truth to that story that when a lover is available you should give your favors to a man who doesn't love you instead, because he is in control of himself while the lover has lost his head. That would have been fine to say if madness were bad, pure and simple; but in fact the best things we have come from madness when it is given as a gift of the god." The passage goes on to praise the Delphic oracle and other prophetic activities for the good that comes from their "madness" (*Phaedrus* 244A–B).

disruption of awareness of one's surroundings.[127] In contrast, Grudem specifies that:

> [M]erely (i) prophesying in an excited state, or (ii) speaking with strong emotion, or (iii) having a high level of concentration or awareness of the meaning of his words, or (iv) having an unusually strong sense of the presence and the working of God in his mind, I shall not consider to be sufficiently abnormal states to warrant the use of the term "ecstasy."[128]

These sets of positive and negative criteria delimit a rather meager (and unsympathetic) picture of religious ecstasy.[129] First, they would allow for only negative possession "against the will" of the practitioner. Second, they preclude any role for cultural interpretation and societal control of ASC. The possibility exists (and has been observed in field studies) that someone might not exercise conscious control of some aspects of behavior (such as demonstration of "strong emotion" or filtering of speech) while simultaneously controlling others (such as whether or not to enter an ecstatic state). Behind Grudem's dichotomy is the false assumption that religious ecstasy is only a loss of control. Third, this description fails to recognize the neurological basis of all the experiences described in these verses. There is nothing incorrect in reserving the term "ecstasy" for so-called third-stage neurological tuning, but it seems tendentious to begin by positing two wholly different experiences and a difference in the core character of two sets of behavior – one of which is marked by an awareness of God and the other by violent raving. Is it possible for readings of confessional interest to entertain the possibility that profound and religiously significant insight can grow out of more than one kind of consciousness?

Other purported distinctions have also been offered as the barrier to comparison. For example, Christopher Forbes argues that Christian prophecy cannot be compared to the Greco-Roman forms because the former was unsolicited and the latter was always in response to an inquiry from a client. As support, he shows that between 100 BCE and 100 CE there were "at most" six cases of "unsolicited and inspired prophecy known from our evidence."[130] Furthermore, he suggests that Christian prophecy relies on "inspiration," whereas the Greco-Roman form is "predominantly

---

[127] Grudem, *Gift of Prophecy in 1 Corinthians*, 150.

[128] Ibid., 151.

[129] Allen Rhea Hunt (*Inspired Body*, 125) similarly asserts that Paul does not think of prophecy as a "state where the human vessel is unresponsive to his or her surroundings or where voluntary human functions are replaced by autonomic ones."

[130] Forbes, *Prophecy and Inspired Speech in Early Christianity and Its Hellenistic Environment*, 307.

technical." This distinction is untenable. It is of the same ilk as the accusations that another group performs magic, whereas one's own group uses prayer. As discussed earlier, many types of activities (i.e., "techniques") are capable of inducing ecstatic states of consciousness. Is fasting not a technique? Is the singing of hymns purely inspiration as opposed to method? The case of Emilio, described in Section 4.1.2, demonstrates the line at which "inspiration" became "technique" for one practitioner. At the same time, it also demonstrates the unhelpfulness of such value-laden comparisons. From Emilio's perspective, the ecstasy he sought by squeezing his ribs was as equally "inspired" by the Holy Spirit as the one he obtained formerly when singing and standing in the midst of other glossolalists who were sufficient driving forces to inspire his own speech.

The final and most substantive sticking point in assessing the nature of prophetic activity is Paul's distinction between mind (*nous*) and spirit. Indeed, the terms are a significant indication of the nature of the intended prophetic activity in Corinth. Part of the interpretive difficulty lies in the fact that Paul sometimes uses πνεῦμα (*pneuma*), with no modification, to designate the one divine possessing spirit and at other times to identify an aspect of human being. In these cases, only the context of his comments indicates which use he has in mind. For the most part, Paul's distinctions pose no difficulties. For example, in 1 Cor 2:10b–12, he speaks of the human spirit and divine spirit, both of which are active in a single person. However, a possible point of confusion regarding the identity of *pneuma* exists in 1 Cor 14:32. Here Paul discusses the control that the prophets have over the "spirits of [the] prophets," and some have proposed that he is referring to several possessing spirits.[131] However, for a number of reasons, it seems far more likely that Paul is referring to an aspect of the human practitioners, an anthropological category. For one thing, Paul introduces this section of the letter with pronounced emphasis on the animating control of the one and same spirit in all the *charismata* of the church, including prophecy (1 Cor 12:4–11). It would be quite unexpected for him to shift to the several spirits when he takes up the topic of prophecy later in the discussion. Furthermore, earlier in the passage at hand, he makes reference to his own spirit with regard to his ecstatic prayer (1 Cor 14:14), and that use provides the most likely explanation of his meaning at the end of

---

[131] For example, E. E. Ellis suggests that the phrase "spirits of [the] prophets" refers to several angelic spirits (cf. 11:10) that animate the activity of the prophets. See E. Earle Ellis, "Christ and Spirit in 1 Corinthians," in *Christ and the Spirit in the New Testament*, ed. Barnabas Lindars, Stephen S. Smalley, and C. F. D. Moule (Cambridge: Cambridge University Press, 1973), 275–76.

the discussion as well. Thus, it seems most likely that Paul is referring to an aspect of the prophets themselves.

The distinction between *nous* and *pneuma* as two aspects of the individual is often taken to indicate Paul's preference for rational, coherent speech (that of the mind) and rejection of the irrational, frenzied variety (that of the spirit). Martin demonstrates convincingly the inappropriateness of the rational–irrational dichotomy.[132] In the first place, he shows that ecstatic speech was valued in the ancient world and, where the inspiration was judged to be of authentically divine origin, rationality or the lack thereof was wholly irrelevant. If the prophetic state was from the god, then it was true and useful by that very fact. Second, although the mind is associated with reason, that is not its most salient feature when it is set in antithetical parallel with *pneuma*. Rather, in this case, *pneuma* and *nous* contrast two aspects of human functioning, and the ancients used these very terms in their discussions of spirit possession and other ecstatic states. The *nous* is not abstract rationality but rather an aspect of human being, as is the *pneuma*.[133]

This distinction is illustrated in the quotation from *Timaeus* cited earlier. In that passage, Plato declares that mantic activity was impossible for the person who was *ennous* and that the successful medium could not interpret her own speech precisely because she had not been in her mind. Philo uses *nous* in ways that are even more instructive for Paul's comments, though not exactly parallel.

> This is what regularly befalls the fellowship of prophets. The mind (*nous*) is evicted at the arrival of the divine Spirit, but when that departs the mind returns to its tenancy. Mortal and immortal may not share the same home. And therefore the setting of reason and the darkness which surrounds it produce ecstasy and divine *mania*. For indeed the prophet, even when he seems to be speaking, really holds his peace, and his organs of speech, mouth and tongue, are wholly in the employ of another, to show forth what he wills. Unseen by us that other beats on the chords with the skill of a masterhand and makes them instruments of sweet music, laden with every harmony. (*Quis Rerum Divinarum Heres*, 265–66)

Philo and Paul differ somewhat in the activity that they call "prophecy," but they understand *nous* to function in largely the same way during ecstatic states. For both of them, performing an ecstatic activity without the *nous* requires, or results in, dissociative states of consciousness – in other words, possession trance. Philo talks about the person(ality) being displaced while

---

[132] See the discussion in D. Martin, *Corinthian Body*, 96–103.
[133] Ibid., 100.

the god or spirit is resident in the prophet. But dissociative trance is only one form of ecstatic religious experience, and Paul has also experienced ecstasy *ennous*.

Paul's own use of *nous* elsewhere supports the sense of the word as identity or self-awareness, even though its most basic translation is "mind." The two most important words referring to the mind or capacity to think are *phren* and its cognates and *nous*, and Paul uses them with some degree of consistent distinction. In particular, *nous* is used in a more static sense than *phrēn*. The latter appears in sections of paraenesis (Rom 12:3; 1 Cor 10:15), where its connotations are those of discernment, and in contrast to foolishness (1 Cor 4:10; 2 Cor 11:19), which suggests the applied nature of the thinking as well. Thus, *phrēn* carries connotations of thinking as a dynamic force. The former term, *nous*, seems rather to connote mind or thinking as an established aspect of the personality. Paul uses it along with heart in his benediction in Phil 4:7 ("and the peace of God ... will keep your hearts and minds") to circumscribe the protection of the person. In other occurrences, it typically represents an individual's established or enduring commitment as opposed to their discernment (Rom 7:23, 25; 14:5).[134] But 1 Cor 14:14–20 provides the best test because the two terms appear in a single context. Throughout the contrast in Chapter 14 between two ways of engagement in worship (i.e., one with only the spirit and the other with spirit and mind), Paul uses the term *nous*. However, at the end of the discussion, he shifts the discourse to a direct appeal to choose and to act according to his advice. When he makes the shift from the faculties that function during ecstatic worship to the process of choosing and deciding, he also switches from *nous* to *phrēn*. In short, then, though both terms are related to cognition, Paul treats *nous* consistently as an established feature of identity and uses *phrēn* to denote more dynamic processes of thinking.

These functioning definitions have implications for how we understand Paul's instructions about ecstatic practice. In particular, they disrupt the easy claim that Paul is concerned centrally with rational (and hence non-ecstatic) distinctions. Instead, in his instructions to the Corinthians, Paul is contrasting two kinds of ecstatic functioning – one with *nous* and *pneuma* and the other with *pneuma* only – both of which are enabled by the same divine spirit. One difference between Paul and other ancient writers is that he speaks of the role of the human spirit in ecstatic activity, whereas they speak

---

[134] I would argue that this is the case even when the *nous* changes. For example, in Rom 1:28, Paul suggests that people are punished when God betrays them to a disapproved mind, and this change of mind seems to be part of Paul's attempt to account for enduring difference. Likewise, in Rom 12:2, renewing one's mind sets one in enduring alignment with God.

only of divine spirits.[135] Paul, like many other leaders in ecstatic cults, is trying to teach control of the ASC. In effect, he is talking about two different phases of consciousness and, as supported by the profile of social settings of ASC, he is also talking about two different uses of these states. The first is straightforward spirit possession marked primarily by the phenomenon of glossolalia and accompanied by the displacement of personality and probably the accompanying partial amnesia that is typical of most spirit possession. The break in personality, described by Philo as the displacement of the *nous*, is a classic cross-cultural sign of spirit possession. Paul writes, similarly to Philo, about praying in tongues without the use of the *nous*. The second type of ASC, I would suggest, is most comparable to mediumship because it is marked by moderate control of the trance experience and a different sort of ASC, which Paul describes by using *nous* and *pneuma*. Paul uses the distinctive anthropological language of spirit in order to distinguish the neurological phenomena that are under the control of the prophets – "the spirits of the prophets are subject to the prophets" (1 Cor 14:32). It is this correspondence between the nature of the ecstatic state and its function in the community that is at the heart of Paul's purpose in the chapter.

4.3.2 Paul's Comments

In the midst of his exhortations on Corinthian corporate worship, Paul declares his own superlative practice of ecstatic speech (1 Cor 14:18). At the same time, within the particular epistolary context, he urges a tempering of glossolalia in their public gatherings and an increase in other spiritual (that is, ecstatic) practices: "Now I wish all of you to speak in tongues, but even more that you might prophesy" (1 Cor 14:5a). Alongside his relative ranking of gifts in public settings, at the close of this discourse, Paul interjects the wish that no one should hinder or prevent glossolalia (1 Cor 14:39b). Frequently, 1 Corinthians 12–14 has been read as

---

[135] Martin (*Corinthian Body*, 101) summarizes the prevalent Platonic view that "it is only right that the *nous* get out of the way when the *pneuma* makes its entrance, just as it is only right for clients to give way to patrons, for slaves to give way to owners, and for employees to give way to employers." However, this sense of hierarchy only holds when the *pneuma* is a divine being, not when it is an anthropological feature. As Martin himself clarifies, Paul is using *pneuma* in the latter sense. Martin also suggests that Paul is deliberately playing on the hierarchical differences between these two aspects of the human being. The *pneuma* is routinely considered the higher and purer aspect, but Paul is deliberately upsetting that superiority by privileging the *nous*. In contrast, I do not think that Paul's interests are narrowly anthropological or that his strategy is quite as adroit as Martin's theory would have it.

a single-purpose condemnation of religious ecstasy. If this is so, Paul makes a counterproductive concession to the practice of tongues at the conclusion of his argument. Instead, this "concession" to tongues is among the evidence that Paul's position is more discriminating than often imagined.

Along with the evidence discussed earlier, several additional details of 1 Corinthians 14 indicate that the prophecy Paul has in mind is also an ecstatic state. The first of these is Paul's language. His use of the passive form for the action of revelation ($\dot{\alpha}\pi o\kappa\alpha\lambda\acute{\upsilon}\phi\theta\hat{\eta}$, 1 Cor 14:30) assumes divine inspiration. Furthermore, his instruction that the one who is speaking must cede the floor to the one who receives a new revelation suggests that Paul values and encourages the relatively spontaneous nature of each new inspiration. That fact witnesses somewhat against the normal self-monitoring phase of consciousness.

Furthermore, Winkelman's social anthropological profile of mediumship fits many of the details of Paul's advice to the Corinthians in Chapter 14. Among the most relevant points of contact are the social role of the prophets and the social conditions in which they practice. For example, Paul instructs them to use their prophecy for the sake of the community and not for private devotion or pleasure (1 Cor 14:2–5) and, further, that more than one member should practice prophecy (1 Cor 14:1, 24, 39a) even at the same meeting (1 Cor 14:29–33). These instructions parallel the pattern of mediums as agents working within a guild or group, accessing spirits on behalf of others. Paul's comment that "two or three prophets ought to speak and the others (οἱ ἄλλοι) discern" seems to suggest a circumscribed group within the larger community.[136] So, although the broad thrust of Paul's comment encourages everyone to prophesy, the details of the passage show that he does not expect everyone to be able to. In addition to these points of practice, the sociological profile of Corinth corresponds to the conditions of a society in which one might expect to find mediums. Chief among these social conditions is the presence of political integration beyond the local level. In this regard, I think it is especially noteworthy that Paul attempts to temper their practices by urging the assembly to consider its place among the other christian groups – "all the assemblies of the saints" (1 Cor 14:33b). In so doing, Paul is introducing an awareness of political (in the loosest sense of the term) integration among the christian assemblies themselves. The members of the Corinthian assembly are already imbedded

---

[136] It is interesting to note that Plato also considers it advisable for individuals other than the inspired speakers to interpret or assess the inspired message (*Timaeus*, 72A–B).

in a civic structure with a good degree of integration within the empire. The christian assembly may have been a place of relative independence and freedom,[137] but now Paul is urging them both to think of the "outsiders" (1 Cor 14:11, 16) and also to consider their relationship to other assemblies – however suggestive and informal that "relationship" may be. His efforts in regard to the collection for Jerusalem have the same effect (1 Cor 16:1–4; also 2 Corinthians 8 and 9). In these ways, Paul attempts to breach the boundaries that isolate the Corinthian assembly from those outside, while at the same time he urges a shift toward a different focus in their ecstatic practice.

So, if Paul is not merely quenching an ecstatic practice, what is the nature of his intervention and how was it expected to help? The careful and sympathetic fieldwork of both Goodman and Wedenoja includes examples of the efforts of societies to train ecstatics in the use of their ASC. Goodman discusses several examples that indicate degrees of behavioral control even during obvious dissociation trance. For example, she describes people who were in dissociative states, complete with involuntary muscle cramping and tremors, and yet were able to hold their very young children without causing them any discomfort.[138] She further describes the strategies used by leaders in a number of communities to stimulate and maintain ecstatic states among uninitiated members. Wedenoja discusses other forms of social control of trance states. He catalogs the vocabulary used by the Jamaican Revivalists to distinguish degrees of communally evaluated authenticity during trance. It is especially noteworthy that this movement is the least tolerant of phases of consciousness that manifest symptoms of indiscriminate neurological stimulations (tremors and the like).[139] They use pejorative vocabulary as one of their means to control religious ecstasy, exercising social pressure and encoding communal values. They also use physical patterning during trance, in which an experienced practitioner will increase his or her activity near a novice. In these ways, communities exert their expectations for ecstatic practice and create a degree of conformity in the actual experience. So, too, they demonstrate the variations in consciousness that can accompany ecstatic states.

So, when Paul urges the Corinthians to become mature and to cease thinking ($\varphi\rho\epsilon\nu\acute{\epsilon}\omega$) like children, he might be insulting them; he might be

---

[137] Perhaps one of the signs of their freedom is their tolerance of the incestuous relationship, which Paul claims would have been offensive even to the broader population (1 Cor 5:1–13).

[138] Goodman, *Speaking in Tongues*, 63–64.

[139] Wedenoja, "Ritual Trance and Catharsis," 286–87.

accusing them of childishness in their pursuit of tongues.[140] But more likely his language is not simply a push from behind but also an urging forward. Paul is not opposed to tongues, but he is in favor of development both in the social organization of the community and in their ecstatic practices. If Esler is right in his reconstruction of the role that glossolalia played in the inception of various communities, then Paul may well view that practice as part of an initiatory phase. In Corinth, it has endured. For this reason, a section of one of Paul's letters to that assembly, he advocates both its continuation and its development into forms that will serve an evolving community.

4.4 IMPLICATIONS: PAUL'S PUBLIC POSITION ON ASC

This chapter has considered ecstasy as part of public *practice*, both Paul's own and that of his communities. Paul's first (extant) letter to the Corinthians offers the clearest evidence of such practice, but ecstatic religious experience was probably a factor in the inception of most of the christian assemblies. Michael Winkelman's work models how such corporate religious experience takes place in specific social contexts and participates in a social "logic" or "economy." The most significant of those findings for understanding the Pauline assemblies is that the practice of ASC varies consistently with the social conditions of the host community. That fact helps to paint a richer and more complex picture of the tensions that attend ecstatic religious practices in Corinth. Glossolalia and even prophecy offered real and symbolic benefits to their practitioners and to the larger host community. The former were largely somatic and aesthetic. The latter include access to neurologically subordinated ways of knowing and discerning. In this final section of this examination, I consolidate this information into three implications for an understanding of formative christianity and Paul's writings.

The first implication concerns the variety in ecstatic religious experience. Paul is not alone in classifying one social practice of ASC as more valuable than another – most cultures that incorporate religious or social ecstatic practice make such distinctions. The sharpest line of demarcation falls between spirit possession and soul journeying. These two general categories define two neurologically different types of experiences that can be summarized as follows:

---

[140] This is the argument made in Hunt, *Inspired Body*, 129.

Soul journey	Spirit possession
Memory of experience retained	Ecstatic amnesia
Displacement of normal embodiment	Displacement of personality
Mastery of spirits	Mastered by spirits
Service of community	Service of spirits
	or personal focus

In assessing Paul's remarks in 1 Corinthians 12–14, the majority of commentators imagine him to be distinguishing between an ecstatic practice on the one hand and a non-ecstatic one on the other. However, it is more likely that he – like members of other societies – is distinguishing between different types of ASC on the basis of their blend of neurological and socially viable characteristics. He values the form of dissociative spirit possession that results in glossolalia (1 Cor 14:5, 18, 39), but he also urges the people to increase the more exceptional phase of consciousness that provides guidance to the assembly and permits integration with various categories of outsiders. In particular, he is urging greater control of and even a change in the character of the ecstatic state.

A number of factors suggest, even more specifically, that Paul is urging a movement beyond the experience of the nervous system that is most generalized, to one that is more neurologically selective. In Chapter 3, I outlined the maladaptive characteristics of so-called temporal lobe syndrome (TLS).[141] They include decreased sexual libido, paradoxically combined with preoccupation with sexual topics and situations; heightened emotions; seeing "cosmic significance in trivial events"; personality changes;[142] and hypergraphia (typically expressed through excessive journaling). Rhawn Joseph connects this sort of self-centeredness with certain functions of the limbic system:

> The hypothalamus, our exceedingly ancient and primitive Id, has an eye that only sees inward. It can tell if the body needs nourishment but cannot determine what might be good to eat. It can feel thirst, but has no way of slaking this desire. The hypothalamus can only say: "I want," "I need," and can only signal pleasure and displeasure.[143]

---

[141] The description is taken from Ramachandran and Blakeslee, *Phantoms in the Brain*, 180–88.

[142] As Ramachandran describes it, these patients often become argumentative, pedantic, and egocentric.

[143] Joseph, *Neuropsychiatry, Neuropsychology, and Clinical Neurology*, 203. Like Ramachandran, Winkelman has suggested a connection between this syndrome and some cases of spirit possession, especially where tremors and other involuntary peripheral nervous system behaviors are present. Wedenoja, too, entertains some degree of overlap between pathological temporal lobe activity and some expressions of religious experience.

It does not seem that much spirit possession is the result of temporal lobe seizures. However, I do think that comparison with TLS is informative in the same way that the study of injured brains informs the understanding of healthy ones. In reflecting on the occurrence of TLS, Ramachandran and Blakeslee state that:

> No one knows why this happens, but it's as though the repeated electrical bursts inside the patient's brain (the frequent passage of massive volleys of nerve impulses within the limbic system) permanently "facilitate" certain pathways or may even open new channels, much as water from a storm might pour downhill, opening new rivulets, furrows and passages along the hillside. This process, called kindling, might permanently alter – and sometimes enrich – the patient's inner emotional life.[144]

The last line of the quotation raises the most important point: Some patients with temporal lobe seizures integrate their neurological experience into their lives in healthy ways and some do not. A similar potential for adaptive and maladaptive appropriations exists in other forms of ecstasy, too. The range of religious ecstasy appears to include a phase that shares some similarities with temporal lobe seizures both in its immediate neurological mechanisms and in its broader psychosocial effects. However, the range also includes forms of ecstasy that do not conform in any significant way to TLS. Either set of forms can be used positively, but the less discrete form of spirit possession seems the most susceptible to difficulties.

A number of factors in Corinth align in ways that suggest an identifiable form of religious experience was taking place. As many commentators have noted, women seem to be of particular interest in Paul's comments about worship practices, and he seems especially concerned that female members of the community should not leave their "unbelieving" husbands as well (1 Cor 7:10–16). In Corinth, the behavior of women as a group seems to be the focus in the veiling of women in the assembly (1 Cor 11:3–16).[145] Indeed, many have suggested that women were the sole or primary participants in the glossolalia group, and the cerebral and neurological as well as sociological differences between men and women may well bear on some of these issues. Parts of the brain, especially regions of the limbic system, are sexually dimorphic; that is to say, there are general physiological and functional differences between male and female brains. Female brains tend to have more abundant and thicker fibers connecting corresponding regions in

---

[144] Ramachandran and Blakeslee, *Phantoms in the Brain*, 180.
[145] It may also be part of their questioning at these gatherings, depending on the status of the disputed (1 Cor 14:33b–35).

the two cerebral hemispheres. Both the corpus callosum (especially where it connects the parietal lobes) and the anterior commissure (which connects the amygdaloid and temporal regions across hemispheres) are up to 18 percent larger in women than in men.[146] Furthermore, in women, the nuclei in the amygdala are also more numerous and more densely arranged than in men. The result of this difference, according to Joseph, is "a condition that would enhance electrical excitability, lower response thresholds, and increase susceptibility to kindling."[147] Other widely recognized gender differences that can be related to brain physiology include more robust areas of linguistic specialization in women and especially those that integrate emotion and language.[148] Even though these measurements might be better understood as "statistical trends than real dimorphisms,"[149] some generalizable difference is supported by this range of studies. In Corinth, it appears that both men and women are practicing prophecy (1 Cor 11:3–10), but it may well be that women are the primary practitioners of glossolalia,[150] as they are in contemporary settings.[151] Certainly, a complex collection of social factors impinges on these distinctions, but the neurology of ecstasy might also be reckoned into the mix. At any rate, Paul's instructions regarding the control of spiritual experience evidence his interest not in ending ecstasy but in refining it. As someone who personally experienced some of the breadth of ecstatic states, he was in a distinct position to offer such advice.

The second major implication of this study concerns the fact that different types of ASC have corresponding social implications. Most of the studies of 1 Corinthians mentioned in this chapter have considered the social

---

[146] R. L. Holloway et al., "Sexual Dimorphism of the Human Corpus Callosum from Three Independent Samples: Relative Size of the Corpus Callosum," *American Journal of Physical Anthropology* 92 (1993), 481–98.

[147] Joseph, *Neuropsychiatry, Neuropsychology, and Clinical Neurology*, 188.

[148] The anterior cingulate gyrus is especially significant in emotional communication and the generation of behavior that is emotionally responsive. This region is nicknamed the "maternal" gyrus. The scientific literature on these differences is vast. Joseph (*Neuropsychiatry, Neuropsychology, and Clinical Neurology*) summarizes the findings on 82–83, 136–37, 188–89, and 244–51.

[149] Carol Rausch Albright, personal communication, June 23, 2005.

[150] Anders Eriksson, "'Women Tongue Speakers, Be Silent': A Reconstruction through Paul's Rhetoric," *Biblical Interpretation* 6 (1998), 80–104, in particular, has made this case.

[151] Goodman (*Speaking in Tongues*, 10, also 67) reports that in many (though not all) of the groups she studied, "women go into glossolalia much more easily than men, and almost all of them are habitual glossolalists." In her study of women in Pentecostal communities in Appalachia, Mary McClintock Fulkerson has likewise observed that women usually comprise more than half of those speaking in tongues even though active female participation in public is discouraged. See Mary McClintock Fulkerson, *Changing the Subject: Women's Discourses and Feminist Theology* (Minneapolis: Fortress, 1994), 245.

implications of glossolalia within that community,[152] but none that I have found consider the role of ecstatic practice for the Corinthian assembly as a society. First, there is a good deal of interest in the use of glossolalia as a tool for social manipulation. These studies typically focus on in-group conflict and status difference, often based on Lewis's type of analysis of spirit possession. Typically, the glossolalists are seen as low-status members of the community who use their ecstasy to promote their own welfare. However, the proper point of reference for the possession cult is not the christian assembly itself but the larger community that would view their behavior as deviant or peripheral. As I have mentioned, Lewis sees spirit possession as a means by which "women and other depressed categories exert 'spiritual' pressures on their superiors in circumstances of deprivation and frustration when few other sanctions are available to them."[153] If this is the case in Corinth, then those pressures would be exerted outside of the christian cult on family members who were not members. Thus, in a different way than is usually proposed, the practice of tongues is a sign to unbelievers (1 Cor 14:22).[154]

Along these same lines, Paul is often seen as begrudging the practice of glossolalia in Corinth. For example, Jerome Neyrey sees a Paul who disapproves of the lack of order in the community and had intervened to impose greater purity control focused on the mouth and speech ("regulation of the oral orifice").[155] For Neyrey, Paul's ultimate goal is greater control on the in group. The details that I have discussed here suggest, in addition, that Paul is concerned with the health of the Corinthian community in light of their relationship to those outside – both their fellow citizens (1 Cor 14:11, 16) and, to some degree, other christian communities. A number of times in this letter – and only in this letter – he appeals to the practice of other assemblies as a way of constraining the behavior of the Corinthians. At these points, Paul's arguments for change in Corinthian practice work partly through

---

[152] Especially Wire, *Corinthian Women Prophets*; D. Martin, *Corinthian Body*; and D. Eriksson, " 'Women Tongue Speakers, Be Slient'. "

[153] Ioan M. Lewis, *Religion in Context: Cults and Charisma,* 2nd ed. (Cambridge: Cambridge University Press, 1966), 318.

[154] My proposal here fits with the assessment of Karl Olav Sandnes that Paul quotes Isa 28:11 to show that tongues will alienate outsiders. Just as God demonstrated alienation from the people by speaking in a foreign tongue, so, too, the Corinthians will show outsiders that they are aliens to the community by speaking a language that the outsiders cannot understand. See Karl Olav Sandnes, "Prophecy – A Sign for Believers (1 Cor 14:20–25)," *Biblica* 77 (1996), 1–15.

[155] Jerome H. Neyrey, *Paul, in Other Words: A Cultural Reading of His Letters* (Louisville, Ky.: Westminster/John Knox, 1990), 128–31.

appeals to a sense of a larger, more complex social reality. He makes that connection in 1 Cor 4:17–20 at the end of his opening appeal for unity. He does so again in 1 Cor 7:17 as part of his appeal to maintain current social ties. In 1 Cor 11:16, his concern is with appropriate dress and in 1 Cor 14:33–35 (if it is authentic) with women's questions, both of which are brought into relation with the practice of other churches. In 1 Cor 4:9–14, his example of "us apostles" is similarly an appeal to an emerging pattern among the assemblies. Likewise, the nature of Paul's appeals to the Lord's command (1 Cor 7:10, 9:14, 11:23–25) signal his sense of a pattern that transcends local governance. At most, he has a sense of the connection between broader political integration and the corresponding shape of magico-religious practice, and he is using the former to influence the latter, or at least the social means by which he has chosen to pressure the Corinthians happen to fit coincidentally with the direction in which he wants them to change in their ecstatic practices.

When Paul urges the move toward mediumship, his language is that of edification (1 Cor 14:3, 4, 5, 12, 17, 26). In addition to indicating purity concerns, as Neyrey suggests, "edification" is literally a structural term and figuratively a political one. It indicates Paul's concern for more robust and complex relationships not only within the community but also between this community and others. So at this point and a number of others, Paul attempts to break the isolation of the Corinthian assembly. As I have shown, mediumship is the form of magico-religious practice that is most naturally associated with increased political integration. As Wire observes, in Chapter 14 "Paul uses mission language . . . against their strictly local reception and dissemination of God's word. They on the contrary see themselves not as receptors of a witness whose agents have come and gone, but as a primary point of Christ's appearance and activity."[156] I do not think that Paul opposes the current practice to the degree that most authors claim. But I do think that Wire's basic claim is correct – Paul is trying to focus Corinthian attention beyond their self-oriented confines or immediate desires. In this case, the private character of religious ecstasy and the insular social location coincide; a certain kind of ecstatic practice is explicitly coupled with a certain kind of political structure. Also in this case, as Winkelman's analysis of ASC societies suggests, a movement away from spirit possession toward mediumship is coupled with an experience of a relatively complex sociopolitical arrangement in which local autonomy is subordinated to a fledgling sense of a network of assemblies

---

[156] Wire, *Corinthian Women Prophets*, 148.

and even the possibility of a loose layer of governance above that collective.[157]

The stereotyped assessment of 1 Corinthians 12–14 is that the Corinthian christians were enthusiasts who had become carried away by their uncontrolled, involuntary, and unintelligible experience of glossolalia. Paul, by contrast, is understood to be the champion of "consciousness and clarity."[158] Although such claims may be true as far as they go, they do not go far enough. The practice of religiously altered states of consciousness has implications for social organization, for personal health, and for societal growth and adaptability. All of these factors impinge on the negotiations Paul carries out with the Corinthians. Given that complexity and the novelty of the situation, the confusion, if it is rightly characterized as such, is as much Paul's doing as theirs.

---

[157] The only clues about the nature of such governance suggest that it might be based on defining teachings that were "from the Lord," a phrase that Paul uses authoritatively a few times in this letter. He also clearly distinguishes that teaching from his own personal discernment about the issues at hand (e.g., 1 Cor 7:10). In addition, the letter hints at a handful of practices that were becoming established among some of the assemblies. In the latter case in particular, the participation of the group in defining the norm is suggested.

[158] Neyrey, *Paul, in Other Words*, 130.

❧

The Whole Paul: A Short Course in (Nondeterministic) Complexity

Experience is never limited . . . it is an immense sensibility, a kind of huge spider-web of the finest silken threads suspended in the chamber of consciousness, and catching every air-borne particle in its tissue.

– Henry James

"Best not to speculate, really," said Aziraphale. "You can't second-guess ineffability, I always say."

– Neil Gaiman and Terry Pratchett

T HIS EXAMINATION BEGAN WITH A DESCRIPTION OF PAUL'S ecstatic experience as a curiosity. By this point in the examination, I hope that it seems much less curious but no less intriguing as a result. The preceding chapters have presented evidence for the widespread and enduring fact of ecstatic religious experience as a meaningful part of the lives of individuals and a contributing factor in the health and growth (as well as some of the conflicts) of their communities. Such positive effects derive in part from the fact that the neurological mechanisms that permit ecstatic experience also provide access to rich ways of knowing that are otherwise often veiled from consciousness. For Paul and these first communities, religious ecstasy helped to make the world meaningful and to orient them in the midst of change and contingency.[1] When they were gathered for worship, their corporate ecstasy became sacred experience and, because the body is inextricably bound to the experience itself, even their bodies were partly redeemed through their participation. Through

---

[1] To some degree, religious ecstasy shares these benefits with other forms of religious experience, even without profoundly altered states of consciousness. See Carol Rausch Albright, "Neuroscience in Pursuit of the Holy: Mysticism, the Brain, and Ultimate Reality," *Zygon* 36 (2001), 485–92.

religious ecstasy, they felt they were in the process of being transformed, as Paul put it, from one glory to another (2 Cor 3:18). This they knew not only as an idea or proposition but also as a set of sensations that demanded description and explanation, even if it also largely defied description. The embodied nature of this form of religious experience provides some of the most powerful and deeply etched forms of knowing that are available. As the anthropologist Janice Boddy puts it, "the body is the ground for legitimating objective knowledge, internalizing it, and making it experientially real."[2] So, in all of these ways, religious ecstasy fleshes out the opening questions about epistemology. It really is a means of coming to know as well as the source of some of the content of what is known.

Paul's letters contain the evidence of a variety of ecstatic religious practices; they also contain his reflections on these events and their significance to him and to the communities to which he writes. These second-order reflections can be categorized as being of different degrees. In some cases, the experience itself appears to be the impetus for reflection as something that demands exegesis or something perceived so powerfully that there is an urge to make it known to others even if the right words have not yet been found. In other cases, the relationship between the embodied knowledge of religious practice, on the one hand, and ideas that are already part of the culture, on the other hand, is quite close. In that set of circumstances, the two dynamics – experience and culture – are quite fluidly mutually reinforcing and not cognitively disruptive. Paul did not have to accommodate a new datum but could elaborate ideas that were already within the cultural repertoire.

Within this latter set of ideas, one might include Paul's Christology and notions of the general resurrection. For instance, concepts of divinity and its apprehension were already available to Paul and others before his visions took place. In particular, the understanding existed that God could be made manifest, and that notion had already been coupled with the idea of *doxa* as the splendor and brilliance of divine manifestation. So, the phenomena of Paul's visions of the risen Christ as a glorious presence of light (e.g., 1 Cor 2:8; Phil 3:21; and especially 2 Cor 4:4–6) coincided with the sorts of claims about God's *kavod* or the formulations of the pre-Pauline hymn of the descent of one who was in the form of God (Phil 2:6–11). At times (e.g., Rom 1:4), Paul even seems to suggest that the resurrection was the means of Christ's divinization, an idea that persisted among some early Christian writers but has since been ignored. Thus, Paul's visions were not necessarily

---

[2]   Boddy, "Spirit Possession Revisited," 425.

the source of such ideas, but they did confirm and amplify Christological reflection on Jesus's divine nature. A second example of the mutual reinforcement of cultural constructs and religious experience is present in Paul's reflections on the resurrection of the dead. The idea of a general resurrection predated the earliest christian formulations, and bodily resurrection was among the ways it was imagined.[3] That possibility received embodied confirmation in Paul's neurochemical transformation in religious ecstasy as he felt his body become like the glorious body of Christ that he had seen in ecstasy. The embodied confirmation of one set of resurrection ideas helps to generate a diverse set of images that Paul uses inconsistently in his writing but that betray a distinctive sense of the significance of the body in its present and redeemed forms. We are being transformed, says Paul (e.g., 2 Cor 3:18), and in other ways he grasps at words for that transitional state. In these ways, experience supplemented existing traditions of thought.

However, in another set of ideas, experience seems to have been the primary source and impetus for Paul's formulations. In other words, religious experience seems necessary to account for the presence of the ideas at all. The central example of this sort is that most Pauline, and least systematic, of themes: Paul's participation theology. His persistent, sometimes seemingly habitual way of speaking about an interrelational existence with Christ punctuates so much of his letters, yet it cannot be explained on the basis of influence from cultural-linguistic parallels. Instead, here it seems that Paul is giving shape to something in the embodied, emotional, and cognitive effects of practices such as prayer or glossolalia or especially powerful ecstatic states of union. Many have observed that the pattern of dying and rising has more than metaphorical value for Paul. He is not saying only that difficulties may be thought of as something like Christ's death; rather, Paul seems to propose that in his own physical traumas he takes part in Christ's sufferings. I have tried to make the case that the "realness" that prompted such understandings results from religious ecstasy. These sorts of religious experiences with their accompanying ASCs are marked by a cognitive vitality and insistence, not to mention their attendant emotions and the extraordinary neurochemical changes in the body. The powerful experiential combination demands explanation, and Christ's part in Paul's religious practice was an immutable component of what appealed to be understood.

For a time, peaking perhaps in the 1980s, it was argued that there is no experience without language. In the introduction, I quoted Margaret Miles's

---

[3]   Among the other options was astral transformation, presented for instance in Dan 12:2–3; 1 Enoch 71; and possibly also Matt 13:43.

critique that much hermeneutical theory is blind to a large proportion of human perception because it construes "reality as verbally constituted" and ignores the "perceptive, affective, and intellectual experience" of the majority of people, whose primary interface "with the world is not verbal."[4] Terry Eagleton makes a related point in his argument with some cultural theorists (and anti-theorists) who place language at the center of knowing. Eagleton points out that "[o]ur physical senses are themselves organs of interpretation" and hence that "all human language is meta-language. It is a second-order reflection on the 'language of our bodies' – our sensory apparatus."[5] The power of Paul's religious experience, as it is signaled in the second-order reflection of his letters, supports this perspective. And that power suggests further that, rather than reading the ideas in the letters as ends in themselves, we would do well to read parts of them as inadequate and even misaligned substitutes for something that was more important to Paul. Furthermore, the importance of experience should not be underestimated, even in cases where Paul is quite content with his words because to cite Eagleton again, "[e]ven when I have language, however, my sensory experience still represents a kind of surplus over it. The body is not reducible to signification, as linguistic reductionists tend to imagine."[6]

For these reasons, attention to religious experience also invites us to take greater notice of the effects on some social phenomena of the early movement. For one thing, it would seem that the assemblies were not founded solely on the basis of preaching but took hold in part because of ecstatic phenomena understood to be directed by the spirit of God. Often Paul explicitly reminds the recipients of some extraordinary corporate manifestation that accompanied their reception of his message (e.g., 2 Cor 12:12; Gal 3:1–3; 1 Thess 1:5), and the surviving correspondence with Corinth suggests that such manifestations were central to the continued participation of some of the members, although troublesome to the community as a whole. Even in the letter to the Romans, written to a community that Paul had not visited, Paul can assume that ecstatic worship is a given (e.g., Rom 8:15–17, 26–27). It is worth considering how great a role this aspect of their gatherings played in attracting people to the movement or even considering that such experience in itself made the assemblies viable among the other options for affiliation that were available in Greco-Roman cities. Furthermore, as Phil

---

[4]   Miles, *Image as Insight,* xi.
[5]   Terry Eagleton, *After Theory* (New York: Basic Books, 2003), 60.
[6]   Ibid., 61. Eagleton goes on to suggest, in a characteristic bit of sardonic humor, that the "overestimating of the role of language in human affairs may spring from the fact that philosophers were traditionally bachelor dons who had no experience of small children."

Esler has argued, glossolalia may well have served to convince the Jerusalem leadership that the time to include Gentiles had arrived.[7] By these means, religious experience had both a motivational and an apologetic force in earliest christianity.

Of course, Paul's ecstasy also served as both motivation and justification for his role as "an apostle of Christ Jesus." The Galatians "call" passage (Gal 1:13–17) has long been recognized as the most significant description of this link. There is consensus that here Paul uses the form of a call narrative to present a more complex set of events. For the sake of comparison, I will distinguish two variations within that general agreement: For some interpreters, those events are the one occasion that is described in the three conversion accounts in Acts; for other interpreters, the background events are a rather longer, unstructured process in which Paul first comes to a new understanding of how God was acting in the world and then orients himself within that understanding. This book shares interests with both views. I agree with the first that something emotionally powerful and viscerally dramatic lies behind the call text (though I would posit multiple events rather than a single one). I agree with the second that Paul's own subjective engagement is a fundamental ingredient in his call. In conversation with both, I would temper the cognicentric focus. Something more than conscious reasoning is at work in Paul's shift in identity, and attention to the nature of religious experience helps to name what that "something" is. Paul's experience of union with Christ during the peak of neurological tuning, as well as his repeated perception that the divine spirit inhabited or possessed him, created in Paul a knowledge of resources beyond his own. That knowledge seems especially strong on occasions such as the period of imprisonment during which he awaited a verdict on his fate (Phil 1:20–26). But the knowledge is also active when Paul proclaims to the Roman christians the benefits of "being in Christ Jesus" (Rom 8:1). Part of what this study proposes is that Paul was moved to his extraordinary project (of founding christian communities, orienting his being and identity to the risen Christ, and articulating a pattern of thought and action) by this sort of experience in particular. So – to put the implications in an extreme, if hypothetical, form – even the "objective" appearance of the "real" risen Christ on the road to Damascus would not have been sufficient for what came of Paul's life. The compelling and embodied knowing of ecstatic experience is necessary (though by no means sufficient) to account for Paul's christianity.

---

[7]   Esler, *First Christians in Their Social Worlds*, 38.

All too often, biblical scholarship can participate in unintentional linguistic reductionism. As mentioned earlier in this study, part of the reticence to explore Paul's religious experience has been the appropriate caution that we cannot know his mind. Yet, although the general caution is warranted, it is not best addressed by simply ignoring or sidestepping the whole category of experience because when we avoid the attempt to examine experience explicitly we do not secure ourselves against the error of pretending we know Paul's mind; in fact, we are still making de facto claims about it, but doing so without theoretical awareness. Our silence is not sufficient to bracket out the internal world because what he has written simply expands to fill the space of his cranium. We end up with statements that catalog all the things Paul somehow "knew"; whatever we can describe "objectively" on the basis of the hard data of rhetoric and philology becomes by default the content of Paul's mind. Thus, in turn, Paul becomes by default someone who read and reflected on texts and picked and chose between cultural elements in much the same way we academics do when we study them. Rhetorical practice, textual parallels, mirror reconstructions, and theological conventions become, in the silence of other factors, the mind of Paul.

However, the aim of this study has not been to replace conventional ways of reading Paul with some sort of neurological reading (assuming that it was even possible to do so) but rather to suggest that we make a greater attempt to add experience – in this case, religious experience – as an impetus for communication and a source of its content. It would be counterproductive to displace analysis of Paul's letters as works of rhetoric, consideration of possible opposing views that he might be refuting, or assessment of the relevance of parallel ideas from surrounding cultures and movements because Paul's words, even in a limited set of texts such as 2 Corinthians 3–5 and Romans 8, are not the product of just one thing, even a thing as rich as ecstatic experience. In fact, Paul's ecstasy itself is not an independent datum but seems to emerge from the complex confluence of many components whose interplay could not have been orchestrated – but neither is it the only possibility that might have emerged from these circumstances. Paul's ecstasy is the coincidence of his physical suffering blended with his reflection on the torturous death of Jesus, the impact of extraordinary ecstatic displays among the Gentile adherents in christian assemblies, familiarity with the religious experience that was practiced in other Greco-Roman movements, Paul's mixed set of leadership skills and their impact on the assemblies, and even his probable neurological predisposition toward ASC. All of these factors, at least, combined in unpredictable measure to create the phenomena reflected in his letters. But, whatever the precise recipe, the experience in itself is an essential ingredient. Hence, part of what this study does argue is that a greater complexity of description is necessary to account for what Paul knew and how he worked among the first assemblies.

So, an examination of Paul's religious ecstasy deviates from many of the issues that traditionally have defined the interpretive crux of the biblical texts. At the same time, this deviation was pursued precisely out of an interest in meaning that is shared by theological readings. Because of this shared interest, comparison with the views of more traditional exegetes of the New Testament are helpful in understanding the focus of the approach of this examination. For example, J. Christiaan Beker reflects in the following way on how meaning is and is not to be found in a study of Paul:

> There is a tendency in recent Pauline scholarship to move away from Paul the theologian, that is, from an inquiry into Paul's theological center and the theological claims of his texts to a psychological and sociological description of Paul. However fruitful the concentration on the descriptive aspects of Paul's person and world is, it entails the danger of displacing the theological claims of the Pauline texts for subtextual concerns. With respect to Paul, we are apt to forget Rudolf Bultmann's insightful summary that the task of New Testament theology is not the "reconstruction of past history" but rather the "interpretation of the New Testament writings"; thus "reconstruction stands in the service of the interpretation of the New Testament under the presupposition that they have something to say to the present."[8]

Beker goes on to say that it is the truth claims of the text that are of utmost importance and that the text "refers primarily" to "God's redemptive action in Christ for faith."[9] What seems most remarkable in these comments is the confidence that those who are seeking God's redemptive action would find it so cleanly separable from social history or psychodynamics – or that we would be interested in whatever it was once it was so severed. What is this redemptive action that does not require history or human experience in order for it to be real or meaningful – or redemptive?

In the course of these discussions, I have alluded to the phenomenon of blindsight, and I take it up again now as a metaphor for the biblical texts. Blindsight, as you will recall, is the capacity of some people who are legally blind (due to tissue damage) to respond to objects in their immediate environment in ways that require knowledge of the physical dimensions

---

[8] J. Christiaan Beker, *The Triumph of God: The Essence of Paul's Thought*, trans. Loren T. Stuckenbruck (Minneapolis: Fortress, 1990), 117.
[9] Ibid., 118.

and positions of the objects. These people cannot, through the ordinary conscious mechanisms of sight, see and describe the object that they reach for and grasp, and yet they "know" its location and shape. Blindsight is a potent reminder that the body knows more than the conscious mind reveals. Likewise, early christianity knew more than the texts reveal. The texts function only as the small amount of knowledge that comes to conscious expression. Sometimes Paul's letters gesture toward this greater knowledge quite consciously and intentionally – like the fingers that separate to just the right distance to grasp the unseen object of their desire. At other times, the precise proportions of this greater knowledge are revealed in the text only through a kind of blindsight that suggests a whole body of knowing that informs, but is not directly expressed in, the texts themselves. The text, like the conscious mind, is kept in the dark about much of the comprehension of the body. Sometimes the text confabulates by imposing the dominant way of understanding over the hidden subordinate knowledge of other (hemi)spheres. At other times, the knowledge never reaches the consciousness of the text in any form. In the end, the fact that a biblical text can still sometimes speak the truth about that wider world of knowing – even in spite of its ostensible ignorance of the facts – is a delight and a mystery.

Bibliography

Abraham, Carolyn. *Possessing Genius: The Bizarre Odyssey of Einstein's Brain*. Toronto: Penguin, 2002.

Achtemeier, Paul J. *Romans*. Interpretation, a Bible Commentary for Teaching and Preaching. Atlanta: John Knox, 1985.

Ahlberg, Nora. "Some Psycho-physiological Aspects of Ecstasy in Recent Research." In *Religious Ecstasy*, ed. Nils. G. Holm, 63–73. Scripta Instituti Donneriani Aboensis ll. Uppsala: Almqvist and Wiksells, 1982.

Akin, D. L. "Triumphalism, Suffering, and Spiritual Maturity: An Exposition of 2 Corinthians 12:1–10 in Its Literary, Theological, and Historical Context." *Criswell Theological Review* 4 (1989): 119–44.

al-Adawiyya, Rabi'a. *Doorkeeper of the Heart: Versions of Rabia,* trans. Charles Upton. Putney, Vt.: Threshold, 1988.

Albright, Carol Rausch. "The 'God Module' and the Complexifying Brain." *Zygon* 35 (2000): 735–44.

— "Neuroscience in Pursuit of the Holy: Mysticism, the Brain, and Ultimate Reality," *Zygon* 36 (2001): 485–9.

Albright, Carol Rausch, and Joel Haugen. *Beginning with the End: God, Science, and Wolfhart Pannenberg*. Chicago: Open Court, 1997.

Alexander, L. "Fact, Fiction and the Genre of Acts." *New Testament Studies* 44 (1998): 380–99.

Alston, William P. "Religious Experience." In *Routledge Encyclopedia of Philosophy,* vol. 8, 250–55. London: Routledge, 1998.

Alvarado, Carlos S. "ESP and Altered States of Consciousness: An Overview of Conceptual and Research Trends." *The Journal of Parapsychology* 62 (1998): 27–64.

American Philosophical Society, Philadelphia Library, and P. Thomas Carroll. *An Annotated Calendar of the Letters of Charles Darwin in the Library of the American Philosophical Society*. Wilmington, Del.: Scholarly Resources, 1976.

American Psychiatric Association Committee on Nomenclature and Statistics. *Diagnostic and Statistical Manual of Mental Disorders*, 3rd ed. Washington, D.C.: American Psychiatric Association, 1980.

Anderson, F. C. "The Call of Saul of Tarsus." *Expository Times* 42 (1930–31): 90–92.

Anderson, Gary. "Celibacy or Consummation in the Garden? Reflections on Early Jewish and Christian Interpretations of the Garden of Eden." *Harvard Theological Review* 82 (1989): 121–48.

— "The Garden of Eden and Sexuality in Early Judaism." In *People of the Body: Jews and Judaism from an Embodied Perspective*, ed. Howard Eilberg-Schwartz, 47–68. Albany: State University of New York, 1992.

Andrews, M. E. "The Conversion of Paul." *Journal of Bible and Religion* 9 (1941): 147–54.

Angus, S. *The Mystery Religions: A Study in the Religious Background of Early Christianity*. New York: Dover, 1975.

Annas, J. E. *Hellenistic Philosophy of Mind*. Hellenistic Culture and Society 8. Berkeley: University of California Press, 1992.

Arnheim, Rudolf. *Visual Thinking*. Berkeley: University of California Press, 1969.

Ashbrook, J. B., ed. *Brain, Culture, and the Human Spirit: Essays from an Emergent Evolutionary Perspective*. Lanham, Md.: University Press of America, 1993.

Ashbrook, James B., and Carol Rausch Albright. *The Humanizing Brain: Where Religion and Neuroscience Meet*. Cleveland, Ohio: Pilgrim, 1997.

Ashton, John. *The Religion of Paul the Apostle*. New Haven, Conn.: Yale University Press, 2000.

Aune, David Edward. *Prophecy in Early Christianity and the Ancient Mediterranean World*. Grand Rapids, Mich.: Eerdmans, 1983.

— *The New Testament in Its Literary Environment*, ed. Wayne Meeks. Library of Early Christianity. Philadelphia: Westminster, 1987.

Austin, James H. *Zen and the Brain*. Cambridge, Mass.: MIT Press, 1998.

— "Consciousness Evolves when Self Dissolves." *Journal of Consciousness Studies* 7 (2000): 209–30.

Azzopardi, J. "Revelation in St. Paul." *Melita Theologica* 24 (1972): 31–39.

Baird, William. *1 Corinthians, 2 Corinthians*. Knox Preaching Guides. Atlanta: John Knox, 1980.

— "Visions, Revelation, and Ministry: Reflections on 2 Cor 12:1–5 and Gal 1:11–17." *Journal of Biblical Literature* 104 (1985): 651–62.

Bamborough, Renford. "Editorial: Subject and Epithet."*Philosophy* 5 (1980): 289–90.

Banquet, J. P., and N. Lesevre. "Event-Related Potentials in Altered States of Consciousness." *Progress in Brain Research* 54 (1980): 447–53.

Barclay, William. *The Letters to the Corinthians*, rev. ed. Daily Study Bible Series. Toronto: G. R. Welch, 1975.

Barnett, Paul. *The Message of 2 Corinthians: Power in Weakness*. Downers Grove, Ill.: InterVarsity, 1988.

Barrett, C. K. "Paul's Opponents in II Corinthians." *New Testament Studies* 17 (1957): 233–54.

— "Christianity at Corinth." *Bulletin of the John Rylands Library* 46 (1964): 269–97.

— *A Commentary on the First Epistle to the Corinthians*. Harper/Black New Testament Commentaries. New York: Harper and Row, 1968.

— *The Signs of an Apostle*. London: Epworth, 1970.

— *A Commentary on the Epistle to the Romans*. London: A. and C. Black, 1971.

— *The Second Epistle to the Corinthians*. Harper's New Testament Commentaries. New York: Harper and Row, 1973.

— *A Commentary on the Second Epistle to the Corinthians*. Black's New Testament Commentaries. London: Black, 1976.

— *Paul: An Introduction to His Thought*. Louisville, Ky.: Westminster/John Knox, 1994.

Barry, H., III, M. K. Bacon, and I. L. Child. "Relations of Child Training to Subsistence Economy." In *Cross-cultural Approaches: Readings in Comparative Research*, ed. C. S. Ford. New Haven, Conn.: HRAF, 1967.

Barth, Karl. *The Epistle to the Philippians*. London: SCM Press, 1962.

Barton, S. C. "Social-Scientific Criticism." In *Handbook to Exegesis of the New Testament*, ed. Stanley E. Porter. Leiden: E. J. Brill, 1997.

Baughen, Michael A. *Strengthened by Struggle: The Stress Factor in 2 Corinthians*. Wheaton, Ill.: H. Shaw, 1984.

Baumgarten, J. *Paulus und die Apokalyptik*. Neukirchen-Vluyn: Neukirchen Verlag, 1975.

Baur, Ferdinand Christian. *Paul, the Apostle of Jesus Christ, His Life and Work, His Epistles and His Doctrine: A Contribution to the Critical History of Primitive Christianity*, 2nd ed., ed. E. Zeller., trans. M. J. Tramo, A. G. Reeves, and M. S. Gazzaniga. A. Menzies. London: Williams and Norgate, 1875–76.

Baynes, Kathleen, and Michael S. Gazzaniga. "Consciousness, Introspection, and the Split-Brain: The Two Minds/One Body Problem." In *The New Cognitive Neurosciences*, ed. Michael S. Gazzaniga, 1355–63. Cambridge, Mass.: MIT Press, 2000.

Baynes Kathleen. "Isolation of a Right Hemisphere Cognitive System in a Patient with Anarchic (Alien) Hand Sign." *Neuropsychologia* 35 (1997): 1159–73.

Beale, G. K. "The Old Testament Background of Reconciliation in 2 Corinthians 5–7 and Its Bearing on the Literary Problem of 2 Corinthians 6:14–7:1." *New Testament Studies* 35 (1989): 550–81.

Bear, David. "Temporal Lobe Epilepsy – A Syndrome of Sensory-Limbic Hyperconnecton." *Cortex* 15 (1979): 357–84.

Beaude, Pierre-Marie. "Psychologie et exégèse paulienne." In *Paul de Tarse*, ed. J. Schlosser. Paris: Éditions du Cerf, 1996.

Beck, Norman A. "The Lukan Writer's Stories about the Call of Paul." *Society of Biblical Literature Seminar Papers* 22 (1983): 213–28.

Beck, R. "The Mithras Cult as Association." *Studies in Religion* 21 (1992): 1–13.

— "The Mysteries of Mithras." In *Voluntary Associations in the Graeco-Roman World*, ed. J. S. Kloppenborg and S. G. Wilson, 176–85. London: Routledge, 1996.

Beets, M. G. J. *Being and Becoming: A Companion to Plotinus' Tractate on Eternity and Time*. Amsterdam: Duna, 1996.

Behrend, Heike, and Ute Luig. *Spirit Possession: Modernity and Power in Africa*. Oxford: James Currey, 1999.

Beker, J. Christiaan. *Paul the Apostle: The Triumph of God in Life and Thought*. Philadelphia: Fortress, 1980.

— *The Triumph of God: The Essence of Paul's Thought*. trans. Loren T. Stuckenbruck. Minneapolis: Fortress, 1990.

Belleville, Linda L. "A Letter of Apologetic Self-Commendation." *Novum Testamentum* 31 (1989): 142–63.

— *Reflections of Glory: Paul's Polemical Use of the Moses-Doxa Tradition in 2 Corinthians 3:1–18*. Journal for the Study of the New Testament Supplement Series 52. Sheffield: Sheffield Academic Press, 1991.

— 2 *Corinthians*. IVP New Testament Commentary Series 8. Downers Grove, Ill.:
   InterVarsity, 1996.

Benson, D. Frank, and Eran Zaidel. *The Dual Brain: Hemispheric Specialization in
   Humans*. UCLA Forum in Medical Sciences 26. New York: *Guilford*, 1985.

Benz, Ernst. *Paulus als Visionär: Eine vergleichende Untersuchung der Visionsberichte des
   Paulus in der Apostelgeschichte und in den paulinischen Briefen*. Verlagder Akademie
   der Wissenschaften und der Literatur. Mainz: F. Steiner Wiesbaden, 1952.

Berger, Peter L., and Thomas Luckmann. *The Social Construction of Reality: A Treatise
   in the Sociology of Knowledge*. Garden City, N.Y.: Doubleday, 1966.

Best, Ernest. *The Letter of Paul to the Romans*. Cambridge Bible Commentary: New
   English Bible. Cambridge: Cambridge University Press, 1967.

— "A Damascus Road Experience." *Irish Biblical Studies* 7 (1985): 2–7.

— *Second Corinthians*. Interpretation, a Bible Commentary for Teaching and Preaching.
   Atlanta: John Knox, 1987.

Betz, Hans Dieter. *Der Apostel Paulus und die sokratische Tradition; eine exegetische
   Untersuchung zu seiner Apologie 2 Korinther 10–13*, Beiträge zur historischen Theologie 45. Tübingen: Mohr, 1972.

— *Galatians: A Commentary on Paul's Letter to the Churches in Galatia*. Hermeneia.
   Philadelphia: Fortress, 1979.

— "Transferring a Ritual: Paul's Interpretation of Baptism in Romans 6." In *Paul in
   His Hellenistic Context*, ed. Troels Engberg-Pedersen. Minneapolis: Fortress, 1995.

Betz, Hans Dieter, and George W. MacRae. *2 Corinthians 8 and 9: A Commentary on
   Two Administrative Letters of the Apostle Paul*. Philadelphia: Fortress, 1985.

Bick, C. H. "EEG Mapping Including Patients with Normal and Altered States of
   Hypnotic Consciousness under the Parameter of Posthypnosis." *International Journal of Neuroscience* 47 (1989): 15–30.

Bieringer, R. "Der 2 Korintherbrief in den neuesten Kommentaren." *Ephemerides
   Theologicae Lovanienses* 67 (1991): 107–30.

— *The Corinthian Correspondence*. Bibliotheca Ephemeridum theologicarum Lovaniensium 125. Leuven: *Peeters*, 1996.

Bieringer, R., and Jan Lambrecht. *Studies on 2 Corinthians*. Bibliotheca Ephemeridum
   theologicarum Lovaniensium 112. Leuven: *Peeters*, 1994.

Bilde, P. "2 Cor 4:4: The View of Satan and the Created World in Paul." In *Apocryphon
   Severini: Presented to Soren Giversen*, ed. P. Bilde, H. K. Nielsen, and J. P. Sorensen,
   29–41. Aarhus: Aarhus University Press, 1993.

Björkqvist, Krista. "Ecstasy from a Physiological Point of View." In *Religious Ecstasy*,
   ed. Nils G. Holm, 74–86. Uppsala: Almqvist and Wiksells, 1982.

Black, Mark C. "1 Cor 11:2–16: A Re-investigation." In *Essays on Women in Earliest
   Christianity*, vol. 1, ed. Carroll D. Osburn, 191–218. Joplin, Mo.: College Press, 1995.

Black, Matthew. *Romans*, 2nd ed. New Century Bible Commentary. Grand Rapids,
   Mich.: Eerdmans, 1989.

Blanke, Olaf, Stéphanie Ortigue, Theodor Landis, and Margitta Seeck. "Stimulating
   Illusory Own-Body Perceptions." *Nature* 419 (2002): 269–70.

Blomberg, C. "The Structure of 2 Corinthians 1–7." *Criswell Theological Review* 4
   (1989): 3–20.

Boas, Franz. "The Limitations of the Comparative Method of Anthropology." In *Race,
   Language and Culture*, 270–80. New York: Macmillan, 1961.

Bockmuehl, Markus N. A. *Revelation and Mystery in Ancient Judaism and Pauline Christianity*. Grand Rapids, Mich.: Eerdmans, 1997.

Boddy, Janice. "Spirit Possession Revisited: Beyond Instrumentality." *Annual Review of Anthropology* 23 (1994): 407–34.

Borchert, G. L. "Introduction to 2 Corinthians." *Review and Expositor* 86 (1989): 313–24.

Boring, M. Eugene. *The Continuing Voice: Christian Prophecy and the Gospel Tradition*. Louisville, Ky.: Westminster/John Knox, 1991.

Bornkamm, Gunther. *Paul*, trans. D. M. G. Stalker. Minneapolis: Fortress, 1971.

Bourdieu, Pierre. *Outline of a Theory of Practice*, trans. Richard Nice. Cambridge Studies in Social and Cultural Anthropology 16. Cambridge: Cambridge University Press, 1997, originally published as *Esquisse d'une théorie de la pratique*. Geneva: Droz, 1972.

Bourguignon, Erika. "The Self, the Behavioral Environment and the Theory of Spirit Possession." In *Context and Meaning in Cultural Anthropology*, ed. Milford E. Spiro. New York: Glencoe, 1965.

— *Cross-cultural Study of Dissociational States*. Columbus: Ohio State University Press, 1968.

— "World Distribution and Patterns of Possession States." In *Trance and Possession States*, ed. Raymond Prince, 39–60. Montreal: R. M. Bucke Memorial Society, 1968.

— "Introduction: A Framework for the Comparative Study of Altered States of Consciousness." In *Religion, Altered States of Consciousness, and Social Change*, 3–35. Columbus: Ohio State University Press, 1973.

— *Religion, Altered States of Consciousness, and Social Change*. Columbus: Ohio State University Press, 1973.

— *Possession*. Chandler and Sharp Series in Cross-cultural Themes. San Francisco: Chandler and Sharp, 1976.

— *Psychological Anthropology: An Introduction to Human Nature and Cultural Differences*. New York: Holt Rinehart and Winston, 1979.

— "Trance and Shamanism: What's in a Name?" *Journal of Psychoactive Drugs* 21 (1989): 9–15.

— "Human Nature as 'Deep Structure': Implications for Comparative Study." In *Personality and the Cultural Construction of Society: Essays in Honor of Milfred Spiro*, ed. D. K. Jordan and M. J. Swartz, 308–25. Tuscaloosa: University of Alabama Press, 1990.

Bousset, W. "Die Himmelsreise der Seele." *Archiv für Religionswissenschaft* 4 (1901): 139–69, 229–73.

— *Kyrios Christos: Geschichte des Christusglaubens von den Anfängen des Christentums bis Irenaeus*, 6th ed. Göttingen: Vandenhoeck and Ruprecht, 1967.

— *Kyrios Christos: A History of the Belief in Christ from the Beginnings of Christianity to Irenaeus*. Nashville, Tenn.: Abingdon, 1970.

Bouttier, M. *Christianity According to Paul*. Naperville, Ill.: Alec R. Allenson, 1966.

Bowker, J. M. "'Merkabah' Visions and the Visions of Paul." *Journal of Semitic Studies* 16 (1971): 57–73.

Boyarin, Daniel. "'Behold Israel According to the Flesh': On Anthropology and Sexuality in Late Antique Judaism." *Yale Journal of Criticism* 5 (1992): 25–55.

— *A Radical Jew: Paul and the Politics of Identity*. Berkeley: University of California Press, 1994.

— "Body Politic among the Brides of Christ: Paul and the Origins of Christian Sexual Renunciation." In *Asceticism*, ed. Vincent L. Wimbush and Richard Valantasis, 459–78. Oxford: Oxford University Press, 1995.

Boyer, L. B. "Notes on the Personality Structure of a North American Indian Shaman." *Journal of Hillside Hospital* 10 (1961): 14–33.

— "Remarks on the Personality of Shamans." *Psychoanalytic Study of Society* 2 (1961): 233–54.

— "Comparison on the Shamans and Psuedoshamans of the Apaches of the Mescalero Indian Reservation: A Rorshach Study." *Journal of Projective Techniques and Personality Assessment* 28 (1964): 173–80.

Brabazon, James. *Albert Schweitzer: A Biography*, 2nd ed. Albert Schweitzer Library. Syracuse, N.Y.: Syracuse University Press, 2000.

Brainard, F. S. "Defining 'Mystical Experience'." *Journal of the American Academy of Religion* 64 (1996): 359–93.

Brandenburger, Egon. *Fleisch und Geist; Paulus und die dualistische Weisheit.* Wissenschaftliche Monographien zum Alten und Neuen Testament 29. Neukirchen-Vluyn: Neukirchen Verlag, 1968.

Brawley, Robert L. "Paul in Acts: Aspects of Structure and Characterization." *Society of Biblical Literature Seminar Papers* 27 (1988): 90–105.

Bray, Gerald Lewis. *1–2 Corinthians*. Ancient Christian Commentary on Scripture, New Testament 7. Chicago: Fitzroy Dearborn, 1999.

Brazis, Paul W., Joseph C. Masdeu, and José Biller. *Localization in Clinical Neurology*, 3rd ed. Boston: Little, Brown, 1996.

Brown, A. R. "The Gospel Takes Place: Paul's Theology of Power-in-Weakness in 2 Corinthians." *Interpretation* 52 (1998): 271–85.

Brown, Colin M., Peter Hagoort, and Marta Kutas. "Postlexical Integration Processes in Language Comprehension: Evidence from Brain-Imaging Research." In *The New Cognitive Neurosciences*, ed. Michael S. Gazzaniga, 881–95. Cambridge, Mass.: MIT Press, 2000.

Brown, Peter Robert Lamont. *The Body and Society: Men, Women, and Sexual Renunciation in Early Christianity*. Lectures on the History of Religions, New Series 3. New York: Columbia University Press, 1988.

Bruce, F. F. *Paul and His Converts: 1 and 2 Thessalonians, 1 and 2 Corinthians*. Bible Guides 17. London: Lutterworth, 1962.

— *1 and 2 Corinthians*. New Century Bible. London: Oliphants, 1971.

— *Paul: Apostle of the Free Spirit*. Exeter: Paternoster, 1980.

Bruce, F. F., and W. Ward Gasque. *Philippians*. New International Biblical Commentary 11. Peabody, Mass.: Hendrickson, 1989.

Brunner, Emil. *Die Mystik und das Wort: Der Gegensatz zwischen moderner Religionsauffassung und christlichem Glauben dargestellt an der Theologie Schleiermachers*, 2nd ed. Tübingen: Mohr, 1928.

Bryan, Christopher. *A Preface to Romans: Notes on the Epistle in Its Literary and Cultural Setting*. Oxford: Oxford University Press, 2000.

Buck, Charles, and Greer Taylor. *Saint Paul: A Study of the Development*. New York: Scribner, 1969.

Bultmann, Rudolf Karl. *Glauben und Verstehen: Gesammelte Aufsätze*. Tübingen: Mohr, 1933.

— *Theology of the New Testament*, Vol. 1. New York: Scribner, 1951.

Burrow, B. J. "Pauline Autobiography: Theological Content, Rhetorical Function, and Biblical Antecedents." PhD dissertation, Baylor University, 1996.

Burton, E. De Witt. "Saul's Experience on the Way to Damsascus." *Biblical World* 1 (1893): 9–23.

Bussanich, John, and Plotinus. *The One and Its Relation to Intellect in Plotinus: A Commentary on Selected Texts*. Philosophia Antiqua 49. Leiden: E. J. Brill, 1988.

Byrne, Brendan. *'Sons of God' – 'Seed of Abraham': A Study of the Idea of Sonship of God of All Christians in Paul against the Jewish Background*. Analecta Biblica 83. Rome: Pontificio Instituto Biblico, 1979.

Byrne, Brendan, and Daniel J. Harrington. *Romans*. Sacra Pagina 6. Collegeville, Minn.: Liturgical Press, 1996.

Callan, Terrance. "Prophecy and Ecstasy." *Novum Testamentum* 27 (1985): 125–40.

— *Psychological Perspectives on the Life of Paul: An Application of the Methodology of Gerd Theissen*. Studies in the Bible and Early Christianity 22. Lewiston, N.Y.: Mellen, 1990.

Campbell, J. Y. "KOINΩNIA and Its Cognates in the New Testament." *Journal of Biblical Literature* 51 (1932): 352–80.

Carrez, M. "Que represente la vie de Jesus pour l'apôtre Paul." *Revue d'histoire et de philosophie religieuses* 68 (1988): 155–61.

Carroll, John T. "Literary and Social Dimensions of Luke's Apology for Paul." *Society of Biblical Literature Seminar Papers* 27 (1988): 106–18.

Carson, D. A. *From Triumphalism to Maturity: A New Exposition of 2 Corinthians 10–13*. Biblical Classics Library 20. Carlisle: Paternoster, 1996.

Cassidy, Richard J. *Paul in Chains: Roman Imprisonment and the Letters of St. Paul*. New York: Crossroad, 2001.

Cecil, R. "The Psychological Aspects of the Conversion of the Apostle Paul." *Union Seminary Review* 9 (1897): 168–76.

Cerfaux, Lucien. *Le Chrétien dans la théologie paulinienne*. Lectio divina 33. Paris: Éditions du Cerf, 1962.

Chafin, Kenneth L., and Lloyd J. Ogilvie. *1, 2 Corinthians*. The Communicator's Commentary 7. Waco, Tex.: Word, 1985.

Charlesworth, James H., ed. *The Old Testament Pseudepigrapha*. London: Darton, Longman and Todd, 1983.

Cheek, John L. "Paul's Mysticism in the Light of Psychedelic Experience." *Journal of the American Academy of Religion* 38 (1970): 381–89.

Chernus, Ira. *Mysticism in Rabbinic Judaism: Studies in the History of Midrash*. Studia Judaica 11. Berlin: de Gruyter, 1982.

Chevallier, M. A. "L'argumentation de Paul dans 2 Corinthiens 10 à 13." *Revue d'histoire et de philosophie religieuses* 70 (1990): 3–15.

Clark, W. H. "William James' Contributions to the Psychology of Religious Conversion." *Journal of Religion and Psychical Research* 3 (1980): 287–96.

Coggan, Donald. *Paul: Portrait of a Revolutionary*. New York: Crossroad, 1985.

Colbert, E. H. *Evolution of Vertebrates*. New York: Wiley, 1980.

Colet, John, Bernard O'Kelly, and Catherine Anna Louise Jarrott. *John Colet's Commentary on First Corinthians: A New Edition of the Latin Text, with Translation,*

Annotations, and Introduction. Binghamton, N.Y.: Medieval and Renaissance Texts and Studies, 1985.

Collange, Jean-François. *Énigmes de la deuxième épître de Paul aux Corinthiens: étude exégétique de 2 Cor. 2:14–7:4.* Society for New Testament Studies Monograph Series 18. Cambridge: Cambridge University Press, 1972.

Collins, John J. "The Heavenly Representative: The 'Son of Man' in the Similitudes of Enoch." In *Ideal Figures in Ancient Judaism: Profiles and Paradigms*, ed. John J. Collins and George W. E. Nickelsburg, 111–34. Chico, Calif.: Scholars Press, 1980.

—— "The Son of Man in First-Century Judaism." *New Testament Studies* 38 (1992): 448–66.

—— *The Apocalyptic Imagination*, 2nd ed. Grand Rapids, Mich.: Eerdmans, 1998.

Collins, J. N. "The Mediatorial Aspect of Paul's Role as Diakonos (2 Cor)." *Australian Biblical Review* 40 (1992): 34–44.

Collins, Raymond F. "Paul's Damascus Experience: Reflections on the Lukan Account." *Louvain Studies* 11 (1986): 99–118.

Collins, Raymond F., and Daniel J. Harrington. *First Corinthians.* Sacra Pagina 7. Collegeville, Minn.: Liturgical Press, 1999.

Conzelmann, Hans. *An Outline of the Theology of the New Testament*, trans. John Bowden. New York: Harper and Row, 1969.

—— *1 Corinthians: A Commentary on the First Epistle to the Corinthians.* Hermeneia. Philadelphia: Fortress, 1975.

Cooper, David A. *Silence, Simplicity, and Solitude.* New York: Bell Tower, 1992.

Corby, J. C., W. T. Roth, V. P. Zarcone, and B. S. Kopell. "Psychophysiological Correlates of the Practice of Tantric Yoga Meditation." *Archives of General Psychiatry* 35 (1978): 571–77.

Corley, Bruce. "Interpreting Paul's Conversion – Then and Now." In *The Road from Damascus: The Impact of Paul's Conversion on His Life, Thought, and Ministry*, ed. Richard. N. Longenecker, 1–17. Grand Rapids, Mich.: Eerdmans, 1997.

Craffert, P. F. "Paul's Damascus Experience as Reflected in Galatians 1: Call or Conversion?" *Scriptura* 29 (1989): 36–47.

—— "Towards an Interdisciplinary Definition of the Social-Scientific Interpretation of the New Testament." *Neotestamentica* 25 (1991): 123–44.

Crafton, Jeffrey A. *The Agency of the Apostle: A Dramatistic Analysis of Paul's Responses to Conflict in 2 Corinthians.* Journal for the Study of the New Testament Supplement 51. Sheffield: JSOT Press, 1991.

Craig, W. L. "Paul's Dilemma in 2 Corinthians 5:1–10: A Catch-22?" *New Testament Studies* 34 (1988): 145–47.

Crapanzano, Vincent, and Vivian Garrison. *Case Studies in Spirit Possession.* Contemporary Religious Movements. New York: Wiley, 1977.

Crook, Zeba A. "Patronage, Loyalty, and Conversion in the Ancient Mediterranean." PhD dissertation, University of St. Michael's College, 2003.

Crossan, John Dominic. *Jesus: A Revolutionary Biography.* San Francisco: HarperSanFrancisco, 1994.

Csordas, Thomas J. "Embodiment as a Paradigm for Anthropology." *Ethos* 18 (1990): 5–47.

Cutton, George B. *The Psychological Phenomena of Christianity.* New York: Charles Scribner's Sons, 1908.

Dalton, W. J. "Is the Old Covenant Abrogated (2 Cor 3:14)." *Australian Biblical Review* 35 (1987): 88–94.

Damasio, Antonio R. *The Feeling of What Happens: Body and Emotion in the Making of Consciousness.* New York: Harcourt Brace, 1999.

— *Descartes' Error: Emotion, Reason, and the Human Brain.* New York: Quill, 2000.

Danker, Frederick W. *II Corinthians.* Augsburg Commentary on the New Testament. Minneapolis: Augsburg, 1989.

d'Aquili, Eugene G. "The Neurobiological Basis of Myth and Concepts of Deity." *Zygon* 13 (1978): 257–75.

d'Aquili, Eugene G., Charles D. Laughlin, and John McManus. *The Spectrum of Ritual: A Biogenetic Structural Analysis.* New York: Columbia University Press, 1979.

d'Aquili, Eugene G., and Hans Mol. *The Regulation of Physical and Mental Systems: Systems Theory of the Philosophy of Science.* Mellen Studies in Sociology 4. Lewiston, N.Y.: Mellen, 1990.

d'Aquili, Eugene G., and Andrew B. Newberg. "Liminality, Trance, and Unitary States in Ritual and Meditation." *Studia Liturgica* 23 (1993): 2–34.

— "Religious and Mystical States: A Neuropsychological Substrate." *Zygon* 28 (1993): 177–200.

— *The Mystical Mind: Probing the Biology of Religious Experience Theology and the Sciences.* Minneapolis: Fortress, 1999.

Dautzenberg, Gerhard. *Urchristliche Prophetie: Ihre Erforschung ihre Voraussetzungen im Judentum und ihre Struktur im ersten Korintherbrief.* Beiträge zur Wissenschaft vom Alten und Neuen Testament 6. Stuttgart: Kohlhammer, 1975.

Davidson, John B. "Religious Experience and the Conversion of the Apostle Paul: Psychological Reflections." In *With Steadfast Purpose: Essays on Acts in Honor of Henry Jackson Flanders Jr.*, ed. Naymond H. Keathley and Henry Jackson Flanders, 327–45. Waco, Tex.: Baylor University Press, 1990.

Davies, Stevan L. *Jesus the Healer: Possession, Trance, and the Origins of Christianity.* New York: Continuum, 1995.

Deissmann, Adolf. *Die neutestamentliche Formel "in Christo Jesu."* Marburg: Elwert, 1892.

— *Paul: A Study in Social and Religious History*, trans. William E. Wilson. New York: Harper and Brothers, 1957.

DeSilva, D. A. "Measuring Penultimate against Ultimate Reality: An Investigation of the Integrity and Argumentation of 2 Corinthians." *Journal for the Study of the New Testament* 52 (1993): 41–70.

— "Meeting the Exigency of a Complex Rhetorical Situation: Paul's Strategy in 2 Corinthians 1 through 7." *Andrews University Seminary Studies* 34 (1996): 5–22.

deSilva, K. A. "'Let the One Who Claims Honor Establish that Claim in the Lord': Honor Discourse in the Corinthian Correspondence." *Biblical Theology Bulletin* 28 (1998): 61–74.

Dibelius, Martin. "Glaube und Mystik bei Paulus." In *Botschaft und Geschichte: Gesammelte Aufsätze*, vol. 2, ed. Martin Dibelius, Heinrich Kraft, and Günther Bornkamm, 94–116. Tübingen: Mohr, 1953.

— "Paulus und die Mystik." In *Botschaft und Geschichte: Gesammelte Aufsätze*, vol. 2, ed. Martin Dibelius, Heinrich Kraft, and Günther Bornkamm, 134–59. Tübingen: Mohr, 1953.

Dibelius, Martin, and Werner Georg Kümmel. *Paul*. Philadelphia: Westminster, 1953.

Dick, M. B. "Conversion in the Bible." In *Conversion and the Catechumenate*, ed. R. Duggan, 43–63. Ramsey, N.J.: Paulist, 1984.

Dobschütz, Ernst von. *Der Apostel Paulus*. Halle (Saale): Buchhandlung des Waisenhauses, 1926.

Dockery, D. S. "Commenting on Commentaries on 2 Corinthians." *Criswell Theological Review* 4 (1989): 153–57.

Dodd, C. H. "The Mind of Paul: A Psychological Approach." *Bulletin of the John Rylands Library* 17 (1933): 91–105.

— *New Testament Studies*. Manchester: Manchester University Press, 1953.

Dodds, E. R. *The Greeks and the Irrational*. Berkeley: University of California Press, 1959.

Dodwell, Peter C. *Brave New Mind: A Thoughtful Inquiry into the Nature and Meaning of Mental Life*. New York: Oxford University Press, 2000.

Donaldson, Terence L. "Israelite, Convert, Apostle to the Gentiles: The Origin of Paul's Gentile Mission." In *The Road from Damascus: The Impact of Paul's Conversion on His Life, Thought, and Ministry*, ed. Richard N. Longenecker, 62–84. Grand Rapids, Mich.: Eerdmans, 1997.

— *Paul and the Gentiles: Remapping the Apostle's Convictional World*. Minneapolis: Fortress, 1997.

Doty, William G. *Letters in Primitive Christianity*. Philadelphia: Fortress, 1973.

Douglas, Mary. *Purity and Danger: An Analysis of Concepts of Pollution and Taboo*. London: Routledge and Kegan Paul, 1966.

— *Natural Symbols: Explorations in Cosmology*. 2nd ed. London: Routledge, [1970] 1996.

— *Purity and Danger: An Analysis of Concepts of Pollution and Taboo*. London: Routledge and Kegan Paul, 1976.

Douglas, W., and J. R. Scroggs. "Some Social Scientific Perspectives." In *Papers from the National Faith and Order Colloquium*, ed. W. A. Norgren, 115–34. Indianapolis: Council on Christian Unity, 1966.

— "Issues in the Psychology of Religious Conversion." *Journal of Religion and Health* 6 (1967): 204–16.

Drury, Nevill. *The Shaman and the Magician: Journeys between the Worlds*. London: Routledge and Kegan Paul, 1982.

Duduit, N. "Preaching on 2 Corinthians." *Criswell Theological Review* 4 (1989): 145–52.

Duff, P. B. "Metaphor, Motif, and Meaning: The Rhetorical Strategy behind the Image 'Led in Triumph' in 2 Corinthians 2:14." *Catholic Biblical Quarterly* 53 (1991): 79–92.

— "Apostolic Suffering and the Language of Processions in 2 Corinthians 4:7–10." *Biblical Theology Bulletin* 21 (1993): 158–65.

— "2 Corinthians 1–7: Sidestepping the Division Hypothesis Dilemma." *Biblical Theology Bulletin* 24 (1994): 16–26.

Dunn, James D. G. "'A Light to the Gentiles': The Significance of the Damascus Road Christophany for Paul." In *The Glory of Christ in the New Testament: Studies in Christology in Memory of George Bradford Caird*, ed. L. D. Hurst and N. T. Wright, 251–66. Oxford: Clarendon, 1987.

— *Romans 1–8*. Word Biblical Commentary 38. Milton Keynes: Word, 1991.

— *First Corinthians New Testament Guides*, ed. A. T. Lincoln. Sheffield: Sheffield Academic Press, 1995.

— *Jesus and the Spirit: A Study of the Religious and Charismatic Experience of Jesus and the First Christians as Reflected in the New Testament*. Grand Rapids, Mich.: Eerdmans, 1997.

— "Paul's Conversion – A Light to Twentieth Century Disputes." In *Evangelium Schriftauslegung Kirche: Festschrift für Peter Stulmacher zum 65 Geburtstag*, ed. Scott J. Hafemann and Otfried Hofius Jostein Adna, 77–93. Göttingen: Vandenhoeck and Ruprecht, 1997.

— *The Theology of Paul the Apostle*. Grand Rapids, Mich.: Eerdmans, 1998.

Dupont, J. "The Conversion of Paul and Its Influence on His Understanding of Salvation by Faith." In *Apostolic History and the Gospel*, ed. W. W. Gasque and R. P. Martin, 176–94. Grand Rapids, Mich.: Eerdmans, 1970.

Dutile, G. "An Annotated Bibliography for 2 Corinthians." *Southwestern Journal of Theology* 32 (1989): 41–43.

Eagleton, Terry. *After Theory*. New York: Basic Books, 2003.

Earle, J. "Cerebral Laterality and Meditation: A Review of the Literature." *Journal of Transpersonal Psychology* 13 (1981): 155–73.

Eberle, Christopher J. "The Autonomy and Explanation of Mystical Perception." *Religious Studies* 34 (1998): 299–316.

Eckel, M. D. "Bearing the Weight of Glory: Pun in 2 Cor 4:17." *Books and Religion* 18 (1991): 5–7.

Edsman, Carl-Martin. *Studies in Shamanism: Based on Papers Read at the Symposium on Shamanism Held at Åbo on the 6th–8th of September, 1962*. Scripta Instituti Donneriani Aboensis 1. Stockholm: Almqvist and Wiksells, 1967.

Ehrlichman, H., and M. Wiener. "EEG Asymmetry during Covert Mental Activity." *Psychophysiology* 17 (1980): 228–35.

Eilberg-Schwartz, Howard. *People of the Body: Jews and Judaism from an Embodied Perspective, the Body in Culture, History, and Religion*. Albany: State University of New York Press, 1992.

— "The Problem of the Body for the People of the Book." In *Reading Bibles, Writing Bodies*, ed. Timothy K. Beal and David M. Gunn, 34–55. London: Routledge, 1997.

Einstein, Albert. *Cosmic Religion with Other Opinions and Aphorisms*. New York: Covici-Friede, 1931.

— *Mein Weltbild*. Amsterdam: Querido, 1934.

Eliade, Mircea. *Birth and Rebirth: The Religious Meanings of Initiation in Human Culture*, trans. Willard R. Trask. New York: Harper, 1958.

— *Shamanism: Archaic Techniques of Ecstasy*. New York: Pantheon, 1964.

— *Le Chamanisme et les techniques archaïques de l'extase*. 2nd ed., revised and augmented. Paris: Payot, 1951.

Elliott, J. H. "Social-Scientific Criticism of the New Testament and Its Social World." *Semeia: Social Scientific Criticism of the New Testament and Its Social World* 35 (1986): 1–33.

— *What Is Social-Scientific Criticism?* Guides to Biblical Scholarship. Minneapolis: Fortress, 1993.

Ellis, E. Earle. "Christ and Spirit in 1 Corinthians." In *Christ and Spirit in the New Testament*, ed. Barnabas Lindars, Stephen S. Smalley, and C. F. D. Moule, 268–80. Cambridge: Cambridge University Press, 1973.

Engberg-Pedersen, Troels. *Paul and the Stoics*. Louisville, Ky.: Westminster/John Knox, 2000.

Engels, Donald W. *Roman Corinth: An Alternative Model for the Classical City*. Chicago: University of Chicago Press, 1990.

Engelsen, N. I. J. "Glossolalia and Other Forms of Inspired Speech According to 1 Corinthians 12–14." PhD dissertation, Yale University, 1970.

Enslin, Morton Scott. *The Ethics of Paul*. Nashville, Tenn.: Abingdon, 1962.

Eriksson, Anders. "'Women Tongue Speakers, Be Silent': A Reconstruction through Paul's Rhetoric." *Biblical Interpretation* 6 (1998): 80–104.

Esler, Philip F. "Glossolalia and the Admission of Gentiles into the Early Christian Community." *Biblical Theology Bulletin* 22 (1992): 261–65.

— *The First Christians in Their Social Worlds: Social-Scientific Approaches to New Testament Interpretation*. New York: Routledge, 1994.

— ed. *Modeling Early Christianity: Social-Scientific Studies of the New Testament in Its Context*. London: Routledge, 1995.

— "Review of D. G. Horrell, The Social Ethos of the Corinthian Correspondence." *Journal of Theological Studies* 49 (1998): 253–60.

— "Models in New Testament Interpretation: A Reply to David Horrell." *Journal for the Study of the New Testament* 78 (2000): 107–13.

Evans, J. W. "Interpretation of 2 Corinthians." *Southwestern Journal of Theology* 32 (1989): 22–32.

Fallon, Francis T. *2 Corinthians, New Testament Message 11*. Wilmington, Del.: Glazier, 1980.

Fee, Gordon D. *The First Epistle to the Corinthians*. New International Commentary on the New Testament. Grand Rapids, Mich.: Eerdmans, 1987.

Fenton, G. W. "Psychiatric Disorders of Epilepsy: Classification and Phenomenology." In *Epilepsy and Psychiatry*, ed. E. Reynolds and M. Trimble, 12–26. New York: Churchill Livingstone, 1981.

Findlay, George Gillanders. *St. Paul's First Epistle to the Corinthians*. In *The Expositor's Greek Testament*, ed W. Robertson Nicoll. New York: Hodder and Stoughton, 1897.

Finley, M. I. *The Ancient Economy*. Sather Classical Lectures 43. Berkeley: University of California Press, 1973.

Fiorenza, Elisabeth Schüssler. "Rhetorical Situation and Historical Reconstruction in 1 Corinthians." *New Testament Studies* 33 (1987): 386–403.

Fischer, David Hackett. *Historians' Fallacies; Toward a Logic of Historical Thought*. New York: Harper and Row, 1970.

Fisher, Fred L. *Commentary on 1 & 2 Corinthians*. Waco, Tex.: Word, 1975.

Fitzgerald, John T. *Cracks in an Earthen Vessel: An Examination of the Catalogues of Hardships in the Corinthian Correspondence*. Society of Biblical Literature Dissertation Series 99. Atlanta: Scholars Press, 1988.

— "Paul, the Ancient Epistolary Theorists, and 2 Corinthians 10–13." In *Greeks, Romans, and Christians: Essays in Honor of Abraham J. Malherbe*, ed. David L. Balch, E. Ferguson, and Wayne A. Meeks, 190–200. Minneapolis: Fortress, 1990.

Fitzmyer, Joseph. "Glory Reflected on the Face of Christ (2 Cor 3:7–4:6) and a Palestinian Jewish Motif." *Theological Studies* 42 (1981): 630–44.

Flaherty, Gloria. *Shamanism and the Eighteenth Century.* Princeton, N.J.: Princeton University Press, 1992.

Forbes, Christopher. "Comparison, Self-Praise and Irony: Paul's Boasting and the Conventions of Hellenistic Rhetoric." *New Testament Studies* 32 (1986): 1–30.

— *Prophecy and Inspired Speech in Early Christianity and Its Hellenistic Environment.* Wissenschaftliche Untersuchungen zum Neuen Testament 2. Tübingen: Mohr [Siebeck], 1995.

Forman, Robert K. C. "Mystical Knowledge: Knowledge by Identity." *Journal of the American Academy of Religion* 61 (1993): 705–38.

— *The Problem of Pure Consciousness: Mysticism and Philosophy.* 1st paperback ed. New York: Oxford University Press, 1997.

Fraade, S. D. "Ascetical Aspects of Ancient Judaism." In *Jewish Spirituality from the Bible through the Middle Ages,* ed. A. Green. New York: Crossroad, 1986.

Fredriksen, Paula. "Augustine and His Analysts: The Possibility of a Psychohistory." *Soundings* 61 (1978): 206–27.

— "Paul and Augustine: Conversion Narratives, Orthodox Traditions and the Retrospective Self." *Journal of Theological Studies* 37 (1986): 3–34.

— *Jesus of Nazareth, King of the Jews: A Jewish Life and the Emergence of Christianity.* New York: Knopf, 1999.

Freyne, Sean. "The Charismatic." In *Ideal Figures in Ancient Judaism: Profiles and Paradigms,* ed. John Joseph Collins, George W. E. Nickelsburg, and the Society of Biblical Literature Pseudepigrapha Group. Chico, Calif.: Scholars Press, 1980.

Fried, I, K. A. MacDonald, and C. L. Wilson. "Single Neuron Activity in Human Hippocampus and Amygdala during Recognition of Faces and Objects." *Neuron* 18 (1997): 753–65.

Friedrich, Gerhard. "Die Gegner des Paulus im 2 Korintherbrief." In *Abraham unser Vater; Juden und Christen im Gespräch über die Bibel,* ed. Otto Betz, Martin Hengel, and Peter Schmidt, 231–53. Arbeiten zur Geschichte des Spätjudentums und Urchristentums. Leiden: E. J. Brill.

— "προψήτης." In *Theological Dictionary of the New Testament,* vol. 6, ed. Gerhard Kittel, trans. Geoffrey Bromiley, 848. Grand Rapids, Mich.: Eerdmans, 1967.

Furnish, Victor Paul. *II Corinthians.* Anchor Bible 32A. Garden City, N.Y.: Doubleday, 1984.

— "Paul and the Corinthians: The Letters, the Challenges of Ministry, the Gospel." *Interpretation* 52 (1998): 229–45.

Gager, J. G. "Some Notes on Paul's Conversion." *New Testament Studies* 27 (1980–81): 697–704.

Garland, D. E. "Paul's Apostolic Authority: The Power of Christ Sustaining Weakness (2 Corinthians 10–13)." *Review and Expositor* 89 (1989): 371–89.

Garrett, Clarke. *Spirit Possession and Popular Religion: From the Camisards to the Shakers.* Baltimore: Johns Hopkins University Press, 1987.

Garrett, S. "The God of this World and the Affliction of Paul: 2 Cor 4:1–12." In *Greeks, Romans, and Christians: Essays in Honour of Abraham J. Malherbe,* ed. David L. Balch, E. Ferguson, and Wayne A. Meeks, 99–117. Minneapolis: Fortress, 1990.

Gaventa, Beverly R. "Paul's Conversion: A Critical Sifting of the Epistolary Evidence." PhD dissertation, University of Michigan, 1978.

— *From Darkness to Light: Aspects of Conversion in the New Testament.* Philadelphia: Fortress, 1986.

— "Galatians 1 and 2: Autobiography as Paradigm." *Novum Testamentum* 28 (1986): 309–26.

Gazzaniga, Michael S. *The New Cognitive Neurosciences*, 2nd ed. Cambridge, Mass.: MIT Press, 2000.

Gazzaniga, Michael S., and Joseph Ledoux. *The Integrated Mind.* New York: Plenum, 1978.

Gazzaniga, Michael S., J. E. LeDoux, and D. H. Wilson. "Language Praxis and the Right Hemisphere: Clues to Some Mechanisms of Consciousness." *Neurology* 27 (1977): 1144–47.

Geertz, Clifford. *The Interpretation of Cultures: Selected Essays.* New York: Basic Books, 1973.

Gellhorn, E, and W. F. Kiely. "Mystical States of Consciousness: Neurophysiological and Clinical Aspects." *Journal of Nervous and Mental Disease* 154 (1972): 399–405.

Genest, O. "L'interpretation de la mort de Jesus en situation discursive – un cas-type: L'articulation des figures de cette mort en 1–2 Corinthiens." *New Testament Studies* 34 (1988): 506–35.

Georgi, Dieter. *The Opponents of Paul in Second Corinthians: A Study of Religious Propaganda in Late Antiquity.* Philadelphia: Fortress, 1986.

Getty, Mary Ann. *First Corinthians, Second Corinthians.* Collegeville Bible Commentary 7. Collegeville, Minn.: Liturgical Press, 1983.

Gieschen, Charles A. *Angelomorphic Christology: Antecedents and Early Evidence.* Arbeiten zur Geschichte des antiken Judentums und des Urchristentums 42. Leiden: E. J. Brill, 1998.

Gilberg, R. "How to Recognize a Shaman among Other Religious Specialists." In *Shamanism in Eurasia*, ed. Mihály Hoppál, Part 1: 21–27. Göttingen: Herodot, 1984.

Gillespie, Thomas W. *The First Theologians: A Study in Early Christian Prophecy.* Grand Rapids, Mich.: Eerdmans, 1994.

Gillman, J. "A Thematic Comparison: 1 Cor 15:50–57 and 2 Cor 5:1–5." *Journal of Biblical Literature* 107 (1988): 439–54.

Glasson, T. F. "2 Corinthians 5:1–10 versus Platonism: Paul's Opponents in Corinth." *Scottish Journal of Theology* 43 (1990): 145–55.

Glazier, Stephen D., ed. *Anthropology of Religion: A Handbook.* Westport, Conn.: Greenwood, 1997.

Glen, John Stanley. *Pastoral Problems in First Corinthians.* Philadelphia: Westminster, 1964.

Gloer, W. Hulitt. *An Exegetical and Theological Study of Paul's Understanding of New Creation and Reconciliation in 2 Cor. 5:14–21.* Mellen Biblical Press Series 42. Lewiston, N.Y.: Mellen, 1996.

— "2 Corinthians 5:14–21." *Review and Expositor* 86 (1989): 397–405.

Goldberg, Arnold, Margarete Schlüter, and Peter Schäfer. *Mystik und Theologie des rabbinischen Judentums.* Gesammelte Studien Texte und Studien zum antiken Judentum 61. Tübingen: Mohr Siebeck, 1997.

Goldstein, L., and N. W. Stoltzfus. "Changes in Interhemispheric Amplitude Relationships in the EEG during Sleep." *Physiology and Behavior* 8 (1972): 811–16.

— "Drug-Induced Changes of Interhemispheric EEG Amplitude Relationships in Man." *Agents and Actions* 3 (1972): 124–32.

Gooch, Peter D. *Dangerous Food: 1 Corinthians 8–10 in Its Context.* Studies in Christianity and Judaism 5. Waterloo: Wilfrid Laurier University Press, 1993.

Gooder, Paula. "Only the Third Heaven? 2 Corinthians 12:1–10 and Heavenly Ascent." PhD dissertation, University of Oxford, 1998.

Goodman, Felicitas D. *Speaking in Tongues: A Cross-cultural Study of Glossolalia.* Chicago: University of Chicago Press, 1972.

— "Apostolics of Yucatán: A Case Study of a Religious Movement." In *Religion, Altered States of Consciousness, and Social Change*, ed. Erika Bourguignon. Columbus: Ohio State University Press, 1973.

— *Ecstasy, Ritual and Alternate Reality: Religion in a Pluralistic World.* Bloomington: Indiana University Press, 1988.

— *How about Demons? Possession and Exorcism in the Modern World.* Bloomington: Indiana University Press, 1988.

Gordon, R. "Reporting the Marvelous." In *Envisioning Magic*, ed. Peter Schafer and H. G. Kippenberg, 65–92. Leiden: E. J. Brill, 1997.

Goulder, Michael. "Vision and Knowledge." *Journal for the Study of the New Testament* 56 (1994): 53–71.

— *St. Paul versus St. Peter: A Tale of Two Missions*, 1st American ed. Louisville, Ky.: Westminster/John Knox, 1995.

Gräbe, P. J. "The All-Surpassing Power of God through the Holy Spirit in the Midst of Our Broken Earthly Existence: Perspectives on Paul's Use of δυναμις in 2 Corinthians." *Neotestamentica* 28 (1994): 147–56.

Grant, Michael. *Saint Paul.* London: Weidenfeld and Nicolson, 1976.

Grassie, William, "Postmodernism: What One Needs to Know," *Zygon* 32 (1997): 83–94

Grech, P. "2 Corinthians 3:17 and the Pauline Doctrine of Conversion to the Holy Spirit." *Catholic Biblical Quarterly* 17 (1955): 420–37.

Grelot, P. "Note sur 2 Corinthiens 3:14." *New Testament Studies* 33 (1987): 135–44.

— "De la maison terrestre a la maison celeste: 2 Corinthiens 4:16–5:10."In *"Ou demeures-tu?": La maison depuis le monde biblique: en hommage au Professeur Guy Couturier a l'occasion de ses soixante-cinq ans*, ed. J. C. Petit, A. Charron, and A. Myre, 343–64. Montreal: Fides, 1994.

Grudem, Wayne A. *The Gift of Prophecy in 1 Corinthians.* Lanham, Md.: University Press of America, 1982.

Gruenwald, Ithamar. *Apocalyptic and Merkavah Mysticism.* Arbeiten zur Geschichte des antiken Judentums und des Urchristentums 14. Leiden: E. J. Brill, 1980.

Gundry, Robert Horton. *Sōma in Biblical Theology: With Emphasis on Pauline Anthropology. Society of New Testament Studies Monograph Series* 29. Cambridge: Cambridge University Press, 1976.

Gunkel, Hermann. *Die Wirkungen des heiligen Geistes, nach der populären Anschauung der apostolischen Zeit und nach der Lehre des Apostels Paulus; eine biblisch-theologische Studie.* Göttingen: Vandenhoeck, 1888.

Gunther, John J. *St. Paul's Opponents and Their Background: A Study of Apocalyptic and Jewish Sectarian Teachings.* Novum Testamentum Supplement 35. Leiden: E. J. Brill, 1973.

Güzeldere, Güven. "The Many Faces of Consciousness: A Field Guide." In *The Nature of Consciousness: Philosophical Debates*, ed. Ned Block, Owen Flanagan, and Güven Güzeldere, 1–67. Cambridge, Mass.: MIT Press, 1997.

Hafemann, Scott J. "'Self-Commendation' and Apostolic Legitimacy in 2 Corinthians: A Pauline Dialectic?" *New Testament Studies* 36 (1990): 66–88.

— "The Glory and Veil of Moses in 2 Cor 3:7–14: An Example of Paul's Contextual Exegesis of the OT – A Proposal." *Horizons in Biblical Theology* 14 (1992): 31–49.

— "Paul's Argument from the Old Testament and Christology in 2 Cor 1–9: The Salvation-History / Restoration Structure of Paul's Apologetic." In *The Corinthian Correspondence: Papers from a Conference Held in Louvain*, ed. R. Bieringer, 277–303. Leuven: Peeters, 1996.

Halperin, David J. *Faces of the Chariot*. Tübingen: Mohr [Siebeck], 1988.

— *The Faces of the Chariot: Early Jewish Responses to Ezekiel's Vision*. Texte und Studien zum antiken Judentum 16. Tübingen: Mohr, 1988.

Hamm, Dennis. "Paul's Blindness and Its Healing: Clues to Symbolic Intent." *Biblica* 71 (1990): 63–72.

Haraway, Donna J. "Situated Knowledges: The Science Question in Feminism and the Privilege of Partial Perspective." In *Simians, Cyborgs, and Women: The Reinvention of Nature*, ed. Donna J. Haraway, 183–201. New York: Routledge, 1991.

Harlow, Mary, and Ray Laurence, *Growing Up and Growing Old in Ancient Rome: A Life Course Approach*. London: Routledge, 2002.

Harner, Michael. "Comments on Richard Noll: Mental Imagery Cultivation as a Cultural Phenomenon: The Role of Visions in Shamanism."*Current Anthropology* 26 (1985): 452.

— "What Is a Shaman?" In *Shaman's Path: Healing, Personal Growth and Empowerment*, ed. Gary Doore, 7–15. Boston: Shambhala, 1988.

— *The Way of the Shaman*, 2nd ed. San Francisco: Harper and Row, 1990.

Harrington, D. J. "Sociological Concepts and the Early Church: A Decade of Research." *Theological Studies* 41 (1980): 181–90.

— "Charism and Ministry: The Case of the Apostle Paul." *Chicago Studies* 24 (1985): 245–57.

Harris, Marvin. "History and Significance of the Emic-Etic Distinction." *Annual Review of Anthropology* 5 (1976): 329–50.

Harrisville, Roy A. *Romans*. Augsburg Commentary on the New Testament. Minneapolis: Augsburg, 1980.

— *I Corinthians*. Augsburg Commentary on the New Testament. Minneapolis: Augsburg, 1987.

Harvey, A. E. *Renewal through Suffering: A Study of 2 Corinthians. Studies of the New Testament and Its World*. Edinburgh: T. and T. Clark, 1996.

Havens, J. "The Participant's vs. the Observer's Frame of Reference in the Psychological Study of Religion."*Journal for the Scientific Study of Religion* 1 (1961): 79–87.

Hay, D. M. *Pauline Theology: 1 and 2 Corinthians*. Minneapolis: Fortress, 1993.

Haykin, Michael A. G. *The Spirit of God: The Exegesis of 1 and 2 Corinthians in the Pneumatomachian Controversy of the Fourth Century*. Supplements to Vigiliae Christianae 272. Leiden: E. J. Brill, 1994.

Hays, Richard B. *First Corinthians*. Interpretation, a Bible Commentary for Teaching and Preaching. Louisville, Ky.: John Knox, 1997.

Headland, Thomas N., Kenneth Lee Pike, and Marvin Harris, eds. *Emics and Etics: The Insider/Outsider Debate*. Frontiers of Anthropology 7. Newbury Park, Calif.: Sage, 1990.

Heckel, Ulrich. *Kraft in Schwachheit: Untersuchungen zu 2 Kor 10–13*. Wissenschaftliche Untersuchungen zum Neuen Testament 2. Reihe. 56. Tübingen: Mohr, 1993.

Heilman, K. M., E. Valenstein, and R. T. Watson. "Neglect." In *Diseases of the Nervous System: Clinical Neurobiology*, ed. A. K. Asbury, G. M. McKhann, and W. I. McDonald, 768–79. Philadelphia: Saunders, 1992.

Heininger, Bernhard. *Paulus als Visionär: Eine religionsgeschichtliche Studie.* Herders biblische Studien 9. Freiburg: Herder, 1996.

Heiny, S. B. "The Motive for Metaphor: 2 Corinthians 2:14–4:6." *Society of Biblical Literature Seminar Papers* 26 (1987): 1–22.

Hellholm, David, ed. *Apocalypticism in the Mediterranean World and the Near East: Proceedings of the International Colloquium on Apocalypticism, Uppsala, August* 12–17, 1979. Tübingen: Mohr, 1983.

Hendrick, Charles W. "Paul's Conversion/Call: A Comparative Analysis of the Three Reports in Acts." *Journal of Biblical Literature* 100 (1981): 415–32.

Hengel, Martin. *Between Jesus and Paul: Studies in the Earliest History of Christianity.* Philadelphia: Fortress, 1983.

— "'Setze dich zu meiner Rechten!' Die Inthronisation Christi zur Rechten Gottes und Psalm 110:1." In *Le Trône de Dieu*, ed. M. Philonenko, 69: 108–94. Tübingen: Mohr Siebeck, 1993. Wissenschaftliche Unterschügen zum Neuen Testament.

Hengel, Martin, and Roland Deines. *The Pre-Christian Paul.* London: SCM Press 1991.

Hengel, Martin, and Anna Maria Schwemer. *Paul between Damascus and Antioch: The Unknown Years.* Louisville, Ky.: Westminster/John Knox, 1997.

— *Paul zwischen Damascus und Antiochien: Die unbekannten Jahre des Apostels.* Wissenschaftliche Untersuchungen zum Neuen Testament 108. Tübingen: Mohr Siebeck, 1998.

Henney, Jeannette H. "The Shakers of St. Vincent: A Stable Religion." In *Religion, Altered States of Consciousness, and Social Change*, ed. Erika Bourguignon, 219–63. Columbus: Ohio State University Press, 1973.

Henney, J. H., and Felicitas D. Goodman. *Trance, Healing, and Hallucination: Three Field Studies in Religious Experience.* New York: Wiley, 1974.

Héring, Jean. *The First Epistle of Saint Paul to the Corinthians.* London: Epworth, 1966.

— *The Second Epistle of Saint Paul to the Corinthians.* London: Epworth, 1967.

Hermann, L. "Apollos." *Revue des sciences religieuses* 50 (1976): 330–36.

Hesselink, I. J. "A Case for a Transitional Body: 2 Cor 5:1–8." *Perspectives* 10 (1995): 10–13.

Hickling, C. J. A. "The Sequence of Thought in II Corinthians, Chapter 3." *New Testament Studies* 21 (1975): 380–95.

Hill, David. *New Testament Prophecy.* London: Marshall Morgan and Scott, 1979.

Himmelfarb, Martha. "The Practice of Ascent in the Ancient Mediterranean World." In *Death, Ecstasy and Other Worldly Journeys*, ed. John Collins and Michael Fishbane, 123–37. Albany: State University of New York Press, 1995.

Hindley, J. C. "Towards a Date for the Similitudes of Enoch: An Historical Approach." *New Testament Studies* 14 (1967–68): 551–65.

Hobson, J. Allan, Edward F. Pace-Schott, and Robert Stickgold. "Consciousness: Its Vicissitudes in Waking and Sleep." In *The New Cognitive Neurosciences*, ed. Michael S. Gazzaniga, 1341–54. Cambridge, Mass.: MIT Press, 2000.

Hock, Ronald F. *The Social Context of Paul's Ministry: Tentmaking and Apostleship.* Philadelphia: Fortress, 1980.

Hodge, Charles. 2 *Corinthians*. Crossway Classic Commentaries. Wheaton, Ill.: Crossway, 1995.

Hoerber, R. G. "Paul's Conversion/Call." *Concordia Journal* 22 (1996): 186–88.

Hof, H. "Ecstasy and Mysticism." In *Religious Ecstasy*, ed. Nils J. Holm, 241–52. Scripta Instituti Donneriani Aboensis. Uppsala: Almqvist and Wiksells, 1982.

Hofstede, Geert. "Empirical Models of Cultural Differences." In *Contemporary Issues in Cross-cultural Psychology*, ed. Nico Bleichrodt and Pieter J. D. Drenth, 4–20. Amsterdam: Lisse, 1991.

Holland, G. S. "Speaking Like a Fool: Irony in 2 Corinthians 10–13." In *Rhetoric and the New Testament: Essays from the 1992 Heidelberg Conference*, ed. Stanley E. Porter and T. H. Olbricht, 250–64. Sheffield: JSOT Press, 1993.

Holloway, R. L. "Sexual Dimorphism of the Human Corpus Callosum from Three Independent Samples: Relative Size of the Corpus Callosum." *American Journal of Physical Anthropology* 92 (1993): 481–98.

Holm, Nils G. "Ecstasy Research in the 20th Century – An Introduction." In *Religious Ecstasy*, ed. Nils G. Holm, 7–26. Scripta Instituti Donneriani Aboensis." Uppsala: Almqvist and Wiksells, 1982.

Holmes, H. Rodney. "Thinking about Religion and Experiencing the Brain: Eugene d'Aquili's Biogenetic Structural Theory of Absolute Unitary Being." *Zygon* 28 (1993): 201–15.

Holsten, C. "Die Christus-Vision des Paulus und die Genesis des Paulinischen Evangeliums." *Zeitschrift für wissenschaftliche Theologie* 4 (1861): 223–84.

Hood, R. W., Jr. "Psychological Strength and the Report of Intense Religious Experience." *Journal for the Scientific Study of Religion* 13 (1974): 65–71.

Hooker, Morna. "Authority on Her Head: An Examination of I Cor. XI. 10." *New Testament Studies* 10 (1964): 410–16.

Hopkins, K. *Death and Renewal: Sociological Studies in Roman History II*. Cambridge: Cambridge University Press, 1983.

Horrell, D. G. *The Social Ethos of the Corinthian Correspondence: Interests and Ideology from 1 Corinthians to 1 Clement*. Studies of the New Testament and Its World. Edinburgh: T. and T. Clark, 1996.

Horsley, Richard A. "Pneumatikos vs. Psychikos: Distinctions of Spiritual Status among the Corinthians." *Harvard Theological Review* 69 (1976): 269–88.

— *1 Corinthians*. Nashville, Tenn.: Abingdon, 1998.

Houde, Olivier, Laure Zago, Emmanuel Mellet, Sylvain Moutier, Arlette Pineau, Bernard Mazoyer, and Nathalie Tzourio-Mazoyer. "Shifting from the Perceptual Brain to the Logical Brain: The Neural Impact of Cognitive Inhibition Training." *Journal of Cognitive Neuroscience* 12 (2000): 721–28.

Howell, Julie Day. "ASC Induction Techniques, Spiritual Experiences, and Commitment to New Religious Movements." *Sociology of Religion* 58 (1997): 141–65.

Hubbard, Moyer. "Was Paul Out of His Mind? Re-reading 2 Corinthians 5:13." *Journal for the Study of the New Testament* 70 (1998): 39–64.

Huby, Joseph. *Mystiques paulinienne et johannique*. Bruges: Desclee de Brouwer, 1946.

Hugdahl, Kenneth. "Cognitive Influences on Human Autonomic Nervous System Function." *Current Biology* 6 (1996): 252–58.

Hughes, J. Donald. *Pan's Travail: Environmental Problems of the Ancient Greeks and Romans*. Baltimore: Johns Hopkins University Press, 1994.

Hughes, Philip Edgcumbe. *Commentary on the Second Epistle to the Corinthians*. Grand Rapids, Mich.: Eerdmans, 1962.

Hultkrantz, Åke. "A Definition of Shamanism." *Temenos* 9 (1973): 25–37.

— "Ecological and Phenomenological Aspects of Shamanism." In *Studies in Lapp Shamanism*, ed. Louise Bäckman and Åke Hultkrantz, 9–35. Stockholm: Almqvist and Wiksells, 1978.

— "Comments on Richard Noll: Mental Imagery Cultivation as a Cultural Phenomenon: The Role of Visions in Shamanism." *Current Anthropology* 26 (1985): 453.

Hunt, Allen Rhea. *The Inspired Body: Paul, the Corinthians, and Divine Inspiration*. Macon, Ga.: Mercer University Press, 1996.

Hunt, Harry T. "Relations between the Phenomenon of Religious Mysticism and the Psychology of Thought: A Cognitive Psychology of States of Consciousness and the Necessity of Subjective States for Cognitive Theory." *Perceptual and Motor Skills* 61 (1985): 911–61.

— "The Linguistic Network of Signifiers and Imaginal Polysemy: An Essay in the Co-dependent Origination of Symbolic Forms." *The Journal of Mind and Behavior* 16 (1995): 405–20.

— *On the Nature of Consciousness: Cognitive, Phenomenological, and Transpersonal Perspectives*. New Haven, Conn.: Yale University Press, 1995.

Hurd, John Coolidge. *The Origin of I Corinthians*. Macon, Ga.: Mercer University Press, 1983.

Hurst, Larry R. "The New Testament Call Narratives: Biographic or Paradigmatic? With Particular Focus on the Conversion of Saul of Tarsus." ThM thesis, Trinity Evangelical Divinity School, 1993.

Hurtado, Larry W. "Convert, Apostate, or Apostle to the Nations: The 'Conversion' of Paul in Recent Scholarship." *Studies in Religion/Sciences Religieuses* 22 (1993): 273–84.

James, William. *The Varieties of Religious Experience*. New York: Triumph, 1991. First published New York: Longmans, Green and Co., 1902.

Jantzen, Grace M. "Feminists, Philosophers, and Mystics." *Hypatia* 9 (1994): 186–207.

Jaynes, Julian. *The Origin of Consciousness in the Breakdown of the Bicameral Mind*. Boston: Houghton Mifflin, 1977.

Jevning, R., R. K. Wallace, and M. Beidebach. "The Physiology of Meditation: A Review. A Wakeful Hypometabolic Integrated Response." *Neuroscience and Biobehavioral Reviews* 16 (1992): 415–24.

Jewett, Robert. *Paul's Anthropological Terms: A Study of Their Use in Conflict Settings*. Arbeiten zur Geschichte des antiken Judentums und des Urchristentums 10. Leiden: E. J. Brill, 1971.

— *A Chronology of Paul's Life*. Philadelphia: Fortress, 1979.

Johnson, Lee A. "Satan Talk in Corinth: The Rhetoric of Conflict." *Biblical Theology Bulletin* 29 (1999): 145–55.

— "The Epistolary Apostle: Paul's Response to the Challenge of the Corinthian Community." PhD dissertation, University of St. Michael's College, 2002.

Johnson, Luke Timothy. *Reading Romans: A Literary and Theological Commentary*. New York: Crossroad, 1997.

— *Religious Experience in Earliest Christianity: A Missing Dimension in New Testament Studies.* Minneapolis: Fortress, 1998.

Johnston, Sarah Iles. *Restless Dead: Encounters between the Living and the Dead in Ancient Greece.* Berkeley: University of California Press, 1999.

Jolivet, Ira J., Jr. "The Lukan Account of Paul's Conversion and Hermgorean Stasis Theory." In *The Rhetorical Interpretation of Scripture: Essays from the 1996 Malibu Conference*, ed. Stanley E. Porter and Dennis L., Stamps, 210–20. Journal for the Study of the New Testament Supplement Series 180. Sheffield: Sheffield Academic Press, 1999.

Jones, A. H. M. *The Roman Economy: Studies in Ancient Economic and Administrative History.* Oxford: Blackwell, 1974.

Jordan, David K., and Marc J. Swartz. *Personality and the Cultural Construction of Society: Papers in Honor of Melford E. Spiro.* Tuscaloosa: University of Alabama Press, 1990.

Joseph, Rhawn. *The Naked Neuron: Evolution and the Languages of the Body and Brain.* New York: Plenum, 1993.

— *Neuropsychiatry, Neuropsychology, and Clinical Neurology: Emotion, Evolution, Cognition, Language, Memory, Brain Damage, and Abnormal Behavior*, 2nd ed. Baltimore: Williams and Wilkins, 1996.

— "The Limbic System and the Soul: Evolution and the Neuroanatomy of Religious Experience." *Zygon* 36 (2001): 105–36.

Judge, E. A. "St. Paul and Classical Society." *Jahrbuch Für Antike und Christentum* 15 (1972): 19–36.

Kaas, Jon H. "The Reorganization of Sensory and Motor Maps after Injury in Adult Mammals." In *The New Cognitive Neurosciences*, ed. Michael S. Gazzaniga, 223–36. Cambridge, Mass.: MIT Press, 2000.

Kandel, Eric R., and James H. Schwartz. *Principles of Neural Science*, 4th ed. Stamford, Conn.: Appleton and Lange, 2000.

Käsemann, Ernst. "Die Legitimität des Apostels: Eine Untersuchung zu 2 Korinther 10–13." *Zeitschrift für die neutestamentliche Wissenschaft und die Kunde der älteren Kirche* 41 (1942): 33–71.

— *Perspectives on Paul*, trans. Margaret Kohl. Philadelphia: Fortress, 1971.

— *Commentary on Romans*, 4th ed., trans. G. W. Bromiley. Tübingen: Mohr, 1980.

Katz, Steven T. "The 'Conservative' Character of Mystical Experience." In *Mysticism and Religious Traditions*, ed. Steven T. Katz, 3–60. Oxford: Oxford University Press, 1978.

— "Language, Epistemology, and Mysticism." In *Mysticism and Philosophical Analysis*, ed. Steven T. Katz, 22–74. New York: Oxford University Press, 1983.

— "Mystical Speech and Mystical Meaning." In *Mysticism and Language*, ed. Steven T. Katz. New York: Oxford University Press, 1992.

Kaye, B. N. "Paul and His Opponents in Corinth: 2 Corinthians 6:14–7:1." In *Good News in History: Essays in Honor of Bo Reicke*, ed. E. L. Miller, 111–26. Atlanta: Scholars Press, 1993.

Kee, Howard Clark. "The Conversion of Paul: Confrontation or Interiority?" In *The Other Side of God: A Polarity in World Religions*, ed. Peter L. Berger, 48–60. Garden City, N.Y.: Anchor/Doubleday, 1981.

Kenney, John Peter. "Mysticism and Contemplation in the Enneads." *American Catholic Philosophical Quarterly* 71 (1997): 315–38.

Kertelge, Karl. *The Epistle to the Romans*. New Testament for Spiritual Reading 12. New York: Herder and Herder, 1972.

— "Buchstabe und Geist nach 2 Kor 3." In *Paul and the Mosaic Law*, ed. J. D. G. Dunn, 117–30. Tübingen: Mohr, 1996.

Kessler, C. "Conflict and Sovereignty in Kelantanese Malay Spirit Seances." In *Case Studies in Spirit Possession*, ed. Vincent Crapanzano and Vivian Garrison, 295–331. New York: Wiley, 1977.

Kilgallen, John J. *First Corinthians: An Introduction and Study Guide*. New York: Paulist, 1987.

Kim, Seyoon. "'The Grace that Was Given to Me': Paul and the Grace of His Apostleship." In *Die Hoffnung festhalten*, ed. Gerhard Maier, 50–59. Neuhausen-Stuttgart: Hänssler-Verlag, 1978.

— *The Origin of Paul's Gospel*. Grand Rapids, Mich.: Eerdmans, 1981.

— "2 Cor 5:11–21 and the Origin of Paul's Concept of 'Reconciliation'." *Novum Testamentum* 39 (1997): 360–84.

— "God Reconciled His Enemy to Himself: The Origin of Paul's Concept of Reconciliation." In *The Road from Damascus: The Impact of Paul's Conversion on His Life, Thought, and Ministry*, ed. Richard N. Longenecker, 102–24. Grand Rapids, Mich.: Eerdmans, 1997.

— *Paul and the New Perspective: Second Thoughts on the Origin of Paul's Gospel*. Grand Rapids, Mich.: Eerdmans, 2002.

King, Sallie. "Two Epistemological Models for the Interpretation of Mysticism." *Journal of the American Academy of Religion* 56 (1988): 257–79.

Kittel, Gerhard, and Gerhard von Rad, "δοκέω, δόξα." In *Theological Dictionary of the New Testament*, vol. 2, ed. Gerhard Kittel, trans. Geoffrey Bromiley, 232–55. Grand Rapids, Mich.: Eerdmans, 1964.

Klass, Morton, and Maxine K. Weisgrau. *Across the Boundaries of Belief: Contemporary Issues in the Anthropology of Religion*. Boulder, Colo.: Westview, 1999.

Knauth Langer, Susanne K. *Mind: An Essay on Human Feeling*, 3 vols. Baltimore: Johns Hopkins University Press, 1967.

Knight, Robert T., and Marcia Grabowecky. "Prefrontal Cortex, Time, and Consciousness." In *The New Cognitive Neurosciences*, ed. Michael S. Gazzaniga, 1319–39. Cambridge, Mass.: Bradford, 2000.

Knox, John. *Chapters in a Life of Paul*. New York: Abingdon, 1950.

Koenig, J. "The Knowing of Glory and Its Consequences (2 Cor 3–5)." In *The Conversation Continues: Studies in Paul & John in Honor of J. Louis Martyn*, ed. Robert Tomson Fortna and Beverly Roberts Gaventa. Nashville, Tenn.: Abingdon, 1990.

Kolenkow, A. B. "Paul and His Opponents in 2 Cor 10–13: THEIOI ANDRES and Spiritual Guides." In *Religious Propaganda and Missionary Competition in the New Testament World: Essays Honoring Dieter Georgi*, ed. Lukas Bormann, Kelly Del Tredici, and Angela Standhartinger, 351–74. Leiden: E. J. Brill, 1994.

König, H. "Wer ist 'Gott in Christus'? Beobachtungen zu den Anfangen der Rezeptionsgeschichte von 2 Cor 5:19 in der fruhchristlichen Literatur." In *Philologia sacra: Biblische und patristische Studien für Hermann J. Frede und Walter Thiele zu ihrem siebzigsten Geburtstag*, ed. Hermann Josef Frede, Walter Thiele, and Roger Gryson. 285–305. Freiburg: Verlag Herder, 1993.

Koslow, Stephen H. Neuroinformatics: Human Brain Project home page. National Institute of Mental Health, http://www.nimh.nih.gov/neuroinformatics/index.cfm.

Kraftchick, S. J. *"Death in Us, Life in You: The Apostolic Medium."* In *Society of Biblical Literature Seminar Papers* (1991): 618–37.

Kreitzer, L. Joseph. *2 Corinthians*. New Testament Guides. Sheffield: Sheffield Academic Press, 1996.

Krippner, Stanley. "The Epistemology and Technologies of Shamanic States of Consciousness." *Journal of Consciousness Studies* 7 (2000): 93–118.

Kroeber, Alfred L. "Psychosis or Social Sanction." In *The Nature of Culture*, ed. Alfred L. Kroeber, 310–19. Chicago: University of Chicago Press, 1952.

Kruse, Colin G. *The Second Epistle of Paul to the Corinthians: An Introduction and Commentary*. The Tyndale New Testament Commentaries 8. Grand Rapids, Mich.: Eerdmans, 1987.

— "The Relationship between the Opposition to Paul Reflected in 2 Corinthians 1–7 and 10–13." *Evangelical Quarterly* 61 (1989): 195–202.

Kümmel, Werner Georg. *Kirchenbegriff und Geschichtsbewusstsein in der Urgemeinde und bei Jesus*. Uppsala: Niehans, 1943.

LaBerge, David. "Networks of Attention." In *The New Cognitive Neurosciences*, ed. Michael S. Gazzaniga, 711–24. Cambridge, Mass.: MIT Press, 2000.

Lachs, Samuel Tobias. "Sexual Imagery in Three Rabbinic Passages." *Journal for the Study of Judaism* 23 (1992): 244–48.

Lakoff, Georgee, and Mark Johnson. *Philosophy in the Flesh: The Embodied Mind and Its Challenge to Western Thought*. New York: Basic Books, 1999.

Lambrecht, Jan. "The Eschatological Outlook in 2 Corinthians 4:7–15." In *To Tell the Mystery: Essays on New Testament Eschatology in Honor of Robert H. Gundry*, ed. Thomas E. Schmidt and Moisés Silva. Sheffield: JSOT Press, 1994.

— "Strength in Weakness: 2 Cor 11:23b–33; Reply to S. B. Andres." *New Testament Studies* 43 (1997): 285–90.

Lambrecht, Jan, and R. Bieringer. "Paul's Boasting about the Corinthians: A Study of 2 Cor 8:24–9:5." *Novum Testamentum* 40 (1998): 352–68.

Lambrecht, Jan, and Daniel J. Harrington. *Second Corinthians*. Sacra Pagina 8. Collegeville, Minn.: Liturgical Press, 1999.

Lampe, Peter, trans. Michael Steinhauser. *From Paul to Valentinus: Christians at Rome in the First Two Centuries*. London: T. and T. Clark, 2003.

Laqueur, Thomas Walter. *Making Sex: Body and Gender from the Greeks to Freud*. Cambridge, Mass.: Harvard University Press, 1990.

Larkin, Marilyn. "Speech and Sign Language Trigger Similar Brain Activity." *The Lancet* 356 (2000): 1989.

Laughlin, Charles D., and Eugene G. d'Aquili. *Biogenetic Structuralism*. New York: Columbia University Press, 1974.

Laughlin, Charles D., John McManus, and Eugene G. d'Aquili. *Brain, Symbol and Experience: Toward a Neurophenomenology of Human Consciousness*. Boston: New Science Library, 1990.

Leary, T. J. "'A Thorn in the Flesh' – 2 Corinthians 12:7: Was Paul Visually Impaired." *Journal of Theological Studies* n.s. 43 (1992): 520–22.

Lessa, William A., and Evon Z. Vogt. *Reader in Comparative Religion: An Anthropological Approach*, 4th ed. New York: Harper and Row, 1979.

Letellier, D. J. "Le Theme du Voile de Moise, chez Origene Exode 34:33–35 et 2 Corinthiens 3:12–18." *Revue des Science Religieuses* 62 (1988): 14–26.

Lettvin, Jerome. "A Sidelong Glance at Seeing." *Sciences* 16 (1976): 1–20.

Leuba, J. "A Study in the Psychology of Religious Phenomena." *American Journal of Psychology* 5 (1896): 309–85.

Levene, Michael J., et al., "In Vivo Multiphoton Microscopy of Deep Brain Tissue." *Journal of Neurophysiology* 91 (2004): 1908–12.

Levine, D. N., R. Calvanio, and W. E. Rinn. "The Pathogenesis of Anosognosia for Hemiplegia." *Neurology* 41 (1991): 1770–81.

Lévi-Strauss, Claude. *Anthropologie structurale*. Paris: Plon, 1973.

Levy, Jerre, Colwyn Trevarthen, and Roger W. Sperry. "Perception of Bilateral Chimeric Figures Following Hemispheric Disconnection." *Brain* 95 (1972): 61–78.

Lewis, Ioan M. "Spirit Possession and Deprivation Cults." *Man* 1 (1966): 307–329.

— *Ecstatic Religion: An Anthropological Study of Spirit Possession and Shamanism*, 2nd ed. Harmondsworth: Penguin, 1971.

— *Religion in Context: Cults and Charisma*, 2nd ed. Cambridge: Cambridge University Press, 1996.

Lewis, Jack Pearl. *Interpreting 2 Corinthians 5:14–21: An Exercise in Hermeneutics*. Studies in the Bible and Early Christianity 17. Lewiston, N.Y.: Mellen, 1989.

Lex, Barbara. "Neurological Bases of Revitalization Movements." *Zygon* 13 (1978): 276–312.

— "The Neurobiology of Ritual Trance." In *The Spectrum of Ritual: A Biogenetic Structural Analysis*, ed. Eugene G. d'Aquili, Charles D. Laughlin, and John McManus, 117–51. New York: Columbia University Press, 1979.

Liddon, Sim C. *The Dual Brain, Religion, and the Unconscious*. Buffalo, N.Y.: Prometheus, 1989.

Lieu, J. "'The Parting of the Ways': Theological Construction or Social Reality." *Journal for the Study of the New Testament* 56 (1994): 101–19.

Lilly, Joseph L. "The Conversion of Saint Paul: The Validity of His Testimony to the Resurrection of Jesus Christ." *Catholic Biblical Quarterly* 6 (1944): 180–204.

Lincoln, Andrew T. *Paradise Now and Not Yet: Studies in the Role of the Heavenly Dimension in Paul's Thought with Special Reference to His Eschatology*. Society for New Testament Studies 43. Cambridge: Cambridge University Press, 1981.

Lipman, J., B. Miller, K. Mays, M. N. Miller, W. C. North, and W. L. Byrne. "Peak ß-endorphin Concentration in Cerebrospinal Fluid: Reduced in Chronic Pain Patients and Increased during the Placebo Response." *Psychopharmacology* 102 (1990): 112–16.

Lohfink, Gerhard. *The Conversion of St. Paul: Narrative and History in Acts*. Herald Scriptural Library. Chicago: Franciscan Herald, 1976.

Lohmeyer, E. *Grundlagen paulinischer Theologie*. Tübingen: Mohr, 1929.

Long, William. "The *Paulusbild* in the Trial of Paul in Acts." *Society of Biblical Literature Seminar Papers* 22 (1983): 87–105.

Longenecker, Richard N., ed. *The Road from Damascus: The Impact of Paul's Conversion on His Life, Thought, and Ministry*. McMaster New Testament Studies. Grand Rapids, Mich.: Eerdmans, 1997.

Loubser, J. A. "Winning the Struggle (Or, How to Treat Heretics) 2 Corinthians 12:1–10." *Journal of Theology for Southern Africa* 75 (1991): 75–83.

Lowie, Robert H. *Indians of the Plains*. New York: McGraw-Hill, 1954.

Lüdemann, Gerd. *Paulus, der Heidenapostel*. Göttingen: Vandenhoeck and Ruprecht, 1980.

Ludwig, A. M. "Altered States of Consciousness." *Archives of General Psychiatry* 15 (1966): 225–34.

Lum, Kenneth Anthony. *Praising His Name in the Dance: Spirit Possession in the Spiritual Baptist Faith and Orisha Work in Trinidad, West Indies*. Studies in Latin America and the Caribbean 1. Amsterdam: Harwood Academic, 2000.

Lyonnet, Stanislas. *Études sur l'epître aux Romans*. Analecta Biblica 120. Rome: Editrice Pontificio Istituto Biblico, 1989.

Lyons, G. *Pauline Autobiography: Toward a New Understanding*. Society of Biblical Literature Dissertation Series 73. Atlanta: Scholars Press, 1985.

Maccoby, Hyam. *The Mythmaker: Paul and the Invention of Christianity*. New York: Harper and Row, 1986.

MacDonald, D. R. "Corinthian Veils and Gnostic Androgynes." In *Images of the Feminine in Gnosticism*, ed. Karen L. King, 283–85. Philadelphia: Fortress, 1988.

MacDonald, George F., John L. Cove, Charles D. Laughlin, and John McManus. "Mirrors, Portals, and Multiple Realities." *Zygon* 24 (1989): 39–64.

MacLean, C. R. K., K. G. Walton, S. R. Wenneberg, D. K. Levitsky, J. V. Mandarino, R. Waziri, and R.H. Schneider. "Altered Responses to Cortisol, GH, TSH and Testosterone to Acute Stress after Four Months' Practice of Transcendental Meditation (TM)."*Annals of the New York Academy of Sciences* 746 (1994): 381–84.

Mageo, Jeannette Marie, and Alan Howard. *Spirits in Culture, History, and Mind*. New York: Routledge, 1996.

Malherbe, Abraham J. *Social Aspects of Early Christianity*, 2nd ed. Philadelphia: Fortress, 1983.

— "'Not in a Corner': Early Christan Apologetic in Acts 26:26." *The Second Century* 5 (1985–86): 193–210.

Malina, Bruce. *The New Testament World: Insights from Cultural Anthropology*. Atlanta: John Knox, 1981.

— *Christian Origins and Cultural Anthropology: Practical Models for Biblical Interpretation*. Atlanta: John Knox, 1986.

— "Reading Theory Perspective: Reading Luke-Acts." In *The Social World of Luke-Acts: Models for Interpretation*, ed. Jerome H. Neyrey, 3–23. Peabody, Mass.: Hendrickson, 1991.

— "Is There a Circum-Mediterranean Person: Looking for Stereotypes." *Biblical Theology Bulletin* 22 (1992): 66–87.

Malina, Bruce J., and Jerome H. Neyrey. *Portraits of Paul: An Archaeology of Ancient Personality*. Louisville, Ky.: Westminster/John Knox, 1996.

Maly, Karl. *Mündige Gemeinde: Untersuchungen zur pastoralen Führung des Apostels Paulus im 1 Korintherbrief*. Stuttgarter biblische Monographien 2. Stuttgart: Katholisches Bibelwerk, 1967.

Marguerat, Daniel. "2 Corinthiens 10–13: Paul et l'experience de Dieu."*Ètudes thèologiques et religieuses* 63 (1988): 497–519.

— "Saul's Conversion (Acts 9, 22, 26) and the Multiplication of Narrative in Acts." In *Luke's Literary Achievement: Collected Essays*, ed. C. M. Tuckett, 127–55. Journal for the Study of the New Testament Supplement Series 116. Sheffield: Sheffield Academic Press, 1995.

Markowitsch, Hans J. "The Anatomical Bases of Memory." In *The New Cognitive Neurosciences*, ed. Michael S. Gazzaniga, 781–95. Cambridge, Mass.: MIT Press, 2000.

Marrow, Stanley B. *Paul, His Letters and His Theology: An Introduction to Paul's Epistles*. New York: Paulist, 1986.

Marshall, Peter. *Enmity in Corinth: Social Conventions in Paul's Relations with the Corinthians*. Wissenschaftliche Untersuchungen zum Neuen Testament 2. Reihe 23. Tübingen: Mohr [Siebeck], 1987.

Martin, Dale B. "Tongues of Angels and Other Status Indicators." *Journal of the American Academy of Religion* 59 (1991): 547–89.

— *The Corinthian Body*. New Haven, Conn.: Yale University Press, 1995.

Martin, R. "The Spirit in 2 Corinthians in Light of the 'Fellowship of the Holy Spirit.'" In *Eschatology and the New Testament: Essays in Honor of George Raymond Beasley-Murray*, ed. Hulitt Gloer, 113–28. Peabody, Mass.: Hendrickson, 1988.

— *Philippians*. New Century Bible Commentary. Grand Rapids, Mich.: Eerdmans, 1980.

— "The Opponents of Paul in 2 Corinthians: An Old Issue Revisited." In *Tradition and Interpretation in the New Testament: Essays in Honor of E. Earle Ellis for His 60th Birthday*, ed. Gerald F. Hawthorne and Otto Betz, 279–89. Grand Rapids, Mich.: Eerdmans, 1987.

Marusich, Alexander A. N. "Religious Conversion: Explorations in Biogenetic Structuralism." PhD dissertation, University of Toronto, 1996.

Marusich, A. Sasha. "A Critical Response to Barbara Lex's Neurophysiological Theory of Trance." *Method and Theory in the Study of Religion* 3 (1991): 47–61.

Matlock, R. B. "Almost Cultural Studies? Reflections on the 'New Paradigm' on Paul." In *Biblical Studies/Cultural Studies: The Third Sheffield Colloquium*, ed. J. Cheryl Exum and Stephen D. Moore, 433–59. Sheffield: Sheffield Academic Press, 1998.

May, D. *Social Scientific Criticism of the New Testament: A Bibliography*. Macon, Ga.: Mercer University Press, 1991.

McCant, Jerry W. "Competing Pauline Eschatologies: An Exegetical Comparison of 1 Corinthians 15 and 2 Corinthians 5." *Wesleyan Theological Journal* 29 (1994): 23–49.

— *2 Corinthians*. Readings, A New Biblical Commentary. Sheffield: Sheffield Academic Press, 1999.

McClintock Fulkerson, Mary. *Changing the Subject: Women's Discourses and Feminist Theology*. Minneapolis: Fortress, 1994.

McGahey, Robert. *The Orphic Moment: Shaman to Poet-Thinker in Plato, Nietzsche, and Mallarmé*. SUNY Series, The Margins of Literature. Albany: State University of New York Press, 1994.

McGinn, Bernard. *The Foundations of Mysticism, Vol. 1: The Presence of God: A History of Western Christian Mysticism*. New York: Crossroad, 1991.

Meeks, Wayne. *The First Urban Christians: The Social World of the Apostle Paul*. New Haven, Conn.: Yale University Press, 1983.

— *The Moral World of the First Christians*. Philadelphia: Westminster, 1986.

Merkur, Daniel. "Unitive Experiences and the State of Trance." In *Mystical Union and Monotheistic Faith: An Ecumenical Dialogue*, ed. Moshe Idel and Bernard McGinn, 125–53. New York: Macmillan, 1989.

Merleau-Ponty, Maurice. *Phenomenology of Perception*, trans. Colin Smith. New York: Humanities Press, 1962, Originally published as *Phénoménologie de la perception*, 15th ed. Paris: Gallimard, 1945.

Metts, R. "Death, Discipleship, and Discourse Strategies: 2 Cor 5:1–10 – Once Again." *Criswell Theological Review* 4 (1989): 57–76.

Metzger, Bruce M. "Methodology in the Study of the Mystery Religions and Early Christianity." In *Historical and Literary Studies: Pagan, Jewish and Christian*, ed. Bruce M. Metzger, 1–24. Grand Rapids, Mich.: Eerdmans, 1968.

Meyer, M. W., ed. *The Ancient Mysteries: A Sourcebook.* Sacred Texts of the Mystery Religions of the Ancient Mediterranean World. San Francisco: Harper and Row, 1987.

—— "Mystery Religions." In *Anchor Bible Dictionary*, vol. 4, ed. David Noe' Freedman, 941–45. Toronto: Doubleday, 1992.

Michael, J. Hugh. *The Epistle of Paul to the Philippians.* London: Hodder and Stoughton, 1946.

Miles, Margaret. *Image as Insight: Visual Understanding in Western Christianity and Secular Culture.* Boston: Beacon, 1985.

Minn, Herbert R. *The Thorn that Remained: Materials for the Study of St. Paul's Thorn in the Flesh: 2 Corinthians XII. vv. 1–10.* Auckland: Institute Press, 1972.

Mitchell, Alan Christopher. "I Corinthians 6:1–11: Group Boundaries and the Courts of Corinth." PhD dissertation, Yale University, 1986.

Mitchell, Margaret M. *Paul and the Rhetoric of Reconciliation: An Exegetical Investigation of the Language and Composition of 1 Corinthians.* Louisville: Westminster/John Knox, 1991.

Montcastle, V. B., B. C. Motter, and R. A. Andersen. "Some Further Observations on the Functional Properties of Neurons in the Parietal Lobe of the Waking Monkey." *Brain Behavioral Sciences* 3 (1980): 520–29.

Moo, Douglas J. *The Epistle to the Romans.* New International Commentary on the New Testament. Grand Rapids, Mich.: Eerdmans, 1996.

Mooneyham, Laura. "The Origin of Consciousness, Gains and Losses: Walker Percy vs. Julian Jaynes." *Language and Communication* 13 (1993): 169–82.

Moore, Robert L. "Pauline Theology and the Return of the Repressed: Depth Psychology and Early Christian Thought." *Zygon* 13 (1978): 158–68.

Mopsik, Charles. "The Body of Engenderment in the Hebrew Bible, the Rabbinic Tradition, and the Kabbalah." In *Fragments for a History of the Human Body*, ed. Michel Feher, Nadia Tazi, and Ramona Naddaff, 48–73. New York: Zone, 1989.

—— "Union and Unity in Kabbalah." In *Between Jerusalem and Benares: Comparative Studies in Judaism and Hinduism*, ed. Hananya Goodman, 223–42. Albany: State University of New York Press, 1994.

Morgan, Robert. *Romans.* New Testament Guides. Sheffield: Sheffield Academic Press, 1995.

Morray-Jones, C. R. A. "Paradise Revisited (2 Cor 12:1–12): The Jewish Mystical Background of Paul's Apostolate. Part 1: The Jewish Sources." *Harvard Theological Review* 86 (1993): 177–217.

— "Paradise Revisited (2 Cor 12:1-12): The Jewish Mystical Background of Paul's Apostolate. Part 2: Paul's Heavenly Ascent and Its Significance." *Harvard Theological Review* 86 (1993): 256–92.

Morris, Leon. *The First Epistle of Paul to the Corinthians: An Introduction and Commentary*, 2nd ed. Tyndale New Testament Commentaries 7. Grand Rapids, Mich.: Eerdmans, 1985.

Mosher, Donald L. "Three Dimensions of Depth of Involvement in Human Sexual Response." *The Journal of Sex Research* 16 (1980): 1–42.

Moule, C. F. D. *The Origin of Christology*. Cambridge: Cambridge University Press, 1977.

Mtsho, Bstan Dzin Rgya et al. *Consciousness at the Crossroads: Conversations with the Dalai Lama on Brainscience and Buddhism*. Ithaca, N.Y.: Snow Lion, 1999.

Müller, Jacobus Johannes. *The Epistles of Paul to the Philippians and to Philemon*. New International Commentary on the New Testament. Grand Rapids, Mich.: Eerdmans, 1955.

Munck, Johannes. *Paul and the Salvation of Mankind*, trans. Frank Clarke. Atlanta: John Knox, 1977.

Murdock, G. P., and D. White. "Standard Cross-cultural Sample." *Ethnology* 8 (1969): 329–69.

Murphy-O'Connor, Jerome. *I Corinthians*. New Testament message 10. Wilmington, Del.: Glazier, 1979.

— "Sex and Logic in 1 Corinthians 11:2–16." *Catholic Biblical Quarterly* 42 (1980): 485–500.

— "'Being at Home in the Body We Are in Exile from the Lord' (2 Cor 5:6b)." *Revue Biblique* 93 (1986): 214–21.

— "Interpolations in 1 Corinthians." *Catholic Biblical Quarterly* 48 (1986): 81–94.

— "Pneumatikoi and Judaizers in 2 Cor 2:14–4:6." *Australian Biblical Review* 34 (1987): 42–58.

— "Faith and Resurrection in 2 Cor 4:13–14." *Revue Biblique* 95 (1988): 543–50.

— "The Date of 2 Corinthians 10–13." *Australian Biblical Review* 39 (1991): 31–43.

— *The Theology of the Second Letter to the Corinthians*. Cambridge: Cambridge University Press, 1991.

— *Paul: A Critical Life*. Oxford: Clarendon, 1996.

Murray, John. *The Epistle to the Romans*. New International Commentary on the New Testament. Grand Rapids, Mich.: Eerdmans, 1959.

Napel, E. T. "'Third Heaven' and 'Paradise': Some Remarks on the Exegesis of 2 Cor 12:2–4." In *Symposuim Syriacum V. K: 1988. Katholieke Universiteit, Leuven, 29–31 caout 1988*, ed. René Lavenant, 53–65. Rome: Pontifical Institute Stud Orientalium, 1990.

Narby, Jeremy, and Francis Huxley. *Shamans through Time: 500 Years on the Path to Knowledge*. London: Thames and Hudson, 2001.

Nathanson, M., P. S. Bergman, and G. G. Gordon. "Denial of Illness." *Archive of Neurological Psychiatry* 68 (1952): 380–87.

Nebes, R. D., and Roger W. Sperry. "Hemispheric Disconnection Syndrome with Cerebral Birth Injury in the Dominant Arm Area." *Neuropsychologia* 9 (1971): 249–59.

Neville, Robert C. *Normative Cultures*. Albany: State University of New York Press, 1995.

Newberg, Andrew B., Eugene G. D'Aquili, Vince Rause, and Judith Cummings. *Why God Won't Go Away: Brain Science and the Biology of Belief.* New York: Ballantine, 2001.

Newberg, Andrew, et al. "The Measurement of Regional Cerebral Blood Flow during the Complex Task of Meditation: A Preliminary SPECT Study." *Psychiatry Research: Neuroimaging* 106 (2001): 113–22.

Newberg, Andrew, M. Pourdhnad, A. Alavi, and Eugene G. d' Aquili. "Cerebral Blood Flow during Meditative Prayer: Preliminary Findings and Methodological Issues." *Perceptual and Motor Skills* 97 (2003): 625–30.

Newman, C. C. *Paul's Glory-Christology: Tradition and Rhetoric. Novum Testamentum Supplement* 69. Leiden: E. J. Brill, 1992.

Newsom, Carol. *Songs of the Sabbath Sacrifice: A Critical Edition.* Harvard Semitic Studies 27. Atlanta: Scholars Press, 1985.

Newton, Natika. *Foundations of Understanding.* Philadelphia: John Benjamins, 1996.

Neyrey, Jerome H. "Body Language in 1 Corinthians: The Use of Anthropological Models for Understanding Paul and His Opponents." *Semeia: Social-Scientific Criticism of the New Testament and Its Social World* 35 (1985): 127–70.

— *Paul, in Other Words: A Cultural Reading of His Letters.* Louisville, Ky.: Westminster/John Knox, 1990.

Niditch, S. "The Visionary." In *Ideal Figures in Ancient Judaism: Profiles and Paradigms,* ed. John Joseph Collins, George W. E. Nickelsburg, and Society of Biblical Literature Pseudepigrapha Group, 153–79. Chico, Calif.: Scholars Press, 1980.

Noll, Richard. "Shamanism and Schizophrenia: A State-Specific Approach to the 'Schizophrenia Metaphor' of Shaminic States." *American Ethnologist* 10 (1983): 443–59.

— "Mental Imagery Cultivation as a Cultural Phenomenon: The Role of Visions in Shamanism." *Current Anthropology* 26 (1985): 443–61.

— "What Has Really Been Learned about Shamanism?" *Journal of Psychoactive Drugs* 21 (1989): 47–50.

Nygren, Anders. *Commentary on Romans.* Philadelphia: Fortress, 1972.

Obeyesekere, G. "Psychocultural Exegesis of a Case of Spirit Possession in Sri Lanka." In *Case Studies in Spirit Possession,* ed. Vincent Crapanzano and Vivian Garrison, 235–94. New York: Wiley, 1977.

Obijole, O. "The Influence of the Conversion of St. Paul on His Theology of the Cross." *East Africa Journal of Evangelical Theology* 6 (1987): 27–36.

O'Brien, Peter T. "Mysticism." In *Dictionary of Paul and His Letters,* ed. Gerald F. Hawthorne, Ralph P. Martin, and Daniel G. Reid, 623–25. Downers Grove, Ill.: InterVarsity, 1993.

O'Neill, J. "The Absence of the 'in Christ' Theology in 2 Corinthians 5." *Australian Biblical Review* 35 (1987): 99–106.

Oosthout, Henri. *Modes of Knowledge and the Transcendental: An Introduction to Plotinus Enneads 5.3(49) with a Commentary and Translation.* Bochumer Studien zur Philosophie 17. Amsterdam: Grüner, 1991.

Orr, William Fridell, and James Arthur Walther. *I Corinthians: A New Translation.* Anchor Bible 32. Garden City, N.Y.: Doubleday, 1976.

Osburn, Carroll D. "The Interpretation of 1 Cor 14:34–35." In *Essays on Women in Earliest Christianity*, vol. 1, ed. Carroll D. Osburn, 219–42. Joplin, Mo.: College Press, 1995.

Osiek, Carolyn. *What Are They Saying about the Social Setting of the New Testament?* New York: Paulist, 1984.

— *Philippians, Philemon*. Abingdon New Testament Commentaries. Nashville, Tenn.: Abingdon, 2000.

Otto, Rudolf. *The Idea of the Holy: An Inquiry into the Non-rational Factor in the Idea of the Divine and Its Relation to the Rational*, 2nd ed., trans. John W. Harvey. London: Oxford University Press, 1968.

Oughourlian, Jean-Michel. *The Puppet of Desire: The Psychology of Hysteria, Possession, and Hypnosis*. Stanford, Calif.: Stanford University Press, 1991.

Overholt, Thomas W. *Channels of Prophecy: The Social Dynamics of Prophetic Activity*. Minneapolis: Fortress, 1989.

Parker, T. H. L. *Calvin's New Testament Commentaries*. Grand Rapids, Mich.: Eerdmans, 1971.

Pate, C. Marvin. *Adam Christology as the Exegetical and Theological Substructure of 2 Corinthians 4:7–5:21*. Lanham, Md.: University Press of America, 1991.

— *The Glory of Adam and the Afflictions of the Righteous: Pauline Suffering in Context*. Lewiston, N.Y.: Mellen, 1993.

Patte, Daniel. "A Structural Exegesis of 2 Corinthians 2:14–7:4 with Special Attention on 2:14–3:6 and 6:11–7:4." *Society of Biblical Literature Seminar Papers* 26 (1987): 23–49.

Pattison, Mansell E. "Behavioral Science Research on the Nature of Glossolalia." *Journal of the American Scientific Affiliation* 20 (1968): 73–86.

Peace, Richard V. *Conversion in the New Testament: Paul and the Twelve*. Grand Rapids, Mich.: Eerdmans, 1999.

Penfield, Wilder, and P. Perot. "The Brain's Record of Auditory and Visual Experience." *Brain* 86 (1963): 595–696.

Perriman, A. C. "Paul and the Parousia: 1 Corinthians 15:50–57 and 2 Corinthians 5:1–5." *New Testament Studies* 35 (1989): 512–21.

Pert, Candace B. *Molecules of Emotion: Why You Feel the Way You Feel*. New York: Scribner, 1997.

Peters, Larry G., and Douglas Price-Williams. "Towards an Experiential Analysis of Shamanism." *American Ethnologist* 7 (1980): 397–413.

Peterson, B. K. "Conquest, Control, and the Cross: Paul's Self-Portrayal in 2 Corinthians 10–13." *Interpretation* 52 (1998): 258–70.

Pfitzner, V. C. *Strength in Weakness: A Commentary on 2 Corinthians*. Adelaide: Lutheran Publishing House, 1992.

Philo. *On the Creation*. Loeb Classical Library. London: Heinemann, 1929.

Pilch, John. "The Transfiguration of Jesus: An Experience of Alternate Reality." In *Modeling Early Christianity: Social-Scientific Studies of the New Testament in Its Context*, ed. Philip R. Esler, 47–64. London: Routledge, 1995.

"Altered States of Consciousness: A Kitbashed Model." *Biblical Theology Bulletin* 26 (1996): 133–38.

— "Psychological and Psychoanalytical Approaches to Interpreting the Bible in Social-Scientific Context." *Biblical Theology Bulletin* 27 (1996): 112–16.

— "Ereignisse eines veränderten Bewusstseinszustandes [BWZ] bei den Synoptkern." In *Jesus in neuen Kontexten*, ed. Wolfgang Stegemann, Bruce J. Malina, and Gerd Tneissen, 33–42. Stuttgart: Kohlhammer, 2002.

Pilch, John J., and Bruce J. Malina, eds. *Biblical Social Values and Their Meaning*. Peabody, Mass.: Hendrickson, 1993.

Pitt-Rivers, Julian Alfred. *Mediterranean Countrymen: Essays in the Social Anthropology of the Mediterranean*. Maison des sciences de l'homme: Recherches méditeranéennes 1. Paris: Mouton, 1963.

Plevnik, J. "Paul's Appeal to His Damascus Experience and 1 Cor 15:5–7: Are They Legitimations?" *Toronto Journal of Theology* 4 (1988): 101–11.

Plummer, Alfred. *A Critical and Exegetical Commentary on the Second Epistle of St. Paul to the Corinthians*. International Critical Commentary on the Holy Scriptures of the Old and New Testaments. Edinburgh: T. and T. Clark, 1915.

Porter, Stanley E. *Handbook of Classical Rhetoric in the Hellenistic Period, 330 B.C.–A.D. 400*. Leiden: E. J. Brill, 1997.

Posner, Michael I., and Marcus E. Raichle. *Images of Mind*. New York: Scientific American Library, 1994.

Price, Craig. "Critical Issues in 2 Corinthians." *Southwestern Journal of Theology* 32 (1989): 11–17.

Price, Robert M. "Punished in Paradise (An Exegetical Theory of II Corinthians 12:1–10)." *Journal for the Study of the New Testament* 7 (1980): 33–40.

— "Review: Drudgery Divine. On the Comparison of Early Christianities and the Religions of Late Antiquity." *Journal of Higher Criticism* 3 (1996): 137–45.

Prince, R. "Foreword." In *Case Studies in Spirit Possession*, ed. Vincent Crapanzano and Vivian Garrison, xi–xvi. New York: Wiley, 1976.

Prior, David. *The Message of 1 Corinthians: Life in the Local Church*. Bible Speaks Today. Downers Grove, Ill.: Inter-Varsity, 1985.

Prokulski, Walenty. "The Conversion of St. Paul." *Catholic Biblical Quarterly* 19 (1957): 453–73.

Proudfoot, Wayne. *Religious Experience*. Berkeley: University of California Press, 1985.

— "Explaining the Unexplainable." *Journal of the American Academy of Religion* 61 (1993): 793–803.

Quast, Kevin. *Reading the Corinthian Correspondence: An Introduction*. New York: Paulist, 1994.

Raina, M. K. *Education of the Left and the Right: Implications of Hemispheric Specialization*. New Delhi: Allied, 1984.

Ramachandran, V. S. "Filling in Gaps in Perception: Part II. Scotomas and Phantom Limbs." *Current Directions in Psychological Science* 2 (1993): 56–65.

Ramachandran, V. S., and Sandra Blakeslee. *Phantoms in the Brain: Probing the Mysteries of the Human Mind*. New York: William Morrow, 1998.

Rambo, Lewis R. *Understanding Religious Conversion*. New Haven, Conn.: Yale University Press, 1993.

Raschke, C. "Revelation and Conversion: A Semantic Appraisal." *Anglican Theological Review* 60 (1978): 420–36.

Reitzenstein, Richard. *Hellenistic Mystery-Religions: Their Basic Ideas and Significance*. Pittsburgh Theological Monograph Series 15. Pittsburgh, Pa.: Pickwick, 1978.

Remus, Harold R. "Sociology of Knowledge and the Study of Early Christianity." *Studies in Religion/Sciences Religieuses* 11 (1982): 45–56.

Reynolds, Frank, Earle H. Waugh, and American Academy of Religion. *Religious Encounters with Death: Essays in the History and Anthropology of Religion.* University Park: Pennsylvania State University Press, 1977.

Ricciotti, Giuseppe. *Paul, the Apostle,* trans. Alba I. Zizzamia. Milwankee, Wis.: Bruce, 1953.

Richard, Earl. "Polemics, Old Testament, and Theology: A Study of 2 Cor 3:1–14:6." *Revue Biblique* 88 (1981): 340–67.

Ritschl, Albrecht. *Theologie und Metaphysik: Zur Verständigung und Abwehr,* 2nd ed. Göttingen: Vandenhoöck and Ruprecht, 1902.

Robbins, Trevor. "The Pharmacology of Thought and Emotion." In *From Brains to Consciousness,* ed. Steven Rose, 29–39. New York: Allen Lane, 1998.

Robertson, A., and A. Plummer. *A Critical and Exegetical Commentary on the First Epistle of St. Paul to the Corinthians.* Edinburgh: T. and T. Clark, 1911.

Robinson, Daniel, ed. *The Mind.* Oxford: Oxford University Press, 1998.

Robinson, John A. T. *The Body: A Study in Pauline Theology.* Studies in Biblical Theology 5. London: SCM Press, 1952.

Rodd, Cyril S. "On Applying a Sociological Theory to Biblical Studies." *Journal for the Study of the Old Testament* 19 (1981): 95–106.

Roetzel, Calvin J. *The Letters of Paul: Conversations in Context,* 4th ed. Louisville, Ky.: Westminster/John Knox, 1998.

— *Paul: The Man and the Myth.* Studies on Personalities of the New Testament. Columbia: University of South Carolina Press, 1998.

Rohrbaugh, Richard L., ed. *The Social Sciences and New Testament Interpretation.* Peabody, Mass.: Hendrickson, 1996.

Rolls, E. T., D. Perret, S. J. Thorpe, A. Puerto, A. Roper-Hall, and S. Maddison. "Responses of Neurons in Area 7 of the Parietal Cortex to Objects of Different Significance." *Brain Research* 169 (1979): 194–98.

Rordorf, Willy. "Paul's Conversion in the Canonical Acts and in the Acts of Paul." *Semeia: Social-Scientific Criticism of the New Testament and Its Social World* 80 (1997): 137–44.

Rowland, Christopher. *The Open Heaven: A Study of Apocalyptic in Judaism and Early Christianity.* New York: Crossroad, 1982.

Rubinstein, Robert A., Charles D. Laughlin, and John McManus. *Science as Cognitive Process: Toward an Empirical Philosophy of Science.* Philadelphia: University of Pennsylvania Press, 1984.

Ruef, John S. *Paul's First Letter to Corinth.* Harmondsworth: Penguin, 1971.

Saake, H. "Paulus als Ekstaiker." *Novum Testamentum* 15 (1973): 153–60.

Safrai, Shemuel, and M. Stern. *The Jewish People in the First Century: Historical Geography, Political History, Social, Cultural and Religious Life and Institutions.* Compendia Rerum Ludaicarum ad Novum Testamentum; section 1. Assen: Van Gorcum, 1974.

Salmon, E. T. *Roman Colonization under the Republic.* London: Thames and Hudson, 1969.

Samarin, William T. "The Linguisticality of Glossolalia." *Hartford Quarterly* 8 (1968): 49–75.

Sampley, J. Paul. "Paul, His Opponents in 2 Corinthians 10–13, and the Rhetorical Handbooks." In *The Social World of Formative Christianity and Judaism: Essays in Tribute to Howard Clark Kee*, ed. Jacob Neusner, Peder Borgen, Ernest S. Frerichs, and Richard A. Horsley, 162–77. Philadelphia: Fortress, 1988.

Sanders, E. P. *Paul and Palestinian Judaism: A Comparison of Patterns of Religion.* Philadelphia: Fortress, 1977.

— *Paul, the Law, and the Jewish People.* Philadelphia: Fortress, 1983.

— "Paul and the Law, His Opponents, and the Jewish People in Philippians 3 and 2 Corinthians 2." In *Anti-Judaism in Early Christianity, Vol. 1: Paul and the Gospels*, ed. P. Richardson and D. Granskou, 75–90. Waterloo: Wilfrid Laurier University Press, 1986.

— *Paul: Past Masters.* Oxford: Oxford University Press, 1991.

Sanders, J. T. "Paul's 'Autobiographical' Statements in Galatians 1–2." *Journal of Biblical Literature* 85 (1966): 335–45.

Sandnes, Karl Olav. *Paul, One of the Prophets? A Contribution to the Apostle's Self-Understanding.* Wissenschaftliche Untersuchungen zum Neuen Testament 2. Tübingen: Mohr, 1991.

— "Prophecy – A Sign for Believers (1 Cor 14:20–25)." *Biblica* 77 (1996): 1–15.

Sarbin, T. R., and N. Adler. "Self-Reconstitution Process: A Preliminary Report." *Psychoanalytic Review* 57 (1970–71): 599–616.

Sargant, William Walters. *Battle for the Mind: A Physiology of Conversion and Brain-washing.* New York: Doubleday, 1957.

— *The Mind Possessed: A Physiology of Possession, Mysticism, and Faith Healing.* Philadelphia: Lippincott, 1974.

Savage, Timothy B. *Power through Weakness: Paul's Understanding of the Christian Ministry in 2 Corinthians.* Society for New Testament Studies Monograph Series. 86. Cambridge: Cambridge University Press, 1996.

Schäfer, Peter. *Geniza-Fragmente zur Hekhalot-Literatur.* Texte und Studien zum antiken Judentum 6. Tübingen: Mohr, 1984.

— "New Testament and Hekhalot Literature: The Journey into Heaven in Paul and in Merkavah Mysticism." *Journal of Jewish Studies* 35 (1984): 19–35.

— *Gershom Scholem Reconsidered: The Aim and Purpose of Early Jewish Mysticism.* Oxford: Oxford Centre for Postgraduate Hebrew Studies, 1986.

— *The Hidden and Manifest God: Some Major Themes in Early Jewish Mysticism.* SUNY Series in Judaica. Albany: State University of New York Press, 1992.

Schäfer, Peter, and Joseph Dan. *Gershom Scholem's Major Trends in Jewish Mysticism 50 Years After: Proceedings of the Sixth International Conference on the History of Jewish Mysticism.* Tübingen: Mohr [Siebeck], 1993.

Schechter. S. "Genizah Fragments." *Jewish Quarterly Review* 16 (1904): 446–52.

Scheff, Thomas J. *Catharsis in Healing, Ritual, and Drama.* Berkeley: University of California Press, 1979.

Schelkle, Karl. *The Second Epistle to the Corinthians*, trans. Kevin Smyth. New York: Herder and Herder, 1969.

Schiffer, Fredric. *Of Two Minds: The Revolutionary Science of Dual-Brain Psychology.* New York: Free Press, 1998.

Schlatter, Adolf von. *Paulus und das antike Judentum.* Wissenschaftliche Untersuchungen zum Neuen Testament 58. Tübingen: Mohr [Siebeck], 1938.

— *Paulus der Bote Jesu: Eine Deutung seiner Briefe an die Korinther.* Stuttgart: Calwer, 1969.

— *Romans: The Righteousness of God.* Peabody, Mass.: Hendrickson, 1995.

Schmithals, Walter. *Gnosticism in Corinth: An Investigation of the Letters to the Corinthians.* Nashville, Tenn.: Abingdon, 1971.

Schneider, Johannes. "στενάξω, στεναγμός, συστενάζω." In *Theological Dictionary of the New Testament*, vol. 7, ed. Gerhard Kittel, trans. Geoffrey Bromiley, 600–3. Grand Rapids, Mich.: Eerdmans, 1971.

Schoder, Raymond V. *Paul Wrote from the Heart: Philippians, Galatians in Straightforward English.* Oak Park, Ill.: Bolchazy-Carducci, 1987.

Schoeps, Hans Joachim. *Paul: The Theology of the Apostle in the Light of Jewish Religious History.* Philadelphia: Westminster, 1961.

Scholem, Gershom G. *Major Trends in Jewish Mysticism.* Schocken Paperbacks SB5. New York: Schocken, 1961.

— *Jewish Gnosticism, Merkabah Mysticism and Talmudic Tradition*, 2nd ed. New York: Jewish Theological Seminary, 1965.

Schott-Billmann, F. *Corps et possession: Le vécu corporel des possédés face à la rationalité occidentale.* Paris: Gauthier-Villars, 1977.

Schrage, Wolfgang. *Der erste Brief an die Korinther.* Evangelisch-katholischer Kommentar zum Neuen Testament 7. Zürich: Benziger Verlag, 1991.

Schreiner, Thomas R. *Paul, Apostle of God's Glory in Christ: A Pauline Theology.* Downers Grove, Ill.: InterVarsity, 2001.

Schröter, Jens. *Der versöhnte Versöhner: Paulus als unentbehrlicher Mittler im Heilsvorgang zwischen Gott und Gemeinde nach 2 Kor 2: 14–7:4.* Texte und Arbeiten zum neutestamentlichen Zeitalter 10. Tübingen: Francke Verlag, 1993.

Schütz, J.H. *Paul and the Anatomy of Apostolic Authority.* Society for New Testament Studies Monograph Series 26. Cambridge: Cambridge University Press, 1975.

Schweitzer, Albert. *Geschichte der paulinischen Forschung von der Reformation bis auf die Gegenwart.* Tübingen: Mohr, 1911.

— *Die Mystik des Apostels Paulus.* Tübingen: Mohr, 1930.

— *The Mysticism of Paul the Apostle*, trans. William Montgomery. New York: Henry Holt, 1931.

— *Paul and His Interpreters: A Critical History*, trans. W. Montgomery. Schocken Paperbacks SB79. New York: Schocken, 1964.

Scott, James M. "The Triumph of God in 2 Cor 2:14: Additional Evidence of Merkabah Mysticism in Paul." *New Testament Studies* 42 (1996): 260–81.

— "Throne-Chariot Mysticism in Qumran and in Paul." In *Eschatology, Messianism, and the Dead Sea Scrolls*, ed. Craig A. Evans and Peter W. Flint, 101–19. Grand Rapids, Mich.: Eerdmans, 1997.

Segal, Alan F. "Paul and Ecstasy." *Society of Biblical Literature Seminar Papers* 25 (1986): 555–80.

— *Paul the Convert: The Apostolate and Apostasy of Saul the Pharisee.* New Haven, Conn.: Yale University Press, 1990.

— "Conversion and Messianism: Outline for a New Approach." In *The Messiah*, ed. J. H. Charlesworth, 296–340. Minneapolis: Fortress, 1992.

— "Conversion and Universalism: Opposites that Attract." In *Origins and Method: Towards a New Understanding of Judaism and Christianity: Essays in Honour of John C. Hurd*, ed. B. H. McLean, 162–89. Sheffield: JSOT, 1993.

— "Paul and the Beginning of Jewish Mysticism." In *Death, Ecstasy and Other Worldly Journeys*, ed. John Collins and Michael Fishbane, 93–120. Albany: State University of New York Press, 1995.

— "Paul's Thinking about Resurrection in Its Jewish Context." *New Testament Studies* 44 (1998): 400–19.

Shaara, Lila. "A Preliminary Analysis of the Relationship between Altered States of Consciousness, Healing, and Social Structure." *American Anthropologist* 94 (1992): 145–60.

Shirokogoroff, Sergei Mikhailovich. *Psychomental Complex of the Tungus*, new ed. Berlin: R. Schletzer Verlag, 1999.

Siikala, Anna-Leena. *The Rite Technique of the Siberian Shaman*. Folklore Fellows Communication 220. Helsinki: Academia Scientiarum Fennica, 1978.

Smart, Ninian. "Understanding Religious Experience." In *Mysticism and Philosophical Analysis*, ed. Steven T. Katz, 10–21. New York: Oxford University Press, 1978.

Smith, Huston. "Is There a Perennial Philosophy?" *Journal of the American Academy of Religion* 60 (1987): 553–66.

Smith, I. K. "Does 2 Corinthians 5:1–8 Refer to an Intermediate State." *Reformed Theological Review* 55 (1996): 14–23.

Smith, James A. *Marks of an Apostle: Deconstruction, Philippians, and Problematizing Pauline Theology*, ed. Gale A. Yee. Semeia Studies. Atlanta: Society of Biblical Literature, 2005.

Smith, Jonathan Z. "In Comparison Magic Dwells." In *Imagining Religion: From Babylon to Jonestown*, 19–35. Chicago: University of Chicago Press, 1982.

— *Drudgery Divine, On the Comparison of Early Christianities and the Religions of Late Antiquity*. Jordan Lectures in Comparative Religion 14. Chicago: University of Chicago Press, 1990.

— "The Temple and the Magician." In *Map Is Not Territory: Studies in the History of Religion*, 172–89. Chicago: University of Chicago Press, 1993.

— "Religion, Religions, Religious." In *Critical Terms for Religious Studies*, ed. Mark C. Taylor, 269–84. Chicago: University of Chicago Press, 1998.

Smith, Morton. *Jesus the Magician*. New York: Harper and Row, 1978.

— "Ascent to the Heavens and the Beginning of Christianity." *Eranos-Jahrbuch* 50 (1981): 403–29.

Smith, W. J. "Ritual and the Ethnology of Communicating." In *The Spectrum of Ritual: A Biogenetic Structural Analysis*, ed. Eugene G. D'Aquili, Charles D. Laughlin, and John McManus. New York: Columbia University Press, 1979.

Snyder, Graydon F. *First Corinthians: A Faith Community Commentary*. Macon, Ga.: Mercer University Press, 1992.

Sperry, Roger W. "Cerebral Organization and Behavior." *Science* 133 (1961): 1749–57.

— "Consciousness, Personal Identity and the Divided Brain." In *The Dual Brain: Hemispheric Specialization in Humans*, ed. D. Frank Benson and Eran Zaidel. New York: Guilford, 1985.

Sperry, Roger W., Michael S. Gazzaniga, and J. E. Bogen. "Interhemispheric Relationships: The Neocortical Commisures; Syndromes of Hemispheric Disconnection." In

Handbook of Clinical Neurology, vol. 4, ed. P. J. Vinken and G. W. Bruyn, 273–90. New York: Wiley, 1969.

Spezio, Michael. "Understanding Biology in Religious Experience: The Biogenetic Structuralist Approach of Eugene d'Aquili and Andrew Newberg." *Zygon* 36 (2001): 477–84.

Spickard, James V. "A Guide to Mary Douglas's Three Versions of Grid/Group Theory." *Sociological Analysis* 50 (1989): 151–70.

Spoerri, Theodor. *Beiträge zur Ekstase*, Bibliotheca Psychiatricaet Neurologica 134. Basel: Karger, 1967.

Springer, Sally P., and Georg Deutsch. *Left Brain, Right Brain: Perspectives on Cognitive Neuroscience*, 5th ed. Books in Psychology. New York: Freeman, 1998.

Squire, Larry R., and Barbara J. Knowlton. "The Medial Temporal Lobe, the Hippocampus, and the Memory Systems of the Brain." In *The New Cognitive Neurosciences*, ed. Michael S. Gazzaniga, 765–80. Cambridge, Mass.: MIT Press, 2000.

Stace, W. T. *The Teachings of the Mystics: Being Selections from the Great Mystics and Mystical Writings of the World*. New York: New American Library, 1960.

— *A Critical History of Greek Philosophy*. London: Macmillan, 1962.

— *Mysticism and Philosophy*. London: Macmillan, 1980.

Stanley, Arthur Penrhyn. *The Epistles of St. Paul to the Corinthians: With Critical Notes and Dissertations*, 5th ed. London: John Murray, 1882.

Stanley, D. M. "Paul's Conversion in Acts: Why Three Accounts?" *Catholic Biblical Quarterly* 15 (1953): 315–38.

Starbuck, E. D. *The Psychology of Religion*. New York: Charles Scribner's Sons, 1899.

Stark, Rodney. *The Rise of Christianity: A Sociologist Reconsiders History*. Princeton, N.J.: Princeton University Press, 1996.

Stendahl, Krister. *Paul among Jews and Gentiles*. Philadelphia: Fortress, 1976.

Stewart, J. S. *A Man in Christ: The Vital Elements of St. Paul's Religion*. New York: Harper and Brothers, 1935.

Stone, Michael E. "Lists of Revealed Things in the Apocalyptic Literature." In *Magnalia Dei, The Mighty Acts of God: Essays in Honor of Frank Moore Cross*, ed. Werner E. Lemke, Patricia D. Miller, and George Ernest Wright, 413–35. Garden City, N.Y.: Doubleday, 1980.

Stott, John R. W. *Romans: God's Good News for the World*. Downers Grove, Ill.: Inter-Varsity, 1994.

Stowers, Stanley K. "The Social Sciences and the Study of Early Christianity." In *Approaches to Ancient Judaism*, vol. 5, ed. W. Green, 149–81. Chico, Calif.: Scholars Press, 1983.

— "Social Status, Public Speaking and Private Teaching: The Circumstances of Paul's Preaching Activity." *Novum Testamentum* 26 (1984): 59–82.

— *Letter Writing in Greco-Roman Antiquity*. Philadelphia: Westminster, 1986.

Strom, Mark. *Reframing Paul: Conversations in Grace & Community*. Downers Grove, Ill.: InterVarsity, 2000.

Sumney, Jerry L. *Identifying Paul's Opponents: The Question of Method in 2 Corinthians*. Journal for the Study of the New Testament Supplement Series 40. Sheffield: JSOT Press, 1990.

Sundermann, Hans-Georg. *Der schwache Apostel und die Kraft der Rede: Eine rhetori-sche Analyse von 2 Kor 10–13.* Europäische Hochschulschriften. Reihe xxiii, Theologie 575. New York: Peter Lang, 1996.

Swartz, Louis H. "Absorbed States Play Different Roles in Female and Male Sexual Response: Hypotheses for Testing." *Journal of Sex and Marital Therapy* 20 (1994): 244–53.

Swartz, Michael D. *Scholastic Magic: Ritual and Revelation in Early Jewish Mysticism.* Princeton, N.J.: Princeton University Press, 1996.

Tabor, James D. *Things Unutterable: Paul's Ascent to Paradise in Its Greco-Roman, Judaic, and Early Christian Contexts.* Studies in Judaism. Lanham, Md.: University Press of America, 1986.

Talbert, Charles H. *Reading Corinthians: A Literary and Theological Commentary on 1 and 2 Corinthians.* New York: Crossroad, 1987.

Tannehill, Robert C. *Dying and Rising with Christ: A Study in Pauline Theology.* Beiheft zur Zeitschrift für die neutestamentliche Wissenschaft und die Kunde der älteren Kirche 32. Berlin: Töpelmann, 1967.

Tarachow, S. "St. Paul and Early Christianity." *Psychoanalysis and the Social Sciences* 4 (1955): 223–81.

Taves, Ann. "Knowing through the Body: Dissociative Religious Experience in the African- and British-American Methodist Traditions." *The Journal of Religion* 73 (1993): 200–22.

Theisohn, J. *Der auserwählte Richter.* Studien zur Umwelt des Neuen Testament. 12 Göttingen: Vandenhoeck and Ruprecht, 1975.

Theissen, Gerd. *The Social Setting of Pauline Christianity: Essays on Corinth.* Philadelphia: Fortress, 1982.

— *Psychological Aspects of Pauline Theology.* Philadelphia: Fortress, 1987.

Thiselton, Anthony C. *The First Epistle to the Corinthians: A Commentary on the Greek Text.* New International Greek Testament Commentary. Grand Rapids, Mich.: Eerdmans, 2000.

Thomas, J. C. "'An Angel from Satan': Paul's Thorn in the Flesh (2 Corinthians 12:7–10)." *Journal of Pentecostal Theology* 9 (1996): 39–52.

Thrall, Margaret E. *The First and Second Letters of Paul to the Corinthians.* Cambridge Bible Commentary: New English Bible. Cambridge: Cambridge University Press, 1965.

— "The Origins of Pauline Christology." In *Apostolic History and the Gospel: Biblical and Historical Essays Presented to F. F. Bruce on his 60th Birthday,* ed. W. Ward Gasque and Ralph P. Martin. Grand Rapids, Mich.: Eerdmans, 1970.

— *A Critical and Exegetical Commentary on the Second Epistle to the Corinthians.* International Critical Commentary on the Holy Scriptures of the Old and New Testaments. Edinburgh: T. and T. Clark, 1994.

— *Introduction and Commentary on II Corinthians I–VII, Vol. 1: A Critical and Exegetical Commentary on the Second Epistle to the Corinthians.* International commentary on the Holy Scriptures of the Old and New Testaments. Edinburgh: T. and T. Clark, 1994.

— "Paul's Journey to Paradise." In *The Corinthian Correspondence,* ed. R. Bieringer, 347–63. Bibliotheca ephemeridum theologicarum lovaniensium, Leuven: Leuven University Press, 1996.

Tilley, Terrence W. "Religious Pluralism as a Problem for 'Practical' Religious Epistemology." *Religious Studies* 30 (1994): 161–70.

Timmis, S. "Power: Playing According to Satan's Rules? Some Reflections on 2 Corinthians 10–13." *Evangelical Quarterly* 11 (1993): 54–61.

Torrey, E. Fuller. "Spiritualists and Shamans as Psychotherapists: An Account of Original Anthropological Sin." In *Religious Movements in Contemporary America*, ed. Irving I. Zaretsky and Mark P. Leone, 330–37. Princeton, N.J.: Princeton University Press, 1974.

Townsend, Joan B. "Shamanism." In *Anthropology of Religion: A Handbook*, ed. Stephen D. Glazier, 429–69. Westport, Conn.: Greenwood, 1997.

Townsend, John T. "Acts 9:1–29 and Early Church Tradition." *Society of Biblical Literature Seminar Papers*, 27 (1988): 119–31.

Tranel, Daniel, Antoine Bechara, and Antonio R. Damasio. "Decision Making and the Somatic Marker Hypothesis." In *The New Cognitive Neurosciences*, ed. Michael S. Gazzaniga, 1047–61. Cambridge, Mass.: MIT Press, 2000.

Trevarthen, Colwyn. *Brain Circuits and Functions of the Mind: Essays in Honor of Roger W. Sperry*. Cambridge: Cambridge University Press, 1990.

Trimble, M. R. "The Gastout-Geschwind Syndrome." In *The Temporal Lobes and the Limbic System*, ed. M. R. Trimble and T. G. Bolwig. Petersfield: Wrightson Biomedical, 1992.

Tucker, David M., R. A. Novelly, and P. J. Walker. "Hyperreligiosity in Temporal Lobe Epilepsy: Redefining the Relationship." *Journal of Nervous and Mental Diseases* 175 (1987): 181–84.

Turner, Max. *The Holy Spirit and Spiritual Gifts: In the New Testament Church and Today*. Carlisle: Paternoster, 1996; repr. Peabody, Mass.: Hendrickson, 1998.

Turner, Victor Witter. "Religious Specialists." In *International Encyclopedia of the Social Sciences*, vol. 13, 437–44. New York: Macmillan, 1968.

—— *The Forest of Symbols: Aspects of Ndembu Ritual*. Ithaca, N.Y.: Cornell University Press, 1967.

—— *The Ritual Process: Structure and Antistructure*. Lewis Henry Morgan Lectures, 1966. Chicago: Aldine, 1969.

Van Rensburg, Johan Janse. "Die Betekenis van Lukas B:10–17 en 2 Korintiers 12:1–10 vir die Okkultism-Diskoers." *In Die Skriflig* 32 (1998): 37–52.

Vernant, Jean Pierre. "Dim Body, Dazzling Body." In *The Body of Engenderment in the Hebrew Bible, the Rabbinic Tradition, and the Kabbalah*, ed. Michel Feher, Nadia Tazi, and Ramona Naddaff, 18–47. New York: Zone, 1989.

—— "Psuche: Simulacrum of the Body or Image of the Divine?" In *Mortals and Immortals: Collected Essays*, ed. Jean Pierre Vernant and Froma I. Zeitlin, 186–92. Princeton, N.J.: Princeton University Press, 1991.

Vincent, Marvin Richardson. *A Critical and Exegetical Commentary on the Epistles to the Philippians and to Philemon*. Edinburgh: T. and T. Clark, 1902.

Vitebsky, Piers. *The Shaman*, 1st American ed. Living Wisdom. Boston: Little, Brown, 1995.

Vos, G. "The More Excellent Ministry (2 Cor 3:18)." *Kerux* 8 (1993): 3–19.

Wackermann, Jiri. "Characterization of States of Consciousness Based on Global Descriptors of Brain Electrical Dynamics." *The Journal of Parapsychology* 63 (1999): 143–61.

Wallace, A. "Mazeway Resynthesis: A Biocultural Theory of Religious Inspiration." *Transactions of the New York Academy of Sciences* 18 (1956): 626–38.

Wallace, Anthony F. C. "Revitalization Movements." *American Anthropologist* 58 (1956): 264–81.

— *Religion: An Anthropological View.* New York: Random House, 1966.

Wallace, Richard, and Wynne Williams. *The Three Worlds of Paul of Tarsus.* London: Routledge, 1998.

Walsh, Roger. "Can Western Philosophers Understand Asian Philosophies? The Challenge and Opportunity of States-of-Consciousness Research." *Cross Currents* 39 (1989): 281–99.

— "Phenomenological Mapping and Comparisons of Shamanic, Buddhist, Yogic, and Schizophrenic Experiences." *Journal of the American Academy of Religion* 61 (1993): 739–69.

— "The Psychological Health of Shamans: A Reevaluation." *Journal of the American Academy of Religion* 65 (1997): 101–24.

Wasserstrom, Steven M. *Religion after Religion: Gershom Scholem, Mircea Eliade, and Henry Corbin at Eranos.* Princeton, N.J.: Princeton University Press, 1999.

Watson, N. M. "'Physician, Heal Thyself': Paul's Character as Revealed in 2 Corinthians, and the Congruence between Word and Deed." In *The Corinthian Correspondence: Papers from a Conference Held in Louvain*, ed. R. Bieringer, 671–78. Louvain: Leuven University Press/Peeters, 1995.

Watts, Fraser. "Cognitive Neuroscience and Religious Consciousness." In *Neuroscience and the Person: Scientific Perspectives on Divine Action*, ed. Robert J. Russell, 327–46. Berkeley, Calif.: Center for Theology and the Natural Sciences, 1999.

Wedenoja, William. "Ritual Trance and Catharsis: A Psychological and Evolutionary Perspective." In *Personality and the Cultural Construction of Society: Papers in Honor of Melford E. Spiro*, ed. David K. Jordan and Marc J. Swartz, 275–307. Tuscaloosa: University of Alabama Press, 1990.

Weiskrantz, Lawrence. *Blindsight: A Case Study and Implications.* Oxford Psychology Series 12. Oxford: Clarendon, 1986.

Weiss, Johannes, Frederick C. Grant, and Rudolf Knopf. *The History of Primitive Christianity.* New York: Wilson-Erickson, 1937.

Welborn, L. L. "On the Discord in Corinth: 1 Corinthians 1–4 and Ancient Politics." *Journal of Biblical Literature* 106 (1987): 85–111.

— "The Identification of 2 Corinthians 10–13 with the 'Letter of Tears'." *Novum Testamentum* 37 (1995): 138–53.

— "Like Broken Pieces of a Ring: 2 Cor 1:2–2:13; 7:5–16, and Ancient Theories of Literary Unity."*New Testament Studies* 42 (1996): 559–83.

Wenham, David. "Being 'Found' on the Last Day: New Light on 2 Peter 3:10 and 2 Corinthians 5:3." *New Testament Studies* 33 (1987): 477–79.

— *Paul, Follower of Jesus or Founder of Christianity?* Grand Rapids, Mich.: Eerdmans, 1995.

Wertenbaker, Christian. "A New Science of Mysticism: Pythagoras in 1999." *Parabola* 24 (1999): 69–76.

Wertheimer, Max. *Productive Thinking.* New York: Harper, 1959.

Wexler, Bruce E. *Brain and Culture: Neurobiology, Idealogy, and Social Change.* Cambridge, Mass.: MIT Press, 2006.

Wikenhauser, Alfred. *Die Christusmystik des Apostels Paulus*, 2nd ed. Freiburg: Herder, 1956.

— *Pauline Mysticism: Christ in the Mystical Teaching of St. Paul*. New York: Herder and Herder, 1960.

Wildman, Wesley J., and Leslie A. Brothers. "Religious Experience." In *Neuroscience and the Person: Scientific Perspectives on Divine Action*, ed. Robert J. Russell, 347–416. Berkeley, Calif.: Center for Theology and the Natural Sciences, 1999.

Williams, Linda Verlee. *Teaching for the Two-Sided Mind: A Guide to Right Brain/Left Brain Education*. A Spectrum Book. Englewood Cliffs, N.J.: Prentice-Hall, 1983.

Wilson, A. N. *Paul: The Mind of the Apostle*. London: Sinclair-Stevenson, 1997.

Wilson, Robert R. "Prophecy and Ecstasy: A Reexamination." *Journal of Biblical Literature* 98 (1979): 321–37.

— *Prophecy and Society in Ancient Israel*. Philadelphia: Fortress, 1980.

Wimbush, Vincent L. *Paul, the Worldly Ascetic: Response to the World and Self-Understanding According to 1 Corinthians 7*. Macon, Ga.: Mercer University Press, 1987.

— *Ascetic Behavior in Greco-Roman Antiquity: A Sourcebook*. Studies in Antiquity and Christianity. Minneapolis: Fortress, 1990.

Wimbush, Vincent L., and Richard Valantasis. *Asceticism*. New York: Oxford University Press, 1995.

Windisch, Hans. *Paulus und Christus: Ein biblisch-religionsgeschichtlicher Vergleich*. Untersuchungen zur NeuenTestament 24. Leipzig: J. C. Hinrichs, 1934–37.

— *Der Zweite Korintherbrief*, Kritisch-exegetischer Kommentar über Neue Testament 6. Göttingen: Vandenhoeck and Ruprecht, 1924.

Winkelman, Michael. "Shamans and other 'Magico-Religious' Healers: A Cross-cultural Study of Their Origins, Nature and Social Transformations." *Ethnos* 18 (1990): 308–52.

— *Shamans, Priests and Witches: A Cross-cultural Study of Magico-Religious Practitioners*. Anthropological Research Papers 44. Tempe: Arizona State University Press, 1992.

— "Altered States of Consciousness and Religious Behavior." In *Anthropology of Religion: A Handbook*, ed. Stephen D. Glazier, 393–428. Westport, Conn.: Praeger, 1999.

— *Shamanism: The Neural Ecology of Consciousness and Healing*. Westport, Conn.: Bergin and Garvey, 2000.

Wire, Antoinette Clark. *The Corinthian Women Prophets: A Reconstruction through Paul's Rhetoric*. Minneapolis: Fortress, 1990.

— "Prophecy and Women Prophets in Corinth." In *Gospel Origins & Christian Beginnings: In Honor of James M. Robinson*, ed. James E. Goehring. Sonoma, Calif.: Polebridge, 1990.

Witherington, Ben III. *Paul's Narrative Thought World: The Tapestry of Tragedy and Triumph*. Louisville, Ky.: Westminster/John Knox, 1994.

— *Conflict and Community in Corinth: A Socio-rhetorical Commentary on 1 and 2 Corinthians*. Grand Rapids, Mich.: Eerdmans, 1995.

Witherup, Ronald D. "Functional Redundancy in the Acts of the Apostles: A Case Study." *Journal for the Study of the New Testament* 48 (1992): 67–86.

Wolfson, Elliot R. "Woman – The Feminine as Other in Theosophic Kabbalah: Some Philosophical Observations on the Divine Androgyne." In *The Other in Jewish Thought and History: Constructions of Jewish Culture and Identity*, ed. Laurence J.

Silberstein and Robert L. Cohn, 166–204. New York: New York University Press, 1994.

Wood, H. G. "The Conversion of Paul: Its Nature, Antecedents, and Consequences." *New Testament Studies* 1 (1955): 276–82.

Woods, L. "Opposition to a Man and His Message: Paul's 'Thorn in the Flesh' (2 Cor 12:7)." *Australian Biblical Review* 39 (1991): 44–53.

Wrede, William. *Paulus*, 2nd ed. Religionsgeschichtliche Volksbücher für die deutsche christliche Gegenwart 1. Reihe, 5/6. Heft. Tübingen: Mohr [Siebeck], 1907.

— *Paul.* Lexington, Ky.: American Theological Library Association Committee on Reprinting, 1962.

Wright, N. T. "Reflected Glory: 2 Corinthians 3:18." In *The Glory of Christ in the New Testament: Studies in Christology: In Memory of George Bradford Caird*, ed. L. D. Hurst and N. T. Wright, 139–50. Oxford: Clarendon, 1987.

— *What Saint Paul Really Said: Was Paul of Tarsus the Real Founder of Christianity?* Grand Rapids, Mich.: Eerdmans, 1997.

Wright, Peggy Ann. "The Nature of the Shamanic State of Consciousness: A Review." *Journal of Psychoactive Drugs* 21 (1989): 25–33.

Yanigita, T. "Self-administration Studies on Psychological Dependence." *Trends in Pharmacological Sciences* 2 (1980): 161–64.

Young, Allan. "Notes on the Evolution of Evolutionary Psychiatry." In *New Horizons in Medical Anthropology: Essays in Honour of Charles Leslie*, ed. Charles M. Leslie, Mark Nichter, and Margaret M. Lock, 221–39. London: Routledge, 2002.

Young, Brad H. "The Ascension Motif of 2 Corinthians 12 in Jewish, Christian and Gnostic Texts." *Grace Theological Journal* 9 (1988): 73–103.

Young, Frances M., and David Ford. *Meaning and Truth in 2 Corinthians.* Grand Rapids, Mich.: Eerdmans, 1988.

Zaidel, Dahlia W. "Adult Commissurotomy: Separating the Left from the Right Side of the Brain." In *Mental Lives: Case Studies in Cognition*, ed. Ruth Campbell, 255–75. Oxford: Blackwell, 1992.

Znamenski, Andrei A. *Shamanism in Siberia: Russian Records of Indigenous Spirituality.* Dordrecht: Kluwer, 2003.

Index of Ancient Sources

Index of Modern Authors

Subject Index